REPUBLICANISM AND
RESPONSIBLE GOVERNMENT

Republicanism and Responsible Government

The Shaping of Democracy in Australia and Canada

BENJAMIN T. JONES

McGill-Queen's University Press
Montreal & Kingston • London • Ithaca

© McGill-Queen's University Press 2014

ISBN 978-0-7735-4361-4 (cloth)
ISBN 978-0-7735-4362-1 (paper)
ISBN 978-0-7735-9206-3 (ePDF)
ISBN 978-0-7735-9207-0 (ePUB)

Legal deposit second quarter 2014
Bibliothèque nationale du Québec

Printed in Canada on acid-free paper that is 100% ancient forest free (100% post-consumer recycled), processed chlorine free

This book has been published with the help of a grant from the Canadian Federation for the Humanities and Social Sciences, through the Awards to Scholarly Publications Program, using funds provided by the Social Sciences and Humanities Research Council of Canada.

McGill-Queen's University Press acknowledges the support of the Canada Council for the Arts for our publishing program. We also acknowledge the financial support of the Government of Canada through the Canada Book Fund for our publishing activities.

Library and Archives Canada Cataloguing in Publication

Jones, Benjamin T., 1982–, author
    Republicanism and responsible government: the shaping of democracy in Australia and Canada / Benjamin T. Jones.

    Includes bibliographical references and index.
    Issued in print and electronic formats.
    ISBN 978-0-7735-4361-4 (bound). – ISBN 978-0-7735-4362-1 (pbk.).
    ISBN 978-0-7735-9206-3 (PDF). – ISBN 978-0-7735-9207-0 (ePUB)

    1. Canada – Politics and government – 19th century. 2. Australia – Politics and government – 19th century. 3. Republicanism – Canada – History – 19th century. 4. Republicanism – Australia – History – 19th century. 5. Democracy – Canada – History – 19th century. 6. Democracy – Australia – History – 19th century. I. Title.

FC461.J65 2014   971.03'9   C2014-901298-5
                                        C2014-901299-3

This book was typeset by Interscript in 10.5/13 Baskerville.

Contents

Acknowledgments   vii

Preface   ix

1 Introduction   3
2 What Is Civic Republicanism?   18
3 1837: The Almost Revolution   39
4 Lord Durham and the Grand Compromise   77
5 Nova Scotia and the New Deal   101
6 The Domino Effect   126
7 The Future America of the Southern Hemisphere: Dr Lang and the Failure of Separatism   148
8 A Colony of Virtue: The Anti-Transportation League   168
9 Eureka Revisited: How Republican Was the Great Stockade?   191
10 Responsible Government: A Liberal or a Civic Republican Legacy?   216

Appendix One: Timeline of the Rebellions of 1837–1838   229

Appendix Two: Timeline of the Eureka Stockade   233

Notes   237

Bibliography   275

Index   295

Acknowledgments

My thinking on the place of civic republicanism has been profoundly shaped and challenged by the work of many noted scholars. I would, however, like to particularly acknowledge Peter J. Smith and Janet Ajzenstat, since their Canadian republican revisionism has had a great influence on my own work. I owe a great debt of gratitude also to Iseult Honohan for her work on the history of civic republicanism and to Mark McKenna, whose pioneering work on republicanism in Australia sparked my interest in this topic. This work has been improved immeasurably by the advice, corrections, and suggestions of Paul Pickering at the Australian National University.

My sincere thanks go to the wonderful staff at the National Library of Australia, the State Library of New South Wales and the Library and Archives of Canada. I have received wonderful support also from the staff at the Museum of Australian Democracy and the Australian Historical Association. The staff at McGill-Queen's University Press have been a pleasure to work with. In particular, I am grateful to my meticulous copyeditor, Ron Curtis, and to Jacqueline Mason for guiding this project to publication.

This work has been made possible by the unconditional love and support of my family. My grandfather, Arthur Neville Shelton, remains my most consistent supporter, and at eighty-eight his sharp eyes and wit to match still examine every article and book I produce. My parents, John and Robyn Jones, have offered unwavering support over many years to see this work go from initial concept to publication. They remain my loyal, unpaid editors and have spared my blushes by discovering many errors before they go to print. My wife, Katrina Jones, has shared this journey with me and is a constant source of joy, encouragement, and inspiration. This book is lovingly dedicated to her.

Preface

Australia and Canada are large, developed, independent nations committed to the principles of democracy and equality for all citizens. As such, it is a political anomaly that they remain constitutional monarchies. The fact that the reverse of every coin, in Sydney or Toronto, bears the image of the British monarch rather than local heroes is symbolic of the awkward relationship both nations have with republicanism. While republicanism as a system of government (or separatist republicanism, as I have coined it) has enjoyed only sporadic and often reluctant support, the role of republicanism as a social and political theory (civic republicanism) warrants further investigation by historians. The more I study the rhetoric and attitudes of colonial reformers in Australia and Canada, the more evidence I find that civic republican ideas shaped their concept of democracy with at least as much force as Lockean liberalism. Identifying the civic republican tradition can unlock some of the seeming contradictions in colonial history and help us gain a better understanding of the reformist crowd and their complex vision of democracy, identity, and Britishness. It is a legacy still clearly visible today.

This work is concerned with the role of civic republicanism within the successful campaign for responsible government in the nineteenth century. It focuses on a small number of key events and is largely confined to just three Canadian provinces and three Australian states. There is far more work to be done on the impact of colonial civic republicanism. It is my hope that this volume might serve to encourage further research into the role of civic republicanism in Canadian Confederation, in Australian Federation, and in twentieth-century politics in both nations. The nexus of religion, civic republicanism, and democratic reform is another area where further research is needed. This work offers the concept of "Christian civic republicanism" to identify democratic reformers who had married their commitment to civic virtue and a politically active polis to their religious ideology and the pursuit of a utopian Christian society. A detailed look at how Christianity shaped leaders in the reformist crowd such as William Lyon Mackenzie and John Dunmore Lang is beyond the scope of this work, but it would provide fertile grounds for further research.

This book certainly challenges the ubiquitous theory of liberalism that is particularly evident in the Australian historiography of progressive colonial politics. Liberalism played a vital role in the democratization of colonial society, but in some histories the concept has become so large that it becomes trite. By introducing civic republicanism as a major philosophical force, this work hopes not to exclude liberalism from the narrative but to gain a clearer idea of its role and its limits. This work is a history of civic republicanism not of civic republicans. It does not seek to label reformers with a republican badge or to deny the influence of other ideologies. Through an examination of the role of civic republicanism, it is hoped that a more complete view of the reformist crowd and their vision can be gained. The story of colonial democracy is far more than a triumph of liberalism. The civic republican tradition, distinct from tory conservatism and Lockean liberalism, shaped democracy in Australia and Canada in the colonial period and continues to do so today.

Sydney, 25 November 2013

REPUBLICANISM AND
RESPONSIBLE GOVERNMENT

1

Introduction

> Republicanism is all too often seen as a province of democratic theory bordering on the large empire of liberalism. But it is historically more correct to regard both liberal and democratic political theory as provinces of republicanism.
>
> Mario Viroli, *Republicanism*

William Shakespeare famously used his star-cross'd lovers to expose the emptiness of titles when he wrote, "What's in a name? That which we call a rose by any other name would smell as sweet." The Bard's musing comes a little unstuck in the context of British colonial politics, where the rose of liberty acquires a distinctly harassing perfume when attached to the name "republicanism." This is not altogether surprising considering the bloody reputation republicanism gained through its use in connection with the English, American, and French revolutions. In fact, more connotations are associated with the term "republic" than with most terms in the British political lexicon. Its meaning in any given context cannot be immediately presumed, since the term has not remained diachronically static with either supporters or opponents. Thus, this book is offered as a history of ideas: that is to say, it is not to be read as either a political or a social history in the conventional sense. It will explore the impact of civic republicanism in Britain's Canadian and Australian colonies in the lead-up to the granting of responsible government in the mid-nineteenth century through the prism of ideas.

"Republicanism" is an ancient term with numerous definitions and implications. Its long and complex history is the type of thing Henry James might have referred to as a "loose and baggy monster." One need only consider our modern nation states to appreciate the diversity of this often revolutionary word. Is the same form of government practised in the French Republic and the People's Republic of China? Or what are the governmental congruencies of the Islamic Republic of Pakistan, the Federal Republic of Germany, the Democratic Republic of the Congo, and the Argentine Republic? The meaning of the word "republic" cannot be immediately presumed, because the definition varies depending on time, place, and context. It is a contested word today, and it was contested also in the nineteenth-century British world.

This book will assess the impact of civic republicanism in the Canadian and Australian colonies at an integral time in their constitutional development. These specific British colonies have been selected because, despite their geographical separation, their political and socio-cultural development was remarkably similar. In 1981 G.K. Raudzens lamented the lack of comparative studies of Upper Canada and New South Wales specifically and of Canada and Australia more generally. Although Raudzens concedes that the official papers and histories pay little attention to one another, contemporary newspapers do reveal that these sister colonies on opposite sides of the world were interested in and educated by the other's news, politics, and development. A brief comparison of the Victorian-era and modern newspapers indicates that the British colonists in Canada and Australia were "more interested in each other's affairs than their descendents are now."[1] While the subsequent three decades have seen some response to Raudzens' challenge, the field as a whole is still young and much illuminating research is yet to be completed.[2] This book is casually called a comparison of colonial Canada and Australia, but its focus is firmly on Upper and Lower Canada, Nova Scotia, New South Wales, Victoria and Tasmania.

The Canadian and Australian colonies represent the British Empire's well-behaved children.[3] Unlike Ireland, the United States, or South Africa, the colonies that would become Canada and Australia never developed a strong anti-monarchical or anti-British republican tradition, which will be termed separatism. It is for this reason people sometimes dismiss their histories as boring.[4] There were no mass nationalist uprisings, no Boston Tea Parties, and no patriotic lullabies to commemorate a day of independence. Does this mean that the people of Australia and Canada have no republican tradition? Certainly not. While separatist republicanism did not enjoy mass support, I will contend that civic republicanism was a major influence on the democratization of the colonies most powerfully landmarked by the granting of responsible government. While the budding flower of colonial democracy was nurtured by a rights-based liberal philosophy, it was equally influenced by community-minded, civic republican ideas.

Civic republicanism can be considered the lost history of Australia and Canada. It is lost because republicanism has become so synonymous with separatism that the classical interpretation of republicanism and its impact on the struggle for responsible government has become largely neglected or forgotten. Although there were no revolutions and no declarations of independence, a short eight-year period from 1848 to 1856 saw responsible government granted to nine North American and Australasian colonies from Nova Scotia to New South Wales. There was undoubtedly a powerful democratic lobby pushing for these reforms. The historiographical orthodoxy has credited this movement overwhelmingly to an imagined domineering prevalence of Lockean liberalism.[5] And yet, what is striking about the rhetoric of the leaders of the reform movement is the reoccurring references to communitarianism, civic virtue, and a fixed notion of the meaning of British citizenship. These concepts find a natural home in the republican tradition. In the history of ideas leading to responsible government in the British world, civic republicanism certainly played a role. This book will examine the impact and influence of civic republicanism, as opposed to liberalism, and trace its role in the reform movement.

As is often the case with under-researched areas, republicanism in Australia and Canada is often the victim of a contextual interpretative flaw. This can be seen in the flurry of books, both advocating and opposing Australian republicanism, that were released during the constitution debates of the 1990s. The introduction to David Headon, James Warden, and Bill Gammage's *Crown or Country: The Traditions of Australian Republicanism* is indicative of the narrow prism through which republicanism was, and is, viewed. The authors note that "this book is about the ideas which shifted Australia away from the Sovereign thought towards the republic. It is about the history of republicanism in Australia and about the people who argued against the odds and against the crown."[6] A historical look at republican thought, however, would suggest that this strict juxtaposition of the Crown and the republic creates a false dichotomy.

The *Crown or Country* interpretation is, of course, a product of its time. The 1990s debate was centred on a minimalist republican model with the primary issue being whether or not to maintain constitutional links to the British royal family in a post–Australia Act period.[7] It is natural enough that books from this period would interpret "republic" as being the antonym of "monarchy." The contemporary republican movement of Canada, although embryonic in comparison to that of Australia, applies a similar binary theory to its interpretation of "republic" and "monarchy." David Smith's *Republican Option* could be considered a Canadian equivalent to the *Crown or Country* thesis. Smith acknowledges the republican agenda of William Lyon Mackenzie, Louis-Joseph Papineau, and the rebels of 1837 and also the republican subtext of the responsible-government reformers. Nevertheless, the lack of anti-monarchical zeal leads him to open his book with the following declaration: "A book about republicanism in Canada labours under the handicap that there is no republican movement in Canada, no believers to extol its worth, no literature to extol the creed."[8]

It is not the case that this interpretation is incorrect, only that is it is limited. Separatism is one branch of the republican tree. Some historical pundits insist that republicanism, to be named as such, must adhere to a stringent anti-monarchical, anti-British means test. It is often the case that all but radical colonial separatists are excluded when tracing Australia's or Canada's republican lineage. The necessary polarization of monarchy and republic, British and Australian or Canadian, within this dictum creates a parochial view of republicanism and excludes many diverse characters and chapters from the narrative. It is ironic that the opening contributor to *Crown or Country* makes the point that this type of thinking can be a forced binary. Mark McKenna notes that it is simply "untrue" and "inaccurate historically" to insist that republicans are necessarily anti-monarchical, anti-British, or anti-Imperialist. He goes on to offer another idea of great importance to the research presented here. He posits that "it may be possible... to argue that the language of British constitutionalism in Australia is a descendent of the political language of classical republicanism."[9] This book will make that very case and draw a sharp distinction between separatist republicanism (constitutional independence from outside forces) and civic republicanism (a classical political and social theory).

One of the chief contentions here is that liberal thought did not monopolize or even dominate the push for greater democracy in the Victorian era. Civic republicanism will be presented as an influence of equal, if not greater, significance. It is crucial to define the terms clearly, however, since they are often contested. This book will draw on the work of three political theorists in particular when identifying liberal and civic republican thought: Isaiah Berlin, Philip Pettit, and Michael Sandel. Drawing on Immanuel Kant, Berlin achieved fame with his celebrated essay "Two Concepts of Liberty," which distinguishes between negative liberty (the absence of things that hinder freedom) and positive liberty (the presence of things that allow freedom).[10] The distinction is particularly useful here since liberalism can be seen as a proponent of negative liberty, seeking to enhance personal freedom by limiting the power of the government, or in this case the governor and colonial office. Civic republicanism on the other hand will be understood as a positive concept of liberty.[11] The primary concern in civic republican thought is not to remove roadblocks to liberty but to institute and encourage things like patriotism, civic pride, community mindedness, and the preservation of virtue.

Philip Pettit offers a variation to Berlin's taxonomy by conceptualizing liberalism as freedom from interference and republicanism as freedom from domination.[12] Again, the distinction is very helpful when applied to the colonial reformers who fought for responsible government in the mid-nineteenth century. Were they seeking to stop interference from Britain, the colonial office, and their local governors, or were they seeking to end imperial domination over the colonies? Michael Sandel offers another important variation in his influential work *Liberalism and the Limits of Justice*. "The fundamental question," argues Sandel, "is whether the right is prior to the good."[13] Taking the example of religious freedom, a liberal view would argue that it is an individual right while passing no judgment on the religion itself. Conversely, a civic republican view would not remain neutral but rather would consider whether the religion in question adds to the harmony and virtue of the community. In this paradigm of thought, liberalism insists that individual rights precede the common good whereas civic republicanism believes the common good precedes individual rights.

This book will understand liberalism to be a negative concept of liberty, promoting freedom from interference and concerned with the protection and advancement of individual rights. In the context of British colonies in the mid-nineteenth century, liberalism is most readily revealed through ideas such as manhood suffrage, elected houses of parliament, and a general rejection of interference in local affairs from the metropole. Civic republicanism will be understood as a positive concept of liberty, promoting freedom from domination and concerned with the production of virtue and the common good. In the lead-up to responsible government, civic republican thought is revealed through a fixed notion in the mind of reformers about what a virtuous British society should look like and how it should be governed. The principal civic republican concern was to establish institutions to counter corruption and produce a community that upheld the best traits of the British race.[14] Both traditions undoubtedly shaped the democratic journey of Canada and Australia. This book seeks to address the overlooked influence of civic republicanism in those heady years immediately before the granting of responsible government.

This understanding of liberalism and civic republicanism is not without its critics. Many historians and political scientists insist that liberalism is too often misrepresented as a cult of individualism. Bruce Curtis has written that "one obvious problem with such attempts to divorce liberalism from republicanism and a conception of the common good, and to equate it to a narrow individualism, in contrast to a 'civic humanist' tradition, is that the leading European intellectuals and activists who came to see themselves as liberals were classically educated, well versed in Greek and Roman history. Like their classically educated Lower Canadian contemporaries, for instance, the English liberals ... were often open admirers of republican democracy."[15] It is certainly true that democratic reformers throughout the British Empire, even those who identified as liberals, actively drew on republican ideas. However, this alone does not justify a concept of liberalism that absorbs the far older republican tradition. By expanding the already wide halls of liberalism in this way, it risks becoming trite. In his influential 2000 essay *The Liberal Order Framework*, which has prompted an important conference and a subsequent book, Ian McKay argues that "liberal assumptions have been so successfully and massively diffused through the population that it is difficult to see... the aliberal positions they have replaced."[16] The same is true of Australian historiography. Prefixes such as Australian, Victorian, and Deakinite are often employed as a point of distinction between the various schools absorbed into liberal terrain.[17]

McKay argues that the Rebellions of 1837–38, the *Durham Report*, and the Act of Union should be seen together as the first phase of the "Canadian Liberal Revolution." McKay sees this period as a high point marked by the "defeat of liberalism's civic humanist adversary."[18] This book will examine these key events as well as important developments in colonial Australia and argue that it was a democratic revolution, driven by civic republican and liberal ideas that created the right conditions for responsible government in these far-flung colonies. Few groups or individuals fit into the neat philosophical boxes academia creates when attempting to make sense of the nineteenth-century British world. The leading reformers in this work, such as William Lyon Mackenzie, Joseph Howe, John Dunmore Lang, and Henry Parkes, drew from many philosophical founts. It will not be argued that these men should be seen as civic republicans but that liberal and civic republican ideas played a key role in shaping the mentality of the reformist crowd.

This work is divided into two sections. The first investigates the role of civic republicanism in Canada between 1837 and 1850. These thirteen years represent a period of extreme change and political evolution. Beginning with the Rebellions of 1837–38, I will trace the impact of the *Durham Report*, the nature of the campaign for responsible government, and the political philosophy of the new constitutions. The second section explores the Australian experience from 1842 to 1856 and discusses the role of civic republicanism in the anti-transportation debates, the pre-constitution debates, and the campaign for responsible government.

The Rebellions of 1837–38 stand out as something of an anomaly in Canadian history. From a military perspective they were on a minute scale when compared with other North American conflicts in the previous half century. They were sometimes viewed as a hiccup of sorts on an otherwise smooth constitutional ride towards responsible government and confederation. This dismissive view fails to account for the enormous popularity of the rebellion leaders, Mackenzie, Papineau, and their more moderate colleagues. It is no small thing for civilians to risk their lives and take up arms against the government. This book conceptualizes the rebellions not as an aberration but as a natural, albeit reluctant, extension of the reform movement's demand for greater democracy. Examining the language of the reform leaders, the case will be made that while the appetite for separatism was not great, the reformers were ravenous for a civic republican style of democracy. They were not asking first and foremost for individual rights but to curtail the perceived corruption of the Family Compact and the Chateau Clique in the interest of the common good. The demands, it will be shown, for an elective legislative council, gubernatorial neutrality, and responsible government were aimed not at advancing personal freedom but at communitarian liberty. To a great extent, the battle of ideas that led to these armed conflicts included a tension not just between toryism and liberalism but with civic republicanism also.

The *Durham Report* is examined in chapter 3 and is christened the grand compromise. Although the *Report* was designed for Canada, it belongs equally to the Australian colonists, who seized upon its reformist message.[19] The case is argued that the *Report* and its recommendation of responsible government were not simply the result of liberal thinking. Despite his short tenure in Canada, Durham exhibited in the *Report* a genius for understanding the dual-patriotism that was so readily evident in the popular consciousness. The colonists were immensely proud of their British heritage. The elderly colonists had lived through two wars that had been fought to maintain the British connection, and the psychological impact of these events cannot be understated. At the same time, the colonists had a firm concept of British citizenship and the rights of British subjects. They were patriots of their own land and would insist in the strongest possible terms, even with the threat of separation, that the British colonists of Canada were entitled to all the honour and privileges of their brethren in England. As democracy became normative in the British colonies of settlement (unlike in Crown colonies and Britain itself) by the middle of the nineteenth century, those privileges increasingly came to mean parliamentary democracy and the obligation of the queen and her ministers to heed the people's voice. The *Report* dissected colonial governance into two parts, local administration and international policy. Durham correctly deduced that if the colonists were granted the former they would be content to submit the latter to the Imperial Parliament. This book will interpret the *Report* not solely as a liberal document granting responsible government but as a civic republican grand compromise allowing the colonists to maintain the British connection while living in a society of virtue based on the principles of mixed government as set out in the British constitution (as the reformers interpreted it).

Following the *Durham Report*, colonial toryism took its last stand in resistance to the principle of responsible government. It would take almost a decade of ideological arm wrestling before Nova Scotia could rightly call herself the first British colony to receive responsible government in 1848. In a year that saw revolution and mayhem engulf Europe, a new deal was established in British colonial policy, revolution was placed permanently on hold, and a new British Empire was born. The fourth chapter of this book will explore the Nova Scotian journey with special attention paid to the role of Joseph Howe in petitioning the British government. With the granting of responsible government, the reformers argued for a virtuous society based on the new democratic orthodoxy in conceptualizing British citizenship.

The final Canadian chapter is titled "The Domino Effect." Although Nova Scotia was the first colony to enjoy responsible government, it was something reformers all over Canada had been petitioning for. With Nova Scotia having set the example, it was not long before the other colonies were granted the same privilege. In the United Province of Canada, the system of responsible government received its sternest test with the passing of the Rebellion Losses Bill. The passing of this controversial legislation and the refusal of the governor to intervene set a precedent that would be followed all over the continent. A new era of colonial democracy began as responsible government was not only accepted in theory but also confirmed in practice. But what kind of democracy was this to be? My argument is that the reform movement's campaign for colonial democracy was often accompanied by a desire to enhance positive liberty and to seek freedom from domination rather than freedom from interference. The grand compromise of Lord Durham had delivered to Canada a civic republican arrangement that would stand the test of time.

On the other side of the world, the Australian colonies had a very different beginning. Rather than United Empire Loyalists, the first Europeans to populate the Australian East Coast were predominately petty criminals. Despite this immense difference, it is remarkable how the universality of the concept of Britishness was able to transform the Australian colonies in such a short period. Dual patriotism was evidenced in Australia almost immediately after white settlement and by the 1830s a proud collection of native-born and free immigrant settlers began demanding rights equal to those enjoyed by their brethren in Canada, Britain, or wherever they might be.

The colonists in New South Wales were determined that they should enjoy the full rights of British subjects. Again, we find the emphasis was not only on promoting individual liberties but also on the collective right of a British society to be governed in a way that allowed the natural virtue of the British constitution to shape the community.

Chapter 6 explores the failure of separatist republicanism to take hold in Australia despite its active promotion by one of New South Wales' leading statesmen, John Dunmore Lang. Lang's career can be seen as something of a paradox in that he was hugely influential and popular as a preacher, author, newspaper editor, and politician, and yet the separatist republicanism for which he is generally remembered had such a limited impact on colonial Australia. This chapter suggests that it was Lang's advocacy of communitarian, democratic, and civic republican ideals, rather than separatism, that gained him such fame. Particularly at a point in history when the Australian colonies were so desperate to establish a respectable identity, Lang's vision of virtuous, protestant immigrants populating a noble British society where all citizens were duty bound to enhance the common good and their international reputation captured the public imagination.

The anti-transportation movement in the Eastern Australian colonies is a prime example of the collectivist, rather than individualistic, bent of the reform movement. The colonists were committed to creating a society of virtue, and they displayed in their rhetoric and their actions an ideology that placed the common good of the community above individual gain. The transportation system was not at all ill-founded from a commercial point of view. The supply of cheap labour to the powerful rural bourgeoisie created enormous wealth for the elite while relieving the pressure on Britain's overcrowded prisons. What is remarkable about the anti-transportation movement is that many landowners acted expressly against their own financial interests by vehemently opposing convictism and refusing to employ former convicts on their runs. Combined with the over-representation of Christian ministers among the leaders, the campaign must be interpreted as moral and spiritual rather than fiscal. Chapter 7 will conceptualize the anti-transportation movement as a civic republican campaign and a struggle to create a British society worthy of the name.

The Eureka Stockade sits uneasily in Australian history. Like Canada's Rebellions of 1837–38, it represents a minor but significant civilian uprising in an otherwise peaceful constitutional development. Australian historiography has seen greatly varied responses to Eureka.[20] It has been dismissed as a petty riot against a local tax and glorified as an Australian revolution. Chapter 8 will examine the ideological roots of the Eureka Stockade and identify a distinct strain of civic republican thinking among the leaders of the rebellion. Victoria was a new colony, largely free from the convict stain of its northern neighbour. The miners saw themselves as a disenfranchised group in a new British society. Their language, demands, and willingness to fight reveal a deeply held conviction about what a free British society should look like and how they should be governed. This chapter will argue that a distinctly civic republican, rather than liberal, idea of democracy, drove the miners to take their fateful stand and resulted soon after in the establishment of responsible government.

One theme that reoccurs throughout this book is the power of Britishness as a cultural identifier. The evolution of Britishness and its contested meaning in Britain itself and the colonies has been chronicled elsewhere.[21] This book looks specifically at how reformers in Canada and Australia married civic republicanism with their idea of Britishness. The concept of the international British family, as opposed to the native English, Scot, Irish, or Welsh, proved to be not only transportable but also central to understanding these new societies. Thomas Humphrey Marshall's influential essay, *Citizenship and Social Class*, outlined the establishment in the nineteenth century of social rights inherent in British citizenship.[22] Although Marshall's theory has been criticized for its narrow focus on males in England, his concept of evolving rights – first civil, then political, and lastly social, is useful for understanding why the demand for reform, specifically responsible government, was so intense in British settler societies.[23] It also goes some way to explaining how fierce protests and reform campaigns, which often included effigy burning and severe denunciations of the British government, were cloaked not in revolutionary but rather in loyalist rhetoric.[24]

In terms of Benedict Anderson's well-known concept of the "imagined community," in which members of all social formations "larger than primordial villages of face-to-face contact" hold in their minds "an image of their communion," the Australian and Canadian colonists imagined themselves to be full British citizens who simply happened to live in "new" worlds.[25] Linda Colley repeatedly calls Britain an "invented" nation, and there was no reason why this invention could not include Canada, Australia, and indeed any part of the world map coloured red.²⁶ The essays collected for Carl Bridge and Kent Fedorowich's *British World* reinforce the argument that Britishness was a transportable idea that accompanied the diaspora to the ends of the earth every bit as much as their physical possessions.²⁷ The editors note that the British world was "a broader and more fluid concept than the British Empire or British Commonwealth" and that it was not held together with economic bonds alone "but also by intricate and overlapping networks and associations of all kinds – family, occupational, professional, educational, religious, and sporting to name a few."²⁸ The nineteenth-century colonists saw themselves without qualification as British and wanted to be treated no differently in Sydney or York than if they lived in London. Protest spectacles, such as singing God Save the Queen while burning an effigy of her governor, reveal a community of dual patriots fighting passionately for the benefit of their new land and still in love with the heritage of the old.²⁹

One final theme worthy of mention here is the powerful role played by the Christian faith in shaping the views of several key reform leaders and the reform movement more generally. The rhetoric of the Nonconformists, in particular, reveals a utopian vision of society, dripping with Biblical imagery. Seymour Martin Lipset argued convincingly in his celebrated work *Political Man* that political values are constructed with twin components: economic values and cultural values.³⁰ The cultural values of the reform movement were undoubtedly coloured by Nonconformist Christianity. Two of the leading characters in this book, William Lyon Mackenzie and John Dunmore Lang, were profoundly shaped by their Scottish Presbyterianism. Lang established the first Scots church on the Australian mainland, while Mackenzie immersed his speeches and editorials with Scripture to the point where his political opponents regularly complained that he was greatly boring them with extensive Bible readings.³¹ In the absence of a father figure, the influence of Mackenzie's devout mother was evident throughout his career. He reminisced in 1824 that "my mother feared God... never in my early years can I recollect that divine worship was neglected."³²

Mackenzie and Lang were thoroughly typical of an age when reformist politics and the Nonconformist conscience were often two sides of the same coin.³³ For many radicals and reformers the quest for salvation and the struggle to usher in the new millennium on earth compelled them to embrace a plethora of "good causes." A fitting example of this world view can be found in the radical Bible Christian minister, James Scholefield, whose congregation regularly sang a hymn with the telling line, "the Common Welfare is our only task." The Scriptures also shaped their sense of the rights of man, producing a heady religiosity of social justice that is nowadays called liberation theology. To again quote Scholefield: "For all the Books that ever were written, none ever flew so full in the face of oppression, and pleaded for justice, mercy and truth, so boldly and repeatedly, as the Bible. In short the Bible is… eminently worthy of being entitled – RIGHTS OF MAN."[34] Lang and Mackenzie (and many others discussed in this work) were "conviction politicians," members of what Alex Tyrrell has called the "moral radical party."[35] The centrality of the religious impulse for some of the reformist politicians discussed here suggests the need for a sub-category of Christian civic republicanism.

The concept of Christian civic republicanism is significant for three reasons. First, it reconciles the frequent inter-textuality of Biblical language in political speeches and documents. This can be readily seen, not just with Mackenzie and Lang, but with Joseph Howe, Daniel Deniehy, John West, and others.[36] Howe read the Bible incessantly, calling it one of "the two great wells of English undefiled" (the other was Shakespeare).[37] The boy orator Deniehy passionately preached against hereditary title, arguing instead for "God's aristocracy" and West, a Congregationalist minister, spoke of the reconciliation between the "laws of God and man."[38]

Second, the Nonconformist nature of the reform movement was partly a response to the over-representation of Church of England members among the colonial elite. This was particularly true in the tory cabals of Canada, where, along with a near-monopoly of desirable government positions, the Church of England also claimed one-seventh of Crown land under a particular interpretation of the 1791 Constitution Act that reserved land for the "Maintenance and Support of a Protestant Clergy."[39] Throughout the British world, large numbers of reformers of all stripes, radical Christians and secularists alike, regarded the Church of England as the corrupt adjunct of a bloated aristocratic state.

Third, and most importantly, a major implication of the marriage of Christianity and reformist politics is that the ideology takes on a distinctly non-liberal character. The rhetoric of reform leaders does not reveal a commitment to individual freedom and non-interference but rather a religious zeal to see their British communities become colonies of virtue. Even when the reformers identify as liberal, in the nineteenth-century progressive sense of the word, there is still a sense that a higher power compels them and that their liberty is to be used not for self gain but for the holier purpose of creating a virtuous society. The *St Thomas Liberal*, for example, printed the following "Rhymes for the People" in the rebellion year of 1837:

> Our King – our government and laws,
> While just, we aye shall love them,
> But Freedom's Heaven-born, holier cause
> We hold supreme above them.[40]

Liberalism and negative liberty most certainly played a role in the advancement of democracy. What will be discussed here is the role of civic republicanism and the specific "holier cause," a vision of a British Christian society dedicated to civic virtue, civic duty, and a civic religion.

Without overlooking or underestimating the importance of a Christian conviction of duty, it is important to see it in terms a broader discourse that was also articulated by those for whom religion was either not prominent or not present in their understanding of the relationship between liberty and duty. The aim of this book is to demonstrate that the reform leaders drew not only from Lockean liberalism but also consistently from a community-minded, civic republican tradition. The rhetoric of the reformers and the nature of the protests themselves reveal a passionate desire to create a specific type of virtuous society. With the focus so strongly on the common good rather than individual rights, this book concludes that civic republicanism was a prominent ideology during the transition to responsible government in Canada first, then immediately after in Australia.

The intention here, it must be stressed, is not to re-brand historical figures as republicans. Such an approach leads easily to historical anachronism, since the protagonists did not apply strict labels to themselves. They did not box themselves in as Lockeans or Hobbesians. Too often the Either/Or logic of the Danish philosopher Søren Kierkegaard is applied to cultural studies, resulting in an unhelpful branding of historical characters.⁴¹ Kierkegaard's theory, of course, has its place. When, however, assessing the politico-ideology of individuals from the mid-nineteenth century British world and the societies they were a part of, it is more useful to employ a Hegelian dialectic.⁴² The human mind, after all, is not an example of linear modality but rather the paragon of a dialectical process in the construction of meaning. The individual mind, and infinitely more so the collective mind, has the capacity, indeed the inclination, to absorb seemingly or blatantly contradictory ideas into a relatively coherent synthesis. Claude Lévi-Strauss contends that through the process of bricolage, societies and the political actors within them draw from many philosophical founts to form their world view.⁴³ This book endeavours to illustrate that civic republicanism was one such fount that has hitherto been hidden from colonial histories.

The goal here is to advocate civic republicanism at the expense, but certainly not the exclusion, of liberalism. It is hoped that the research exhibited in this book will go some way to correcting a mistaken presumption that the mid-nineteenth-century rejection of separatist republicanism in Australia and Canada correlated with a rejection of republican thought. The aim is not to promote civic republican as a new brand name, as it were, with which to stamp Australia and Canada. The postulation is simply that civic republicanism as a political theory was prominent and that many people in these British societies, both laymen and political leaders, borrowed ideas from this tradition in pursuit of the ideal British *common weal*. The project is to assess the impact of this politico-ideology in the lead-up to responsible government in the mid-nineteenth century. The task is not to judge but to understand.

2

What Is Civic Republicanism?

Republicanism is all too often seen as a province of democratic theory bordering on the large empire of liberalism. But it is historically more correct to regard both liberal and democratic political theory as provinces of republicanism.

Mario Viroli, Republicanism

Ideologies do not tend to spring to dominance in a cultural *coup d'état*. Unlike the physical manifestations they produce, which may well appear sudden, the ideology itself is generally the result of a slow evolution in thought. Republican ideology in the Canadian and Australian colonies certainly adheres to this axiom. The philosophical underpinnings of colonial reformation did not appear *ex nihilo*. In order to understand civic republicanism in the 1850s, it is necessary a priori to understand the circumstances that produced it. The classical, Renaissance, and revolutionary traditions of civic republicanism will be briefly outlined before tracing its historiography.

Civic republicanism is an ancient political ideology with roots in classical Athens and Rome. The etymology of the term implies its primary concerns. "Civic" is a derivative of the Latin word *ciuicus*, meaning connection and involvement with fellow citizens. The word was also associated with a garland of oak leaves awarded for saving the life of a fellow soldier in the Roman army.[1] Indeed, soldiers working together and looking out for one another is an apt metaphor for a civic republican utopia. "Republic" comes from *res publica*, meaning activities affecting the whole people, the public good, or the national interest. When added together, civic republicanism means a society of citizens engaging in activities to promote the body politic. It is a philosophy that extols participation in a political community and emphasizes the need to counter the desire for self gain (corruption) with the desire for the greater good (virtue). Like Roman soldiers watching over their comrades, citizens should be concerned about the well-being of their peers and value *bonum commune communitatis* (the common good) over *bonum commune hominis* (the individual good).

The two principal contributors to the theory of civic republicanism from the ancient world are the Greek philosopher, Aristotle (384–322 BCE), and the Roman statesman, Marcus Tullius Cicero (106–43 BCE). In his enduring philosophical tome, *The Politics*, Aristotle famously charged that "man is by nature a political animal" (ζῷον πολιτικόν).[2] Among the animals of the world, man alone possessed *logos* (λόγος), which is translated as both "argument" and "reason". In terms of usage the two are virtually synonymous for the Greeks: Democritus asserts that if something is not arguable it is not reasonable.[3]

Aristotle arrived in Athens during the twilight of their famous democracy. Following the democratic reforms of Cleisthenes, Athens emerged in the late sixth century BCE as the cradle of civic republicanism. Particularly during the Periclean period (mid-fifth century BCE), Athens prided itself on the equality its citizens enjoyed before the law. All citizens, regardless of wealth, were expected to participate in the formation of laws and the running of the state. Such was their belief in civic duty and active participation that an organized police force would roam the streets searching for absent citizens when the *Ekklesia* (ἐκκλησία) was in session.[4] Any citizens found loitering were lassoed with a rope covered in red-dye and dragged to Pynx Hill. The red stain on their tunics would inform the community that this person did not really care about the republic. Magisterial positions were granted by lottery, and the threat of ostracism served to deter potential dictators. In his famous funeral oration, Pericles boasted of the democratic and meritocratic nature of the Athenian *polis* (πόλις). He concluded: "Our government is not copied from those of our neighbours: we are an example to them rather than they to us. Our constitution is named a democracy, because it is in the hands not of the few but of the many. But our laws secure equal justice for all in their private disputes, and our public opinion welcomes and honours talent in every branch of achievement, not for any sectional reason but on grounds of excellence alone."[5] Aristotle saw the art of politics in general and the ethos of civic republicanism in particular as central to Athens' success.

Aristotle's *Politics* is famous for its scientific dissection of various constitutions, which concludes that power may reside in the hands of the many, the few, or a single person. If the government serves the common good then these forms are called polity, aristocracy, and monarchy. If, however, the government seeks its own profit against the common good the forms degenerate into democracy, oligarchy, and tyranny. Even the good forms for Aristotle are not ideal by themselves. If a state has popular rule he warns, "suppose the poor, because they are the majority, divide up the property of the wealthy; is this not unjust?" Conversely he questions, "is it just for the minority and the rich to rule? So if these also do the same things and ravage and take away the possessions of the multitude, it will be just?" Aristotle's solution to this dilemma is a mixed constitution. Although men are not equal and not all can obtain high office, all should participate in public life and civic institutions. Every citizen should contribute in some way, "for each of them, though many, could have a part of virtue and prudence, and just as they could, when joined together in a multitude, become one human being with many feet, hands, and senses, so also could they become one in character and thought."[6]

Aristotle contends that man is the only animal with the ability to contribute to politics, that is, to things concerned with the *polis* or community.[7] Politics, therefore, is the most virtuous of pursuits, since it distinguishes man from other animals. Aristotle notes, however, that the raison d'être of politics is to serve the common good: "Therefore, the Good of man must be the end of the science of politics. For even though it be the case that the Good is the same for the individual and for the state, nevertheless, the good of the state is manifestly a greater and more perfect good, both to attain and to preserve. To secure the good of one person only is better than nothing, but to secure the good of a nation or a state is a nobler and more divine achievement."[8] The Aristotelian ideal is to create a society of virtuous citizens who engage in politics to benefit the state.

Cicero, writing more than two and a half centuries after Aristotle's death, placed a similar emphasis on the need to promote virtue and counter corruption. He argued that the highest realization of *virtutem* (virtue) was achieved through defending the *communem salutem* (common safety) and contributing to *civitatus gebernatio* (governing the state). He writes: "I will content myself with asserting that Nature has implanted in the human race so great a need of virtue and so great a desire to defend the common safety that the strength thereof has conquered all the adherents of pleasure and ease."[9] This is a remarkable, and very idealistic, statement suggesting that civic republicanism can produce a state with such virtuous citizens that individual "pleasure and ease" are seen as secondary to the common good. Cicero believed, however, that the choice represented a false dichotomy, since the prudent path and the virtuous path were always the same.

This idealism is perhaps unsurprising. Cicero, like Aristotle, was writing at a time when democracy seemed to be fading (mid-first century BCE). The principles of the Roman republic were under ever-increasing attack from the ambitious power lust of Caesar, Mark Antony, Octavian, Pompey, and others. Cicero looked to the Greek Stoics and the Peripatetics (the Aristotelian school of thought) and sought a utopian civic republican solution. His works, *On the Commonwealth* and *On the Laws*, written between 54 and 51 BCE, sought to adapt Greek political thought to the Roman republic.[10]

Cicero saw the law, rather than active participation in politics, as the great defender of a just republic. Freedom was defined not by creating the laws but by a citizen's *aequalitas* (equality) under the law. Nevertheless, Aristotle and Cicero highlight many of the same ingredients as necessary for a successful and happy state. The production of virtue is a key binding element. Active citizens must be encouraged through civic institutions to embrace the state and to seek common profit rather than individual gain. A sense of communalism is both natural and necessary. Good laws are essential and must be geared towards protecting the state from tyranny, be it external or internal. For Aristotle the citizens should participate in the creation of laws; for Cicero citizens need only to be protected from domination by them. These two variations of civic republicanism would continue through the centuries, and civic republican thinkers from other times can be categorized as either neo-Grecian or neo-Roman.

Although of less impact than Aristotle and Cicero in the formation of classical republican thought, two other ancients are worthy of mention here: the historians Polybius (203–120 BCE) and Livy (59–17 BCE).[11] Polybius was a strong supporter of Aristotelian mixed government and argued in his *Histories* that the strength of the Roman republic lay in its separation of powers between the consuls, the senators, and the people. He notes that the powers of each element "had been regulated with such a scrupulous regard to equity and equilibrium, that no one could say for certain, not even a native, whether the constitution as a whole was an aristocracy, or democracy or despotism."[12] The works of Polybius, though not celebrated in his own time, would prove to have an enormous impact on the authors of the United States constitution. Many of the Founding Fathers considered the Roman republic to be the closest humans had come to an ideal state and Polybius, whose writings went through five editions in the late eighteenth century, was their main source of Roman knowledge.[13] The primacy of separation of powers in the constitution and the staunch apologia for the principle in John Adam's *Defence of the Constitutions of Government* bears the mark of Polybian thinking.[14]

Like Polybius, Livy was called on regularly by the American founders as they debated how to emulate Rome yet avoid her fate. M.N.S. Sellers comments that "Livy's project was exactly that of America's new statesmen – to quarry history for models both to imitate and to avoid, so as to create a republic by forestalling the dangers of avarice, luxury and passion which had ruined the republic in Rome."[15] Livy, who was sixteen when Cicero was murdered, shared with him a firm belief that the essential element of a free republic was *imperia legum potentior fuerunt quam hominem* (the power of the law being stronger than that of men).[16] The heroes of Livy's *History of Rome* were paragons of civic republican virtue who lived, and in some cases died, not for themselves but for the *communem salute.* Livy and Polybius, along with Aristotle, Cicero, and others, were rediscovered during the Italian Renaissance and played a major role in shaping republican thought there.

The next major innovator and contributor to the civic republican tradition was the Florentine diplomat and political philosopher Niccolò Machiavelli (1469–1527). Two of Machiavelli's posthumously released works, *Il Principe* (*The Prince*) and *Discorsi sopra la prima deca di Tito Livio* (*Discourses on the First Ten Books of Livy*) would serve as a staple for republicans for centuries to come. Jean-Jacques Rousseau went so far as to describe *Il Principe* as "a handbook for republicans."[17] As with Aristotle and Cicero, civic republicanism for Machiavelli meant a constant struggle to counter corruption with virtue in the citizenry. While the precise meaning of both terms does vary between the three thinkers, the general motif that corruption serves the individual good whereas virtue serves the common good is maintained. Unlike Cicero, however, Machiavelli has no faith in natural virtue but, rather, suggests that "it must be taken for granted that all men are wicked." For Machiavelli, participation in civic institutions, such as religion or the military, serves as a safeguard against "the malignity that is in [the people's] minds."[18] Participation is therefore crucial, since it allows civic republicanism to produce civic virtue within the citizenry.

Machiavelli's works were produced as the last of the Italian republics were succumbing to autocratic rule. Even his beloved Florentine republic was to be consumed by the powerful House of Medici in 1512 and, following a republican revival in 1527 (the year of his death), again in 1530. Machiavelli looked back to the Roman republic, just as Cicero had looked to the Athenian republic, in search of the ideal state. Machiavelli concludes that popular government is preferable to monarchical reign because "if you put the populace in charge of protecting liberty, it is reasonable to believe that they will do a better job, and since they cannot hope to monopolise power themselves, they will ensure nobody else does."[19] Like the classical civic republicans, Machiavelli saw virtue as key to the survival of the state. Even if a corrupt people somehow obtained freedom in a republic, they would likely lose it. Only the production of civic virtue could ensure the success of civic republicanism.

In a pre-Enlightenment context, Aristotle, Cicero, and Machiavelli are generally accepted as the three leviathans within the civic republican pantheon. These writers provide the basis of civic republican thought. It is important to emphasize that the classical and Renaissance authors of the civic republican tradition never argued against the presence of monarchy. Many modern commentators have tried (largely in vain) to highlight that in terms of political ideology, monarchy and republic are not mutually exclusive. Bill Galligan argued during the republican debates of the 1990s that "Australia is already a republic."[20] Examining American political thought, John Koritansky describes the possibility of a "republican monarchy."[21] Patrick Collinson sparked a wave of new research with his essay "The Monarchical Republic of Queen Elizabeth I."[22] Significantly, even the eighteenth-century pamphleteer Thomas Paine, whose works were so influential in the American Revolution, made the point that "what is called republic, is not any particular form of government."[23]

The classical civic republican authors were generally in favour of a mixed government with powers shared between the three Aristotelian good forms; monarchy, aristocracy, and polity. Machiavelli writes in *Discorsi* that if a constitution combines *Principato* (Principality), *Ottimati* (Aristocracy) and *Popolare* (Democracy), "each would keep watch over the other."[24] In the Polybian tradition, the monarchic element need not be a traditional, hereditary monarch. A Roman consul, Greek magistrate, or any powerful political leader could fulfil the monarchic role so long as their power was curtailed by that of parliament and, by extension, the people. John Adams and many of America's Founding Fathers saw the role of the president as a de facto monarch, with the senate representing the aristocracy and the congress the people.[25] The intelligentsia of Tudor and Stuart England reconnected with the concept of a mixed constitution in a powerful way. Whig historians came to consider mixed government as an ancient English right. The seventeenth-century struggle between parliament and the monarchy would serve to entrench the civic republican tradition in the English *polis*.

The ultimate victory of the Roundheads and the execution of Charles I on 30 January 1649 resulted in the creation of an eleven-year republic (1649–60). Civic republicanism was a powerful politico-ideology during this turbulent period. The most articulate expression of this theory was to come from the pen of James Harrington (1611–77). Harrington's most famous work, *The Commonwealth of Oceana*, was released in 1656, the mid-point of England's republican experiment. *Oceana* was both a rebuttal of the *Leviathan* by Thomas Hobbes (1588–1679) and a prospectus for a new republican state. Having witnessed the catastrophic schism between the monarchy and parliament resulting in a bloody civil war, Harrington was searching for a new social contract. The works of Harrington and Hobbes can be seen as foundational texts in the respective republican and tory canons. Both men were writing in response to the calamitous civil war and both sought to reconcile the authority of the state with the freedom of the individual in a new political symbiosis.

Released in 1651, Hobbes' *Leviathan* put forward the case that society must surrender various freedoms to an absolute monarch in exchange for peace and security. Hobbes dismisses the logic of Aristotle and Cicero as "nothing else but captions of words, and inventions how to puzzle." He is particularly scathing of Aristotle, insisting that nothing could be more "repugnant to government than much of that he hath said in his Politics, nor more ignorantly, than a great part of his ethics." Hobbes contended that individual freedom was synonymous with pre-societal anarchy, "for as among masterless men, there is perpetual war, of every man against his neighbour; no inheritance, to transmit to the son, nor to expect from the father; no propriety of goods, or lands; no security." In order to obtain security and harmony, a monarch must be obeyed and empowered, "to be judge both of the means of peace and defence, and also of the hindrances, and disturbances of the same; and to do whatever he shall think necessary to be done."[26]

The antithesis to Hobbes' view, the contention that ruling power must be limited to protect liberty, would be most famously pronounced in John Locke's *Two Treatises of Government*.[27] Harrington's republican response to the English political crisis sits somewhere in between Hobbesian absolutism and Lockean liberalism. Harrington, like Hobbes, suggests that individual freedoms must be forfeited. Unlike Hobbes, however, he suggests they be surrendered to a free republic, the laws of which the people themselves help form. A republican utopia would follow the tradition of Aristotle and Livy and produce an "empire of laws and not of men." Harrington saw the Greek and Roman republics as high points in civil administration and sought a return to the "ancient prudence" of those societies.

Machiavelli's theory of civic republicanism is particularly praiseworthy according to Harrington, who describes the Italian as the "learned disciple" of ancient prudence.[28] Like Machiavelli, Harrington highlights the twin needs of a republican utopia: strong civic institutions and a virtuous citizenry to participate in them. Civic virtue, according to Harrington, can be best instilled through religion, education, and the military.[29] Along with participation in civic institutions, citizens of Harrington's commonwealth are able to participate in forming laws and running the state. Iseult Honohan notes, "Harrington emphasises that participation should be widely open and that upward mobility should be possible on a meritocratic basis – 'where a man from the lowest cannot rise... the commonwealth is not equal.'"[30]

The glory of civic republicanism is the provision of political liberty and the protection it offers citizens from tyranny. For this reason

Harrington hastens to dispute Hobbes' claim that the citizens of a republic do not enjoy greater freedom than the subjects of a monarch. Hobbes writes that "whether a commonwealth be monarchical, or popular, the freedom is still the same." In Lucca, he continues, the word *Libertas* is engraved in the city's turrets, and yet citizens there have no more liberty than in Constantinople.[31] Harrington forcefully rejects Hobbes' assertion. The critical difference is that the people of Lucca are subject to laws put in place to serve the common good. The people of Constantinople are forever at the mercy of an absolute monarch who may act with impunity against the common good. Harrington notes that even the "greatest bashaw" of Constantinople is a mere tenant of the monarch, whilst the poorest landowner of Lucca remains a freeholder and is "not to be controlled but by the law." Unlike the arbitrary decrees of a monarch, the laws of a republic are not a source of domination, since they are "framed by every private man unto no other end... than to protect the liberty of every private man, which by that means comes to be the liberty of the commonwealth."[32]

Somewhat to Harrington's dismay, Hobbes never actively engaged with him, offered a rebuttal, or acknowledged his critique. One republican, however, whose "very ill reasoning" Hobbes did consider worthy of his criticism was John Milton.[33] It is debateable whether Milton chose republicanism or if it chose him. Thomas Corns notes that "before the execution of the king, there is no evidence that he had added constitutional radicalism to the array of heterodox and oppositional opinions he had shown in his pamphlets of 1641–5." In any case, Milton became an apologist for the regicide and was appointed secretary of foreign tongues in the new republic. Milton drew on Aristotelian logic in arguing against absolute monarchy: "For every Common-wealth is in general defin'd, a societie sufficient of itself, in all things conducible to well being and commodious life. Any of which requisit things if it cannot have without the gift or favour of a single person, or without leave of his privat reason, or his conscience, it cannot be thought sufficient of itself, and by consequence no Common-wealth, nor free."[34]

Milton's principal concern was the preservation of liberty. As William Morison notes, "the exaltation of liberty was his *unum ago* [sole urge]. With his right hand and his left, by his poetry and his prose, he laboured in it."[35] In Milton's own words, "Mortals that would follow me / Love virtue, she alone is free."[36] The endangerment of English liberty by the corrupt government of Charles I proved to be a "Machiavellian moment" for Milton.[37] While it has been suggested that he was a regicide rather than a republican and the critic of a king rather than kings, the radical response of Milton to the English political crisis bears the mark of civic republican ideology.[38] When monarchy degenerates into tyranny and mixed government becomes despotic rule, action must be taken to preserve the liberty of the commonwealth.

The republic of England was dissolved in 1660 when the Stuart dynasty was restored under Charles II. The most radical republican writer following the restoration was Algernon Sidney (1623–83). Like Harrington, Sidney's chief text, *Discourses concerning Government*, was written partly in response to a monarchical apologia, in this case Sir Robert Filmer's *Patriacha*.[39] Filmer's Hobbesian defence of the divine right of kings was anathema to Sidney's republican mind and was the catalyst for his passionate rebuttal. He states, "I hope to prove, that of all things under the sun, there is none more mutable or unstable than absolute monarchy; which is all that I dispute against, professing much veneration for that which is mixed, regulated by law, and directed to the publick good."

Like Harrington, Sidney was a great admirer of Machiavelli and a firm believer that civic virtue goes hand in hand with liberty, while corruption is the nurse of tyranny. He notes that "Machiavelli, discoursing of these matters, finds virtue to be so essentially necessary to the establishment and preservation of liberty, that he thinks it impossible for a corrupted people to set up a good government, or for a tyranny to be introduced if they be virtuous… [This] being confirmed by reason and experience, I think no wise man has ever contradicted him." Sidney was also in keeping with Harrington and Machiavelli when he insisted that an absolute monarch is likely to have private interests that oppose the common good, whereas a popular government has no agenda but to serve the public. Sidney highlights the animosity that these conflicting interests can produce: "In absolute monarchies the matter is quite otherwise. A prince that sets up an interest in himself, becomes an enemy to the public: in following his own lusts he offends all, except a few of his corrupt creatures, by whose help he oppresses others with a yoke they are unwilling to bear, and thereby incurs the universal hatred. This hatred is always proportionable to the injuries received, which being extreme, that must be so too; and every people being powerful in comparison to the prince that governs, he will always fear those that hate him, and always hate those he fears."[40]

Sidney drew widely from both ancient and biblical prudence in supporting his republican thesis. He called on both the Greco-Roman tradition (Plato, Aristotle, Livy, Cicero, *et alia*) and the Christian tradition (St Paul, St Augustine, Kings of Israel and Judah) to support his claims against absolute monarchy and for a civic republican mixed government. The timing of Sidney's writings (1681–83), however, proved to be fatal. Having survived the horrors of the Civil War and the tumultuous republican decade, the Stuart monarchy had little patience for a man who described the regicide of Charles I as the "justest and bravest act... that ever was done in England, or anywhere." A governmental crackdown on revolutionaries in 1683 led to Sidney's arrest. His unpublished *Discourses* were seized and used against him in the subsequent trial. Sidney used his defence as a further opportunity to attack the government and articulate his ideas. He was executed on 7 December 1683.[41]

The execution of Sidney served only to increase the fame of both the author and his work, which would be posthumously published in 1698. Following the displacement of the Stuart dynasty during England's Glorious Revolution of 1688, Sidney's legacy was transformed from traitorous to trail-blazing. Jonathan Scott notes that "the debate between Filmer and his opponents is of great significance because it helped set the terms for the thought of the eighteenth century, not only in England, but in Europe, America and still in much of the western world today."[42] The ensuing debates of the eighteenth century, both in England and America, have been seen largely as a struggle between Lockean liberalism and Burkean conservatism.

John Locke's *Two Treatises of Government* introduced a powerful alternative to republicanism in the fight against perceived tyranny. The first treatise would argue against Filmer's writing and the second would oppose Hobbes. Unlike the republican thesis, however, Locke did not seek public participation but public protection. Rather than freedom from domination, Locke argued for freedom from interference. Hence, the author places huge importance on the protection of property. Locke's influence in both exciting thirteen American colonies for revolution and forming a political philosophy for the new nation is well documented. Indeed there was a time when the motto of eighteenth-century American studies was

*Locke et praeterea nihil.*⁴³ The civic republican tradition, however, was also being advocated and warmly received during this period.

The Glorious Revolution caused a schism within the Whig party. Several civic republican thinkers who felt the revolution had not gone far enough rebelled against the mainstream and referred to themselves as the "real Whigs," or Commonwealthmen. The Commonwealthmen were a loose alliance of writers who sought to keep alive in the eighteenth century the revolutionary flame that had burned so brightly in the seventeenth. Naturally enough, Sidney was the perfect martyr and hero for their purpose. The influence of the Commonwealthmen in their native England was limited. J.W. Gough even questions whether the Commonwelathmen had much influence on nineteenth-century English radicals.⁴⁴ The impact, however, of these writers in Ireland, Scotland, and especially British America was enormous. The Revolution of 1776 can be interpreted as the ultimate manifestation of Commonwealthman ideology.

The best and most influential example of Commonwealthmen thinking can be found in the 144 short essays known as *Cato's Letters*. Penned by John Trenchard and Thomas Gordon, the letters were originally published in the *London Journal* and *British Journal* between 1720 and 1723.⁴⁵ The *Letters* were both republican and revolutionary, suggesting that tyrannical governments may expect the violent wrath of its citizens. The emotive language is typified by letter eight: "But when, through the Ignorance of their Pillagers, the Courfe of Juftice is entirely ftopt, when the abufed and enraged People can have no Remedy, either real or imaginary, nor one Victim to their Fury, they will naturally and neceffarily look higher; and then who can forefee where their Vengeance will end?" ⁴⁶ The *Letters* could be found in libraries all across eighteenth-century America, including those of the Founding Fathers. Clinton Rossiter even suggests that the *Letters* – and not Locke's writings – were the "most popular, quotable, esteemed source of political ideas in the colonial period."⁴⁷ While the Commonwealthmen sought to connect with the republicans of the seventeenth century, they were also the flag bearers of a civic republican tradition that can be traced back to classical Athens and Rome. The canon of civic republicanism continued to endorse the countering of corruption with virtue, the encouragement of participation in a political community, an emphasis on civic institutions, and the rejection of tyranny.

One final theorist worthy of mention here is the French noble Baron de Montesquieu (1689–1755). Like Locke, Montesquieu was not a republican, but his works did have a profound impact on political thought in Europe, North America, and, eventually, Australasia. Writing for the *Edinburgh Review* in 1827, prominent whig historian Thomas Macaulay opined that "Montesquieu enjoys, perhaps, a wider celebrity than any political writer of modern Europe."[48] A meticulous researcher and aficionado of ancient texts, Montesquieu spent years reading and evaluating various political systems. Fearing censorship, in 1748 he anonymously released what would become his seminal work, *De l'esprit des lois* (The Spirit of the Laws). Like Aristotle, Montesquieu identified different constitutional forms (republicanism, monarchy, and despotism). Also like Aristotle, he claims that each form can fall into corruption (although he notes that despotism is "even in its nature corrupt").[49]

Montesquieu strays from classical civic republican thought by downplaying the importance of civic virtue in an ideal society (be it monarchic, aristocratic, or democratic). As Honohan notes, civic virtue is seen as "admirable but anachronistic."[50] Montesquieu defines it as "not a moral, nor a Christian, but a political virtue." While patriotism is desirable, it is not essential, as it was for Machiavelli. Montesquieu, like Cicero, believed that *aequalitas* was the key to liberty. Equality before the law is the cornerstone of his notion of freedom. It was not, however, freedom without limits, since he warns, "we must continually present to our minds the difference between independence and liberty." Real liberty required law-abiding citizens, lest the liberty turn to anarchy.

Montesquieu championed the notion of separation of powers and constitutional checks and balances. He argued that "there is no liberty, if the judiciary power be not separated from the legislative and executive." Writing after the Glorious Revolution, Montesquieu lauds the English for separating the powers of the king and parliament. England could "be justly called a republic, disguised under the form of monarchy."[51] For Montesquieu, it was not the form of government but rather the preservation of liberty and equality before the law that made a constitution truly great. Montesquieu's influence in America was profound as the independent colonists considered how best to preserve their own newly won liberty. Melvyn Richter states that "at the time of the American Revolution, few other theorists could rival Montesquieu's prestige in the English-speaking world."[52] In the loyal colonies also, Montesquieu was read and quoted as debates raged about the merits of responsible government and the meaning of the British constitution.

British North America was born out of the 1783 Treaty of Paris, with British settlement with Australasia following just five years later, in 1788. Colonial reformers from New South Wales to Nova Scotia displayed many of the best characteristics of the civic republican tradition in their campaign for responsible government. Colonial libraries were not necessarily furnished with the writings of Sidney, Harrington, and Trenchard, but the reformist press in both hemispheres did extol a spirit of communitarianism that upheld Commonwealthmen ideology.[53] Although his connection to Australia and Canada has been largely overlooked, the civic republican teachings of Italian statesman Giuseppe Mazzini were also regularly reproduced in the reform press.[54] The fact that the Australasian and Canadian colonies never resorted to a war of independence does not mean that civic republicanism had no impact. By the mid-nineteenth century, responsible government had been successfully petitioned for in the majority of cases. This book will seek to locate the connections between the political ideology and the political manifestations.

The historiography of civic republicanism is often murky, since the definition of key terms has been contested. The first contest concerning the *Crown or Country* thesis has already been alluded to. Australian and Canadian historians have been reluctant to use the term "republican" with regard to mid-nineteenth-century political thought. With the exception of blatant colonial separatists, Australian democratic agitators have been deemed popular constitutionalists or minimal monarchists, or described in more ideologically neutral terms as reformists. None of these terms, however, can claim to be *le mot juste*, since they do not identify the political tradition to which the subjects belong. Historians have traditionally seen the political development of Canada in whiggish terms, with Lockean liberalism, tempered by tory communalism, leading the colonists down the road of democracy. Perhaps the academic nearsilence concerning the republican tradition owes something to the popular epigram that Canada draws its identity from not being the (republican) United States.[55]

The absence of a republican narrative is doubtless tied to the extreme negative connotations the term carried in the nineteenth-century British world. Owing, in part, to the perceived barbarity of the French Revolution, the word "republic" was associated with a savage, nearly anarchic regime that was juxtaposed sharply with the peaceful civility of the British constitution. In Canada especially, "republic" was also inextricably linked to the government of its southern neighbour. The British government was obviously keen to portray American republicanism in an unfavourable light and, particularly during the War of 1812, employed a propaganda campaign to this effect. It is not surprising that progressive reformers in both Canada and Australia appealed to the British constitution and the Glorious Revolution when championing their cause. Henry Parkes' *Empire* expressed its frustration at the "bugbear" of republicanism, insisting that the American system of government was in fact very close to that of Britain. He noted that "those who raise such an outcry against Yankeeism in government, little imagine, or else if they do imagine it they hypocritically conceal it, that they are really opposing all that is valuable in the British constitution." Parkes' exacerbation was well justified. He bemoaned the "imbecility" of being terrified by the "horror of names," yet this was the political reality in both Australia and Canada.[56] Republicanism was a frightening term, and the vast majority of democratic reformers avoided it at all costs.

Recognizing the *realpolitik* does not mean that reformers were cynically clouding their separatist republican aspirations in the convenient fog of a venerable notion of British rights. This book will seek to show that, while the reformers of the day did not employ the term, their activism and their concept of British citizenship reveals the influence of civic republican thinking. Civic republicanism was not a term used in contemporary debate, and its ancient advocates were rarely invoked by name on the platform, in parliament, or in the columns of the press. But that is not the point. As McKenna deftly reminds us, "in an Australian context, those who employed this [classical republican] language did not consciously perceive it as republican."[57] Nevertheless, civic republicanism is the most accurate ideological term to describe the non-liberal push for democracy in the lead-up to the granting of responsible government. Liberalism, of course, played its role; however there is much in the reformers' rhetoric that is difficult to account for with this Lockean, negative view of liberty. From the rebellions of 1837–38 to the rebellion at Eureka, there is a wealth of communitarian thinking and of calls not just for the advancement of individual rights but for a new system to serve the common good. "Civic republican" is used in this book, rather than simply "republican," in order to distinguish the concepts being dealt with from the anti-monarchical, separatist republican tradition. The word "civic" is also apt, for the heart of this theory is the support of civic participation and the production of civic virtue.

The second typological contention concerns the historiographical debate between civic humanism and civic republicanism. Civic humanism entered the historiographical lexicon as the English equivalent of *Bürgerhumanismus*, a word born out of the Weimar republic. The term is epitomised by Hannah Arendt's *vita activa* and holds that freedom and civic virtue require active participation in public life.[58] Hence, Isaiah Berlin's binary would categorize civic humanism as a theory of positive liberty. Civic humanism is associated with the work of the German Renaissance historians, the Cambridge school (J.G.A. Pocock in particular), and the Atlantic republican tradition.

Civic republicanism is viewed by some as radically distinct from civic humanism. Frank Lovett, for example, interprets the two as diametrically opposed: civic humanism is tied to a positive view of liberty and civic republicanism to the negative.[59] This stance, however, is problematic, as Lovett admits. If civic republicanism is viewed as a strictly negative concept of liberty, it loses most of what distinguishes it from modern liberalism. Republicanism, as Mario Viroli has argued, is the larger theoretic domain inside which liberalism and democratic theory both take up residency.[60] This book will interpret civic republicanism as a broader concept that, rather than opposing civic humanism, encompasses it. Civic republicanism will be understood as a large narrative concept including both neo-Grecian and neo-Roman thought. With this conception in mind, a brief outline of the civic republican historiography will be sketched.

The pioneering research into the Italian republics of the Renaissance period was conducted under the banner of civic humanism, rather than republicanism. The foundation of Italian humanist studies was laid by Jacob Burckhardt and Georg Voigt.[61] The struggle between *den Päpsten und den Hohenstaufen* (the Papacy and the Germanic dynasty that ruled much of Italy) resulted in an unstable environment and the rise of diverse political units ranging from republics to despots. Of the post-feudal Italian poleis, Burckhardt notes, "In ihnen erscheint der moderne europaische Staatsgeist zum erstenmal frei seinen eigenen Antreiben hingegeben" (In them, the modern European political spirit is seen for the first time, freely propelled by its own instincts).[62] The key contribution of Burckhardt and Voigt was their interpretation of the Italian Renaissance as an epochal transition from a medieval conciseness to a nascent modernity. It was, however, another German historian who most clearly articulated the ideological phenomena that underpinned the spirit of the age.

Hans Baron's influential tome, *The Crisis of the Early Italian Renaissance*, highlighted the role of civic republicanism as a political tool during the turbulent early Quattrocento.[63] The Florentine humanists, Baron argued, equated the decline of ancient Roman culture with the decline of the Roman republic. The revival of Italian cultural life in the Renaissance was seen by republicans as a result of the rise of free communities.[64] For civic republicans, the philosophy they extolled was not a mere system of government but a complete weltanschauung encompassing both culture and politics.

The beginning of the Quattrocento was dominated by the aggressive expansionist policy of Giangaleazzo Visconti, duke of Milan. Visconti's attempts to unite the northern Italian city-states led to a military campaign against Florence. Baron's work interprets this event very much as a struggle between republican liberty and monarchical tyranny. He writes, "Florence was taking up arms for the defence of her own liberty and for the liberty of the peoples under the yoke of the Visconti. According to another Florentine proclamation: 'Ours is a commonwealth not of noblemen... but free – the most hateful and abominable thing to the Duke."[65] It has been suggested that Baron's crisis thesis was an exegesis, drawing heavily on his own experience as a Jewish academic working in Nazi Germany; however, Riccardo Fubini and Ronald Witt have both noted that the origins of his argument are found back in the Weimar period.[66]

Some of Baron's critics argue that he overemphasizes the sociocultural changes of the Renaissance period and fails to acknowledge the pre-existing humanist elements of medieval Italy. Nevertheless, his reconstruction of Renaissance republicanism as a humanist response to a political crisis fundamentally changed the way historians conceptualized the period. Furthermore, Baron's work inspired historians of the Anglophone world to reassess the impact of civic republicanism, Machiavelli in particular, in their own crisis moments. Wallace Ferguson opined in 1958 (three years after *The Crisis* was released) that "it may be that [Baron's] most important contribution will prove to be the stimulus his ideas will give to future research."[67] This certainly proved to be prophetic, since Baron's works are still cited half a century later as key texts in the study of Italian humanism.

Bernard Bailyn's *Ideological Origins of the American Revolution* carried Baron's crisis thesis into the eighteenth-century Atlantic world. Published in 1967, *Ideological Origins* was founded on a meticulous study of revolutionary pamphlets that suggested to Bailyn that the call to arms in 1776 was motivated by ideological opposition to perceived political corruption. He writes that "the American Revolution was above all else an ideological, constitutional, political struggle and not primarily a controversy between social groups undertaken to force changes in the organization of the society or the economy" (vi).

Bailyn's work transformed the way people conceptualized the American Revolution by insisting that the ideological – indeed moral and ethical – concerns of the thirteen colonies were of greater significance than their economic opposition to the Intolerable Acts. According to Bailyn, the colonists "saw about them, with increasing clarity, not merely mistaken, or even evil, policies violating the principles upon which freedom rested, but what appeared to be evidence of nothing less than a deliberate assault launched surreptitiously by plotters against liberty both in England and in America. The danger to America, it was believed, was in fact only the small, immediately visible part of the greater whole whose ultimate manifestation would be the destruction of the English constitution, with all the rights and privileges embedded in it" (95). The American colonists felt the ministry of George III had been corrupted and was geared against the public good. Consequently, it was their duty to rise against the tyranny of George III, just as their ancestors had risen against Charles I. Bailyn sees this as a central goad to colonial wrath: "The balance of the constitution had been thrown off by a gluttonous ministry usurping the prerogatives of the crown and systematically corrupting the independence of the Commons. Corruption was at the heart of it – the political corruption built on the general dissoluteness of the populace, so familiar in the history of tyranny and so shocking to observers of mid-eighteenth-century England" (130).

Bailyn highlights the numerous references that were made to the classical and English republican traditions in the revolutionary pamphlets. This in turn poses the question: might not the same be true in other English-speaking places? He notes the civic republican terminology of Arthur Lee, who worried in 1768 that "unchecked taxation would lead to a total corruption of free government in America, with the result that the colonies would 'experience the fate of the Roman people in the deplorable times of their slavery'" (102). Commonwealthmen ideology also played a clear role, with Bailyn writing, "This distinctive influence had been transmitted most directly to the colonists by a group of early-eighteenth-century radical publicists and opposition politicians in England who carried forward into the eighteenth century and applied to the politics of the age of Walpole the peculiar strain of anti-authoritarianism bred in the upheaval of the English Civil War."[68]

In his celebrated tome, *The Machiavellian Moment*, J.G.A. Pocock elucidated further on the links between the civic republican tradition and the revolution in America. Pocock draws a clear epistemological link between revolutionary thought in America and the civic republican tradition. He notes that, "a political culture took shape in the eighteenth-century colonies which possessed all the characteristics of neo-Harringtonian civic humanism" and further that the American Revolution was "anchored in the Aristotelian and Machiavellian tradition."[69]

The orthodox account of American historiography had held that Lockean liberalism, with its theory of negative liberty, was the dominant impetus driving the revolution. Athanasios Moulakis writes that this paradigm of thought was so entrenched that it was "identified not as Lockeanism or liberalism but rather as 'Americanism.'"[70] Pocock's republican revisionism presented a powerful challenge to Locke's status as the "patron saint of American values." His interpretation "stresses Machiavelli at the expense of Locke; it suggests that the republic – a concept derived from Renaissance humanism – was the true heir of the covenant and the dread of corruption the true heir of the jeremiad."[71]

Where Pocock saw the revival of neo-Grecian civic republicanism, the other notable contributor to the Cambridge school, Quentin Skinner, saw neo-Roman civic republicanism. Re-examining the anti-Medicean writings of late Quattrocento and early Cinquecentro Florentine theorists, including Francesco Patrizi, Alamanno Rinuccini, Antonio Brucioli, Francesco Guicciardini, Donato Giannotti, and, of course, Machiavelli, Skinner concludes that the binding element is the authors' allegiance to political liberty. This allegiance, however, belonged to a pre-humanist republican tradition. Although freedom from monarchic tyranny is stressed by all these writers, whether the republic should be governed by all or primarily by the elite (*governo largo o stretto*) was for Skinner a more complex question.

While Machiavelli and Giannotti stressed the value of an inclusive *Consiglio Grande*, which would extend to the ordinary *popolani*, Patrizi and Guicciardini argued that the plebeians were simply incapable of making important governmental decisions. Guicciardini notes that because "the city has always been free" and is "attached to liberty," it is natural enough that the people of Florence would revolt against despotism. This does not necessarily mean, however, an endorsement of *vita activa*.[72] For Skinner the primary concern of Florentine republicans was not the revival of Aristotelian participatory democracy but the return of classical Roman jurisprudence. Thus the emphasis was on preserving liberty in the negative sense.

Although Skinner highlights the role of negative liberty in the republican tradition, he also broadens the philosophical lens through which the concept is viewed. This is perhaps his greatest contribution to republican historiography. In his own words: "I shall try to show that, in an earlier and now discarded tradition of thought about social freedom, the negative idea of liberty as the mere non-obstruction of individual agents in the pursuit of their chosen ends was combined with the ideas of virtue and public service in just the manner nowadays assumed on all sides to be impossible without incoherence."[73] The symbiosis of non-obstruction and public service is uncomfortable, since it presumes that a citizen's personal interest and public duty will face the same direction. This book views the promotion of civic institutions, patriotism, virtue, and an active campaign to regulate society for the greater good as clear evidence of positive liberty. Unlike Skinner, civic republicanism will be viewed as a positive conception of liberty.

The role of civic republicanism in Britain's Australasian and Canadian colonies has gone almost entirely without investigation. The dominance of the *Crown or Country* thesis has led generations of historians to conclude that there is no republican tradition to investigate.[74] In 1995 Janet Ajzenstat and Peter Smith's *Canada's Origins* drew upon the Bailyn-Pocock tradition and challenged this powerful orthodoxy. The question posed in the subtitle of this work, *Liberal, Tory, or Republican?*, marks a new way of conceptualizing the development of political thought in Canada. The authors assert that, "the challenge to nineteenth-century liberalism arose from a republican ideology on the political left, rather than toryism on the right."[75] Interestingly, while Smith maintains that the place of civic republicanism has not been fully acknowledged, Ajzenstat has adjusted her position somewhat. Concerning the founding of Canada, she now sees the clear impact of Locke's hand.[76] Although, the responsible-government debates took place some twenty years before the confederation debates, this book will challenge the assumption of Lockean dominance by seeking out evidence of the civic republican tradition opposing both liberalism and conservatism in the pursuit of responsible government in Canada and Australia. Beginning with the Rebellions of 1837–38 and concluding with the Eureka Stockade, this work is bookended with riot and revolt. It is, however, the lack of violence that is remarkable when considering the revolutionary changes that took place in such a short time. How did civic republicanism shape the reform movement? Is responsible government a civic republican legacy? The next four chapters will explore the Canadian experience before attention is turned to Australia.

3

1837: The Almost Revolution

> The contest to be waged in this Province is between Monarchy and
> a Republic. There are of course men professing all shades of opinion,
> but the time draws nearer every day, where they must either declare
> their attachment to the British Constitution, or venture on the bold
> and dangerous step of signing a Declaration of Independence.
>
> *Royal Standard*, 9 November 1836

Conventional semantics tells us that a rebellion and a revolution are both attempts to dramatically alter a system of government that is deemed to be intolerable, the difference being that a revolution is successful while a rebellion is not. It is, however, one of history's long-running ironies that many revolutions, though technically successful, actually failed to achieve their goals, while many rebellions, though technically unsuccessful, managed to achieve their objectives in the long run. From a military point of view, the Rebellions of 1837–38 in Upper and Lower Canada were a tragicomedy. Nevertheless, the philosophy that underpinned the failed *coup d'état* did not evaporate or follow the rebellion leaders in seeking exile. This chapter will suggest that the rebellions were the result of a great desire not for separatist republicanism but for greater democracy. Further, the type of democracy pursued was more civic republican in its form than liberal. The grievances that spurred the movement received immediate attention in the form of the *Durham Report* and ultimate satisfaction a decade later when Nova Scotia became the first colony in the empire to enjoy responsible government.

In 1995, Allan Greer published an article calling for the Rebellions of 1837–38 to be reconsidered.[1] Greer felt attempts to better understand the rebellions were being "bedevilled by a particularly advanced case of historiographical apartheid." This binary approach to understanding the two provinces is as old as the rebellions themselves. Addressing the grand jury in 1838, Chief Justice John Beverley Robinson found the actions of the Upper Canadians "incomprehensible" but found the Lower Canadians' actions unsurprising.[2] Greer laments that too many works see "no connection between the two rebellions, as if it were pure coincidence that Mackenzie attacked Toronto just after fighting broke out in the Montreal region." A second major obstacle, according to Greer, is "the comparative isolation of Canadian historiography from larger international currents." This chapter offers civic republicanism as one possible solution to the myopic historiography of the rebellions. The rebellions were by no means identical, but there was a common desire by reformers in both provinces to achieve a more democratic constitution. This desire, it will be argued throughout this work, was part of a broader democratization of the British Empire as colonists from Montreal to Melbourne debated what it meant to be a British subject.

This chapter will pay particular attention to the political philosophy of the reform movements led by radical Scottish journalist and statesman William Lyon Mackenzie and the French Canadian leader Louis-Joseph Papineau. Both these men achieved infamy for their prominent roles in the Rebellions of 1837–38. It will be argued here that for many of their supporters, democracy and civic republicanism were primary concerns and separatist republicanism was an option they felt driven to, not one they wholeheartedly embraced. Mackenzie and Papineau are two of the most controversial figures in Canadian history. Papineau continues to be revered as a cult figure of French Canadian resistance to forced assimilation, while Mackenzie was seen for decades after his death as the champion of democratic reform.[3] Were these men democratic liberals? This chapter will suggest that the reform movement they led, while doubtless influenced by liberalism, can be better understood through the prism of civic republican ideology. Long before the trouble, in 1834, Mackenzie stated that Canada "has not the dignity, the texture, nor the independence of the British Constitution – it is far beneath, in point of efficiency, purity and liberality, that form adopted in the neighbouring Republic."[4] This was a period of political frustration for reformers, who felt their rights under the British constitution were being ignored. Although few sought separatist republicanism, the longing for greater democracy caused some to look enviously at the United States. It was not so much a quest for individual rights, however, that spurred the reformers to contemplate rebellion but rather a desire to see the British provinces governed by the principles of virtue, positive liberty, and a philosophy that sought the common good over individual gain.

At the height of its power in the eighteenth century, British America stretched from Florida to Newfoundland on the Atlantic Seaboard. The loss of the thirteen colonies in the Revolutionary War was an extreme psychological blow to the empire that stood as master of North America following the Treaty of Paris of 1763. After two short decades, a new Treaty of Paris in 1783 would see the bulk of the continental empire lost, with ramifications that would reverberate even into the new century. In early 1783, King George III mused in an unpublished paper, "America is lost! Must we fall beneath the blow? Or have we resources that might repair the mischief?"[5] The spectre of 1776 would stalk British policy towards Canada and Australia, and indeed the entire colonial empire, right through to the granting of responsible government.

The Continental Congress by no means had universal support in America. British Loyalists were to be found in all thirteen colonies and all social classes. As Gerald Craig notes, "their numbers can never be certainly known, for there were almost infinite degrees of positive and passive loyalism, but those who worked and hoped and fought for the defeat of the rebellion made up a quarter of the nearly two million residents in the Thirteen Colonies."[6] The nature and legacy of the loyalists has been contested. Thomas Allen characterizes them as "tories," instinctively conservative opponents of the revolution.[7] Maya Jasanoff offers a more nuanced description, noting that "loyalism cut right across the social, geographical, racial and ethnic spectrum of early America."[8] Most loyalists simply accepted the new American republic and moved on with their lives. Some fifty thousand, however, mainly farmers, emigrated north, mainly settling in southern Quebec with government grants of land.

Amateur historian William Canniff said of the loyalists, "this noble class... would live anywhere, endure any toil... so long as they were in the King's dominion, and the good old flag waved over their head."[9] The 1774 Quebec Act was still in place, and this caused great tension among the newly arrived loyalists and the traditional French inhabitants of the province. The Quebec Act recognized and protected what the British saw as the three pillars of French

Canadian culture: the Roman Catholic faith, the French language, and French civil law. Reginald Coupland described the measure as crucial for avoiding in Canada "a re-enactment of the Irish tragedy."[10] The drafters were doubtless concerned about avoiding the Acadian tragedy as well.[11] The act ended discrimination against Roman Catholics by allowing them to stand for public office and removed references to Protestantism from the controversial oath of allegiance. It also reinstated French civil law in Quebec, including the semi-feudal Seigneurial system of land distribution.[12] This act was one of the so-called Intolerable Acts that spurred the American Revolution. It was intolerable also to the loyalists, and the British parliament debated an alternative arrangement.

In April and May 1791 there was a heated debate between Charles Fox, the leading whig, and Prime Minister Pitt, leader of the tories. Pitt was seeking to pass a bill that would become the Constitution Act (also known as the Canada Act). The purpose of the bill was to separate Quebec into a French north and a British south and to provide a British-style constitution to both provinces. The bill, originally authored by Lord Grenville, was given a major amendment by Pitt. Clauses XXXV to XLII dictated that one-seventh of the land in Upper Canada would be reserved for the "Maintenance and Support of a Protestant Clergy" and every township should reserve land for a rectory "according to the establishment of the Church of England."[13] Fox argued both that this was far too generous and that the Roman Catholic Church or even the Church of Scotland had a better claim to public support according to the population make-up.[14]

Fox's main attack, however, was centred on the legal structure of the bill. The new province of Upper Canada was geographically next door to the newly established United States of America. Fox stressed that the Loyalists who had fought for Britain in the Revolutionary War must not feel that their situation was worse than that of their neighbours. He worried that the undemocratic nature of the constitution and the considerable power the unelected Legislative Council held over the popular Legislative Assembly would create an unfavourable comparison with the United States. He informed the Commons in April:

> You offer the Canadians the privilege of representation, but when we come to examine into this representation, we find that the Assembly of Lower Canada is to consist of thirty

Members, and that of Upper Canada of sixteen Members only. Is this a popular Assembly? Is this a representation? Or is it representation burlesqued?... While you have limited the popular Assemblies of Canada (if it be not ridiculous to call them by that name) to the number of 30 and 16, you have thought it proper to leave the Members of the Council unlimited. The Members of the Council are the creatures of the Governor who has the power of creating them at his pleasure, and who of course will not fail to gain over to his interest the whole aristocracy of the province. Will a popular Assembly of thirty or sixteen Members form a counter-balance to this aristocracy?[15]

Fox suggested an elected council with a restrictive franchise or, at the very least, with councillors chosen for life, but without the hereditary element. Pitt was unmoved and countered that the constitution should mirror the constitution of Britain as closely as possible and that a hereditary council would act like a de facto House of Lords. Fox made one last attempt to derail Pitt's plans on 9 May. This time he argued that the province should not be divided at all, claiming the tories were "separating [Britain's] interests, which ought to be combined, and widening instead of closing the division between the ancient French inhabitants, and the recent settlers." Edmund Burke leaped to Pitt's defence insisting that the "lesser inconveniences" highlighted by Fox must "give way to greater advantages."[16] Defeated and outnumbered, Fox bitterly told the Commons on 12 May that he hoped "it would no longer be attempted to be said that we gave Canada even a sketch of the British constitution, or anything like it." The Constitution Act was given royal assent on 19 June 1791.

The act allowed for, but did not technically dictate, the separation of Quebec into a Protestant, English-dominated Upper Canada and a Roman Catholic, French-dominated Lower Canada. It gave both provinces a bicameral legislature. The Legislative Council would be appointed by the governor, and councillors would hold seats for life. The King was empowered to grant hereditary titles of honour. The Legislative Assembly would consist of elected members serving a maximum term of four years. Rural citizens could vote if they possessed freehold property worth forty shillings per annum or more. Urban citizens would have to own property worth five pounds per annum or rent property at a rate of ten pounds per annum.[17]

The phraseology of the Westminster debates reveals that the meaning of the British constitution was bitterly contested. This great war of ideas would eventually see battles and skirmishes not only in London but in Manchester, Montreal, Melbourne, and every place in the empire where freemen and women discussed their rights and liberties as British subjects. The conservative Pittites in Britain and the colonies took a traditional Hobbesian, tory position, insisting on the necessity of a strong centralized government. It was natural enough to give the colonists a system of government similar to that of Britain. The Foxite camp countered that the meaning of the constitution had been distorted. The social contract had been bent in favour of the aristocracy, and the ancient mixed constitution was neglecting the popular arm. In short, the battle was for the place of democracy in the British constitution.

What is often lost in the examinations of the Pittite-Foxite clash is that the latter camp was petitioning for a specific type of democracy that can be best described as civic republican. It can be assumed quite reasonably that the whigs were not separatist republicans. It will be argued in subsequent chapters that even within the radical camps in the colonies there were few who supported political separation. Significantly though, it was not simply a liberal democracy for which the Foxites campaigned. The reformers petitioned for a specific type of democracy with a strong emphasis on communalism and on civic virtue. The Constitution Act would be found intolerable and would ultimately spark an armed rebellion. The act was despised because it allowed for widespread corruption by placing power in the hands of a small tory cabal, the "creatures of the Governor," as Fox put it.[18] This above all, the reformers would claim, was anathema to the civic republican spirit of the British constitution.

The debates concerning the 1791 Constitution Act reveal the nearly religious veneration Britishers in both the United Kingdom and the Canadas held for the British constitution. The editor of Upper Canada's *Royal Standard* captured the sentiment that was as true for whig as it was for tory: "The original form of our Constitution is almost divine; to such a degree, that no state of Rome or Greece could ever boast one superior to it; nor could Plato, Aristotle, nor any Legislator, even conceive a more perfect model of a state. The three parts which compose it are so harmoniously blended and incorporated, that neither the flute of Aristoxenus, nor the lyre of Timotheus ever produced more perfect concord."[19] It was suitable then that the opening of Upper Canada's first session of parliament at Newark in October 1792 was marked with praise for the constitution by Lieutenant-Governor John Graves Simcoe: "This province is singularly blessed, not with a mutilated Constitution, but with a Constitution which has stood the test of experience, and is the very image and transcript of that of Great Britain."[20]

While the British constitution was undoubtedly revered, there were grave doubts that it was being reflected in the governance of Canada. The Constitution Act led to the creation of an entrenched oligarchy in both provinces. This oligarchy was called the Château Clique in Lower Canada and in Upper Canada, the Family Compact. Despite the name, members were not always related. More often than blood ties, what they had in common was that they were generally wealthy, upper-class, conservative Anglican elites. The Family Compact and Château Clique were able to effectively control the Canadas through their position in the Executive Councils. Members were given positions for life in this unelected body. The Compact and Clique developed into a powerful cabal especially after the War of 1812 and would use their influence on the governor to appoint like-minded people to every important civil post. Because the cabal often had members in both the Executive Council and the Legislative Council, they could veto any bill they disagreed with and rendered the elected Legislative Assembly relatively powerless.

A reform movement developed in the Canadas in reaction to the perceived corruption and greed of the ruling tories. Katherine Fierlbeck has argued that, although "hardly a coherent idea," toryism in colonial Canada was "the belief that the common good was more important than individual rights." She goes on to describe "tory collectivism" as the belief that "too much liberty" would lead to corruption and self-interest.[21] Fierlbeck takes her lead from Gad Horowitz, who described Canada's unique political philosophy as a marriage of toryism and socialism (or red toryism) in contradistinction to America's liberal tradition.[22] The trouble with this interpretation is two-fold. First, the notion that the common good must surpass individual rights is already well established in the civic republican tradition, a tradition that predates toryism by centuries.

Second, and more importantly, as this chapter will attempt to show, it was the reformers who used collectivist language and charged the tories with corruption and neglecting the public good. Aileen Dunham has commented that the radicals were "resentful of this class of men [the tory elite] because of the political monopoly which they enjoyed."[23] The reformers of colonial Canada were both democratic and British. They were influenced not by toryism but by a collectivist civic republican ideal that they argued was a truer interpretation of the British constitution.

Despite the inherent flaws in the Constitution Act, a general belief remained that the British constitution was the best system available. The unbridled democracy of the American system led to a "spirit of party" that ultimately worked against the public good. An article published in the *Kingston Gazette* on 29 January 1811 is typical of the view held by many in Upper Canada:

> The characteristic evil of their democratic system is its tendency to foster an uncontrollable spirit of party. Their frequent popular elections of all branches of their government furnish fuel and fan the flame. The rage of their parties has become intolerable. In their mutual struggles to oppose and crush each other, they spare neither feelings nor characters. If their newspaper publication were to be credited, we should think that almost every man of any prominence among them guilty of the blackest vices and crimes...
>
> In this Province, whose government is the English constitution reduced to a smaller seal; our courts and juries, like those of the mother country, are distinguished by impartiality. Whatever imperfections there may be in our Provincial system, we are happily exempt from those overwhelming tides of party passion and prejudice, which prevail in more popular governments. Let us, then, not envy our neighbours, but be contented with and improve our own condition, and, in obedience to the apostolic injunction, lead peaceable and quite lives in all godliness and honesty.[24]

This sentiment was as true for the reformers as it was for the conservatives. Even Mackenzie, arguably the wildest of them all, was initially convinced of the superiority of the British constitution to

American republicanism.[25] The question was how to counter the corruption of the ruling tory. The answer was democracy.

William Baldwin, who along with his son Robert would provide one of the most powerful voices for responsible government, informed the electors of York in 1820 that "in the breast of the American citizen [is] a spirit of personal ambition unknown to an Englishman."[26] The republican government of the "barbarous Americans" was seen as too selfish, too party-dominated, too individualistic, and too liberal. The British reformers of Canada would advocate a civic republican democracy geared towards the public good. By the 1820s the reform movement in Upper Canada was steadily increasing in size and stature.[27] It was spurred by issues general and specific. For non-Anglicans the institutionalized Church of England monopoly over Crown lands was a chief grievance. For those outside the aristocracy, the exclusion from public offices drove dissent, since the Family Compact would allow important positions to go only to men who were ideologically congruent with the government. For many democratic reformers, control of money was a central issue. The Constitution Act had given the executive enormous powers by allowing certain funds to be entirely at their control. This clause effectively removed the elected Legislative Assembly's biggest bargaining chip. Even if the Assembly chose to block supply, the executive and the governor would be financially able to keep running the province. All cases, however, share a common civic republic thread in that the reformers perceived corruption by the tory elite and felt the need to infuse the *polis* with virtue.

In Lower Canada there was even more reason for dissatisfaction. Along with the complaints they shared with the Upper Canadian reformers, the largely French population of Lower Canada felt discriminated against by the English minority who dominated the Château Clique. In 1806 the reformist newspaper *Le Canadien* began weekly publications. Although the authors used aliases such as *Un Spectateur* and *L'Ami de la Justice,* the paper was the mouthpiece for the French reformist Parti Canadien, which dominated the popularly elected Legislative Assembly.[28] Although *Le Canadien* fought to preserve French culture, especially against the advances of Anglicanism, the authors embraced the transplanted British constitution of 1791. England was even referred to as *la mère-patrie* (the mother country).[29] *Le Canadien* in print, along with the more radical *La Minerve* and *Vindicator*, and the Parti Canadien in the Assembly fought for the ancient British and civic republican, right, so that the voice of the third estate would be heard along with the other two. After all, they reasoned, "Tous les habitans de la province ne sont-ils pas Sujets Britanniques?" (Are not the habitants of this province British subjects?).[30]

In the late 1820s and early 1830s, an increasing number of moderate and some extreme reformers won seats in Upper Canada's Legislative Assembly. Much to the chagrin of the tory oligarchy, the election for the tenth parliament of Upper Canada in July 1828 saw a good return of the increasingly vocal reform movement. Among the elected reformers was the fiery and razor-tongued Scot, William Lyon Mackenzie. As the editor of the *Colonial Advocate*, Mackenzie made regular stinging attacks on the Family Compact, leading to regular and personal reprisals from the tory *Courier of Upper Canada* and Francis Collin's *Canadian Freeman*. Exacerbated by Mackenzie's success, the latter publication ran an article under the headline "Alarming Crisis!!!" which demanded of the people of York, "why did you vote for such an unprincipled scoundrel as MacKenzie?"[31]

The Reform Party enjoyed even greater success at the 1834 election as they won control of the House. There was some friction between the radical and moderate reformers; however, they held a reasonably consistent argument, demanding an elective Legislative Council, a responsible Executive Council and full control of funds for the Assembly. Mackenzie was well on the path to radicalism and, hinting at things to come, changed his newspaper's name from the *Colonial Advocate* to simply the *Advocate*. During the election campaign the *Advocate* created much controversy by publishing a black list of "uncompromising enemies of the peace, happiness, and welfare of the people of U. Canada, and of free and enlightened political institutions."[32] The comprehensive list included four categories; reformers, doubtful, unknown, and enemies of civil and religious liberty.[33] The British government was uneasy with these democratic developments. In 1835 a new lieutenant-governor was commissioned to replace Sir John Colborne. Sir Francis Bond Head was dispatched with a warning that this was an "era of more difficulty and importance than any which has hitherto existed in the history of that part of His Majesty's dominions."[34]

Head was given a long list of instructions by Lord Glenelg as to what his approach should be as governor. He was ordered to review the policy of Crown patronage, make appointments based on qualification, not politics, and to adhere to the wishes of the Assembly wherever possible. Glenelg spoke positively of the Assembly, calling it a place where, "the discussion of public grievances, whether real or supposed, has always been conducted with an earnestness and freedom of inquiry, of which, even when occasionally carried to exaggeration, no reasonable complaint can be made."[35] In general, Glenelg wanted conciliation with the Reform Party and wanted, as far as possible, to show that Britain was willing to hear the colonist's grievances and act on them. Although he tried to impress this on the new governor, after landing in Upper Canada in early 1836, Head ignored his instructions and set about governing the province as he saw fit.[36]

It is ironic that the reformers of Toronto cheered the arrival of the new governor with banners reading, "Sir Francis Bond Head, A Tried Reformer."[37] A staunch conservative, he soon revealed how wrong this perception was. Head flatly refused the reformers' requests, claiming that "the people of Upper Canada detest democracy: they revere their Constitutional Charter, and consequently are in staunch allegiance to their King."[38] He felt that "strong Republican Principles... leaked into the country from the United States" had infected the reformist Assembly, which did not represent the "general Feelings and Interests of the inhabitants."[39] He referred to the Reform Party as the Republican Party and insisted that it did not represent the views of the majority of the population.[40] David Mills has noted that it was the high tories of the early nineteenth century who "frame[d] the official definition of loyalty."[41] Republicanism was essentially an insult, a charge of Americanism and disloyalty in the contemporary nomenclature. Antagonisms grew quickly and on 15 April the Assembly, finding the new governor intolerable, voted to block supply. A month later, Head dissolved the legislature.

A bitterly fought election campaign ensued in which Head assumed control of conservative forces. He proved to be a master of *divide et impera* and went to enormous effort to paint all reformers as republicans, American sympathisers, and traitors to Britain. Head drew a very clear line in the sand, claiming that all men loyal to Britain and the British constitution must support the conservatives, who began to refer to themselves as the constitutionalists. The constitutionalists even argued that they were better able to carry out reform than the reformers. Honest reform was fine, they argued, but to support the

Reform Party was to support revolution and separation from the mother country. This tactic proved superbly successful and the election was a landslide for the conservatives. In the new Assembly, constitutionalists outnumbered reformers by about two to one.

The electoral victory by the conservative forces doubtless owed a great deal to the effective campaigning of the new governor. He was, however, enthusiastically assisted by the Irish Orangemen.[42] The first Orange lodges in Upper Canada were founded in the 1820s and their numbers increased sharply under the pro-immigration policy of Lieutenant-Governor Sir John Colborne in the early 1830s. The Orangemen were naturally drawn to Head's call for loyalty. With Catholic French above them and Republican Americans beneath, everything within their power must be done to preserve Upper Canada as a British province. These "infuriated demons" where renowned for employing intimidation and violence as political tactics.[43] An unnamed historian of Middlesex, Ontario, noted that the "Orange legions" led by John Jennings would regularly use "batons or arms" to disrupt reformist meetings while crying, "the constitution is in danger."[44]

The progressive press lamented the thuggish behaviour of the typical "low bred Orangeman" and the seeming complicity of Head's government during the election campaign:

> It is painful to reflect upon the desperate character of the low, Orange Irish; and it is painful to reflect on the palpable neglect of duty, and the total disregard of riot and bloodshed manifested by our Tory Magistrates, and *State-Paid* Ministers of the Gospel, during the Election who if they did not all directly encourage the miscreant mob to acts of riot, bloodshed and MURDER, by their continued presence among them, yet they winked at all these things, and did not, in the slightest degree, interpose their authority to save the lives of men.
>
> Every day of the Election there was more or less rioting. Every man known to be a conspicuous Liberal was insulted; and many persons were grossly abused, kicked, dragged and beaten by the Orange Tory mob.[45]

The radical British press also condemned the conservatives' tactics. The *Manchester Advertiser* commented on 27 August: "Sir Francis has discovered the use and application of the old bludgeon and vote splitting system which has gone out in England. The worst methods of outrage and intimidation have been adopted. His government has multiplied votes to infinity, by issuing, on the instant, crown grants of land, some of them for a quarter of an acre, and letting in his ruffianly body of mushroom voters to the utter subversion of the real electors. Government has accordingly carried the election and got a house of commons suited to the views of the sage and humane pauper hunter at its head."[46]

Foul play by Head and the Orangemen does not alone account for the wild electoral turnaround from 1834 to 1836. With the election framed so clearly by Head as a contest between loyal and disloyal people, most Protestants and even many Catholics sided with the conservatives. The significant Methodist minority also, who had often been pro-reform, voted for the Constitutionalists when push came to shove. In London, Lord Glenelg wrote to Head, "I perceive with much satisfaction that these elections have terminated in such a manner as to testify, on the part of the inhabitants of that city [Toronto], their confidence in your policy, and the approbation of the measures which you have adopted to promote the general welfare of His Majesty's subjects in Upper Canada."[47] The ruling whigs in London would incorrectly interpret the election result as evidence that the fight for popular representation had waned.

The reformers were particularly outraged because they had developed a strong democratic ideal and felt that the British constitution itself demanded that the governor act as a neutral adjudicator to the parties in the Assembly.[48] The fact that Head had been so vocally supportive of the tories and had failed to intervene against the "infernal conduct of the Orangemen" led Mackenzie to a frightening conclusion. With great significance he launched a new paper, *The Constitution*, on 4 July. He bitterly asked his readers: "Can there be truth or justice or humanity in the Tory system which is supported, *and which requires the support of such unjust means and such inhuman monsters?* Monsters that regard the life of a fellow creature no more than they regard the meanest insect that crawls on the ground!"[49] This was where the moderate and radical reformers parted company. The radicals gave up hope that the British whigs were any more likely to grant them democratic reform than the tories. The *Spectator* concluded, "the transition state of home politics seems to have thoroughly *Toryfied* them."[50] The *Constitution* agreed: "after all is said and done, the British Whig Government are as faithless and treacherous as any that went before them."[51] A new battle cry was formed: "the people are determined to have their rights; peaceably if they can: at all hazards if they must."[52]

The contest between the reformers and the Governor can be seen as representative of the battle of ideas that was taking place all over the British Empire. Some four decades later, the Pittites and Foxites were still engaged in heated debate. What is noteworthy from the reformers' language is that by the 1830s the democratic question had been answered in the affirmative. It was assumed knowledge for these latter-day Foxites that democracy held a central place in the British constitution. That is precisely why it was so outrageous that Head should be anything other than an impartial adjudicator maintaining the dignity of the Crown. The ultimate result of this electoral loss would be the radicalizing of some reformers and a new belief that the grievances of the Upper Canadians could never be addressed constitutionally when the constitution itself (as they interpreted it) was not being honoured.

It is important to remember that the reformers were not naturally predisposed towards separatist republicanism. Quite the contrary, they saw their British heritage as the Biblical pearl of great price.[53] They saw the civic republican ethos of serving the common good as the rudder of a virtuous ship of state. It was not a joyous but rather a sad revelation to Mackenzie that he was now forced to choose between severing ties with Britain or abandoning the noble civic republican principles that made his homeland great. Mackenzie's thinking was intensely radicalized in the 1830s. In 1833 he claimed to want simply to "enjoy something like a 'Constitution the very image and transcript of that of Great Britain.'"[54] The following year he proudly declared that "after wearing the dress of a Whig for some years, I conscientiously adopted that of a radical reformer."[55] Finally he would defer to the logic of Rousseau in championing republics over monarchies as "a man of real merit is as rarely to be found in the ministry of a king, as a blockhead at the head of a republic."[56] Together with fellow exacerbated reformers, he determined to declare war for the sake of civic republican democracy. It was their commitment to civic republicanism that saw them reluctantly embrace separatist republicanism, and it was their love of Britishness that would see them rebel against Britain.

The 1836 conservative landslide saw Mackenzie lose his seat. It is reported that he wept uncontrollably at a friend's house and was ever since a visibly different man. His return to journalism was marked by a new level of intensity and aggression as he let out all his reformist frustrations at the Family Compact, the Anglican monopoly, and most of all, his chief nemesis Sir Francis Bond Head. He declared: "Tories! Pensioners! Placemen! Profligates! Orangemen! Churchmen! Brokers! Gamblers! Parasites! Allow me to congratulate you. Your feet are at last on the people's necks."[57] The title of his new paper, *The Constitution*, is just as telling as the auspicious date of its launch, 4 July. He clearly felt he was fighting for the true communal spirit of the British Constitution. Mackenzie was a Scottish highlander whose grandfathers had fought with the infamous '45ers for Bonnie Prince Charlie.[58] Once again, it seemed, the Mackenzie clan was at war with England.

Back in London, Lord Glenelg made another plea for Head to pursue a course of conciliation with the Reformers. He reminded him in August that the role of the British government was to "put a stop to the irritation and violence which party processions are calculated to produce," not to inflame them. Glenelg attempted to impress on the governor the importance of neutrality, stating, "I have however felt it incumbent on me to call your attention to [the numerous letters of complaint from the Reform Party], in the full confidence that it is your purpose to administer the government which His Majesty confided to you with the strictest impartiality, and with the single object of advancing the real interests of every class of His Majesty's subjects in the province."[59] Head, however, was not in the least bit interested and Glenelg eventually retired in frustration. The election result was a clear vindication, in Head's mind, of his policy of conceding nothing to the reformers. Conciliate with them, he argued, and you will have the House full of disloyal republicans. Attack them and the loyal majority will follow your lead. He commented in 1839, "I was sentenced to contend on the soil of America with Democracy, and if I did not overpower it, it would overpower me."[60]

Meanwhile, in Lower Canada the reformers led by Louis-Joseph Papineau, an "extraordinary man," according to English radicals, continued their campaign for greater representation.[61] The Parti Canadien had renamed themselves the Parti Patriote and took a radical turn in an attempt to achieve their reformist platform.

In 1832 the Patriotes in the Assembly voted to block supply until their grievances, chiefly against the tory Legislative Council, were addressed. On 21 February 1834 Papineau presented the Ninety-Two Resolutions to the Legislative Assembly which were then sent to London, where their London agent John Roebuck presented them to the Commons. The Resolutions was an eclectic document detailing many concerns; chiefly the abuses of the Legislative Council, discrimination against the French, fiscal issues, land regulation, and the administration of justice. Allan Greer notes that despite the legalistic nature of the document, "the revolutionary thrust of the Ninety-Two Resolutions was not lost on Lower Canadians of all political persuasions. Debated in the Press, discussed in the taverns and on church doorsteps, they served to accelerate the polarization of an already divided province."[62]

Papineau was one of the chief architects of the Ninety-Two Resolutions, and a keen insight into his political philosophy can be gained by examining it. The first resolution is one of the more significant. It reminded the British parliament that Lower Canada was a loyal part of the British Empire. The province had proved the "strongest attachment" to Britain, first by refusing to join the American Revolution and then by defending British North America against American aggression. It noted also that all British subjects were their "brethren" and were welcome to emigrate to their province "without any distinction of origin of creed."[63] Papineau and his fellow drafters were keen to assert that they were not against the British race or any English-speaking people. They were openly against the Château Clique because it was a small, corrupt body of aristocrats that they judged to be acting against the growing tide of democracy and against the common good. This kind of argumentation stems not from liberal but from civic republican thinking. They went to some length to frame their fight as constitutional not racial, and their common cause with the Upper Canadian reformers goes some way to legitimizing this claim.

The Ninety-Two Resolutions went all the way back to the debates on the 1791 Constitution Act, and the drafters identified themselves with Fox. Like their hero, they argued that the unelected Legislative Council, and the unmitigated power it gave the governor and the Clique, meant that the people of Lower Canada had no true representation but only "representation burlesqued."[64] This "exorbitant power" was in complete opposition to the British constitution.

This above all, was the "most serious defect," the "radical fault," the "most frequent cause of abuses of power," and it was all "foretold by the Honourable Charles James Fox at the time of its adoption." The result of this "power unlimited" was that a "spirit of monopoly and despotism" reigned and it was "never in favour of the public interest."[65] Papineau and the Patriotes again borrowed from Fox, who had demanded of the Commons in 1791 not to boast that "we gave Canada even a sketch of the British constitution, or anything like it."[66] Resolution fourteen made clear its concurrence, stating that the British government had "unreasonably and erroneously asserted, that it has conferred on the two Canadas the institutions of Great Britain."

The Ninety-Two Resolutions was clearly a call for greater democracy and a sure indicator of the general mood for democratic reform, which would become manifest right across the British Empire in the middle portion of the nineteenth century. It is clear also that this was not in any way a call for separatist republicanism. But was it necessarily a liberal document? As a whole, the tenor of the document was not merely a complaint against interference or an assertion of the rights of the people. The document reflected the strong sense of community in Lower Canada and its desire to be governed in the public interest. Lower Canada panted for democracy not because it would establish individual rights but because "preference [is] given at free elections to virtue."[67] Papineau was known in Britain as the O'Connell of Canada.[68] This was the highest possible accolade the reformers could bestow. Earlier in the year, the *Correspondent and Advocate* had hailed O'Connell as "the actual hinge whereupon turns the whole ministerial policy of England."[69] Like the great Irish politician, Papineau was vehemently against arbitrary domination but happy and willing to work within the British system to achieve substantial political improvements for his community. The Legislative Council of Lower Canada was no true parliament. It was dismissed by Papineau as an "impotent screen between the Governor and the people." Responsible government was needed so that the people could call on "honest, contented and devoted men" to replace the "richer men, of whom they may think less highly."[70] This was not a call for French nationalism but civic republicanism.

Following the United Kingdom's general election in 1835, Viscount Melbourne became prime minister for the second time and replaced the tory government of Robert Peel. Melbourne was a weak, albeit gentlemanly, leader, who delegated much of his policy power to the whig's official spokesman in the Commons, Lord John Russell.[71] Russell, whose father, the Sixth Duke of Bedford, was close friends with Charles Fox during the Constitution Act debates, was a moderate reformer. Nevertheless, Russell rejected the Patriotes' key demands that the Legislative Council be elective and that the Executive Council be answerable to the Assembly, not the Governor. In dismissing the first demand, Russell informed the Commons on 6 March 1837 that "to make the Legislative Council elective would be to produce a second assembly, exactly like the first, simply an echo." With regard to the second demand, Russell drew on Jean-Louis De Lolme's theory of government. Only at the seat of empire could ministers be answerable to parliament; "otherwise we should have separate, independent powers existing, not only in Great Britain, but in every separate colony. Each colony would in effect be an independent state."[72] De Lolme had warned in 1775 that the power of the democratic arm must be kept in check, for "should the parliament exert their privilege to its full extent, the prince, reduced to despair, might resort to fatal extremities; or that the constitution, which subsists only by virtue of its equilibrium, might, in the end, be subverted."[73] Russell, then, did not want to give the democratic arm unnecessary power, especially not more power than it had in England. The question remained how best to transplant the spirit of the ancient constitution of Britain to foreign soil.

Russell saw the problems in Lower Canada as a direct result of the bastardized constitution of 1791. The backdrop to the Constitution Act was formed, of course, by the French Revolution and the passionate debates (typified by Edmund Burke and Tom Paine) concerning the merits of monarchic and republican government.[74] These issues were reflected in the Pitt-Fox debates in parliament. Unsurprisingly, Russell blamed the tories for producing this untenable "anomaly in colonial government" and suggested a return to the ancient constitution. He believed the real cause of tension in Lower Canada was the anglophone bias in the Executive and Legislative Councils, noting that "it has been too much the practice to appoint them almost entirely from amongst persons of the English extraction who form but a small minority in the province."[75] Russell offered Ten Resolutions for the Canadas which not only failed to strengthen the Assembly but actually weakened it by removing the power to block supply.

The Resolutions were easily passed in London on Friday, 14 April but roundly rejected in the Canadas.[76] They were branded the "Coercion Bill."[77] To emphasize the repugnance of one resolution (an original suggestion of the whig turned conservative, Lord Stanley) the *Constitution* reported it in all capital letters:

IF THE GOVERNMENT OF CANADA FOUND THAT THE ASSEMBLY WOULD NOT CONSENT TO THESE PROPOSALS AND THAT THEY COULD NOT, IN CONSEQUENCE, TRANSACT THE BUSINESS OF THE COLONY, THAT THEN THE GOVERNMENT SHOULD BE ABLE TO CONTINUE FOR ANY INDEFFINATE TIME INDEPENDENTLY OF THE CONSENT OF THE ASSEMBLY.[78]

La Minerve described it as "new acts of oppression." It asked,"Is it considered that we must succumb to the weight of this force, bow our heads shamefully under the yoke? No, our position as a people is simply strengthened, since such measures should help us pursue more actively than ever this struggle which will end in success for American principles." One of the "American principles" alluded to was the revolutionary battle standard of 1776, "no taxation without representation." *La Minerve* was outraged that without the consent of the people's Assembly, "the mother country is putting its hand in our coffers."[79] The *Spectator* concurred: "these resolutions not only negatived all the demands of the Colonial suitors for justice, but authorized robbery."[80]

For its part, the British government did genuinely try to appease the popular party in both provinces. Helen Manning has observed that with the exception of Edward Stanley's term as secretary of state for war and the colonies (1833–34), there was "a consistent effort between 1830 and 1837 at conciliation."[81] Paul Scherer agrees, noting that "the British were full of good will toward Canada, but their knowledge of Canadian conditions was scanty."[82] Be that as it may, the Lower Canadian Patriotes gave up all hope of an agreement. Papineau incited the people to "protest against the atrocious measures of coercion which Lord John Russell and the British aristocracy are preparing for this democratic colony." The radical English press noted that shouts of "Vive Papineau" accompanied him wherever he went and that "banners, laurels, and the ladies await the presence of this great man."[83]

Late on Tuesday night, 6 June, Papineau arrived at Saint Benoit to be a guest at an anti-coercion meeting on Thursday. Having Wednesday free, he wandered the streets and was struck by what he saw. All the houses had been decorated with flags, banners, and colourful flowers in his honour. Maple leaves and flowers were gaily arranged and "nothing could equal the warmth of feeling with which this good and tried friend of Colonial rights was everywhere received."[84] The home of Papineau's host, J.J. Girouard, was exquisitely adorned with maple branches and a white silk banner that read "Honneur à Papineau!" Wherever Girouard's carriage took him that day, it was followed by merry cries, "Vive Papineau!"

The meeting itself was an extremely colourful and theatrical display. Whether by design or by fate a procession of ninety-two carriages (a number of significance not lost on the editor of the *Montreal Vindicator*) slowly made its way up a hill in Saint Scholastique. Along the way, the women who lined the streets and cheered from the windows waved their handkerchiefs. Two cavaliers accompanied Papineau's carriage, one holding a banner reading, "Honor to Our Representatives," the other a banner reading, "Honour to the O'Connell of Lower Canada." One of the centrepieces was a large flag bearing a gruesome black skull with the title "Legislative Council." Piercing the ears of the skull was the reformer's cry, "elective institutions." The skull was surrounded by the titles of bills that had passed the Assembly only to be blocked by the Council. The demand for democracy is clear. But the demand for liberalism is less so.

The gathering was a community affair held in a spirit of communalism and civic goodwill. The speakers did threaten separatist republicanism, and they did call on the memory of the American Revolution as an example, but this was not their chief project. There were countless flags and banners, and it is helpful to consider some of the messages they bore. The *Vindicator* lists some of the slogans: "A bloody struggle rather than the oppression of corrupt powers." "Shame on Lord John Russell!" "The people will resist Coercion." "Gratitude to our Agent, Roebuck, and to the minority of the house of Commons. Long live Leader!" "Honor to the working-men of London. Long live Hoare, Chapman, Molesworth, Thompson, Harvey, Wade, Murphy, O'Conner." "Liberty, The bread of the people and the will of God." "Union of all parties for the common defence of the liberties of the country." "Death before slavery."[85]

The mixture of slogans reveals the protest to be a push for democracy, not French nationalism or even separation. If there was to be secession from Britain it would be, as with the Upper Canadians, a last resort to gain the kind of civic republican democracy they desired and believed to be their right. If the protest had been anti-British, rather than pro-democratic, it would have been strange indeed to see so many British radicals honoured. As the protestors sang their songs and raised their banners, they were living the Aristotelian ideal of virtuous participation in politics. They were living Hannah Arendt's *vita activa*.[86] One further flag succinctly phrased the Patriote's agenda: "No more hands plunged in the public chest, and then the Canadians will be happy."[87]

The failure of Lord Russell's Ten Resolutions drew the battle lines for conflict. There was a strong sense in both provinces that the tory monopoly of the Family Compact and Château Clique existed not to preserve the British constitution but to entrench their own oligarchy. The time of the moderate reformers had passed and the radicals stepped up. Robert Davis made the following observations in 1837:

> The word radical is heard with trembling, by every Orangeman, every Tory, every fat-fed tax eater. And why is a Radical so terrible an enemy to a Tory? Because a Radical is exerting himself to bring political matters to their primitive, original state; to elevate man from his degraded situation to that lofty state he was destined to fill. A Radical Reformer is the best friend of human nature. If the pensions, the sinecures, and the fat offices of the Tories were taken from them, they would be Radicals themselves. When Lord Gosford came to Lower Canada, and manifested a desire to do right, the Tories took up their rifles against the king and the people. Fine constitutionalists indeed! But Radicals are not for the sword, but for reason and peace.[88]

By July 1837, the Upper Canadian reformers were watching events in the north with great excitement. Mackenzie's press began printing copies of Paine's *Common Sense*. As a clear indication of hopes for wide distribution they could be bought singularly for 7½ shillings for a single copy or for a dollar per dozen.[89] The reformers held meetings all over the province and revolutionary resolutions were passed. The language of the meetings is telling. First and crucially, democracy was taken as an accepted and righteous principle. But what type of democracy was being endorsed? It is clear that the liberalism of John Locke and the American experience played some role, but it is tempered by the need to promote the common good and the need to use democratic civic institutions as a safeguard to ensure virtue and not corruption in public officials. Just as the Commonwealthmen and *Cato's Letters* influenced the Americans, so too did civic republicanism influence these radical Canadians.

On 19 August, the reformers of Vaughan met at the German Church on lot 11. With Robert McNair as chairman and Michael Fisher as secretary the group first sought to "express public sympathy with Lower Canada." Mr Handlan noted that "we accord our need of praise to the gallant conduct of the people and assembly of Lower Canada; who, with their able leader, Mr. Speaker Papineau, are taking the stand we would have gladly taken here." It was claimed time and again that corruption reigned in the Legislature and that "the friends of reform have as yet been baffled in their honest efforts to bring about a better state of things."[90] Corruption, of course, had been a consistent theme since the election. Mackenzie had collected evidence of electoral corruption but poor health prevented him from presenting it to the Assembly. Dr Charles Duncombe, who had won a seat in Oxford Country for the reformers, took a petition to London complaining of widespread corruption. Having received advice from Head, Glenelg refused to see him.[91] The reformers of Vaughan were livid. Dr William John O'Grady, who had taken over the editorship of Mackenzie's *Advocate* in 1834, gave a long and stirring speech climaxing with the following resolution, which was met with great cheers: "Government is founded on the authority, and is instituted for the benefit of a people, or community, and not for the benefit, honour, or profit, of any man, or any class of men, who are only a part of that community."

The language of the meeting reflected a strong belief in positive liberty and communalism. Contrary to the doctrine of individualism, the Canadian reformers emphasized that they were a community and must have laws and leaders who acted in the interest of the commonweal. This was an ideal they were willing to fight for, and O'Grady added to his first resolution that "the doctrine of non-resistance to arbitrary power is slavish, absurd and discreditable to a people who can appreciate their privileges." Again taking their lead from the Americans before them, they vowed to boycott British goods: "We solemnly pledge ourselves to abstain, as far as possible, from the purchase or use of British goods which have paid taxes to a government which openly declares its bad faith, by resolving to rob the exchequer of the sister colony, and keep her people without education, and by continuing from year to year to plunder us of many thousands of pounds annually, for the worst of purposes."

The day before, a similar meeting was chaired in York by James Davis, with William Poole as secretary. Again the treatment of the Lower Canadians was heavily criticized. The meeting ended by declaring to the government in Upper Canada and in Britain that "the people of this township are more than three to one in favour of reform – they have always been considered as radical reformers."[92] On 9 August reformers at Caledon met at the house of George Bells. Chaired by William Clarke with Miles Bacon as secretary they declared, "This meeting resolves to stand by the Democratic principle of our constitution, being assured that we have no other safeguard to the fruits of our labour, we will never sacrifice it but to overwhelming force; and we would desire rather to be independent altogether of a government that would countenance or connive at the imposition of such a wrong or the like alternative."

The following day at the mansion home of John Campbell, the reformers of Chinguacousy made "common cause" with the reformers of both provinces. With John Watson as chairman and James Robson as secretary, it was resolved "that the present House of Assembly is an idle and expensive mockery, which neither has the will nor the power to do the country any good – neither do the reformers of Chinguacousy expect the least good from any pretended representation of the people, got up as this was, by the grossest bribery, corruption, and a violation of all law and usages of Great Britain, by a non-responsible governor and his dumb and irresponsible council called the executive council." The sentiments were expressed again on 14 August at Hull's Tavern. The former member for Halton was chosen chairmen of the Trafalgar meeting with a boasted attendance of some six hundred people. Lord Russell was accused of "virtually destroy[ing] the constitution of 1791." Papineau, John Rolph, M.S. Bidwell, and Dr Morrison were all honoured as men who had, "always proved themselves the fearless asserters of our privileges."[93]

By October the resolutions had become even more revolutionary. The grievance ceased be concerned with local administrative issues but with the very political connection to Britain. The radical reformers urged their supporters to do as the Americans did:

> This, People of Upper Canada, is your government!! In the name of God! Is this a Government fit for freemen or enlightened Englishmen or Americans? Can the people have no better government? Can the majority of the people ever flourish under a Government whose sole object is oppression! monopoly!! gross partiality!!! And individual persecution?

> If this Province and Lower Canada were a state of the great neighbouring Union, property everywhere would increase in value, the population would double every few years, our markets would be always good, our enterprise would be vastly increased, the resources of the Province would be called up and enjoyed, and the bickering of party would subside in the great ocean of Republicanism, Government offices would not then be sought for on account of their worth and value so much as for their honour and trust.[94]

These events were watched with great interest by the radical press in England. The *Bristol Mercury* noted that the language at these meeting revealed the "detestation of the tyrannical conduct of Earl Gosford, in Lower Canada, and the no less oppressive sway of Sir Francis Head, in Upper Canada."[95] Head not only refused to negotiate with the reformers; he somewhat pigheadedly refused to believe they existed in any significant numbers. Convinced of the people's loyalty, an opinion that was hardly shared in London, he moved all British troops out of the province and stationed them in Lower Canada where rebellion was brewing.

On 13 November 1837, a convention of farmers, mechanics, labourers, and other residents of Toronto met in the Committee Room of the Royal Oaks Hotel and approved a new constitution for the province, "should the British system of government... be positively denied us." The drafters listed their political mentors as Henry Grattan, John Locke, Algernon Sidney, and Benjamin Franklin. This short list of influences is telling. While the liberal hand of Locke is acknowledged, it is countered by the republicanism of

Sidney, Franklin, and Grattan. The constitution borrowed generously from the American Declaration of Independence. Like the American document, Mackenzie's declaration separated church from state, protected the right to bear arms, the right of assembly, and the freedom of the press. It also upheld traditional English liberties like habeas corpus and trial by jury. The real energy behind the document comes from Mackenzie's utter conviction that democracy was the way forward. The document proudly insisted that the people alone would have the authority to elect the governor and that he would be answerable to the elected parliament. Mackenzie followed the American example of looking back to the Romans and renamed the Legislative Council the Senate. This never-to-be-used constitution was radically democratic. Although liberalism did outline some sections, such as those concerning the rights of property owners, the communalism and emphasis on virtuous public participation make it a very republican document.[96]

On 23 October the *Assemblée des six-comtés* met in Saint-Charles. Fernand Ouellet notes that "there were armed militiamen, a liberty pole, and flags and banners bearing inscriptions of every kind, announcing to the 4000 attending that the moment of great decisions was approaching."[97] The chairman of the *Assemblée* was the English Patriote Wolfred Nelson. Nelson's maternal grandfather was a wealthy New York landowner who had lost his possessions during the American Revolution. Despite his Loyalist heritage, Nelson became a vociferous advocate of French Canadian rights. Addressing the crowd at Saint-Charles he boldly declared that "whenever any form of government becomes destructive... it is the right of the people to alter or abolish it."[98] One observer commented that "the applause of the crowd from which there came not a single disapproving voice showed clearly that already a revolution had taken place in [their] hearts and all that was left was to proclaim it."[99]

The great crowd reassembled on 24 October to hear an address that would often be referred to as Canada's Declaration of Independence. Just as Mackenzie's declaration had done, the one read by Nelson drew heavily on and acknowledged the influence of the "wise and immortal" framers of the United States Declaration of Independence. While Mackenzie had looked to Grattan, Locke, Sidney, and Franklin, the Six Counties Address saw the works of radical republican Thomas Paine as it inspiration. The address echoed the United States Bills of Rights in asserting that it was "self-evident" that "GOD created no artificial distinction between man and man" and that "government is but a mere human institution" that must always "give satisfaction to the People, the sole legitimate source of power." The address goes on to decry the lack of democracy in Lower Canada. The Legislative Council had become a small, corrupt body that existed to serve its own oligarchy rather than the public good. Instead of the common weal, the 1791 constitution worked to the "advantage of the favourites, creatures and tools of the government." Nelson and his fellow Patriotes concluded that precedents for the current arrangements were "to be found only in the darkest pages of British history."[100]

Despite the radical rhetoric and the frequent summons of the ghost of 1776, the Patriotes' address was constitutional, not revolutionary. Like their Upper Canadian co-sufferers, with whom they so frequently pledged solidarity, the reformers can be seen as latter-day Foxites, still arguing that the Constitution Act had not provided them with their rights as British subjects. Nelson, recalling the public meetings in 1851, insisted that a "bold, constitutional, and truly British feeling pervaded every bosom." Nelson's apologia suggests that the aim was not to create a republic for the liberal aim of ending interference but to end the domination of corrupt officials and establish their British rights, a civic republican agenda. Nelson continues, "while it was the object of the leaders to employ the most unequivocal terms of remonstrance, it was not their intention to overstep the limits of legitimate discussion and reproval."[101] The Scottish journalist William Tait agreed, noting that "the only offence committed by the people, or their leading friends, was that of peaceably assembling, setting forth their grievances, passing and publishing resolutions [and] addressees." Tait expressed outrage that the flimsy pretext of the liberty pole was used to justify the charge of treason, which caused many respectable men to be "hunted down like wild beasts, by the myrmidons of power."[102]

Following his replacement by Head as lieutenant governor of Upper Canada, Sir John Colborne was appointed commander-in-chief of British forces in the Canadas.[103] Alarmed by the acceleration in rebellious sentiment, he wrote to Governor Gosford in early November asking for military reinforcements, an armed police force for Montreal, and the banning of *La Minerve* and the *Vindicator*.[104] Of particular concern to Colborne was the founding in September of the *Société des Fils de la Liberté* under the leadership of Thomas Storrow Brown. Similar in name and sentiment to Samuel Adams' Sons of Liberty in 1776, they were a "society both civil and military."[105] Within days, the young men of Upper Canada formed an equivalent to the Fils de la Liberté at Nelson's Hotel. They declared, "Canada must triumph over her enemies. The young blood of the country is aroused. The bone and sinew of the land have taken the determination to rescue the colony from the fangs of the vampyre now preying on its vitals."[106]

The increasing tensions in Lower Canada served to polarize the province. Royalist or constitutionalist clubs emerged to counter the Patriotes and the *Fils de la Liberté*. In particular, Adam Thom's Doric Club emerged as the fierce counter in Montreal to the *Fils de la Liberté*. On 6 November the two groups engaged in a bloody street fight, with the constitutionalists winning the day. Gosford determined that he must act to quell the poisonous atmosphere. He decided that a pre-emptive strike was the best course of action and prepared arrest warrants for the Patriote leaders, charging them with high treason. Word of this plan was leaked, however, and the Patriote chiefs of Quebec and Montreal went into hiding.[107] Papineau and Edmund Bailey O'Callaghan resisted arrest by joining Nelson in a fortified Saint-Denis.[108]

The main source of Patriote strength was in the rural areas of Lower Canada. Although there was no grand plan for a military *coup d'état*, local militia groups were organized at Pointe-à-la-Mule, Saint-Denis, Saint-Césaire, Terrebonne, Vaudreuil, Saint-Benoit, and Saint-Eustache, along with a large insurgent camp at Saint-Charles. Allan Greer notes that the random placement of the camps does not correspond with a plan to sack Montreal or anywhere else. The resistance was essentially symbolic, "like the charivari and the community meeting in the rectory, the military camp formed part of the heritage of French Canada; it seems only natural that the embattled peasants and villagers of 1837 would draw upon their historical experience [such as the War of 1812] in this way."[109]

On 23 November, three hundred British soldiers attacked the Patriote camp at Saint-Denis. The camp was defended by some eight hundred rebels with around two hundred guns. Papineau and O'Callaghan disguised themselves as peasants and fled when the fighting began at around nine in the morning, leaving Nelson to command the Patriote forces. For six hours the two sides exchanged fire. Although there were no heavy causalities on either side, Colonel

Charles Gore ordered the British troops to retreat at three in the afternoon. The falling rain, then snow, had left the British at a considerable disadvantage. Gore reported that the men's clothes were starting to freeze onto their skin and that his medical officer advised they were at risk of death in another half hour.[110] The *Northern Star* commented that the "British Invincibles" had been "driven back ignominiously."[111] This was a great symbolic victory. The Patriote farmers and workers had, with the assistance of a bitterly cold Canadian winter, kept the world's best-trained soldiers at bay.

Two days later, the British, now numbering four hundred, attacked Saint-Charles. Thomas Storrow Brown, still nursing bruises from the 6 November street fight, led the resistance. The superiority of the British in terms of arms and military discipline was immediately apparent, and one of Brown's chief tasks was to stem the flow of Patriote deserters. As the British guns rained down, Brown himself took flight. After an hour of heavy fire, the British stormed the town. In his memoires one "old soldier" paints a gruesome picture:

> When I got up we brought our right shoulders forward, and with three cheers bore down upon the barns and breastworks, which were still lined with rebels... On entering the town there was little quarter; almost every man was put to death; in fact, they fought too long before thinking of flight. Many were burned alive in the barns and houses, and the picture that presented itself the following morning to my eyes was terrible. A number of swine got loose, and were eating the roasted bodies of the enemy who were burned in the barns and killed in the streets: these brutes were afterwards shot. The loss of the rebels was great; their position was strong, and they defended it with desperation; but they were totally routed, and received a lesson they are not likely to ever forget.[112]

News that an armed insurrection had broken out in Lower Canada electrified the Upper Canadian Radicals. Mackenzie, convinced public support was on his side, set a date for rebellion. He recounted the plan in a memoir:

> It was determined that on Thursday the 7th of December, our forces should secretly assemble at Montgomery's Hotel, three miles back of Toronto, between six and ten at night, and

proceed from thence to the city, join our friends there, seize 4000 stand of arms, which had been placed by Sir Francis in the city-hall, take him into custody, with his chief advisors, place the garrison in the hands of the liberals, declare the province free, call a convention together, to frame a suitable constitution, and meantime appoint our friend Dr. Rolph, provincial administrator for the government. We expected to do all this without shedding blood, well knowing that the vice regal government was too unpopular to have many *real* adherents.[113]

Mackenzie printed a final copy of the *Constitution* on 6 December 1837. He also used a smaller press to distribute a revolutionary handbill. Riddled with religious rhetoric, he made a case for the fast-approaching rebellion:

There have been nineteen strikes for independence from European tyranny on the Continent of America. They were all successful! Brave Canadians! Do you love freedom? I know you do. Do you hate oppression? Who dare deny it? Do you wish perpetual peace, and a government founded upon the eternal heaven-born principle of the Lord Jesus Christ? Then buckle on your armour, and put down the villains who oppress and enslave our country... We have given Head and his employers a trial of forty-five years – five longer than the Israelites were detained in the wilderness. The promised land is now before us – up then and take it – but set not the torch to one house in Toronto, unless we are fired at. We cannot be reconciled to Britain – we have humbled ourselves to the Pharaoh of England, to the Ministers and great people, and they will neither rule us justly or let us go. Up then, brave Canadians! Get ready your rifles, and make short work of it. Woe be to those who oppose us, for "In God is our trust."[114]

Clearly Mackenzie saw no other course but rebellion at this stage. The language of the handbill was designed to stir emotions and rouse actions. Steeped in religious imagery and Biblical intertextuality, it could be called Christian civic republicanism. Mackenzie's dream for a new society clearly took it for granted that Christianity would be the foundational civic religion and a source of identity and morality. The rest of the paper was much more philosophical and offers an intriguing insight into the author's mind at the time.

The final issue of the *Constitution* was hastily put together without the normal advertisements on Tuesday night for publication the following morning. The first article was written, likely by Mackenzie, under the pseudonym of Philonothus. It was a much calmer and more contemplative work than the hectic pieces that populated the columns throughout the year. If it was written by Mackenzie, he was well aware that the events of that day would be momentous, and he wished to reflect on the conflict he could not possibly avoid. The article took a classically whig interpretation of the progress of history, marvelling at the limitless capacity of the human mind to develop to an ever higher understanding of the world. "What was the difference," asked Philonothus, "betwixt the mind of a Newton, Derham, Boyle, or an Archidemus, Plato, Cicero, or a Demosthenes, from that of others in an infantile state?" These men were content not only with learning existing knowledge but with "pressing forward" and making "practical improvements." Standing in the way of human advancement were the "tyrannical governments" that burdened Canada and many parts of the world.

"What a cruel state of slavery is ignorance," lamented the *Constitution*. The Family Compact were accused of acting against the common good and attempting to keep the people in a state of ignorance in order to "promote the aggrandisement of and ambition of a set of high fed and unjustly exalted villains." The article called on Biblical language and insisted that the destiny of the Christian British reformers was to lead the empire and the world into a new state of enlightened democratic freedom greater than even the revered ancients could have imagined. The article noted that "among the heathens a Solon, Plato, a Cicero and Pythagoras, though in midnight darkness, investigated with much earnestness this sublime subject, but nature's light showed them no sure path… Not so with those who are favoured with a Bible." It is difficult to conclude from this grand narrative language that the reformers were concerned merely with establishing liberal democratic rights as normative. The fight was to bring the whole community into a state where virtue was encouraged and expected.

There was, in Mackenzie's paper at least, a passionate description and defence of what the common good looked like and the glorious destiny of the Canadian people to progress to a civic republican promised land. When the wisdom of the ancients concerning communalism and public virtue combined with the "sacred volume" of the Bible, "what a pleasing and delightful field is here opened for the young tyro." The last issue of the *Constitution* ended with a parable on punctuality. A man is fifteen minutes late for an appointment with his eight colleagues. The dismissive man is reprimanded with the revelation that through wasting the other men's time also, he had in fact consumed two hours and only one-eighth of that was his own property.[115] With the confrontation inevitable, this was a clear warning that the tardiness of some could jeopardize the lives of all. The fight was set to begin, and all hands were needed.

Dr John Rolph was a respected reform leader who in a rare attempt at conciliation by Head, briefly served on the Executive Council.[116] Although committed to reform, his support for armed revolt was less certain. Learning of an arrest warrant for Mackenzie and paranoid that the government knew of the plan, he sent an urgent message to the rebels, bringing the date forward to Monday, 4 December. Mackenzie could not be found immediately, and the message was delivered to two of the rebel leaders, Samuel Lount and Anthony Anderson, who began marching with their men. When Mackenzie was finally reached, he tried to reverse the order and keep to the original date. It was, however, too late, since the men were on the march. The last-minute change had disastrous consequences for the rebellion, since many hundreds of would-be participants found out about it too late. Among these was the man who was to command the popular forces, the Napoleonic War veteran Colonel Anthony van Egmond. The rebellion half-heartedly began at Montgomery's Tavern with a few hundred men and virtually no guns and without their military commander. To further darken the mood, news also arrived that the rebellion in Lower Canada had been crushed.

The rebels approached the northern outskirts of Toronto on Tuesday night, 5 December, and were spotted by the sheriff who was patrolling with twenty-seven men. When they were within sight the sheriff's men fired and then promptly dropped their weapons and ran away into the night, fearful of reprisal from the larger force, and leaving only the sheriff himself hiding in a garden. Lount ordered the rebel's riflemen to return fire. Once the first line had done so, they dropped to the ground to allow the second line to fire. The dark of the night and the smoke from the gunfire confused the pikemen and other rebels toward the back. When they saw the riflemen at the front go down, they presumed they had all been shot and killed by a large government force. Consequently, they broke rank and fled out of the city, which meant that the riflemen had no choice but to retreat as well. Mackenzie screamed at his army, but to no avail. They ran as fast as their legs would carry them and eventually ended up all the way back at Montgomery's Tavern. The sheriff emerged from the garden where he was hiding and surveyed the empty battlefield. With one dead man on either side, he would not have realised that he had effectively stopped the rebellion. Two days later, the government militia stormed the tavern, and the rebel army dispersed.

In Lower Canada a substantial Patriote force remained in the county of Deux-Montagnes, particularly in the village of Saint-Eustache. Boosted by a local volunteer corps and an additional regiment from Quebec, Colborne led over a thousand troops against the village on 14 December. Much like the events in the siege of Saint-Charles, many of the Patriotes fled, leaving those who remained to face the wrath of a superior force. Again the "old soldier" paints a horrific picture of the "town in flames" and the piercing screams of rebels, "many of them being roasted alive." The next day, Colborne's men marched to the last Patriote outpost, Saint-Benoit. This time the Patriotes grounded their weapons and surrendered before the British were even in sight. Nevertheless, as the "old soldier" explains, "being one of the chief seats of their disloyalty for years back, we burned the whole town, church and all, and then retraced our steps to Montreal, bringing home 108 prisoners, many of them wealthy men, and leaders of the blind."[117]

The rebellions continued in the new year, but on a diminished and erratic scale. On 14 December, Mackenzie and his supporters took possession of Navy Island in the Niagara River and declared it a republic. Boosted by support from American sympathisers, the 450 rebels were forced to retreat to the United States on 14 January.[118] In Lower Canada sporadic raids from exiles in the United States were easily put down. The last significant rebel assault took place in November 1838 when the city of Beauharnois was attacked. This too was easily put down by alert British forces. In December 1837, George Arthur, who had served as lieutenant-governor of the penal colony of Van Dieman's Land (now the Australian state of Tasmania) was appointed lieutenant-governor of Upper Canada. He oversaw the hanging of 20 rebel leaders, including Lount, despite receiving petitions for clemency signed by some 30,000 people. A further 92 were transported to his old colony of Van Dieman's Land.[119] From Lower Canada, 58 men were transported to New South Wales, taking their ideas on responsible government with them.[120] The Sydney suburb of Canada Bay serves as a reminder of the colonial connection between the two countries. The chief agitators for rebellion fared much better. Both Papineau and Mackenzie were eventually pardoned, in 1844 and 1849 respectively. Significantly, both were re-elected to parliament. The rebellions themselves enjoyed only limited and tentative support, but the reasons behind them were widely accepted as legitimate. Papineau and Mackenzie remained popular men.

The Rebellions of 1837–38 leave historians with something of an enigma. On the military face of it, the rebellions were a tragicomedy. A few hundred farmers led by middle class politicians never had much hope against the might of the British army. Compared with the scale and commitment of the American or French revolutions, the Canadian rebellions seem rather inconsequential. The huge numbers of deserters and turncoats in both provinces does not indicate that these were popular insurrections. It is tempting to conclude that they represent little more than a bump in the relatively smooth colonial development of the Canadas, the unfortunate climax of some excitable radicals. Does this interpretation do justice to the rebels and Patriotes who lost their lives in 1837? Does this interpretation explain the mass support for the Reform Party and the Parti Patriote? Does this explain how Mackenzie managed to elude capture despite a £1,000 reward on his head and safely escape to America?[121] There clearly was a popular movement in the Canadas and the utter failure of the rebellions helps us to understand the nature of that movement. The people sought freedom not from Britain but from domination. The people sought not to sever the British connection but to claim the civic republican liberties that they saw as their British rights.

David Mills has argued that "Upper Canadians appealed to Burke and not to Paine, to British and not to American models, to moderate and not to radical objectives."[122] The last two claims certainly match the evidence. The hagiography of Britain and the British constitution was clear in the language of both sides. The confused and lethargic call to arms suggests that moderate rather than radical reform was desired. As Shaun McLaughlin has noted, "most colonists remained loyal to the Queen despite their disgust with the colonial government."[123] Paine and separatism was the preferred option of few, but does that leave Burkean thought as the dominant political philosophy? A conclusion like this is certainly congruent with Horowitz's argument that, unlike the exclusive liberal philosophy that dominated America, the "legitimate ideological diversity" of the Canadian tradition married toryism and socialism.[124] Mills provides this statement from the *Upper Canada Gazette* in 1800 as representative, "I pause to admire and gratefully contemplate that noblest fabric of human wisdom, the British Constitution."[125] What passes without comment is that the anonymous author used the moniker Cato.[126] *Cato's Letters* was the hugely popular civic republican work of Commonwealthmen, John Trenchard and Gordon Thomas.[127] A hero of the Roman republic, Cato was the alter ego of choice for letter writers throughout the British world, but almost exclusively from the reform side, not the conservatives.[128] The argument here is that along with toryism and liberalism, civic republicanism was a key political philosophy and that many reformers called for positive liberty and a collectivist mindset as a British community abroad.

The nature of the reform movement of the 1830s points to a contest over the meaning of the constitution and the right to legitimate opposition. The commitment by both tories and reformers to the British constitution is readily seen. On 18 March 1822 Justice Campbell expressed this sentiment to the Grand Jury of Upper Canada:

> Our Constitution is the tried and perfected production of
> many ages, effected by the valour and wisdom of our Ancestors;
> we are indebted to the Saxons for its most valuable parts, from
> their time to the present, it has undergone various modifica-
> tions, and received such improvements as were suggested
> by experience, and best adapted to the circumstances of the
> immediate times, and the progress of civilization and litera-
> ture, and of Agriculture, Manufactures and Commerce, and
> the consequent more refined and enlarged views of civil, polit-
> ical, and religious liberty. At the Norman conquest it encoun-
> tered a severe shock, and suffered an almost entire eclipse by
> the introduction of the Feudal System, but it still retained the

germ of freedom, that genial, that celestial principle which eventually overcame all obstructions, and by means of Magna Charta, the Reformation, the Revolution, the Bill of Rights, and above all, of the Habeas Corpus Act, has now put us in possession of it unencumbered by any base alloy, and in a state of perfection unparalleled in the annals of the world.[129]

The constitution was perfect and to be revered. So much so, in fact, that when a corrupt administration perverts the natural harmony of the three arms, the duty of all people loyal to the constitution is to rebel.

Legitimate rebellion was a concept embedded in British history. The *Colonial Advocate* emphasized this moral prerogative as early as 1829 in an article titled "The Lessons of 1688 and 1776 Compared":

> From that day on which the glorious revolution of 1688 dawned upon benighted Britain, Englishmen regarded themselves as the arbiters of their destiny. "From that day they considered the institutions of their country as made for them and not them for the institutions. From that day, the right of thinking, and of delivering their thoughts, both respecting government, and respecting religion, they assumed as their own; and spurned the advocates of slavery, who would rob them of that invaluable possession." The government of William III, and still more strongly the government of the House of Hanover, nourished this spirit among the people, and advocated the propriety of revolting against established power... hence the ability, high-toned independence and manly feeling displayed in the address of Congress in February 1776, to their friends and countrymen and fellow subjects. They were firmly attached to the first and best principles of the British constitution: so are we; so are the inhabitants of British America.[130]

The comparison to revolutionary America is a fair one and one that would be used by radicals in Australia also.[131] In the Commons, radical John Leader chastised Russell for having "forgotten or disregarded the warning indelibly stamped by [the American Revolution] on the tablet of history."[132] The language of Mackenzie, Papineau, and other radicals bore no small similarity to that of the Commonwealthmen. Paine and Locke were called on frequently in making their arguments. The rebels were not anti-British; it was their Britishness that compelled them to rebel.

The Upper Canadians wanted greater democracy within the blended constitution but, largely, did not want to separate from Britain. It is worth remembering that as recently as 1812 the Upper Canadians jumped to Britain's defence against the United States. Many people had parents, grand-parents, and other relatives who had fought for Britain in the Revolutionary War and the Seven Years War. These ties ran deep and go some way to explaining the seemingly schizophrenic nature of the populace, so eager to reform but so loathe to revolt. The historical experience of Quebec is often seen as being unique compared to the other Canadian provinces. With respect to the rebellions of 1837, however, the similarities between the Lower Canadians and the Upper Canadians, not the differences, are striking. The Upper Canadian reformers regularly spoke in support of their Lower Canadian brethren and their "manly, constitutional and truly independent stand."[133] It was not French nationalism that goaded the movement but a commitment to responsible government and greater democracy. It may be coincidental that it was Wolfred Nelson who fought and Louis-Joseph Papineau who fled the Battle of Saint-Denis, but it speaks volumes as to the interracial nature of the reform movement. The Patriote cause was neither French nor English; it was a battle over the spirit of the British constitution.

Reformer leaders in both provinces used civic republican language to highlight the inherent corruption in the bastardized constitutions. The malfeasance and nepotism of the tory oligarchies aroused great feelings of indignation. Many of them classically educated, the reform leaders echoed Cicero's defiant declaration, "if there are some who are found to be dishonest, then I promise to you... that only death – by Hercules! – will prevent me from opposing their corruption with vigour and perseverance."[134] Mackenzie had been denouncing the corrupt nature of the Family Compact for a decade by the time rebellion broke out. In 1828 he commemorated the second anniversary of the vandalism of the *Colonial Advocate*'s office by a mob of young tories by releasing a pamphlet with the sub-title *Official Corruption and Hypocrisy Unmasked*.[135] Charles Lindsey, who married Mackenzie's daughter Janet, reminisced that from their first meeting, Mackenzie spoke "with great earnestness and animation on the claims of justice, the odiousness of oppression, and the foulness of corruption."[136] It was a reoccurring theme for Papineau also. Drawing on the well-used mantra of colonial reform that demanded the substance not the shadow of the British constitution, Papineau spoke of the wheels of government being "clogged by corruption."[137] Writing to George Bancroft from the safety of the United states in December 1837, he denounced the Canadian judiciary as "*mercenaire, asservi, corrompu ou partisan*" (mercenary, servile, corrupted or partisan).[138] But if corruption was the disease, what was the cure? Ultimately, it would be responsible government, but in the heady atmosphere of 1837, radical reformers insisted that separatist republicanism was the only way forward.

Following the announcement of Lord Russell's Ten Resolutions, the radicals in both provinces hijacked the reform movement. It is important, though, not to let the separatist republican rhetoric of 1836 and 1837 overshadow the civic republican ethos that was both older and more strongly supported. Calls for responsible and local government were flavoured by a desire for a civic republican democracy. Reform was desperately needed to weed out individual corruption and to promote civic virtue and the common good. Before becoming radicalized, even Mackenzie called not for separation but for "limited monarchy."[139] The political participation of virtuous citizens, epitomized by the popularly elected Legislative Assembly, was not being encouraged in the Canadas. Between the governors, the Family Compact, and the Château Clique, the voice of the commons was being ignored, as was ancient prudence.

Beyond the specific details any piece of legislation, there was for civic republican thinkers something called the spirit of the law. In his treatise *On the State*, Cicero discussed the spirit of true law: "Its validity is universal; it is immutable and eternal... Any attempt to supersede this law, to repeal any part of it, is sinful; to cancel it entirely is impossible. Neither the Senate nor the Assembly can exempt us from its demands."[140] This is how the civic republican thinkers in the Canadas, indeed throughout the British world, viewed the British constitution. The spirit of the British constitution was ancient and eternal; it was a higher law to which even the king was subject. In 1836 both reformers and conservatives claimed to be fighting for the British constitution.[141]

The reformers of Upper and Lower Canada reached many of the same conclusions civic republican thinkers in America had reached in the late eighteenth century. To achieve the Polybian ideal of a mixed constitution and to censure the greed and corruption of the local oligarchies, responsible government was needed at local level. The move in 1836 from civic to separatist republicanism was an uneasy and ultimately disastrous one. Even Wolfred Nelson complained: "I am vexed by Mr. Papineau's and Mackenzie's admission that we have decided to rebel. It gives justification to our adversaries."[142] Although many reform leaders, like Nelson, and many lay people ultimately fell in line with the separatists, it seems clear that the majority wanted to peaceably advance the cause of democracy and, through popular political participation, restore virtue to its rightful place.

The Rebellions of 1837–38 were a shock to the British government. The radical press chastised the administrators for either ignoring or being ignorant of the large degree of dissatisfaction in the provinces. The rebellion in Lower Canada could perhaps be explained away by the racial divide between the populace and the ruling power. The rebellion in Upper Canada had no such excuse. It must be seen as political agitation, as Ireland's *Freeman's Journal* gloated: "After all, it does not appear that Sir Francis Head is such a jewel of a governor as his Tory friends fancied. Neither does it appear that Upper Canada is so loyal or so well disposed – so peaceable or so contented under his *energetic* administration of the law – as his admirers would fain persuade us to believe."[143]

John Leader soberly informed the Commons in December 1837 that "the North American provinces are now strong enough to take care of themselves and they know it."[144] The government responded by dispatching Lord Durham to investigate the mischief. His conclusions would have ramifications for the colonial administration of the entire British Empire. The battle for the British constitution was set to continue.

4

Lord Durham and the Grand Compromise

Lord Durham a leader, forsooth!... We who hear the laugh of scorn with which the Ex-Dictator's name is received, even by the Radicals of this, his own locality – we have some little knowledge on the subject, and we tell our friends in Dublin, that if there be one aristocrat in Great Britain more despised, more spat upon than another, that man is Lord Durham.
Northern Liberator, 1 December 1838

He is the most proud, imperious, haughty, and tyrannical despot breathing. Where is the neighbour, tenant, or servant, who ever liked Lord Durham!
Champion and Weekly Herald, 22 July 1837

Lord Durham's 1838 *Report on the Affairs of British North America* is a document of such importance in the British world that it has evoked its own mythology. It is rarely, if ever, cited by British world historians without a colourful prefix such as "famous," "influential," or "great." Following its Canadian publication in February 1839 the reformist *Spectator* made the somewhat prophetic statement that "Lord Durham's report... is, without any exception, the most interesting state paper that we ever saw; and will prove, we venture to predict, scarcely less important in its consequences."[1] The *Report* reached the Australian colonies in June, when the *Sydney Monitor* stated that "Lord Durham's report... ought to be read by every man in New South Wales who can think as well as read."[2] On printing an abridged version some 125 years later, the editor commented that the *Report* "has come to occupy such a central place in the history of the Commonwealth of Nations that no apology is needed for making it readily available to students and readers, both inside and outside the schools and universities."[3]

Although the micro-political objective of the *Report* was to respond to the 1837 Rebellions in Lower and Upper Canada, the macro-political objective was nothing less than a reworking of British policy towards conquered and colonized societies. In 1912 Sir Charles Lucas released a three-volume version of the *Report*. In the "introduction," which occupies the entire first volume, Lucas comments on the enormous ramifications of Durham's work, which spread far beyond the specific time and place of the author's words: "The words apply beyond Canada and beyond America. The spirit of them transcends the sphere of settlement, it is the living force of the whole British Empire. The words are the message of a great Englishman to his fellow countrymen, that the one thing needful is to leave behind a legacy of what is permanently sound and great. If England continues to be inspired by what Lord Durham taught so well, then as Great Britain has grown into Greater Britain, so Greater Britain will grow into Greatest Britain, to the glory of God the Creator, and to the well-being of mankind."[4] It is entirely without controversy to state that the impact of the *Report* spread far beyond the borders of Lower and Upper Canada. What then was the political theory that underpinned this document? What was the inspiration and what would be the ramifications?

At the heart of Lord Durham's *Report* lie two distinct and controversial policies. The first is the principle of responsible government for the British North American colonies, and the second prescribes the union of Upper and Lower Canada and a process of assimilation to bring the French Canadians in line with British cultural norms. Professors and students of Canadian history have tended to condemn the second aspect of the *Report*. The orthodoxy both in the academy and in society at large is to view Durham's treatment of the French Canadians as either ignorant and misguided or prejudicial and racist.[5] According to Mason Wade, Durham was "blinded by the very racism he disowned."[6] More sympathetically, Gerald Craig pleads ignorance, reminding his readers that "Lord Durham could not know as clearly in 1839 what we know today."[7] In either case, it is rejected in the modern, popular Canadian consciousness. Although the second principle of the *Report* certainly lends itself to criticism, revisionists, chiefly Janet Ajzenstat, challenge the claim that Durham's recommendations were either racist or ignorant.[8]

This chapter will argue that the first recommendation was seen as a necessity to introduce the second and that the second was the great enabler of civic republican democracy. There can be no doubt that liberalism guided Durham's hand to some degree, but was this the only political philosophy at work? Did the colonists in Canada and Australia interpret the *Report* through a strictly liberal prism? The principle of responsible government was a grand compromise between Britain and Canada. It would afford colonists the local self-determination they so desperately wanted while maintaining the warmth of connection to the British Empire. As Christopher Bayly notes, "new methods of political control" were needed in response to unrest in Canada and Australia.[9] The *Report* would provide a blueprint for a new British Empire. Limited autonomy would find the balance between full independence and full subjection. Colonial parliaments from Nova Scotia to New South Wales, housed with the inhabitants of the land, would make decisions to increase the wealth and happiness of the people. This would be done, however, under the flag of Great Britain, and it required, in Durham's summation, a people who not only enjoyed British laws but who were culturally British also. Although separated by oceans and in some cases hemispheres, the colonists would be reminded that they were a British community with British institutions and values. The fact that the British Queen is still enshrined on the currency of Canada and Australia is a remarkable testimony to the robustness of Lord Durham's central ideas outlined in the *Report*. This chapter will examine the degree to which civic republican political theory influenced his thinking and the colonies he would impact.

Lord Durham was born John George Lambton on 12 April 1792 in Berkeley Square, London. There was perhaps something auspicious about his birth year coinciding with the declaration of the revolutionary French Republic, since the future Earl of Durham would come to be known as Radical Jack.[10] Indeed Lambton's radical pedigree was second to none. His father, William Lambton, was an extreme Foxite Whig and chairman of the infamous Society of the Friends of the People.[11] At age six Durham was placed under the care of Bristol physician and radical supporter of the French Revolution Thomas Beddoes.[12] Lambton was elected to the House of Commons on 20 September 1813, describing himself as a "reformer."[13] On 9 December 1816 he married Lady Louisa, the eldest daughter of Whig-convert, reformer, and future prime minister, the second Earl Grey. According to Trevelyan it was this union that "brought modern democracy into the heart of the Whig consuls."[14] Lambton further cemented his radical reputation by forcefully denouncing the Peterloo Massacre on 22 October 1819, stating, "the fact could not be denied that English blood had been shed; and it was the duty of Englishmen to see that not one drop should be illegally or wantonly wasted."[15]

Following the aftermath of Peterloo, Lambton, along with Lord John Russell, began petitioning for parliamentary reform. Poor health restricted Lambton's effectiveness in the Commons, and on 29 January 1828 he became Baron Durham and prepared for the House of Lords. On 16 November 1830 Earl Grey became prime minister, and Durham was commissioned to draft a reform bill. He worked closely with a small coterie, including Russell, Lord Duncannon, and Sir James Graham at his London house, 13 Cleveland Row, and on 14 January 1831 presented Grey with a plan for sweeping reform.[16] In a letter to Grey the drafters outlined their chief objective: "we propose to grant representatives to all the large and populous towns of more than 10 000 inhabitants, of which there are unrepresented now in England about thirty, the right of voting."[17] The first and second versions of the bill would falter, but the third incarnation became the Great Reform Act on 7 June 1832. Despite vocal complaints to Grey that the eventual bill was not radical enough, Durham, as one of the chief drafters, was one of the four commissioners when the royal assent was granted.

On 14 March the following year, Durham resigned from Grey's cabinet. Their long-standing relationship had been strained over the issue of Irish policy and Grey's support for Edward G. V. Stanley; however, Durham claimed that poor health had forced his resignation.[18] Although away from parliament, Durham remained active in radical politics and in July 1835 accepted the post of ambassador to St Petersburg under the Melbourne Whig government. As trouble in Canada began to mount, Melbourne called upon Durham for another diplomatic task. The radicals and liberal whigs in England, much like the reformers in the Canadas, had become frustrated with the government's lethargy in political reform. Sir William Molesworth typified many radicals when he complained that the whig government were the "miserablest brutes that God Almighty ever put guts into."[19] In 1836 Molesworth along with Joseph Parkes and other liberal whigs took Durham's idea and founded the Reform Club.[20] Many in the radical faction saw Durham as their natural leader and hoped, returning from Russia, he would challenge Melbourne and lead the third party. The *Weekly Chronicle* certainly held this hope, noting that "he and he alone, can now organize the Radical party."[21]

With the return of Lord Durham to England, Melbourne saw an ideal opportunity to kill two birds with one stone. The growing discontent in the Canadas had become a rallying cry for English radicals. Lord Russell's Ten Resolutions were roundly rejected by the radicals, and John Arthur Roebuck gave a vehement denunciation in the Commons: "The instant you have passed the resolution of the noble lord, a wide and impassable gulf will be opened between you and your colony; the time for reconciliation will be gone forever; repentance will be in vain – our loss will be irreparable – shame, defeat and ignominy will be our portion; and we shall leave forever the shores of America, amid the hootings and reviling, and exultation of the many millions of her people who we have successively injured and insulted."

Jeremy Bentham's iconic catchphrase delivered at the National Convention of France in 1793, "Emancipate Your Colonies," was again called upon. Reprinted in 1838 by an unknown radical under the alter ego "Philo-Bentham," it acknowledged that the Canadian problem was "one of the precious legacies left us by Toryism." Nevertheless, "fields of blood and disgrace" would be the legacy of the whig Melbourne government for "late obedience to Bentham's great precept of honour and peace."[22] From Melbourne's point of view, with Lord Gosford recalled, Durham was the perfect man to address the Canadian problem. Such an appointment would appease the radicals on a contentious issue, keep the tories out of power, and remove a general menace from London. Diarist, Charles Grenville would later recall a conversation with MP Charles Buller, who suggested the government could increase their popularity only if they were wise. "I wonder what you call being wise?" asked Grenville. "Take in Durham," was the reply.[23]

Durham initially rejected the Canadian posting but reconsidered following news of the rebellions in November and December. In January 1838 he formally accepted the post of high commissioner and governor-general of British North America. Lord Russell introduced a bill to suspend the constitution of Lower Canada, allowing Durham and a Special Council of his choosing to create laws. On 13 April at Windsor Castle, Victoria outlined these instructions to her "Right Trusty and Right Well beloved Cousin and Councillor": "Whereas by an Act passed in the First Year of Our Reign Intituled 'An Act to make temporary provision for the Government of Lower Canada,' it is amongst the other things enacted that it shall be lawful for Us by any Commission or Commissions to be from times to time issued under the Great Seal of our United Kingdom or by any Instructions under Our Signet and Sign Manuel, and with the advice of Our Privy Council, to constitute a special Council for the affairs of Our said Province of Lower Canada, and for that purpose to appoint... not less than Five Special Councillors."[24] Durham's power in Lower Canada was nearly absolute. In addition, he was given full administrative power when physically present in any other province and also the power to pardon those accused of treason. Durham left for Canada with more official power than any previous British governor, prompting Lord Brougham to "terrify" the Lords by comparing Durham's mission to Canada to that of Pedro de la Gasca's mission to Peru.[25]

Lord Durham's appointment was greeted, according to Queen Victoria's journal, with "great delight" by the radicals and "sarcastic cheers" from the tories.[26] New comments that in Westminster "there was no criticism of Durham's appointment, most of the speeches expressed hearty approval of it."[27] Durham did face some criticism in the press for seemingly compromising his radical politics for whig favour. Richard Cobbett, son of the famed journalist William, accused Durham of being a pseudo-Radical: "And some of the Radicals, we are sorry to say, have been toasting his Lordship as one of their number. It is extremely puzzling to us, who are not learned in the subtleties and mysteries of party, to guess at what there is about Lord Durham to make him worth scrambling for. What has he ever done? What peculiar talent has he ever shown himself to be possessed of? His speeches are mere throwings up of gall, clothed, perhaps, in sufficiently well-tuned language; but gall it is, and gall it must be, for gall is the chief characteristic of his Lordship's mind and body."[28] The *Times* was more succinct: "here stands Lord Durham, who bids highest?"[29] The Lower Canadian press, with the exception of some English party papers, were more enthusiastic. *Le Canadien* was typical of the French papers in its enthusiasm for the hero of the Great Reform Act. It happily concluded, "if the Home-Government had been ill-disposed towards us, it would not have sent us the most liberal men to set our affairs in order."[30]

Despite the gravity of the Canadian situation, Durham delayed his departure till 24 April, not arriving till 29 May.[31] His team included thirty-one-year-old chief secretary, Charles Buller. A onetime pupil of Thomas Carlyle, Buller was a Benthamite, an acquaintance of John Stuart Mill, and the Member for West Looe.[32] The next most important man was the colonial theorist Edward Gibbon Wakefield, author of the infamous tome *A Letter from Sydney*.[33] Published in 1829, the British public accepted the book as a genuine account from an Australian colonist. The work was in fact written by Wakefield, who had never been to Sydney and was serving three years in Newgate prison for tricking the young daughter of a wealthy manufacturer into marrying him. Following his release, Wakefield became influential in both the South Australia Association and the New Zealand Association, promoting systematic British colonization. Wakefield, however, was not the only potential liability in Durham's team. His legal advisor, Thomas Turton achieved notoriety in 1831 when he became one of the first men in Britain to be successfully sued for divorce by his wife. He was found guilty of incest for having sex with his sister-in-law.[34] Using it as a pretext to attack the "Morality of the English Aristocracy," Mackenzie noted that Turton was "pretty well hauled over the coals for being a whoremonger and adulterer."[35] Despite this scandalous reputation, Durham, fiercely loyal to his old Eton friend, who had also helped him on the Reform Bill, insisted Turton join him on his mission to Canada.

Lord Durham's mission was perhaps doomed to failure. The polite pessimism of the *Times* proved to be accurate: "we sincerely wish Lord Durham success in his mission: we certainly do not venture to predict it."[36] Ireland's *Freeman's Journal* was cautiously optimistic, stating that "Lord Durham, no doubt, will exercise his dictatorial powers with generous forbearance, and endeavour to remedy the evils which a vicious policy, and still more vicious men, have inflicted upon unfortunate Canada."[37] The mutual antipathy between Durham and several leading whigs, not least the prime minister, meant that his support from London, despite grandiose promises, would always be precarious. His violent temper and sharp tongue served to alienate him even from men who should have been political allies. Lord Holland notes in his journal, "no two men are more unlike than Durham when in good humour, and Durham in his angry, tetchy and, I am afraid one must add, usual mood."[38]

Bruce Curtis has described him as a man with a "predisposition to condescension."[39] Whilst Durham's biographers Stuart Reid and Chester New blame the failure of the Canadian mission on the whigs, Ged Martin suggests that his own proud and arrogant behaviour was at fault.[40] On 9 October 1838 Durham resigned his post, returning to England on 1 November.[41] He had been in Canada for just over five months.

Durham's time in Canada began well enough. He was highly successful in handling a border dispute with the United States and went a long way towards improving relations with British North America's southern neighbour. He also created a police force for Lower Canada along the lines of Sir Robert Peel's bobbies. The most pressing, yet sensitive, political problem, however, concerned the 161 rebels still in prison.[42] The situation was highly delicate since ordinary trials could not take place. A Lower Canadian jury selected in the usual manner would be predominately French Canadian and would almost certainly acquit the rebels. Colborne and the Lower Canadian officers argued that courts martial should be used since impartial trials were not possible, but Glenelg rejected this suggestion, insisting that British justice and ordinary juries must be used. Unless the "failure of ordinary tribunals [was to be] established," Durham was stuck with them.[43] Durham examined the prisoner list and identified eight for punishment, including Wolfred Nelson, who, seemingly repentant, described his decision to challenge a force "powerful enough to crush Bonaparte" as "madness."[44] After consulting with the English party and securing their approval, an ordinance was enacted on the coronation day of Queen Victoria, 28 June 1838. The ordinance read that the eight prisoners would be sent to Bermuda and, along with sixteen others in exile, including Papineau and O'Callaghan, would be forbidden from entering Lower Canada. If any of the prisoners or exiles "shall at any time hereafter, except by permission of the Governor General of Her Majesty's Provinces on the continent of North America… be found at large, or come within the said Province without such permission as aforesaid [they shall be found guilty of high treason] and suffer death accordingly."[45]

Durham's decision was generally applauded by both the French and the English factions. It was certainly approved by the eight prisoners, who reportedly toasted Durham on board the *Vestal*, which sailed for Bermuda on 3 July.[46] Buller gloated of the reception throughout North America the ordinance received:

> The British population of Lower Canada, after a few partial indications of dissatisfaction, universally acquiesced in it. The French, who were not disposed to be satisfied with anything but an entire concession to all their most unreasonable views, were awed by the decision, and conciliated by the lenity of the Act. After a while they ceased to murmer at it. But its reception in the United States was most satisfactory. All parties agreed in extolling it as a noble, wise, and liberal act. The very newspapers that had previously been most violent in assailing the British Government changed their tone for a while…
> From that hour the disaffected in Canada ceased to derive any aid from the public opinion of our neighbours, and among our difficulties we had no longer to contend with the chance of war with the United States.[47]

Buller certainly overstates the case by suggesting Durham's ordinance prevented war with the United States. Be that as it may, the warmth of reception in Canada is noteworthy for its stark juxtaposition with elsewhere. Writing in exile in New York, Mackenzie lambasted the "autocrat of the Canadas" for banishing the "best lovers of their country" to appease the "cravings of the Ultra Tories."[48] When the news hit England the response was no kinder.

Durham had exceeded his authority in passing the ordinance. His power was restricted to British North America and certainly did not extend to Bermuda. He had no right to sentence men to banishment without a trial and even less so to execute them should they return. Lord Brougham took no small pleasure in announcing that should an execution take place, Durham "would be guilty of no less a crime than murder."[49] His inattention to the technical limits of his powers aroused great interest in the press also. John Murray's *Quarterly Review* revelled in the whig's embarrassment. It condemned the "despotic" Durham: "The selection of such a man as Lord Durham – so headstrong, so wayward, so impracticable, that they could not keep him in their own cabinet – for duties of such distant and complicated responsibility – is undoubtedly the strongest trial that ministers could make of Tory patience, and of the dutiful respect of the Tory leaders for the Queen's name and for the constitutional principle of leaving to those who are responsible for measures the unfettered choice of their own instruments."[50]

The affair was causing the whig leadership to come under scrutiny. *Fraser's Magazine for Town and Country* dismissed the whole Melbourne government: "With a prime minster, notorious for nothing but courtesy, nonchalance, and abandoned Toryism; with a home-secretary, of meagre ability, and the closest prejudices; with a colonial minister, of universally confessed incapacity; and with a governor of the great Indian empire, fitted for nothing higher than the enjoyment of a sinecure at Greenwich." Fraser was no kinder with respect to the Bermuda ordinance, noting, "We candidly own that Lord Durham's plan was original, if nothing else... he did not remember Dr. Kitchiner's injunction to the cook who had to dress a live hare, 'first catch the hare, *then* proceed.' Oh, no! Lord Durham is for 'no compromise.' He published an ordinance (shade of Charles X. lie still!) declaring these untried men guilty of high treason, and sentencing them to banishment for life to Bermuda, on pain of death. But his Lordship, it appears, has no control at Bermuda; and, besides that, we happen to have some old-fashioned notions here in England, that no one must be treated as guilty, much less banished for life, to a place we have no right to send him, without full and fair trial by jury."[51] Durham's actions certainly were defensible. Government lawyers determined that the only technical illegality in the ordinance was the transportation to Bermuda, not the banishment without trial. Melbourne could have introduced a bill allowing Durham to detain prisoners at Bermuda. Lord Howick and Lord Glenelg were keen to fight Brougham. Melbourne, however, never a fan of Durham and influenced strongly by Lord Russell, chose to support the Indemnity Bill.[52]

It was unfortunate that Lord Durham first learned of his betrayal through a New York newspaper on 19 September.[53] The Lower Canadians rallied behind Durham, burning an effigy of Brougham at Place d'Armes on the twenty-fifth.[54] The *Montreal Herald* notes the great theatre that took place as the citizens voiced their disapproval of Melbourne's actions: "Two transparencies, each six feet by nine, were mounted on a carriage and drawn by some jackasses, and followed by a transparent coffin, born by pall-bearers, who carried lighted torches. On the coffin the word 'Brougham' was painted. One of the transparencies represented Lord Brougham seated on a jackass, with his face to the animal's tail, an imp of darkness leading the ass and exclaiming, 'come along, old boy!' while his Lordship says, 'I protest against the legality of this ordinance'... A fingerpost, stuck up at a short distance, having on it the words 'Road to Hell.'"[55] Despite these scenes, Durham resigned on 9 October. It is unlikely the failure of the ordinances so much as the palpable lack of support from Melbourne and the whigs that guided this decision. With his health again deteriorating, Durham returned to England, determined to be "the plaintiff and not the defendant."[56]

Durham's short time in Canada was made notorious by the scandals. With the benefit of hindsight, however, his tenure is remarkable for the fundamental shift in gubernatorial attitude towards a British colonial population. Far from the rigid, militaristic mindset of Sir Francis Bond Head, Durham represented a new democratic approach that acknowledged the legitimacy of the people. As a governor, Durham wasted no time implementing his program of conscientious reform. He effectively destroyed the old Château Clique by refusing to reappoint the old executive councillors. Charles Buller in his 1840 memoir, praised this as the "wisest course of conduct": "The strange system of colonial government, by which every person once in office was held in practice to be forever irremovable, had had the effect of filling the Executive Council with some of the oldest men of every clique that had in succession ruled the Province... being men of little strength of character, or position in public life, [they] were likely to be very docile agents of the one or two persons who really managed the government. No one of them possessed the confidence of the British population."[57] Lower Canadian reformers welcomed the "refreshing breeze" that accompanied Lord Durham's arrival.[58] The *Montreal Transcript* typified the response of many: "the days of reform have indeed dawned upon this colony."[59]

Durham was attempting to reconcile the colonists' desire, especially that of the English-speaking population, both to stay within the British orbit and to exercise a degree of independence. Durhamite democracy, however, cannot be completely accounted for in the philosophical halls of liberalism. There was more to it than the recognition of individual rights, the removal of imperial interference, and the promotion of democratic principles. Durham's democracy required duty and virtue also.[60] It required a commitment to the greater good by a community who saw themselves united as one people, neither French nor English (nor Irish, Scottish, Welsh, or American) but British. History did not allow Durham to put his ideas into practice. Instead he would achieve immortality through articulating a theory of government centred on a virtuous but, crucially, homogeneous and British people. This system was hinged on civic institutions promoting a British mono-culture. It is in this communal emphasis that the civic republic bent of Durham's *Report* is revealed.

The meaning of Britishness was contested, and contemporaries in the nineteenth century understood it differently. In an essay from 1603, regularly reprinted in Britain in the nineteenth century, Francis Bacon spoke of the need to surrender small tribal identities to the greater collective. Referring specifically to the union of England and Scotland, he stated: "But when the island shall be made Britain, then Scotland is no more to be considered as Scotland, but as part of Britain; no more than England is to be considered as England, but as a part likewise of Britain... let us imagine... that Britain had never been divided, but had ever been one kingdom."[61] This popular concept of Britishness was applied not only to Scotland but to the rest of the Isles and to colonists at the farthest reach of the empire. Linda Colley has noted that Great Britain itself was an "invented nation superimposed, if only for a while, onto much older alignments and loyalties." The prolonged wars with France helped the British forge a new national identity. As Colley notes, "a powerful and persistently threatening France became the haunting embodiment of the Catholic Other."[62] These ideas are readily seen in Durham's *Report*. Having witnessed the cultural divide between English and French Canada, he was convinced that only a British state could hope to achieve unity and harmony.

It is easy to forget that Durham was sent to Canada not to write a report but to govern. London's *Monthly Magazine* certainly picked up on this in 1839: "Lord Durham's Report to Her Majesty *after* he had *resigned* his office! – What were the terms of the royal commission whereby he was appointed? It directed him to 'enquire into and *adjust* all questions depending in the said province': not to enquire into and *report* upon them. More easy to sit down snugly in Cleveland-Row, and write about the grievances of a people, than on the other side of the Atlantic to cure them."[63] Since then, however, such has been the acclaim given the *Report*, the Magna Carta of the Second British Empire, to use Reginald Coupland's cant phrase, one could be forgiven for thinking it was birthed from success rather than failure.[64] Durham had broken an important governmental protocol by storming out of Canada before receiving an official recall. According to the *Church of England Quarterly Review*, upon his return the "puerile ministry" enacted a petty revenge "consistent with their own peculiar paltry meanness" by accepting Durham's resignation on the ship, thus depriving him of the salute he would have been owed had he landed as governor general.[65]

Just two days after Durham left Quebec a second, albeit minor, rebellion broke out in Lower Canada. News of the rebellion certainly dampened claims that the mission had been a success.[66] Durham was seen by many in whig circles as an embarrassment to the government and he received a duly cold reception upon his return. According to McGilchrist, "the indignity and injustice destroyed him, and he returned to England only to die."[67] When he sat down in December to write the *Report*, he was in many ways attempting to prove he had been of use to both the government and the colonies and that, despite Russell's sardonic suggestion, his departure from Canada was not "such a blessing to the Province that he could not delay it till he received the answer of the Govt."[68]

What emerged two months later was a document of over one hundred thousand words assessing the problems in British North America and suggesting the twin solutions of responsible government and assimilation of the French. A work of this magnitude, produced so quickly, was probably not the work of a single author. However, the old epigram "Wakefield thought it, Buller wrote it, Durham signed it" is unfair to the *Report*'s eponymous hero. Lucas makes the point that "to maintain that Lord Durham, of all men in the world, allowed somebody else to dictate what he was to recommend is ridiculous."[69] Although there is ample circumstantial evidence to believe that Buller indeed penned great chucks of the *Report*, we have no reason to doubt that Durham was actively involved, dictating, editing, and approving and that the final result was indeed his not only in name but in spirit too.[70]

Turning first to the *Report*'s assessment of the French population and the union of the Canadas, there is certainly ample evidence for those who wish to decry Durham as either racist or ignorant. Durham, never one to be sensitive about other people's feelings, makes a series of blunt and negative comments concerning the French Canadians (whom he sometimes refers to simply as the Canadians). In one of the more famous lines in the *Report*, Durham explains: "I expected to find a contest between a government and a people: I found two nations warring in the bosom of a single state: I found a struggle, not of principles, but of races;

and I perceived that it would be idle to attempt any amelioration of laws or institutions, until we first succeed in terminating the deadly animosity that now separates the inhabitants of Lower Canada into the hostile divisions of French and English."[71] Bearing in mind that the *Report* was never guaranteed to become a public document until it was leaked to the *Times*, Durham certainly makes it clear which race should yield and which should dominate Canada.[72]

Durham's assessment of the French Canadians is severe:

An utterly uneducated and singularly inert population, implicitly obeying leaders who ruled them by the influence of a blind confidence and narrow national prejudices, accorded very little with the resemblance which had been discovered to that high-spirited democracy which effected the American Revolution.

The superior political and practical intelligence of the English, cannot be for a moment disputed. The great mass of the Canadian population, who cannot read or write, and have found in few of the institutions of their country, even the elements of political education, were obviously inferior to the English settlers.

The only power that can be effectual at once in coercing the present dissatisfaction, and hereafter obliterating the nationality of the French Canadians, is that of a numerical majority of a loyal and English population; and the only stable government will be one more popular than any that has hitherto existed in the North American Colonies.

The whole interior of the British dominions must, ere long, be filled with an English population, every year rapidly increasing its numerical superiority over the French. Is it just that the prosperity of this great majority, and of this vast tract of country, should be for ever, or even for a while, impeded by the artificial bar which the backward laws and civilization of a part, and a part only, of Lower Canada, would place between them and the ocean?

> And is this French Canadian nationality one which, for the good merely of that people, we ought to strive to perpetuate, even if it were possible? I know of no national distinctions marking and continuing a more hopeless inferiority. The language, the laws, the character of the North American Continent are English; and every race but the English (I apply this to all who speak the English language) appears there in a condition of inferiority. It is to elevate them from that inferiority that I desire to give to the Canadians our English character. [73]

These comments and others like them are the staple of what has become the orthodox school of thought. Describing the French as inferior and backward and calling for their obliteration lends itself to criticism. The *Report*, however, must be read in its entirety and understood in terms of Durham's ultimate, civic republican ambition.

Durham's *Report* was undoubtedly influenced by Alexis de Tocqueville's revered tome, *De la démocratie en Amérique*. Indeed, the "beautiful" and "accurate" French writer alluded to in the *Report* is almost certainly Tocqueville.[74] Released in French in 1835 and immediately translated into English by Henry Reeve, many of Tocqueville's conclusions would be reiterated by Durham. Speaking of the French in America, Tocqueville says this:

> There was once a time at which we also might have created a great French nation in the American wilds, to counterbalance the influence of the English upon the destinies of the New World... But a concourse of circumstances, which it would be tedious to enumerate, have deprived us of this magnificent inheritance. Wherever the French settlers were numerically weak and partially established, they have disappeared; those who remain are collected on a small extent of the country, and are now subject to other laws. The 400,000 inhabitants of Lower Canada constitute, at the present time, the remnant of an old nation lost in the midst of a new people. A foreign population is increasing around them unceasingly and on all sides, which already penetrates among the ancient masters of the country, predominates in their cities, and corrupts their language. This population is identical to that of the United

States; it is therefore with truth that I assert that the British race is not confined within the frontiers of the Union, since it already extends to the North-east.

For Tocqueville, the battle for America was not so much racial as ideological. The primary cause behind the success of New England and the failure of New France was the former's embrace of democracy and ultimately republicanism. "Nations which are accustomed to free institutions," he argues, "are better able than any others to found prosperous colonies."

When Tocqueville speaks of the British race, he is referring specifically to the British democratic tradition, in which civic republicanism plays a major role. The American inheritance of Commonwealthman ideology is seen as a major factor in what made the British race prosper. He notes that "the habit of thinking and governing for oneself is indispensable in a new country". He includes both the Americans and the English Canadians in the British race because they were both bound to a certain way of thinking. It is the idea and not the "race" (in the way we understand the term today) that earns such high praise from this French scholar: "It cannot be denied that the British race has acquired an amazing preponderance over all the other European races in the new world; and that it is very superior to them in civilization, in industry, and in power."[75]

Durham follows Tocqueville to the letter, both figuratively and literally, as he opts for the term "English race," which is a translation closer to the French original, *la race Anglaise*.[76] More importantly Durham shares a belief that the British democratic ideas, shared by Americans and the English Canadians alike, rather than race, is the source of superiority. A repeated theme in the *Report* is that social cohesion requires shared civic institutions producing civic virtue. This is central to the civic republican rather than the liberal democratic tradition. To Durham's mind, that spirit of civic duty, so crucial to a harmonious society, was impossible to achieve with a racial fault line and a division between French Lower Canada and English Upper Canada. As unpalatable as Durham's phraseology may appear to modern readers, there can be little doubt that his energy was spent in the *Report* articulating a pro-democratic rather than an anti-French position. Even Mason Wade, who condemns Durham's "racist outlook" concedes that the "terms" rather than the substance of the *Report* "produced a sense of injustice and injury in French Canada which has survived in some measure to the present day."[77]

Durham's desire to see the French language become extinct in North America, anathema as it was to French Canadians then and now, was in line with Tocqueville's favoured prophesy of a homogenous British character dominating the whole continent.[78] Durham perceived that the French Canadians were in fact not French at all, since they had been "separated by eighty years of a foreign rule, and still more by those changes which the Revolution and its consequences have wrought." Similarly, the English Canadians, joined though they were in culture and spirit, were not really English. Rather, the two sides needed to come together as one, neither French nor English but a new kind of British. Durham's arguments for a single language reveal a clear civic republican disposition. The language barrier bred a "hereditary enmity" that retarded the creation of patriotic citizens. Not only did it restrict the average French Canadian from full intercourse in the British political arena, Durham also spoke of things like literature and theatre.[79] It is through a shared culture and active participation in civic institutions that virtuous citizens can be produced. Durham wanted them to be no longer an "old nation lost in the midst of a new people" but equals in his true project; a government, "more popular than any that has hitherto existed in the North American Colonies."[80]

Did Durham fully appreciate the attachment of the Lower Canadian masses to the French language and other aspects of French culture? Most likely he did not. Nor, it would seem, did he anticipate the tenacity of the *La Survivance* movement. Be that as it may, his arguments for a single language need not necessarily be seen as racist or ignorant. It is a basic principle of civic republicanism that virtuous citizens need to actively participate in a political community. This, Durham stresses, is unlikely to occur under linguistic apartheid:

> The difference of language produces misconceptions yet more fatal even than those which it occasions with respect to opinions: it aggravates the national animosities, by representing all the events of the day in utterly different lights. The political misrepresentation of the facts is one of the incidents of a free press in every free country; but in nations in which all speak the same language, those who receive a misrepresentation

from one side, have generally some means of learning the truth from the other. In Lower Canada however, where the French and English papers represent adverse opinions, and where no large portion of the community can read both languages with ease, those who receive the misrepresentations are rarely able to avail themselves of the means of correction. It is difficult to conceive the perversity with which the misrepresentations are habitually made, and the gross delusions which find currency among the people; they thus live in a world of misconceptions - in which each party is set against the other, not only by diversity of feelings and opinions, but by an actual belief in an utterly different set of facts.[81]

Janet Ajzenstat has argued that Durham's prescriptions in the *Report* were "grounded in a thorough understanding of the British liberal tradition."[82] This, of course, is true. Durham's adherence to the liberal whig and radical traditions has already been commented upon. Durham's political philosophy was also influenced heavily by the civic republican canon. It was no less an authority on the *Report* than Lucas who compared Durham's Canadian mission with that of Aristotle in writing *The Politics*.[83] The conclusion reached by both men, separated by centuries, is remarkably similar. The best constitution would require a division of powers representing the three estates and a community of virtue. Although the assimilation program may have been contentious, it was a necessary precursor, in Durham's mind, for responsible government; the civic republican grand compromise.

Durham's time in British North America was spent almost exclusively in Quebec. He made only a brief sojourn to Upper Canada and neglected the other provinces under his jurisdiction completely. Nevertheless, it needs to be acknowledged that Durham's ultimate project both as governor general and through the *Report* was much larger than the Canadas. Durham's commission authorized on 31 March 1838 by Writ of Privy Seal was effectively three-tiered. First, he was "Governor-in-Chief in and over each of Our Provinces of Lower Canada, Upper Canada, Nova Scotia and New Brunswick, and in and over Our Island of Prince Edward."[84] Second, he was made "Our High Commissioner for the adjustment of certain important questions depending in the said Provinces of Lower and Upper Canada respecting the form and future government of the said Provinces." Finally, he was made governor general of all provinces, Prince Edward Island and Newfoundland also.[85] Although the emphasis of Durham's mission is the Canadas, it is no accident that his powers extended across the whole of British North America.

The rebellions of 1837 had taken place in only two provinces. The causes of the rebellions, however, were common to all British North America. Indeed, Durham opens his *Report* claiming he had found "common causes, requiring common remedies." The imminent danger was restricted to the Canadas, but it was inevitable that without drastic measures the other provinces, faithful as they were, would become jealous of the superior condition of their American neighbours. The greatness of the American republic and the negative juxtaposition with British North America was a constant concern for Durham.[86] In Craig's words, "the shadow of the United States hovered over nearly every page of the *Report*."[87] Even in the quiet maritime provinces, the connection to Britain could not be maintained by mere nostalgia: "But even this feeling [of affection] may be impaired, and I must warn those in whose hands the disposal of their destinies rest, that a blind reliance on the all-enduring loyalty of our countrymen may be carried too far. It is not politic to waste and cramp their resources, and to allow the backwardness of the British Provinces every where to present a melancholy contrast to the progress and prosperity of the United States."

Durham's *Report* suggested remedies far beyond the immediate problems in Lower and Upper Canada. He was proposing a reworking of empire based on civic republican principles. Durham gives a scathing account of the Family Compact in Upper Canada: "For a long time this body of men, receiving at times accessions to its numbers, possessed almost all the highest public offices, by means of which, and of its influence in the Executive Council, it wielded all the powers of government... A monopoly of power so extensive and so lasting could not fail, in process of time, to excite envy, create dissatisfaction and ultimately provoke attack; and an opposition consequently grew up in the Assembly, which assailed the ruling party, by appealing to popular principles of Government – by denouncing the alleged jobbing and profusion of the official body – and by instituting inquiries into abuses, for the purpose of promoting reform." Durham concludes that the "great struggle" in Upper Canada, which he perceives will be common to all British North America, concerned the question of "responsibility of the Executive

Council." At first glance Durham is only promoting what the Upper Canadian reformers, Robert Baldwin in particular, had been agitating for years before the rebellion. On closer inspection, however, Durham has very firm ideas about what powers should be extended to the popular arm and which should be reserved for the Crown in a new Canadian constitution.

Durham's recommendations are classically republican in that they propose a division of power between the monarchic, aristocratic, and democratic arms, with each looking over the other. To this extent, he is in keeping with the ideas of Aristotle, Plutarch, and Machiavelli. Durham did not believe in republicanism as a form of government; that is to say, he did not endorse the separatist republicanism of Mackenzie, Papineau, or Bentham. Rather, he endorsed the social and political theory of civic republicanism. Having founded and maintained the British North American provinces "at a vast expense of blood and treasure," Durham was loath to see the connection between the mother country and her colonies broken. He describes himself as "perfectly aware" of the value of the colonies and "strongly impressed with the necessity of maintaining our connection with them." Nevertheless, his commitment to democracy led him to conclude that local power must be in local hands: "the British people of the North American Colonies are a people on whom we may safely rely, and to whom we must not grudge power."

Durham is both specific and selective about which powers need to be reserved for the representatives of the Crown and which would be given over to the democratic arm. According to the *Report*, "the constitution of the form of Government – the regulation of foreign relations, and of trade with the mother country, the other British colonies and foreign nations, and the disposal of the public lands, are the only points on which the mother country requires a control." The bulk of administrative and legislative power, however, should be surrendered. He writes, "I admit that the system which I propose would, in fact, place the internal government of the colony in the hands of the colonists themselves... I know not in what respect it can be desirable that we should interfere with their internal legislation in matters which do not affect their relations with the mother country."

At its heart, the *Report* seeks to extend to British subjects abroad the same rights as British subjects in England. In place of aristocratic tory cabals, Durham wanted the colonists to enjoy the benefit of a British-style cabinet that would be responsible to the popularly elected Assembly. The parliamentary conditions grudgingly endured by British North Americans would be completely unacceptable to free Englishmen. Durham gives a vivid example: "Let it be imagined that at a general election the opposition were to return 500 out of 658 members of the House of Commons, and that the whole policy of the ministry should be condemned... Let it be supposed that the Crown should consider it a point of honour and duty to retain a ministry so condemned and so thwarted... it will not be difficult to imagine the fate of such a system of government. Yet such was the system, such literally was the course of events in Lower Canada, and such in character, though not quite in degree, was the spectacle exhibited in Upper Canada, and, at one time or another, in every one of the North American colonies."[88] With the spectre of the United States constantly before them, democracy was the only way forward for the Canadas and for the other provinces too. Through a civic republican style of democracy, the grand compromise of responsible government was possible.

The grand compromise would, in time, come to be the model for British colonies around the world. With democracy fast becoming normative, responsible government was seen as a basic liberty for free British subjects. As Jack Greene notes, "Britons, in the far peripheries as well as at the centre of the British Empire, still regarded liberty as the essence of Britishness."[89] Colonists were able to retain their connection to the British Empire while wielding the reins of their own affairs. The patriotic pride and sense of identity was allowed to continue, since the civic republican tradition highlights this as necessary for the production of virtuous citizens. Under Durham's plan, however, the voice of the third estate was to be elevated. Durham was keenly aware that the tide of public opinion, especially on the American continent, was quickly turning and that democracy was soon to be not the exception but the rule. It is quite likely true that if Durham had been in America in 1775, there would have been no revolution in 1776.

New's assessment of the *Report* is worth considering. He opines that "the greatest weakness of the *Report* – all the more striking because it marked Durham's only failure in the sphere of political prophesy – is its treatment of the French-Canadians."[90] Readers of Canadian history would do well to consider this aspect of the *Report* as a weakness rather than a display of racism or ignorance. Durham dreamed of a union of the Canadas where virtuous citizens would actively engage in the body politic valuing above all *bonum commune communitatis*. The *Report* repeatedly displays his desire to see French Canadians engaging in the political process and embracing British culture. This desire was realized in a way Durham would not have anticipated or approved of, since French Canadian politicians used the very British institutions he was so keen to establish to protect French culture and identity. Influenced of course by aspects of liberal ideology, Durham's thesis is essentially civic republican. The French and English, he hoped, would one day stand together in a new kind of British polis.

The response to the *Report* was in many ways as one would expect. The Canadian tories were naturally incensed at a proposal to destroy the influence of the Family Compact. Head wasted little time in producing his *Narrative*, defending his administration and insisting Durham was misleading "our youthful Queen" in suggesting that Upper Canadians were "dissatisfied with their institutions." "It really seems to me," Head concluded, "that Lord Durham has looked upon British North America in general, and upon the province of Upper Canada in particular, through a glass darkened."[91] The *Eclectic Review* sarcastically dismissed Head's apologia for his own conduct, commenting that "he is by no means the Machiavel that he would fain represent himself to have been."[92] Chief Justice of Upper Canada and "bone and sinew" of the Family Compact, John Beverley Robinson, also rushed to release a counter to the *Report*.[93] Steeped in Burkean conservatism, Robinson insisted the Family Compact was needed to defend the province from the "rash and unwise popular body."[94] Robinson strongly rejected Durham's plan to unite the Canadas, preferring instead that Upper Canada would annex Montreal, prompting Patrick Brode to remark that "if Durham's plans for French Canada were somewhat harsh, Robinson's were positively draconian."[95]

The reformers of Canada, on the other hand, were delighted with the *Report*. Even the Lower Canadian reformers, who certainly had cause for grievance with the assimilation program, welcomed the principle of responsible government. The *Report* was welcomed with eagerness in Nova Scotia, which would distinguish itself as the first colony in the British Empire to achieve responsible government. Politicians in Australasia studied the *Report* with great care. Thornton Leigh Hunt ventured to predict on 26 June 1839 that if the principles of the *Report* were applied to the Antipodean colony, "how much more reason will the millions of Britons in New Zealand have to honour the name of Durham, than the Virginians that of Elizabeth?"[96] In Britain, the *Belfast News-letter* called it, "the most ably drawn state paper that has, for half a century at least, been submitted to a British Parliament."[97] The *Bristol Mercury* praised the "deliberate judgement, acute perception, and extended but wise liberality of feeling which characterize his entire report."[98]

In London, the Melbourne government embraced the *Report*. Were the cabinet ministers attempting reconciliation with the governor they had let down, or were they more interested in courting the radicals in order to have a working majority? Probably the latter. Nevertheless, as early as 3 May the government introduced legislation to unite the Canadas. On 3 June none other than Lord Russell, so firmly against responsible government when he handed down his Ten Resolutions two years earlier, spoke approvingly of the *Report* and the idea that the popular Assembly should retain control of public revenue. Although the proposals were delayed, the writing was on the wall for the British North American tories. On 6 September Charles Poulett Thomson, later Baron Sydenham, was made governor-in-chief of British North America. A disciple of Durham, Bentham, and David Hume, it was clear that Poulett was sent to pave the way for the recommendations in the *Report*.[99]

Lord Durham, loud and opinionated though he was, proved himself a team player for the whigs. His health had been battered by the physical and emotional turmoil that marked his mission to Canada, a mission he only took, it should be remembered, out of a sense of whig duty. On 26 July he rallied his strength for a final speech in the House of Lords. New summarizes it well by stating, "he spoke briefly but forcibly in defence of the Government that had treated him so badly." Durham's health would fluctuate but generally deteriorate for just over a year. Gravely ill, he received a letter from Charles Buller on 28 July 1840, informing him that the bill to unite the Canadas was to be passed immediately. Buller also delighted in telling his old mentor that the principle of responsible government would inevitably be introduced also: "You told the British Government that it could never hope to govern the Colonies quietly unless it brought its Executive into harmony with the Colonial Legislature. From the hour in which you said this, the people in every colony of Gt. Britain took it up as the true and wise principle of colonial government. The Ministers here pretended to differ from you. But what has their whole conduct been but a gradual though unwilling concession to your principles?"[100] Durham died hours later. It is widely claimed his last words were, "Canada will one day do justice to my memory." The Canadians did not fail him. From 1840 to the present day, who has laid more honour at the feet of this great reformer than the people of Canada?

Durham's *Report on the Affairs of British North America* was to be the ideological building block on which a new British Empire would be built. The civic republican grand compromise would prove to be contagious. From Nova Scotia to New South Wales, the British colonies, like dominoes, would one after the other clamber to achieve this new kind of society. Durham lived just long enough to welcome in the Victorian era, yet his ideas would become crucial in shaping it. It was the Edwardian scholar A.H. Snow who compared Durham's contribution to colonial science to that of Grotius to international science.[101] The comparison does both men justice, since both were able to pioneer and articulate ideas that would outlive their own epochs and can be readily seen in practice even to this day. The ideological battle between conservatism, liberalism, and civic republicanism would continue to shape the political development of the British colonies in North America and Australasia. For placing them on a path to democracy that would avoid the valleys of revolution and civic war, the Earl of Durham deserves no small thanks.

5

Nova Scotia and the New Deal

The planets that encircle the sun, warmed by its heat and rejoicing in its effulgence, are moved and sustained, each in its bright but subordinate career, by the same laws as the sun itself. Why should this beautiful example be lost upon us? Why should we run counter to the whole stream of British experience; and seek, for no object worthy of the sacrifice, to govern on one side of the Atlantic by principles the very reverse of those found to work so admirably on the other. The employment of steamers will soon bring Halifax within a ten days' voyage of England. Nova Scotia will then not be more distant from London, than the north of Scotland and the west of Ireland were a few years ago. No time should be lost, therefore, in giving us the rights and guards to which we are entitled; for depend upon it the nearer we approach the mother country, the more we shall admire its excellent Constitution, and the more intense will be the sorrow and disgust with which we must turn to contemplate our own.

Joseph Howe

By 1841 the Canadas had been united, fulfilling one-half of Lord Durham's dream for British North America. The Family Compact and the other tory cabals, however, were by no means going to concede the second half, responsible government, without a fight. The reformers, especially in Upper Canada, had been morally decimated by the 1837 Rebellions. They had been branded disloyal and were forever being painted by the tories as (separatist) republicans and general traitors. The endorsement of the Queen's High Commissioner was exactly the boost they needed to carry on. The talk of rebellion and revolution needed to be dropped if the reformers were to achieve their goals. The reformers' struggle for the most part of the decade would be to peaceably move to responsible government, something Durham had shown to be a most British and constitutional goal.

A battle of ideas was taking place in British North America, and the very meaning of the constitution was at stake. The reformers were essentially arguing that the British constitution was the enabler of a communal form of democracy that can be understood in civic republican terms. They insisted that the Aristotelian ideal had matured into perfection in British hands and that a mixed constitution was an example to the world; the king was revered, the elite were respected, and, most significantly of all, virtuous citizens of all ranks were called on to participate in the body politic. Adam Shortt and Arthur Doughty theorized in 1913 that the constitutional problem for Canada in the wake of the *Durham Report* was "virtually the same as that which confronted England after 1688."[1] Howe certainly agreed with this assessment, noting that elections were a "mockery" in "England down to the period of the revolution... as it was in Nova Scotia down to 1840."[2] Over a century of constitutional evolution separated the Glorious Revolution and the development of responsible government in Britain. Having set the example, Canada would not wait as long, but the battle of ideas still lasted almost the whole span of the "vibrant and hungry" 1840s before reaching resolution.[3] As the 1830s wound to a close it was clear that a fundamental shift in psychology was taking place. No longer was it the fringe reformers who panted for responsible government, but rather it was the fringe tories who most vocally opposed it. By the close of the decade the battle for the meaning of the constitution would be decided.

As the great boon of responsible government was fought for and won in the Canadian colonies, it needs be considered what type of democracy was being championed and also why it was being championed. The reformers were by no means second-rate patriots when compared to their tory counterparts. It was British heritage, British institutions, and the British constitution that they saw as the bastion of virtue that they wanted their adopted land to share in. The speeches and demands of the reformers do reveal liberalism in that they wanted to manage their own local affairs without interference. Together with that, however, must be seen the great influence of civic republicanism, which guided their interpretation of the *Durham Report*. They wanted to maintain the British connection and all the immense social and cultural capital that accompanied it.

They wanted also to rid themselves of the corruption of oligarchic power centres, which acted, in their summation, contrary to the common good. It was responsible government and Durham's grand compromise that allowed the colonists to have their civic republican cake and eat it too.

Had he lived another year or so, Radical Jack would have noted with pleasure the emergence of Durham Meetings in North America and the incredible way in which the *Report* had split the once solid tory bloc in Upper Canada. Former members and affiliates of the Family Compact came to be convinced of the principle of self-rule. It was "absolutely necessary," argued William Hamilton Merritt, "that a vigilant watch be maintained by persons on the spot – by our own legislators," as the "Imperial Parliament is too much occupied with other affairs."[4] This soft toryism came to look surprisingly similar to the ideas of moderate reformers. Both sides insisted their support for Durham was completely alien to the Mackenzie-Papineau school. Another tory convert, Egerton Ryerson, stated this plainly. For him there was "as much difference between the 'responsible government' advocated by Mackenzie and his associates in 1835–36 and Lord Durham's 'responsible government,' as there is between independent democratic Republic and a subordinate Limited Monarchy."[5] The message was clear: the responsible government these loyal reformers wanted was by no means a separatist republican agenda. Separatist republicanism would only isolate the colonists from the traditions, customs, and institutions they instinctively preferred. Civic republicanism revealed through responsible government would allow them to reconcile their love of liberty with the sacred feelings of warmth and connection within the British family. The call was against domination not connection.

The newly created United Province of Canada would not be the place to test Durham's grand compromise. The implementation of his assimilation program proved arduous and was ultimately abandoned. The fact that the capital city was changed six times in the province's twenty-six-year history is indicative of the precarious political situation. What was needed was a quiet province, somewhere politically stable and venerably loyal. It would be Nova Scotia that would set the example to follow, not only in Canadian colonies, but in colonies all across the empire. Following the devastation of the Seven Years' War and the tragedy of the Acadian Great Expulsion, Nova Scotians had carried on their affairs in a comparatively calm and peaceful manner. The province, although courted, chose not to be the fourteenth colony in the American Revolution. Neither was it prone to the revolutionary talk that had made Mackenzie and Papineau famous men in the Canadas and abroad. This alone, however, was hardly enough to guarantee responsible government. That prize would be won only through determined and statesmanlike petitioning. And it was another tory convert who would prove the most influential of all in achieving this goal: Joseph Howe.

The Howe family had come to America in the mid-seventeenth century and was well established by 1776. Joseph's father, John Howe, was a Boston printer who claimed to have witnessed Samuel Adams board the tea ships on 16 December 1773.[6] Unlike the rest of his family, John Howe was staunchly opposed to the Revolution and dedicated his publications to the Loyalist cause. On 17 March 1776 the British evacuated Boston, and John Howe left with great sadness. He would settle eventually in Nova Scotia and found the *Halifax Journal*. Like most New Englanders, John Howe was no fan of George III or Britain's treatment of her American possessions. Nevertheless he was committed heart and soul to the British connection. It was a huge emotional and financial sacrifice for Howe to trade the sophistication of the Boston Common for the "miserable village" of Halifax.[7] The intensity of his love for the British constitution and his determination to live and die under the good old flag would leave an indelible mark on his son.

Joseph Howe was born on 13 December 1804 at the Northwest Arm on Halifax Harbour. Although John Howe would eventually become postmaster general and the King's Printer in Halifax, he would never be a wealthy man, and, consequently, young Joseph enjoyed little formal education. Nevertheless, he was an edacious reader with a keen mind and a strong Protestant work ethic. In a letter from January 1824, the nineteen-year-old Joseph articulates his love of the written word: "My books are very few, but then the world is before me – a library open to all – from which poverty of purse cannot exclude me – and in which the meanest and most paltry volume is sure to furnish something to amuse, if not to instruct and improve."[8]

Howe took an active interest in his father's trade and by the age of thirteen he began assisting the King's Printer. At the age of twenty-three he acquired his own paper and began publishing the *Arcadian*. Within a year, however, he began publishing the paper that would bring him fame, the *Novascotian*. The influence of the *Novascotian* in its eponymous province with Howe behind the reigns cannot be overstated. As Chester Martin has said, Howe is "perhaps the first in Canadian history to inspire a cult."⁹ As the political voice of Nova Scotia he was *sans pareil*. Yet Daniel Cobb Harvey was right to ponder in a Dalhousie lecture in 1933 to what extent Howe had sprung "Minerva-like from the rocks of the North-West Arm, or how far he was the embodiment of the spirit of his age in Nova Scotia."

Nova Scotia in the 1830s was a province in transition. Harvey has described the period from 1835 to 1848 as the intellectual awakening of Nova Scotia.¹⁰ It was the period where the people of Nova Scotia discovered and embraced, in the words of Archibald MacMechan, their "Nova-Scotia-ness."¹¹ The awakening was undergirded by the same civic republican spirit of which the great Greco-Roman philosophers spoke. A sense of civic pride swept over the province and, importantly, the common people began to actively engage in and discuss the politics of the day. There was in a very real sense a cultural transformation at play, as evidenced by the emergence of libraries and schools, museums and galleries, and, significantly, newspapers and political reporting.

The British victory at Waterloo on 18 June 1815 was heartily celebrated in Halifax, as it was right across the British world. The following year a veteran of the Napoleonic Wars who served under the Marquess of Wellington arrived as the new lieutenant-governor.¹² The governorship of George Ramsay, the ninth Earl of Dalhousie, saw the seeds of the intellectual awakening sown. Although Dalhousie is remembered for his commitment to improved roads and agriculture, his passion for non-sectarian education is particularly noteworthy. Nova Scotia could boast in King's College, founded in 1789, the oldest university in English Canada. Its doors, however, were not open to all. Following the large Scottish migration in the early nineteenth century, some four out of five Nova Scotians were excluded.¹³ Modelled on the University of Oxford, King's required a submission to the Anglican Church's Thirty-Nine Articles at matriculation. In 1816 Pictou, with its dense concentration of Scots, established its famous academy as a liberal non-sectarian college. Governor Dalhousie also fought for an institution to be modelled on the University of Edinburgh. In 1818 the university that bears his name was established, although it would suffer for lack of finances and not offer instruction till 1838.

Pictou Academy was to play a major role in the education and cultural development of Nova Scotia. Established by the eccentric

Presbyterian clergyman, Thomas McCulloch, the academy in many ways embodied the intellectual awakening. Of McCulloch, Harvey wrote, "he it was who stirred his illiterate countrymen into action... [and] left to Pictou country and the Nova Scotian Scots that intellectual tradition of which they are so justly proud."[14] Nevertheless, the academy was constantly frustrated by its inability to secure government funding. Although McCulloch's fiery and uncooperative nature may have been to blame, those within the academy felt they were being persecuted by the largely Anglican Executive Council. Phillip Buckner notes that "seven times between 1825 and 1830 the Council rejected bills initiated by the assembly for the support of the academy."[15] The ire of the academy was turned into critical journalism courtesy of the Howe-dubbed Pictou Scribblers. These pro-reform commentators represented the very eidolon that McCulloch hoped would be the trademark of academy graduates. In a lecture titled *The Nature and Uses of a Liberal Education*, McCulloch emphasized his hope that with the academy a new educational paradigm would reign in Nova Scotia. He concluded: "This institution is partly an experiment of the value of literature: friends and foes are waiting for the result with anxiety; and much depends upon your improvement and conduct. The approbation of your best friends, the honour of this seminary, your reputation, your prospects in life, are at stake. What an honourable field for activity is here presented! Should these motives, arousing exertion, conduct you to excellence, how noble the result!"[16]

Along with education, agriculture and commerce improved markedly. Coming out of a postwar depression in the early 1820s, by the end of the decade business was being carried out with greater levels of sophistication than hitherto seen in the province. At the turn of the century, Nova Scotian commerce was still conducted largely in doubloons, pistareens, old guineas, dollars, and Spanish money.[17] The establishment in 1826 of the old Halifax Banking Company was indicative of the burgeoning economy of Nova Scotia. The bank was not established through legislation but rather as a joint-stock company. The great success of this private enterprise led to the creation in 1832 of the Bank of Nova Scotia. Business was indeed booming. In Harvery's words, "agriculture, fishing, lumbering and shipbuilding forged ahead; and the minds of the young Nova Scotians were quickened both by economic rivalry and by the literature of knowledge that was written about their province and its industries."

Immigration and natural growth saw the population of Nova Scotia steadily rise from 80,000 in 1817 to 120,000 in 1827 and some 200,000 in 1837. Increasingly the English, Scottish, and French inhabitants, combined with the significant number of American migrants, developed a provincial identity and saw themselves as Nova Scotians. A new social awareness and political interest is evidenced in particular by the growth in local media. The emergence and success of the *Arcadian Recorder* in 1813 and the *Free Press* in 1816 signified a growing market of politically aware and active readers. Within twenty years the number of newspapers jumped from three to nine.[18] In 1824 the *Nova Scotian or Colonial Herald* was established by twenty-two-year-old George Renny Young. On 3 January 1828 Joseph Howe, just twenty-four himself, took over the paper.

Having worked previously for the *Arcadian* and before that with his father, it was clear from the outset that Howe viewed the role of editor with extreme gravity. He had very specific and deeply held convictions about the proper role of the press and the ethical implications of owning a newspaper. The press was, to his mind, a vital civic institution and the most powerful tool of civic education available. He opined that an editor "cannot be bought by the wealthy… awed by the powerful… [or] alarmed by the sudden ebullitions of popular feeling."[19] The prospectus for the new *Novascotian* revealed an unabashed love for the British connection and constitution, doubtless an inheritance from his father, but also the seeds of a reformist nature that would ultimately germinate and amaze the whole British Empire:

> The motto on our title page in part explains our political creed, which may be resolved into this, the Constitution, the *whole* Constitution, and *nothing but* the Constitution. We are no cold approvers, but ardent admirers of the system under which we live. We are not blind to its blemishes, but feeling alive to its excellence; like a candid critic, who in contemplating the numberless beauties of a work, looks mildly onto its imperfections. Whatever goes to extend or to secure the advantages which of right ought to flow to the People, from the wholesome operation of the system, we shall steadily and fearlessly uphold. But the Press, like a two edged sword, waving round the Constitutional Tree, should defend it alike from the misguided zeal of the People, the dangerous

encroachment of Rulers; and he who would timidly shrink from the performance of this double duty is unfit to put his hand to the hilt. We will therefore as steadily defend the Government when its acts are just, as we will boldly warn the People when they are unjust.

With Howe at the helm the *Novascotian* became the most important newspaper in the province. Howe would personally report between 150 and 200 columns of Assembly debate each session, and in the words of his biographer J. Murray Beck, "the *Novascotian* became an instrument both for his own self-education and for the education of his readers."[20] While the other provincial newspapers would give brief summaries of the Assembly's debates, Howe prioritized them, dedicating vast quantities of space to their publication. The philosophical impetus driving Howe's editorship can certainly be understood as civic republican. The *Novascotian* did not simply advocate reform or democratic rights as a political principle. It made a considerable effort to raise the level of political knowledge in the province and forge a community of virtuous and politically aware citizens. The goal went far beyond the realms of liberalism. Howe hoped through his paper to endorse a form of positive liberty where active and educated debate was considered normative for the ideal British citizen in Nova Scotia. In 1834 alone, Howe dedicated some 172 columns to parliamentary debate.[21] It was not without justification that Howe claimed that without his reports, "the country would have been left in almost total ignorance... and have been about as incapable of judging of the conduct of their Representatives, as if they had assembled in the moon."[22]

Howe began his editorship of the *Novascotian* as a natural ally of the tory official party. His observations of parliament, however, though doing nothing to diminish his view of the British constitution, led him to question its application in British North America. Influential also was the intellectual outpouring from the Pictou Scots. While the conservative Scots subscribed to the *Observer*, the academy students voiced their reformist mantra through the *Colonial Patriot*. Edited by Jotham Blanchard, the *Patriot* was the first liberal-radical paper in Nova Scotia. Blanchard was no champion of separatist republicanism and the motto of his paper was, *Pro rege, pro patria*. It was reform, democracy, and, it will be argued in this chapter, a civic republican bent that captured the imagination of many.

Although initially hostile, Howe was slowly won over by the reformist arguments to the point where, entering the *Patriot* office during the election campaign of 1830, he is reported to have joked that "the Pictou scribblers (as he used to call the writers in the *Patriot*) have converted me from the error of my ways."[23]

Howe's disillusionment with the Council was evident as early as 1830, when he spoke with disdain of their behaviour during the Brandy Dispute.[24] By 1835 he was disillusioned with the Assembly, local administrators, and the general conduct of government also. Under the alias The People, on 1 January he published a letter penned by his friend George Thompson. The People indignantly declared that the "poor and distressed" of Nova Scotia were being systematically robbed by their magistrates. For the past three decades, The People snarled, "the Magistracy and Police have, by one stratagem or other, taken from the pockets of the people, in over exactions, fines, etc. etc., a sum that would exceed in the gross amount of £30,000."[25] Whether consciously or not, in publishing this letter Howe crossed an ideological Rubicon and committed himself, in Beck's words, to the transition from "mild Tory to reforming assemblyman."[26] On 4 February, the attorney-general informed Howe that he was being sued for criminal libel.[27]

Howe entered the Supreme Court on 4 March and found that, along with members of the Halifax establishment, the gallery was filled with supporters and well-wishers.[28] James F. Gray made a simple case for the Crown. The *Novascotian*, under Howe's editorship, had made "false, infamous, defamatory, and malicious" statements designed to "injure, degrade, and bring into disgrace, the magistrates of the town of Halifax."[29] Howe defended himself and insisted that his motive was not to disturb the peace but to serve the province through frank and fearless reporting.[30] It was his "public duty" to report "an even line of which no consideration could sway [him] to the right or to the left."[31]

Howe's defense was a showcase of Demosthenic talent and emotional manipulation. In the words of W.S. Macnutt, "Nova Scotia had found not only its John Wilkes but also its Charles James Fox."[32] He finished by proclaiming in no uncertain terms that an English jury would acquit him, for "the victim may be bound, and prepared for sacrifice, but an English jury will cast around him the impenetrable shield of the British law." Howe also pressed strongly that the future of a free press in Nova Scotia rested on their decision. Tears were visible on the jurors' cheeks as he made his closing remarks: "Will you, my countrymen, the descendents of these men; warmed by their blood; inheriting their language; and having the principles for which they struggled confided to your care, allow them to be violated in your hands? Will you permit the sacred fire of liberty, brought by your fathers from the venerable temples of Britain, to be quenched and trodden out on the simple alters they have raised?... Your verdict will be the most important in its consequences, ever delivered before this tribunal; and I conjure you to judge me by the principles of English law, and to leave an unshackled press as a legacy to your children. You remember the press in your hours of conviviality and mirth - oh! do not desert it in this its day of trial."[33]

The jury took less than ten minutes to return a verdict of not guilty. The breathless silence, "was broken by shouts of applause from the immense crowds in and around the courthouse." The news sparked immediate celebrations in the city: "On leaving the Province building [Howe] was borne by the populace to his home amidst deafening acclamations. The people kept holiday that day and the next. Musical parties paraded the streets at night. All the sleds in town were turned out in procession, with banners; and all ranks and classes seemed to join in felicitations on the triumph of the press.[34]

Howe celebrated by joyfully and incorrectly declaring in the next issue of the *Novascotian* that "the press of Nova-Scotia is Free."[35] Armed with legal protection, the democratic flame would only grow. The argument to be advanced here, is that civic republicanism matched liberalism as an influence on this nascent democracy. Howe was determined to shape Nova Scotia into a community, both politically aware and active in promoting the common good. Positive liberty and the championing of civic institutions, public education, and community-minded thinking were central elements to Howe's dream. These ideals were completely in keeping with the education revolution, the intellectual awakening, and the emergence in popular consciousness of Novascotianess. Reporting and discussion of the province's political affairs would become more intense as the people pursued a greater sense of participation and involvement for the third estate.

Although elated, Howe could see clearly that the rights of free British subjects, as reformers across the continent had come to understand them, could not be secured through journalism alone.

The time had come for him to no longer report the news but rather to make it. On 9 November 1836, Joseph Howe accepted a nomination to the Legislative Assembly for the county of Halifax. He stated his reasons for running plainly in the *Novascotian*: "The Press has done much in informing and arousing the people; but the conviction has slowly, yet steadily deepened over my mind, that all its efforts must be useless until a majority is formed in the Assembly, who will follow out a system of rational reform. If suitable materials for forming and combining that majority were more abundant, I should not have ventured out of the ordinary paths of my profession."[36] In a Musquodoboit speech on polling day, 5 November, Howe made it clear that he intended to champion the cause of responsible government. He declared to the electors, "Gentlemen, all we ask is for what exists at home – a system of responsibility to the people."[37]

The events of 1837, climaxing with the twin rebellions, were, naturally, watched with great interest in the Atlantic provinces. Although clearly a reformer, Howe and his colleagues were not as radical as their Upper or Lower Canadian counterparts. Howe drew up Twelve Resolutions to address the grievances of Nova Scotia. Unlike Robert Baldwin, who was petitioning for a responsible executive, the lynchpin of Howe's reforms was a responsible Upper House. This was outlined in the final resolution: "*Resolved*, That, as a remedy for these grievances, His Majesty be implored to take such steps, either by granting an elective Legislative Council, or by such other reconstruction of the local government, as will ensure responsibility to the Commons, and confer upon the people of this Province, what they value above all other possessions, the blessings of the British Constitution."[38] The wild events in Upper and Lower Canada and the short-lived governorship of Lord Durham did nothing but strengthen Howe's belief in responsible government.

Although committed to peaceful reform within the British sphere, Howe's language had a radical tone on occasion. In keeping with the spirit of the age, Howe spoke of a patriotic duality of British subjects and Nova Scotian (eventually Canadian) nationals: "I feel, I trust, as a British subject should feel, proud of the History and Literature and Science of the Mother Country, of belonging to that Empire, which presents to the world, in all its phases, an example of greatness and glory. But, Sir, here in the country of my birth – this little spot, between Cape North and Cape Sable, is dear to me, as a

Nova Scotian, above every other place – and while priding myself in the glories of the Empire, I respect, as a native should do, the soil on which I tread." The language here is a classic manifestation of the awakening and a reminder of the civic pride and sense of place that is central to the spirit of civic republicanism. As a Nova Scotian, Howe was duty bound to fight above all for the *commune bonum* of Nova Scotia. The public good and the effective management of the province required most powers to be in local hands and in hands that held popular confidence. If Nova Scotia was to remain part of the empire, it must be granted, "the fullest extent of British constitutional freedom."[39]

One of Howe's key allies in the House was another Loyalist's son, Herbert Huntington of Yarmouth. Contemporary reverend and amateur historian John Roy Campbell described the one-time militia leader as "a man of uncommon pretention, and robust intellect, brusque in manner, but acknowledged by all, to have been foremost in the rank of the most fearless and incorruptible of Nova Scotian politicians."[40] At much the same time as Howe was being converted by the Pictou Scribblers, Huntington was witnessing first-hand the abuse of power and blatant tory partisanship of country officials. In 1830 he was elected to the House and set naturally in the company of reformers. The electrifying impact of the *Durham Report* in both Britain and the North American colonies has been discussed in the previous chapter. Huntington, committed heart and soul to the principle of responsible government, was naturally elated by the endorsement of such a high-ranking minister. In Huntington's summation, Durham was "the best friend these colonies ever had."[41] Following the publication of the *Report*, Huntington and William Young went to London to argue for its immediate implementation in British North America. But while the reformer's lobbyists made handy contacts in Charles Buller and Henry Labouchere, Lord Russell was less easily swayed.

Although Russell had agreed with Durham's recommendations for uniting the Canadas and showed great empathy to the rationale behind responsible government, he remained convinced that its implementation would be a contradiction in terms for a British colony. The new governor-in-chief for British North America, Poulett Thomson, 1st Baron Sydenham, received two famous dispatches from Russell outlining his position. The first dispatch was dated 14 October 1839 and was a rejection of responsible government. Of the governor, Russell wrote, "if he is to obey his instructions from England, the parallel of constitutional responsibility entirely fails; if, on the other hand, he is to follow the advice of his council, he is no longer a subordinate officer, but an independent sovereign."

The second dispatch, dated 16 October 1839, was to sound the death knell for the tory cabals across the provinces. Russell advised Sydenham that he was authorized to remove executive councillors who had previously held their seats for life. The implications of this dispatch were two-fold. First, governors were free to break up local oligarchies and remove councillors who might otherwise reject their policies. The second implication was both more subtle and profound. By allowing the removal of councillors "as often as any sufficient motives of public policy may suggest the expediency of that measure," Russell was directing at least one of the governor's ears towards the *vox populi*.[42] It will be outlined later how Sydenham and some of the provincial governors would use this power to attempt reconciliation between the reformers and the tories.

London's *Colonial Gazette* was quick to highlight the mixed message being presented by Russell. On the one hand he maintained his theoretical objection to responsible government, yet on the other he was taking a great step towards seeing its practical accomplishment. The *Gazette* noted in January 1840:

> On the publication of Lord Durham's Report, Lord John seized the first opportunity of declaring that he did not agree with Lord Durham in his views of Responsible Government. Subsequent consideration appears to have induced him to take the trouble of *understanding* Lord Durham's views, and to refrain from dwelling on theoretical differences of opinion rather than the practical agreement in policy. He now ends the matter by issuing one despatch which takes the only *practical* step which Lord Durham ever proposed, or could have taken were he in Lord John's place, – namely the substitution of tenure at pleasure instead of the present permanent tenure of office; and another despatch, in which he declares that he "sees little of no objection to the practical views of Colonial government recommended by Lord Durham, as he understands them." With one who comes to so right a conclusion we will not quarrel for a few sophistries, by which he tries to make out the consistency of saying "No" and acting "Yes."[43]

In Nova Scotia, Howe was intrigued by Russell's conduct.

Although he was doubtless upset by the 14 October dispatch, there is scant evidence to believe that Howe viewed Russell as a political enemy. Rather, he saw in him a fellow moderate reformer whose caution concerning responsible government needed to be overcome by sound reason. In any case, Howe told Russell he was satisfied that "once convinced that the great principles of the British Constitution can be more widely extended, without peril to the integrity of the empire – you will not hesitate to lend the influence of your great name and distinguished talents to the good old cause."[44] Howe seems to have appreciated that the new Colonial Secretary was simply an adherent to the Biblical logic that no man (or in this case governor) can serve two masters. Imperial logic suggested that power must run downwards from the seat of empire and that the governor must be held responsible to the Crown above not the Assembly below. Howe skilfully articulated in his famous *Letters* to Russell the colonial response to this long-standing axiom. Chester Martin praises the *Letters* as the one of the great political treatises in the English language. He notes: "By common consent Howe's four open *Letters* to Lord John Russell have been accepted as the colonial counterpart of Durham's *Report* and Charles Buller's *Responsible Government for Colonies*. To be grouped with these is to be enshrined in the political literature of the English language. Over both of these, however, the *Letters* had one great advantage. Howe's method was empirical, and he wrote with authority from the colonial point of view... the *Letters* were addressed to a British Minister, but the wealth of the imagery, the flexibility of the argument, and the vigour of the language all betrayed an appeal as wide as the political instincts of the race."

Howe's *Letters* methodically countered the Russellite arguments. He began by addressing the perceived elephant in the room, the French Canadians. The lead-up to and the aftermath of the 1837 Rebellions had left the colonial office geared towards restricting freedoms in French-speaking Canada rather than granting them in the other provinces. If the governor was made responsible to the assembly in one province, would not that same freedom have to be granted in all? Russell clearly dreaded the result of such an arrangement in a "ministry, led by M. Papineau."[45] Howe's simple yet powerful retort was to assert the inherent injustice of applying what, to his mind, was a collective punishment to British North America.

Why should "large bodies of British subjects" be denied the full blessings of the British constitution simply because they inhabit the same continent as the Lower Canadians? Surely, Howe exclaims, there is no reason why the people of Upper Canada, Nova Scotia, New Brunswick, Prince Edward Island, and Newfoundland should be denied responsible government. Emphatically, he concludes, "If the Frenchmen in one Province do not understand, or cannot be entrusted with this valuable privilege, why should we, who are all Britons, or of British descent, be deprived of what we do understand, and feel that we can never be prosperous and happy without?"

Although Howe had clearly been, at the very least, partially converted from the toryism of his youth, he remained attached as ever to constitution, the whole constitution, and nothing but the constitution. Howe emphasized that the demand for responsible government was both "extremely simple and eminently British." "It seems strange," he muses, "that those who live within the British empire should be governed by principles other than those of the British Constitution, yet it is true."[46] In these musings, Howe reveals his deep convictions about the meaning of Britishness and the universal British family. He clearly identified certain standards of living and of government as suitable for a British community and roundly condemned anything less. W.S. Macnutt has noted that "Howe could envisage his own forum in Nova Scotia as no less respectable than that of the Parliament of Great Britain."[47] In the same way, he viewed himself and his fellow colonists as no less British than the citizens on Leeds or Edinburgh. He was convinced that, if rightly informed, the parliament and people of Britain would never force British colonists to "live under a system so absurd, so anti-British, so destructive of every manly and honourable principle of action in political affairs."

The *Letters* emphasize that the *vera causa* of the colonists of Nova Scotia and the other provinces is simply to secure the same rights and freedoms enjoyed by their brethren at home. Could it be, pondered Howe, that Melbourne's whigs were so accustomed to the rights of British subjects that they no longer appreciated their value? Had they become like "the cabman who drives past St Paul's a dozen times a day [but] seldom gazes at its ample outline or excellent proportions?" Of the 658 seats in the House of Commons, the whigs may enjoy a majority of just ten and yet those in Britain are "simple enough to believe" they possess the confidence of the country. How would Russell react if, despite having a majority of seats, his party was excluded from power and all cabinet positions were given to his opponents? Howe laments, "this would be absurd at home; and yet it is the height of wisdom in the Colonies." The provincial governors routinely ignore the wishes of reform parties, though they control two-thirds of the popular assembly. This for Howe was the greatest of the "absurd anomalies and wretchedness of our system."

There is also a sense of indignation in the *Letters,* since the Russellite argument infers that the colonists of British North America are so nonchalant in their opinion of Great Britain that, were it not for the influence of some dozen executive councillors, the provinces would be immediately swept up in a tide of separatist republicanism. What a suggestion to be made to the sons and daughters of loyalists, who had given up land and money to remain in the King's dominion. Howe considers this attitude "a libel against upon the Colonist, and upon the Constitution he claims as his inheritance." He insists that the colonists are as devoted and loyal as any subjects in the British Empire:

> I have ever held, My Lord, and still hold to the belief, that the population of British North America, are sincerely attached to the parent State; that they are proud of their origin, deeply interested in the integrity of the empire, and not anxious for the establishment of any other form of government here than that which you enjoy at home; which, while it has stood the test of ages, and purified itself by successive peaceful revolutions, has so developed the intellectual, moral and natural resources of two small Islands, as to enable a people, once comparatively far behind their neighbors in influence and improvement, to combine and wield the energies of a dominion more vast in extent, and complicated in all its relations, than any other in ancient or modem times.
>
> Why should we desire a severance of old ties, that are more honorable than any new ones we can form? Why should we covet institutions more perfect than those which have worked so well, and produced such admirable results?... Why should it be taken for granted, either by our friends in England, or our enemies elsewhere, that we are panting for new experiments;

or are disposed to repudiate and cast aside the principles of that excellent Constitution, cemented by the blood and the long experience of our fathers, and upon which the vigorous energies of our brethren, driven to apply new principles to a field of boundless resources, have failed to improve?

Howe's *Letters* defend the Durham solution to the hilt. If the central thesis of the *Report* was acted on and the governor became responsible to the Assembly, "Where is the danger? Of what consequence is it to the people of England... Would the stocks fall? Would England be weaker, less prosperous or less respected, because the people of Nova Scotia were satisfied and happy?" The genius of the *Letters* is that they paint the colonists as no different from any other British subjects. It is their loyalty rather than their disloyalty that demands responsible government. It would be unthinkable for Westminster to try to dictate local policy in Glasgow or Aberdeen. Why then try to do so in Nova Scotia? After all, "what else is a Province, like Nova Scotia, than a small community, too feeble to interfere with the general commercial and military arrangements of the government; but deeply interested in a number of minor matters, which only the people to be affected by them can wisely manage?" Howe finishes his first letter by reminding Russell that the advent of the steamer put Halifax only ten days travel from London.[48] If New Scotland is virtually as close to the heart of empire as Old Scotland, why should British subjects enjoy freedom in one place but not the other?

As will be discussed in the next chapter, Nova Scotia was hardly the only province whose appetite had been whetted by Durham for responsible government. Nonetheless, by the dawn of the 1840s nowhere else had made the issue such a central concern. Significantly, in February 1840 the influential tory John Boyle Uniacke joined the Reform Party. In July, Howe, Uniacke, and two other reformers were invited to join members of an Official Party, leader James William Johnston, and four other tories in a makeshift coalition in the Executive Council. The plan was the brainchild of Governor Sydenham. An admirer and acquaintance of Lord Durham, perhaps Sydenham saw the unity governments, which he also created in other Atlantic provinces, as the precursor to responsible government. In any case, his hand in removing the more sectarian lieutenant-governor Sir Colin Campbell to be replaced by

Lord Falkland suggests Sydenham was genuinely interested in producing a more harmonious relationship between the executive and the people's representatives.

The reformers, though not nearly content, were generally satisfied for the moment. Things were at least heading in a positive direction. The *Colonial Gazette* noted, however, that Sydenham's reasonably successful attempts to undermine political factionalism resulted in an increase of his personal power. It commented in October 1841: "It was Lord Sydenham's policy to break up all existing parties, to deal rather with individuals than with parties, and so to get the whole conduct of the executive government into his own hands. He was his own Executive Council and his own Chief Secretary – a sort of Louis Philippe for Canada, whose constant aim, in which he was entirely successful, was to *individualize* the Government, and let no importance, no responsibility exist save his own."[49] Following Sydenham's death on 19 September 1841, there was some speculation and uncertainty about his replacement, Sir Charles Bagot. Despite this, Howe relished his new-found importance as both a member of the Executive Council and speaker of the House. The coalition lasted for three years until disputes between Howe and Johnston led Falkland to dissolve the House on 26 October 1843.

When the Assembly met again on 8 February 1844 it became clear that party politics had returned to Nova Scotia (as though they had ever truly disappeared). Howe and the reformers, or the "Great Liberal Party," as they were dubbed by the *Times*, refused to rejoin the Executive Council, thus denying the illusion of a unity government.[50] The reformers had been outraged by the partisan behaviour of Falkland, who had appointed Mather Byles Almon, a tory and brother-in-law of Johnston, to both the Executive and the Legislative Councils. The early votes in the House were largely along party lines, and with the defection of the member for Argyle, John Ryder, to the tory ranks, it was the Official Party that narrowly had the numbers.[51] Nonetheless, loose fish in the tory ranks allowed Howe and Huntington to dictate play from the opposition.

Although the reformers were sometimes known as liberals it is important to be clear on how that term was used. In the nineteenth-century British world, "liberal" was often used as a euphemism for "democrat." Especially in the heady atmosphere before the granting of responsible government, the terminology of the reformers was a delicate matter. The words "republicanism" and "democracy" had highly negative connotations and were directly linked to both the American and the French Revolutions. Sir Francis Bond Head had summarized the tory position well when he claimed to have been sent to Canada to do battle with democracy. Democracy was seen as the antonym of constitutionalism, while republicanism was seen as traitorous separatism. "Liberal" was thus adopted as a respectable alternative term for a loyal reformer. As a political philosophy, liberalism was of some significance among Canadian reformers. With the benefit of historical hindsight, it is argued here that the agenda of the reformers and particularly their emphasis on positive liberty, community, and the common good is more in line with classic civic republican ideas.

By 1846 events seemed to swing decidedly in favour of the reformers. In Westminster, Melbourne's whigs had been out of power since the general election of 1841. By 1846, however, the intense debate over the Corn Laws split Prime Minister Robert Peel's tories. On 25 June the peelites and the whigs combined to repeal the Corn Laws; however, the very next day the whigs backed the protectionists to defeat Peel's Irish Coercion Bill. Unable to control the Commons, the Queen called on Lord Russell to form a government. The return of the whigs to power in England roughly coincided with the appointment of a new governor-general favouring responsible government for British North America, Lord Elgin. That same year saw the arrival of a new lieutenant-governor for Nova Scotia. Falkland was replaced by Sir John Harvey, who had previously served Prince Edward Island, New Brunswick, and Newfoundland. Harvey's track record had shown an adherence to the Sydenham philosophy of non-partisanship government, and he would attempt to continue this pattern in Nova Scotia by reconciling the reformers and the executive.

The Russell ministry included a new pro-reform colonial secretary, Viscount Howick, 3rd Earl Grey. Grey's despatch to Harvey on 3 November 1846 was to be the decisive move that, in the words of Ronald Stewart Longley, would cut the "Gordian knot" on the issue of responsible government.[52] Grey advised Harvey that Britain had "no interest whatsoever in exercising any greater influence in the internal affairs of the colonies, than is indispensable either for the purpose of preventing any one colony from adopting measures injurious to another, or to the Empire at large."[53] Grey confirmed the decision on 31 March of the following year, when he instructed Harvey that he should do all in his power to make sure that "the tenure of offices in the public service [were] dependent on the result of party contests."[54]

Harvey still attempted to form a tory-reformer coalition government in Nova Scotia, but with Russell as prime minister and Grey as colonial secretary the reformers had little interest. With no less a disciple of Lambton than Charles Buller in frequent communication with Howe, the tides of change appeared irreversible. In Martin's words, "while Harvey and his councillors were exploiting for the last time the barren subtleties of a coalition, the Reformers, with Charles Buller as liaison office, were perfecting their historic alliance with the British Durhamites, now in the Colonial Office."[55] Howe declined the new governor's cordial offer and requested he dissolve the House. He also wrote to Buller requesting that he pressure Grey to order Harvey to comply, as the result would be "no more troubles in Nova Scotia for the next four years."[56] Perhaps seeing the bigger picture, Grey refused Howe's request. Buller reasoned with Howe that a governor should dissolve parliament only under extraordinary circumstances; otherwise he would, in effect, be acting outside the principles of responsible government.[57]

By late November it was general knowledge that an early dissolution would not be sanctioned. The elated tories continued to press for a unity government. The *Novascotian* mocked their desperation, commenting that "the Harts never panted for the water brooks more ardently than do the Tories, just now, for another coalition."[58] Howe was steadfast that there could be no coalition between men whose views on the constitution were so utterly polar. On 17 December he released a joint statement with Laurence O'Connor Doyle, James McNab, and George Young:

> Because, though we shall be at all times ready to act with gentlemen with whom we can agree on common measures and in whose patriotism and discretion we confide, with the members of the existing Council we can enter into no political alliance, until the people of Nova Scotia decide between them and us, upon various matters drawn into controversy during the last three years. Though they now desire to make it appear that there are "no questions of public moment" dividing parties in Nova Scotia, they well know that:

While the Liberals have sought to introduce into the Province the system of government suggested by Lord Durham and sanctioned by Lord Sydenham and his successors, the Conservatives have as steadily opposed it, practically denying to the people the power which should result from the possession of representative institutions.[59]

So the path chosen was to wait till the election next year. Giving up on the coalition, Harvey merely requested that Howe not block any tory bills directed towards the public good. Given that the sword of Damocles was hanging by a single hair over the tory cabal and the old system in general, it was a request Howe happily agreed to.

The election campaign was fiercely contested by both sides. The rhetoric of the reformers highlights the magnitude of the change taking place in Nova Scotia. The move to responsible government was not an accident of history, nor was it a mere alteration of a political system. A democratic revolution was taking place that would set a new model for the running of empire. It would be the people, politically active and educated, who would ultimately determine what was best for the community and the province, an ideal civic republican democracy. Howe did not blush from comparing the Nova Scotian awakening and its political and social repercussions to Great Britain's Glorious Revolution of 1688: "The distinction is marked – the change presents the evidence of a revolution, as great as ever appeared in the history of any country: a revolution, won for you, without a blow or a drop of blood, by peaceful and constitutional means, and which conferred upon you privileges, analogous to those which our brethren in Britain have exercised, with so much advantage for the past 160 years."[60]

The election took place on 5 August 1847. The reformers carried the day in twelve of the seventeen counties, resulting in a majority of seven in the fifty-one seat house.[61] Much to the chagrin of Howe, Johnston refused to accept defeat and remained in office for five more months, perhaps hoping still for a coalition. When the new House met on 22 January 1848, Johnston objected in vain to the election of the reformer George Young as speaker. Two days later the former tory Uniacke made the historic amendment that would see the people's representatives dismiss an administration for the first time outside of Britain. Uniacke moved that "we consider it our humble duty respectfully to state that the present Executive Council does not possess that confidence so essential to the promoting of the public welfare." The debate continued till 25 January, when the no confidence vote was passed twenty-eight to twenty-one. Johnston and the Executive Council resigned immediately. Howe delivered a rather ungracious speech choosing to vent his annoyance at Johnston rather than mark the historic occasion. He sneeringly remarked: "I had hoped that the gentlemen opposite would have folded their robes around them and submitted with dignity. The last fight of faction was as unnecessary as it was unavailing. Had the members of the administration submitted gracefully, we might at least have said of them that 'Nothing in office became them like the leaving of it.'"

On 2 February 1848 the first responsible ministry in a British colony was formed. Uniacke was to be leader of the government and attorney-general, with Howe as provincial secretary. The new ministry also included Huntington, Doyle, McNab, Young, Michael Tobin, Hugh Bell, and William F. Desbarres. In the words of Joseph Chisolm: "Responsible government was now secured to British America. Principles and rules of administration, defined and illustrated by the conflicts of the past four years, were clearly apprehended and could be misstated and mystified no longer. The right of any party commanding a parliamentary majority to form a Cabinet and administer public affairs; the right of ministers to be consulted, to resign when they were not, and to go into opposition without injury to the prerogative in fact, nearly all the points upon which there had been so much controversy, were now settled and disposed of."[62] The tide of change was now irreversible. Once established in Nova Scotia, responsible government would soon be demanded in all colonies in British North America. Within a decade, British colonies in the furthest reach of the empire would request the same.

The first issue of the *Novascotian* following the historic day was surprisingly non-triumphant about the first responsible ministry in the British Empire. It included much lengthier articles on random points of interest, such as the evolution of the English language and the great advances in astronomy. Although the trademark reporting on the goings-on at the Legislative Assembly was present, it was followed by little analysis. A short article titled "The New Cabinet" merely noted the appointment of Uniacke, Howe, and their comrades. Apart from the suggestion that the tories continued to frustrate and delay the appointment to the end (the paper opined that, left to themselves, the reformers could have settled matters in an hour) little more was said.[63] Perhaps there is something to be read into the fact that the same issue included a lengthy article about the Christ-like wisdom of Oliver Cromwell.[64] It is likely that the muted response was a reflection of the political apprehension of the time and reveals a fear that the tories might somehow overturn the great principle yet. If William Annand had known with certainty that the principle of responsible government was secure, perhaps the pages of the *Novascotian* would have been more jubilant. Similarly, the British press noted the new appointments without commenting on the extraordinary circumstances that produced them.[65]

Joseph Howe's life in many ways personifies the collective struggle for responsible government. During his libel trial he made his famous statement that encapsulated every ideal of the ancient civic republican thinkers: "My public life is before you; and I know you will believe me when I say, that when I sit down in solitude to the labours of my profession, the only questions I ask myself are, What is right? What is just? What is for the public good?"[66] It is fitting that the central theme of the annual Joseph Howe lecture at the University of King's College is the public good.[67] Like his father, Howe believed passionately that the common weal was more sacred than any individual rights. His pursuit of what is right, good, and in the public interest led him to abandon the toryism of his youth. He was no closed-minded ideological apparatchik. The fact that the Pictou Scribblers were able to convert him is testament to an open mind. Though loyal to the British connection and constitution, Howe, like so many of his countrymen, came to believe that there were serious faults in the provincial government that required serious reform rather than superficial amendments. S.F. Wise has rightly said, "Howe's whole public life was testimony to his ardent admiration of Great Britain; his political model was the reformed constitution."[68] Again, Howe exemplified his province by allowing curiosity concerning Durham's *Report* to evolve into committed adherence. Finally he would entertain the Sydenham model of unity government before refusing to accept anything less than responsible government.

Howe's contribution to the triumph of 1848 was extraordinary. Through his newspaper and speeches he educated the public and convinced them that his cause was indeed their cause. It was he who transformed the Assembly's reformers from a loose coalition to a disciplined

Reform Party that would succeed so magnificently at the 1847 election. Howe hoped that the civic republican democracy won in Nova Scotia would provide a blueprint for other colonies. At a banquet in Halifax on 23 November 1840, he said this: "This little Province has more influence and power than could be imagined, looking at her geographical extent alone. She has influence in New Brunswick, in Prince Edward Island, in Lower and Upper Canada; and my pride and hope is that we shall make Nova Scotia, by her loyalty, intelligence and spirit, as it were, a normal school for British North America, to show how far British liberty may be assumed in a colony and at what point it should stop, and the people be content."[69] No one did more than Howe to ensure responsible government was granted in Nova Scotia, but it must be remembered that he was still just a figurehead of a larger movement. He was the voice of a civic republican democratic trend that would soon engulf the Canadian provinces.

Howe was acutely aware that he was simply championing a movement that had appeared quite independently. He wrote to his half-sister on 22 September 1844 that "the rising of a people is like the rising of the Nile." The intellectual awakening in Nova Scotia revealed a people both interested and active in the politics of empire. The Nova Scotians of Howe's generation came to view the British constitution as the protector of civic republican democracy, and they were not satisfied that they were receiving the rights and liberties that they were entitled to. The battle in all the Canadian colonies was essentially the same, a battle to give the third estate political teeth in the Aristotelian mixed constitution and a battle to create virtuous British communities abroad, patriotic about both the land of their birth and the land of their heritage. By the mid-1840s the awakening was in full flight, and Howe was convinced that if the legislature would adhere to the people's wishes, the "true" intention of the constitution would be realized for the first time in the history of British occupation on the North American continent. He concluded the letter to his half-sister with this statement: "The first appeal to the People will set all to rights, and in the meantime we are sustained by the assurance of their cordial and enthusiastic sympathy. The waters have risen and there will be corn in Egypt yet."[70]

There can be little doubt that the reformers felt they were fighting, in the purest sense of the terms, to replace the corruption of the tory compacts with the virtue of responsible government. By 1847 the awakening had peaked, and the civic republican interpretation of the constitution had been accepted in London, cheerfully by some, begrudgingly by others. Lord Elgin commented that the governor-general must now exert a "moral influence" in consequence of his loss of power. The new democratic and civic republican paradigm would allow the colonists to engage in politics and to truly take ownership of the land they possessed. At the same time the "quasi-monarchical relation," as Elgin termed it, would allow Britishers around the world to continue their connection to the mother country they loved so dearly.[71]

The precedent having been set, it would not be long till colonies from New Brunswick to New Zealand would follow the Nova Scotian example. The next chapter will explore how the domino effect saw a new British Empire established with remarkable speed. A new deal had been established between Britain and her colonies in which democracy would be normative. Howe took pride above all in the fact that the changes had been made in a peaceable and eminently British fashion. When Falkland broke up the tory cabal in the Executive Council, Howe boasted, "by the peaceful agitation of four years, in which, from one end of the country to the other, there has not been a blow stuck or a pane of glass broken, great changes have been wrought."[72] With the granting and implementation of responsible government an even greater and more lasting change was wrought, and again, no blows were struck and no glass was broken. The zeitgeist of the intellectual awakening was soon to spread democratic civic republicanism to the four corners of the empire on which the sun did not set.

6

The Domino Effect

The Crown is certainly a strong tie, but the constitution is a stronger tie. If we assimilate our constitution to that of England, the tie will last for all time.
    Legislative Council and Legislative Assembly of Victoria, Debates 1868

The first half of the nineteenth century can certainly be conceptualized as a contest of ideas that cut to the very heart of citizenship in the British Empire. The essence of Britishness was a social contract enshrined in the venerated constitution. To be a true Britisher required a person to live a life of civic virtue, to stand in the shade of the good old flag and to value the common good over individual gain. The contract, however, included obligations on the part of the government. The governors, politicians, and administrators were required similarly to act always for the common good. For the Canadian reformers, Machiavelli's advice that it must be "taken for granted that all men are wicked," rang true when applied to the tory oligarchies.[1] Responsible government had been won in Nova Scotia, and it would immediately face and pass its sternest test in the United Province of Canada. From there the domino effect would see Durham's grand compromise spread to the furthest reaches of the British world.

    The fight for responsible government in itself reveals only a shift away from Hobbesian authoritarianism and towards democratic freedom. But what did it mean to these British communities to be free? If it was liberal freedom, with communities seeking to live a life free from interference, then they needed only to emigrate individually or cede en masse to their great southern neighbour. Yet this was by no means the case. Quite the contrary, the Canadian colonies were populated with loyalist immigrants from the United States, and they took up arms in 1812 to protect their British identity. For the Canadian reformers, enjoying freedom was most often articulated as being free from domination. They wanted to maintain the British connection and their British institutions and to create a virtuous British society. At the same time, they wanted to be free to govern themselves and to let local people attend to local issues. The Canadians were dual patriots, lovers of both the land of their birth and the land of their imagination. Durham's civic republican grand compromise allowed them to embrace both.

On 10 September 1852, Earl Grey penned a letter to Lord John Russell outlining a history of his administration's colonial policy. Grey described the events of the previous six years as the dawning of a new epoch in British North America. Grey was particularly proud that "their system of government, which was previously in a state of great doubt and uncertainty, may be said to have been established on what there is good reason to hope may be a permanent footing, and the difficult and embarrassing questions which had arisen, as to the rules to be observed in conducting their affairs, have received a solution in which all parties have practically acquiesced... we may congratulate ourselves."[2] Grey acknowledged the Canadian colonies as the most important of Britain's dependencies and was particularly gratified that the whigs had implemented a new system that would do as much as possible to assure their continuing loyalty and connection.

The push for responsible government was happening simultaneously across British North America. While Nova Scotia is acknowledged as the first colony to exercise responsible government, a spirit of democracy shaped by civic republicanism was evident in many places. This spirit gave birth to a colonial feeling of dual nationalism or dual patriotism. Although there was great loyalty to and love for the richness of British institutions, history, and achievements, this was coupled with a sense of civic pride and civic duty in the place they lived. This chapter will outline the growth of civic republicanism in the United Province of Canada as the demand for responsible government came to be met by the middle of the century.

The Act of Union was a messy, compromised arrangement that pleased few of the affected parties. Passed by the British parliament on 23 July 1840 and implemented the following year, the act allowed for a new Province of Canada comprised of the former Upper and Lower provinces, to be governed along the basic lines of the 1791

Constitution Act. The act was directly influenced by Lord Durham's *Report,* which had stated that "the first object ought to be that of making it an English Province; and that, with this end in view, the ascendancy should never again be placed in any hands but those of an English population."[3] The old provinces of Upper Canada and Lower Canada would be renamed Canada West and Canada East, respectively, and section XII stipulated that, despite the Canada East holding a numerical advantage of some two hundred thousand, both would receive an equal number of seats in the united Assembly. Section XXXV insisted that all members of both Houses must take an oath of allegiance to Queen Victoria asserting that the new province is "dependent on and belonging to the said United Kingdom." The Durhamite commitment to an English ascendency was most poignantly illustrated in Section XLI, which insisted that all "written or printed Proceedings, of what Nature soever... shall be in the English Language only."

The French Canadians had just cause to feel aggrieved with the Act of Union. Lower Canada, effectively debt free in 1840, was burdened by the union with the debts of Upper Canada. Section XXX allowed the governor to choose the site for the Houses of Parliament and insult was added to injury when Lord Sydenham selected Kingston in Canada West.[4] Many Upper Canadians, however, were also far from pleased. In the wake of the *Durham Report,* the reformers of Upper Canada were panting for responsible government. To be left with essentially the same constitutional arrangements that had been unsuccessfully operating for half a century left many incensed. Even though he had spent almost no time there as governor, Durham's *Report* had electrified the reformers of Upper Canada. 1839 saw some sixteen large Durham Meetings in various parts of the province, all advocating the principle of responsible government.[5] The reformers greeted the Act of Union with disappointment but determination.

The very design of the Act of Union made clear its Durhamite objective: to assimilate the French Canadians into a British nation. Durham had famously stated in his *Report* that he found in Canada "two nations warring in the bosom of a single state." Yet the actions of the popular reform parties in Canada West and Canada East suggest that the situation was more complex than this. Durham found in Canada "a struggle, not of principles, but of races."[6] And yet, for a majority in both former provinces, the struggle was not against a rival race but against Downing Street for the principle of responsible government. French Canadian radicals did call for a complete rejection of the union, just as Upper Canadian tories rejected responsible government. The success of the Baldwin-La Fontaine ministry, however, speaks volumes about the unity between the two ancient tribes in their joint bid for a democracy shaped not only by liberalism but by civic republicanism also.

Robert Baldwin was born in Toronto on 14 May 1804 with a wonderful pedigree for a future reformer. His grandfather for whom he was named, Robert Baldwin Sr, had published Ireland's *Volunteer Journal*, which the family boasted was favourably spoken of by Charles James Fox.[7] Narrowly avoiding his nation's uprising, in 1798 Robert Sr immigrated to Upper Canada, where his son, William, would become a leading voice for responsible government. William Baldwin was noted for his whiggish politics in Upper Canada's Legislative Assembly and led the calls for reform of the administration of Sir Peregrine Maitland. Young Robert Baldwin grew up watching and admiring his father. At a by-election in 1829, he would take his own seat in the Assembly. Responsible government would hence be a great boon agitated for by father and son alike.

When Sir Francis Bond Head arrived in Toronto on 23 January 1836, the new governor asked Robert Baldwin to join his Executive Council. Baldwin accepted only with the greatest reluctance and on the condition his friend and fellow Reformer Dr John Rolph join him. Both were to quickly resign in disgust. Baldwin's conviction that responsible government was a principle demanded by the constitution was matched for intensity by Head's refutation. Baldwin left for England and argued the case for responsible government with the Colonial Office. During this time, his letters of introduction and connections through his cousin, the member for Cork, Dr Herbert Baldwin, saw him meet and dine with London's progressive elite. With his numerous connections to Canada, the member for Bath, John Roebuck, expressed his desire to see an elective Legislative Assembly. Baldwin famously wrote that this was "merely grasping at the shadow and losing the substance."[8] Baldwin was more impressed with Joseph Hume and his friend James McGregor, who he felt were not only supporters but men who understood the principle of responsible government in its "true light."[9]

Following his return early in 1837, Mackenzie and his rebels did not bother asking Baldwin to join their ranks. Rather, he and Rolph appeared on the governor's behalf attempting to broker a truce. Baldwin had no interest in separatist republicanism and remained convinced throughout the turbulent 1830s that responsible government was the solution to the young province's oxymoronic desire for both independence and connection. Following the untied province's first election in March 1841, Baldwin, as the natural leader of Canada West's reformers, took the seat of Hastings in the Legislative Assembly and a seat on Sydenham's Executive Council.

Louis-Hippolyte La Fontaine was born just three years after Baldwin on 4 October 1807. The son of a carpenter, La Fontaine was called to the bar in 1828 and, following his marriage into a wealthy, connected family, entered politics in 1830 as the member for Terrebonne in Lower Canada's Legislative Assembly. La Fontaine was a passionate and vocal supporter of Papineau and a leader of the Parti Patriote. Gérard Bergeron notes that *Les deux girouettes, ou l'hypocrisie démasquée* from 1834 and *Notes sur l'inamovibilité des curés dans le Bas-Canada* written in the rebellion year 1837 bear testament to his skill and influence as a Patriote pamphleteer.[10]

Yet La Fontaine was at heart much like Baldwin, a moderate reformer, not a revolutionary. His biographer Jacques Monet commented that he would "prove to have a profound understanding of the principles of the British constitution and of their importance for the survival of French Canadians."[11] The battle for La Fontaine was not physical or even racial; it was constitutional. Rather than taking part in the rebellion, La Fontaine followed Baldwin's example from the previous year and spent time in London, meeting with fellow reformers. Despite his efforts to avoid conflict, when rebellion flared a second time in November 1838, La Fontaine was briefly arrested, although no charges were laid. It was in this period that La Fontaine emerged as the great mediator between the French Canadian radicals and the British government. He worked closely with Buller and Wakefield during the brief Durham administration and was the intermediary between the government and the exiles to Bermuda. Through his contact with Joseph Hume, Lord Gosford, and others, La Fontaine would articulate most clearly to Westminster the causes of Lower Canada's grievances and the constitutional remedy. Francis Hincks went some way to addressing the absence of a radical press following Mackenzie's exile when he began printing the *Examiner,* with its Durhamite motto, "responsible government."[12] It was Hincks who would introduce La Fontaine and Baldwin and, in doing so, help form the multi-cultural reformist coalition that would ultimately crush the tory oligarchy and usher in a new democratic era.[13]

Should Baldwin and La Fontaine be considered the champions of liberalism? It is hard to make such a claim without ignoring the fact that both men argued not against government intervention in itself but against the counterproductive government intervention coming from British politicians who did not understand Canada's unique condition. Both men were, of course, influenced by liberalism, but they were not purebred liberals. Rather, they were deeply concerned that once power was wrestled from the British governors and their tory acolytes, a form of positive liberty be maintained. While the tories spoke of commerce and the Lockean liberals spoke of individualism, the Baldwin-La Fontaine ministry urged policy directed towards the public good; a civic republican pillar.

Baldwin had always admired the British constitution (or his interpretation of it). After 1837, La Fontaine came to a deep appreciation of it as well. Through the civic republican interpretation that demanded mixed government, the production of virtue and government that actively seeks the common good, La Fontaine saw the formula to save the French Canadians. The battle, despite having racial elements, was not predominately racial but political and ideological. The battle was to secure democracy in general and specifically a civic republican form of positive liberty for all the people of British North America. In his numerous letters to Francis Hincks, La Fontaine confirmed his commitment to a political party based on principle, not race. This was further enforced by his election to the English-speaking seat of York on 23 September 1841. To his new constituents he said: "Apart from the considerations of social order, from the love of peace and political freedom, our common interests would alone establish sympathies which, sooner or later, must have rendered the mutual cooperation of the mass of the two peoples."[14]

Just over a year later the favour would be returned as the 95 percent French-speaking constituency of Rimouski elected Baldwin on 30 January 1843.[15] This step may be seen as symbolic, but it speaks volumes of the unity of the reformers under the leadership of La Fontaine and Baldwin. The fact that some twenty-five French members had offered to resign their seats for Baldwin is a strong indication that the struggle for liberty was not curtailed by a racial divide.[16] Just as English and French speakers took arms together in the rebellions of 1837–38, they now sided together in the political battle for responsible government. There was a clear understanding among moderate reformers that their strength lay in unity and in peaceful agitation to create a specific type of free British society. The separatism and breast-beating of Papineau had been tried and found wanting.

Charles Poulett Thomson, soon to be Lord Sydenham, arrived in Quebec City as British North America's new governor in chief on 19 October 1839. He went quickly to work dissolving the separate legislatures of Upper and Lower Canada and drafting what would become the Act of Union. Following elections in March and April 1841, Lord Sydenham, raised to the peerage the previous year, opened the first parliament of the Province of Canada on 14 July. Although the political infrastructure in the Province of Canada was similar to that which had descended into rebellion just three years before, the attitude of the governor was markedly different. Before 1837, a general pattern was in place in which the governor would invariably align himself to the local tory oligarchy, which would form his Executive Council. Sydenham broke this mould by selecting an Executive Council not made up of appointed Legislative Councillors but of elected men in the Legislative Assembly. The members of the Executive Council were given various portfolios and became a sort of pseudo-cabinet to a governor who was effectively the prime minister of the province also. Despite the immense power the governor held over the Executive Council, the fact that he chose to surround himself with the people's elected representatives was another step in the direction of responsible government.

It can only be hypothesized how the constitutional battles in Canada would have played out had Sydenham's administration not suddenly ended following his death from a riding accident on 19 September 1841. Sydenham clearly did not support the kind of responsible government Joseph Howe would soon petition for. The governor insisted in Russellite terms that he could not serve both the imperial and colonial government, yet he was under clear instructions to cede to the Assembly as much as could be done safely. Consequently, Sydenham walked a constitutional tightrope, balancing on one hand the desire to appease the reformers and on the other his own position of authority. His replacement seemed far more resigned to the fact that the only way to avoid another rebellion was to yield local power to the local government.

Sir Charles Bagot virtually conceded in 1842 that responsible government was inevitable. Although personally wary of both men, Bagot felt he had no choice but to invite Balwin and La Fontaine into his Executive Council. The consequences of not inviting men who held the people's confidence seemed too dire for Bagot:

> There was but one way to avoid it – by appointing a new Executive Council prepared to act without the sympathy and against an overwhelming majority of the House of Assembly: by denying *in toto* the principle of Responsible Government, and refusing to act upon it, at a crisis which would immediately have brought the question to an issue unfavourable to the government. But having before me the Act of Union, Lord John Russell's despatch of the 14th October 1837, Lord Sydenham's avowed policy, the Resolutions of the House of Assembly last Session, and the present feeling and temper of its members, I was not prepared, to adopt such a policy. The consequences would have been disastrous. The Assembly would have stopped the supplies about to be voted – the questions which led to the former troubles of Canada would have been revived – all attempts to resist the power of the Assembly and the tide of public opinion would have failed, and Canada would have again become the Theatre of a wide spread rebellion, and perhaps the ungrateful separatist or the rejected outcast of British Dominion.[17]

The lesson of 1837 had been well learnt by Bagot, who saw in opposing the wishes of a popular Assembly the futility of King Cnut ordering the tide to halt and not wet his feet.

Although the writing appeared to be on the wall to some, the debate over responsible government continued in England. Following the general election in 1841, Robert Peel's conservative government was returned, and Lord Stanley replaced Lord Russell in the Colonial Office. On 30 March 1843, Sir Charles Theophilus Metcalfe officially replaced Bagot. In Metcalfe, Stanley felt he had chosen a man skilled in the art of conciliatory leadership. Metcalfe had satisfactorily governed Jamaica from 1839 to 1842, overseeing the political conflict between the newly emancipated slaves and the plantation owners. The conservatives felt Bagot had conceded too much to the reformers and were keen for Metcalfe to return the status of imperial sovereignty to its rightful place.

Metcalfe's governorship of Jamaica and his long stint in India, the land of his birth, had given him great sympathy for the grievances of native populations under British rule.[18] Consequently, he arrived in British North America with an open ear to the French Canadian leaders and a conciliatory spirit. He gained the admiration of some in the French bloc by rejecting the Durhamite recommendation of forced anglicization and describing the former exclusion of the French Party from power as an "injustice."[19] Metcalfe petitioned to change the capital from Kingston to Montreal, he argued for a general amnesty for the rebels of 1837-38 (except those accused of murder), and in general he looked favourably on a greater French Canadian presence in government circles. Metcalfe's attitude towards the French Canadians earned him the ire not only of Canada West but also of Peel and Stanley, who did not share his liberal attitude.

Metcalfe's administration was under constant pressure, since it was effectively fighting a war on two fronts. The Colonial Office and the conservatives in London were opposed to what they felt was an overly accommodating policy towards the French Canadians. In Canada, the reform leaders of both Canada East and Canada West continued to campaign for responsible government. Metcalfe struggled to counter the spirit of party government and to act as an independent Crown representative appointing government positions on merit. As George Wilson has noted, in the influential editor of the Methodist *Christian Guardian*, Egerton Ryerson, Metcalfe could not have asked for a "more powerful or able defender."[20] Refuting the claims of Baldwin and the Toronto Reform Association, Ryerson released a pamphlet in the governor's defence.[21] Despite his best attempts, however, the organization and discipline of the reformers and the demand for responsible government was too strong for this to be anything but a temporary situation. It was perhaps a mercy that ill-health forced Metcalfe's resignation in 1845. He would not have survived another year in the post anyway, since the controversy over the repeal of the Corn Laws resulted in a return to office for the whigs and the appointment of Earl Grey to colonial secretary.

It is tempting to view the change of prime minister from Peel to Russell, of colonial secretary from Stanley to Grey, and of governor-in-chief of Canada from Metcalfe to Elgin (separated by the brief rule of military governor, Charles Murray Cathcart) as decisive moves from an anti- to a pro-responsible government administration, yet the lines of battle were not so clearly drawn. Responsible government as a colonial demand was something both whig and tory alike were coming to terms with in London. It was, after all, Russell who as colonial secretary had shown such reluctance to grant the second of Durham's twin principles. The contrast between Stanley and Grey has been particularly exaggerated. Although Grey attempted to write his own history, his reminiscences do not quite match the facts and, as Phillip Buckner argues, he was slow and cautious as he yielded to the inevitable.[22] Nonetheless it was Grey who had the foresight to know which way the colonial winds were blowing, and he adjusted the governmental sails accordingly in his famous despatches.

The previous chapter has already mentioned the despatch from Grey to the lieutenant-governor of Nova Scotia, Sir John Harvey, on 3 November 1846. Although it contained on one level specific instructions to one governor in one province, its meaning and significance stretched beyond the little Atlantic peninsula. The lessons of 1837 had been learnt and the wisdom of Lord Durham acknowledged. Grey could just as easily have been speaking of New Brunswick or New South Wales when he declared the futility of attempting to govern large colonial populations in opposition to their wishes. The role of the governor was henceforth to be that of a neutral mediator between the various parliamentary parties, and only with the "greatest possible discretion" was he to challenge the wishes of an Executive Council that possessed the confidence of the people. Grey concluded: "A refusal to accept advice tendered to you by your council is a legitimate ground for its members to tender to you their resignations – a course they would doubtless adopt, should they feel that the subject on which a difference had arisen between you and themselves was one upon which public opinion would be in their favour. Should it prove to be so, concession to their views must sooner or later become inevitable; since it cannot be too distinctly acknowledged that it is neither possible nor desirable to carry on the government of any of the British provinces in North America in opposition to the opinion of the inhabitants."[23]

The universality of these words was highlighted when George Verney Smith quoted them in the Victorian Legislative Assembly in 1868 when pursuing a reformist agenda. It applied, not just to Nova Scotia, but to all matured British colonies with a British population when Grey advised Harvey that "any transfer that may take place of political power, from the hands of one party in the province to those of another, [must be] the result, not of an act of yours, but of the wishes of the people." The argument put forward by Victorian reformers also could just as easily have come from progressive lips in Canada; what they wanted was not separatist republicanism but the mixed civic republican constitution of Britain. Smith continued: "With reference to one of the strongest arguments used by our adversaries – that we intend doing, or that we are aiming at something which might in some way cause separation from England – I say that nothing is more fallacious. I don't want to use strong terms, but I cannot conceive anything more likely to bind us indissolubly to England than the maintenance of our rights under the English constitution. The Crown is certainly a strong tie, but the constitution is a stronger tie."[24]

Grey's appointment of James Bruce, 8th Earl of Elgin and 12th Earl of Kincardine, as governor general of Canada in 1847 was symbolic of the change of role that post now entailed. Lord Elgin was a former tory member of parliament, yet he was personally aligned to the whigs through his marriage to Lady Mary Louisa Lambton, Lord Durham's daughter and Grey's niece. Such was to be the model for future governors, a neutral representative of the Crown adjudicating the party contest. Elgin was to prove be a governor to whom Alexander Pope's satire of Horace could be faithfully applied: "in moderation placing all my glory, while Tories call me Whig, and Whigs a Tory."[25] Elgin was committed "frankly and unequivocally" to responsible government as proposed by Durham. On 11 March he correctly predicted to his wife, that if responsible government was successfully implemented, her father's "reputation as a statesman will be raised beyond the reach of cavil." He wrote: "I told you formerly that I thought it ought to be possible (not easy) to govern Canada under the system introduced by Lord Durham, and that if it was found to be possible to carry on the Government under that system, his title to be considered a great benefactor to his country would no longer be disputed. I am forfeited in these convictions by all that I have learnt since I came here."[26]

On 13 July, Elgin penned a letter to Grey that outlined the new colonial policy that would prove to be the dawning in practical application of Durham's second empire. Elgin urged the Colonial Office not to be surprised at initial recklessness by the Assembly but to exercise patience and hold faith that the principles of the British constitution would deliver government worthy of British subjects in British North America. Elgin acknowledged that the government of the colonies would henceforth be only "quasi-monarchical." If not for the strong use of the word when describing the colonies' southern neighbour, Elgin could well have described the new arrangement as civic republican. In any case, the mixed constitution so favoured by the ancients and by Machiavelli was to be put in place.

Elgin foresaw that as the democratic arm secured a more political role, the Crown was destined to fulfil a moral role in the second empire. He went to some lengths explaining this to Grey: "My course in these circumstance, is, I think, clear and plain. It may be somewhat difficult to follow occasionally, but I feel no doubt as to the direction in which it lies. I give my ministers all constitutional support, frankly and without reserve, and the benefit of the best advice that I can afford them in their difficulties. In return for this, I expect that they will, in so far as it is possible for them to do so, carry out my views for the maintenance of the connexion with Great Britain and the advancement of the interests of the province. On this tacit understanding we have acted together harmoniously up to this time, although I have never concealed from them that I intended to do nothing which may prevent me from working cordially with their opponents, if they are forced upon me." In this statement, which sounds so modest to modern ears, Elgin is making two important distinctions. First, he is conceptualizing the role of governor in much smaller terms than had previously been the case. The governor seeks, not to dictate local policy, but to ensure the British connection is maintained. More significantly, Elgin does not feel obliged to maintain the tory oligarchy against the wishes of the people and states his willingness to work with either side of politics.

Elgin goes further and describes the party system, which previous governors had fought so valiantly against, as central to British constitutional government. He informs Grey:

> That ministers and oppositions should occasionally change places, is of the very essence of our constitutional system, and it is probably the most conservative element which it contains. By subjecting all sections of politicians in their turn to official responsibilities, it obliges heated partisans to place some restraint on passion, and to confine within the bounds of decency the patriotic zeal with which, when out of place, they are wont to be animated. In order, however, to secure these advantages, it is indispensible that the head of the

Government should show that he has confidence in the loyalty of all the influential parties with which he has to deal, and that he should have no personal antipathies to prevent him from acting with leading men.

I feel very strongly that a Governor-General, by acting upon these views with tact and firmness, may hope to establish a moral influence in the province which will go far to compensate for the loss of power consequent on the surrender of patronage to an executive responsible to the local parliament.

The Durhamite understanding of colonial governance is clearly on display here. The governor is to surrender actual power for moral influence. This may well have been a brave, if not reckless, move at the time. History would vindicate the shift in mentality and Canada would see out, not only the nineteenth century but the twentieth also, constitutionally attached to Great Britain.

Elgin worried that his path would be narrow and slippery as he negotiated the new constitutional path, attempting to fall neither into the "*néant* of mock sovereignty" nor the "dirt and confusion of local factions."[27] The litmus test for Elgin's new role and for responsible government in the Province of Canada was to come early in 1849 when the Baldwin-La Fontaine ministry introduced the Rebellion Losses Bill. The bill was designed to compensate property owners for damages incurred as the military put down the rebellion. A similar bill had appeased Upper Canadian property owners in 1841. Since it was impossible to determine whether claimants were loyalists or rebel sympathisers during 1837–38, compensation would be payed to all except convicted rebels. For the Canadian tories, the bill was controversial to the point of being scandalous. The bill would inevitably compensate some men who were at least tacit supporters of Papineau and the rebels. As a result, the tories argued, the bill would effectively reward acts of treason. The prospect of taxes taken from loyalists in Canada East and West being used to reward those who warmly, though not actively, supported the champions of disloyalty was unpalatable.

Charles Smith published a satirical play to arouse opposition to the bill. His piece called *Rebels Rewarded?* typified the indignation felt by a conservative element that must have sensed the winds of change and a loosening grip on power. A lengthy poem addressed to loyal Britons of all stripes asked if they were now betraying the legacy of their noble ancestors:

> Up-spoke a man of spirit in the crowd,
> Shall we be slaves my friends? He cried aloud;
> Shall we submit to tyrants? Men, he said,
> Whilst rebels are rewarded, aye, and paid,
> For powder, shot and bullets made of lead;
> That they in times gone by hurl'd at the head
> Of every Loyalist that lov'd his Queen,
> Both French and English, Scotch, and Irish green...
>
> Did Wolfe and his brave fellows bleed in vain,
> Before Quebec on Abraham's bloody plain,
> Did they lay down their lives that we should be
> Bondsmen to Frenchmen! Sold to slavery!

The play went on to parody the Rebellion Losses Bill, referring to it as "An act to benefit 'French Canadians' at the expense of 'Anglo Saxons!!'"[28] This intensely personal brand of propaganda cut to the heart of a very sensitive issue and raised passions and resentment among the conservatives. Nevertheless, in the House, the tories appeared a defeated force and their attempts to halt the bill by legitimate means were continually frustrated by their modest numbers and Elgin's stalwart neutrality.

The tories were well and truly on the back foot by the time the Rebellion Losses Bill was read for the second time on Friday night, 9 March. There was more than a touch of desperation in the speech given by Bartholomew Conrad Augustus Gugy in opposition to the bill. The old colonel, who had led a cavalry unit for the Crown against Saint-Charles and Saint-Eustache during the rebellions in Lower Canada, gave an extremely lengthy performance that according to the *Montreal Pilot's* correspondent, touched on "every imaginable topic excepting the one before the House." Gugy's oratory included everything from lessons from history, such as Hector and the siege of Troy, to personal anecdotes including how the governor general used to pat him on the head as a boy. The *Pilot* observed that during Gugy's speech, the gallery thinned to almost nothing and the members themselves steadily trickled out the door until just half a dozen remained on the government side, "and they, with two exceptions, were peaceably slumbering." The moment Gugy resumed his seat, "the Members flocked in from the lobbies and the newsrooms," and the tory amendments were rejected.[29]

On 26 April 1849 Lord Elgin, accompanied by some cavalry, rode to Parliament House and gave his assent to the Rebellion Losses Bill. As Jeffrey McNairn states, the passage of this bill was the "final, inescapable recognition of self-government."[30] The immediate consequences of this decision were dire. Ultra-tory loyalists assembled at the Champ de Mars, and cried out "to the Parliament House." At eight o'clock in the evening the members were still debating. They were horrified to be interrupted by a hail of stones that broke nearly every window. As the members rushed to escape, the rioters entered the building. One rioter sat in the speaker's chair and declared to his fellow vigilantes, "I dissolve this House."[31] The building was then set on fire. The military eventually dispelled the mob, but the House, along with its libraries and public records, could not be saved. Contemporary historian John Mercier McMullen lamented this wanton destruction: "The Paris mobs, in the midst of revolution and anarchy, respected public buildings, the libraries, and works of art; and it remained for the vandalism of Montreal rioters to inflict a public injury on themselves, of a character adopted by the Saracens and Huns, and other barbarians of the middle ages, to punish their enemies."[32]

The *Pilot*, which, under the editorship of Francis Hinks, had become the chief mouthpiece of the reformers, reported with "deep regret" that "the metropolis of Canada has been disgraced by one of the most wanton and scandalous riots that has ever taken place in any civilized country."[33] It was reported that the following day the houses of Hincks and LaFontaine were attacked by a "mob of men and boys."[34] Riots had already taken place in Toronto in response to the bill. Having been granted amnesty earlier in the year, William Lyon Mackenzie returned to Canada and was lodging with his friend and fellow Scottish-born reformer John McIntosh. It must have been a terrifying welcome for the old rebellion leader to see thousands of rioters gather outside the home and burn his effigy. Screaming abuse, the excitable tory mob assailed the home "with stones and all manner of missiles, completely riddling the windows." With an effigy of Baldwin also, the rioters proceeded to the homes of several other reform leaders.[35]

The radical press in Britain roundly denounced the needless violence. The *Examiner* lamented, first, the "strong party bias in favour of the insurgents," which characterized many of the reports on the riots. It went on to describe in graphic detail Lord Elgin running a gauntlet of tory rioters with his face smeared by rotten eggs.[36] The *Manchester Times* described the riots as "exciting, but... not alarming."[37] It dismissively concluded that "well drilled and disciplined as the Canadian Tories are in tumult and disorder, they would not have been true to their nature had they suffered such an opportunity to pass... without resorting to violence."[38] Under a banner taken from Cicero, *Salus populi lex suprema* (the common good of the people is the supreme law), the *Liverpool Mercury* used the occasion to attack the British tories and support the principle of responsible government.[39] It noted: "It is quite characteristic of the man and the party he represents, that Lord Stanley should... have attempted to hold her Majesty's Government accountable for the doings of his own Canadian friends. On his Lordship's theory, the Government should have burked the obnoxious bill; and all would have been well." The *Mercury* had completely accepted the Durhamite principle. The "only conceivable instance" in which Elgin, or any governor, could withhold assent, is when a bill "conflicts with imperial legislation." The Rebellion Losses Bill was a "purely Canadian question" making it "neither our business or policy to interfere." If the governor interferes with local politics then "responsible government signifies nothing." The article ends with a staggering hypothetical. Even if the whole rebel party of 1837 were elected, "what has England to do with this?" It would simply be "the fault of the Canadian Tories, who should have mustered in larger numbers at the poll."[40]

Despite this violent destruction, the Durhamite grand compromise was now immovable and could not be destroyed by stones or fire. The *Pilot* captured the spirit of the new democratic orthodoxy in its Friday editorial, the morning after the riot. It acknowledged that some bills may be "exceedingly obnoxious to the minority in and out of Parliament; but no good argument has been, or could be adduced to warrant the Representative of the Crown to interpose his prerogative to prevent the constitutionally expressed wishes of the people being carried into effect." A new democratic paradigm was in place. As something of an auspicious sign for responsible government, the flames that destroyed the parliament buildings and its library, incredibly, did not consume the Rebellion Losses Bill itself. The *Pilot* trumpeted that "all the mischief has been done by the Tories without accomplishing their object."[41]

The tories let out the most vehement public howl imaginable. Riots took place, Baldwin's effigy was burnt in the streets, and yet the decision would not be altered.[42] There would no longer be a government party, as it were, but merely a conservative one, unaided, officially at least, by the governor. An apologia for Elgin's decision was speedily produced by Alexander Mackay and published in London to persuade the British parliament not to veto the bill and consequently undermine the principle of responsible government and legitimize the rioters. This was not an imperial issue, the pamphlet insisted, since "the bill merely contemplates the appropriation of local funds for a local purpose." Further, the pamphlet reinforced the contention that English and French Canadian reformers had been proposing since the 1830s. The cause of tension and ultimately of rebellion was that the people had been promised a constitution that was to mirror that of the mother country. Referring specifically to the Upper Canadians, who had no racial fault line to distract administrators, Mackay writes, "they were promised Parliamentary Government, instead of obtaining which, they were almost immediately handed over to the tender mercies of a local oligarchy."[43]

There were calls by some, frustrated by the constitutional melee of the 1840s, to wilfully have their province annexed to the United Sates. Observing events from England, the influential Scottish Presbyterian minister Dr John Dunmore Lang argued that Canada's British population should flee the "tyranny of the French majority" and embrace the "go-a-head" principle of America.[44] The famous *Annexation Manifesto*, first published in the *Montreal Gazette* on 11 October 1849, warmly adopted this thinking.[45] Although a number of French names were on the document, the majority of the signatures came from English tories. Under the presidency of Scottish industrialist John Redpath, the Montreal Annexation Association, which penned the *Manifesto*, acknowledged its strange alliance with some French radicals but concluded that for the greater economic interest parties of all "origins and creeds" must unite.[46] The movement came to nothing. It failed to gain support in Canada, and it is unclear if the United States would have supported it either.

As Baldwin's daughter Maria opined in a letter to him, if the Americans wanted to increase their territory, they would more likely look "to the south than to the north."[47] It is worth considering the flaws in the dichotomy pressed so firmly by Head and the tory press, namely, that the conservatives represented loyalty and that the reformers, especially French reformers, were disloyal, separatist republicans. The cooperation of some French radicals and English tories, but more importantly, the popularly supported coalition of moderate French and English reformers, suggests that the issue of race should not be overstated.

Despite the best attempts of Smith and other hardline tories to represent the bill as a severe blow to English Canadians in a racial war, support, if not for the bill, at least for the principle of responsible government, could be readily seen among the English speakers. One of the conservative papers noted that "bad as the payment of the Rebellion losses is, we do not know that it would not be better to submit to pay twenty rebellion losses, than have what is nominally a free constitution fettered and restrained." Similarly, the Scottish St Andrews Society of Toronto was unlikely to have supported the bill. Nevertheless, at their meeting on 10 May 1849, they warmly praised Elgin, the society's patron, for his "most admirable impartiality, firmness and adherence to the Constitution guaranteed to us by the Imperial authority." Elgin, doubtless touched by this support, wrote to the society that he was determined to "steadily adhere through evil report, through disaster, even through defeat, to the cause which I know to be a right one."[48] A decade earlier, London's *Examiner* had noted of the Rebellions of 1837–38 that "others than French Canadians are striking for liberty; that the Anglo-Saxons are now aroused; that Protestantism and Catholicism are marching arm in arm; that there are Papineaus and Browns in every town."[49] At the height of the Rebellion Losses Bill debates, the *Daily News* concluded that "nothing could be more palpably unjust than to characterize the present contest in Canada as a war of races."[50] Just as English and French rebels had supported each other in the late 1830s, English and French reformers did so again in the late 1840s. Race was important but democracy was more so.

In passing the Rebellion Losses Bill, Canada trumpeted to the world that a new epoch in British colonial administration had begun. What Durham put down in theory a decade earlier had now been put into practice, calmly in Nova Scotia and dramatically in Canada. Ultimately what the reformers achieved was victory in a battle of ideas concerning that most sacred of institutions, the British constitution. As the *Novascotian* commented in 1847: "Those who read the trash that the Tories sprout and scribble would suppose that Toryism is but another name for loyalty... Liberals and Whigs have ever been rebels at heart – disturbers of society, and men upon whom the Government could place no real dependence. Is this true? History flatly denies it, and tells us that, but for the Whigs and Liberals of the Mother Country, there would have been no order – no rational liberty – only an unrestrained hereditary tyranny, for the Tories to admire, and the people to obey."[51]

In the wake of the violent riots, the *Globe* similarly claimed that toryism could no longer be considered synonymous with loyalty. It noted, "The Tory merchants whose lip loyalty was wont to be displayed before the world, have for the last two years fallen on bad times, commerce, ally, and their loyalty has at once evaporated."[52] Writing in the 1930s, George Wilson also referred to this period as a great "cooling of Tory loyalty" and, like Hincks, would highlight economic reasons for this fair-weather loyalty.[53] No longer would support for the 1791 constitution be considered support for the mother country writ large. The reformers and whigs had won the battle for responsible government, and whig historians would glorify the tide of progress from the tyranny of old to the enlightened and prosperous future.

Interpretations of the shift to responsible government have varied greatly in the twentieth century. One prevailing misconception is that the transition was somehow a safe and calculated compromise, a watered-down version of Mackenzian republicanism. This view miserably fails in doing justice to the brobdingnagian change (as Jonathan Swift might have phrased it) the reformers had brought about. It would have been a grand shift in Canadian history if the rebels had been victorious in 1837; however, there was never any guarantee that one oligarchy would not simply replace another one. Although the British connection remained, the transition to responsible government did represent a seismic shift in the nature of colonial governance. Two questions then remain to be answered: did the impetus for this change come from Britain or Canada and did the change away from toryism represent a shift towards liberalism or civic republicanism?

Before 1975 the historical orthodoxy was to view the granting of responsible government in the Canadian colonies as something of a cause-and-effect happening as Britain's economic platform changed from mercantilist to free trade.[54] In 1846 the infamous Corn Laws were finally repealed after a lengthy campaign. In 1849 the repeal of the Navigation Laws marked the end of the old colonial system of trade. Historically, of course, the embrace by the British government of a system of free trade does coincide with the granting and exercising of responsible government in Nova Scotia and the Province of Canada. The extent, however, to which the two events are related has been grandly overstated.

Buckner has argued convincingly that the movement for responsible government was not created in Britain and that although it may have been coincidentally goaded by the British free trade movement, its real impetus was purely colonial. "Events in London and in the colonies each had a momentum of their own," writes Buckner, adding that "either could have developed without the other."[55] Just as the British free traders had little desire to see a fundamental reform of colonial governance, the colonial reformers would not have welcomed an end to the preferential system of trade. The most that can reasonably be concluded is that the change in British trade policy was advantageous to the cause of responsible government. It can be seen as an accelerator but not the catalyst.

What, then, was behind the great change that birthed the new British Empire? The previous chapters have already suggested that civic republicanism played a significant role in the unfolding drama of the mid-nineteenth century. That is not to suggest that the liberalism of John Locke's school was not also a driving force in calling for greater democratic freedoms. Rather, it needs to be acknowledged that a third political philosophy was at play. Civic republicanism, with its strong emphasis on collectivism, the production of civic virtue, and the protection of the common good, shared some traits with the toryism that was so prevalent in the early nineteenth century. Civic republicanism was a third way of thinking, a middle ground between the conservatives and reformers, since it held things in common with both sides.

There are historians who interpret the role of liberalism as something of a guiding light in Canada, just as (they claim) it was in the United States.[56] The whole process has been one of a gradual movement away from the hierarchical and communal toryism towards the democratic and individualistic tenor of liberalism. The problem with this interpretation is that it offers little explanation for why Mackenzian separatist republicanism failed to take root. There is little in the liberal tradition that endorses communalism or an emphasis on the common good, and there is virtually nothing, save a nostalgic impulse, to explain the overwhelming desire among the colonists to maintain a political connection to Great Britain. If Lockean liberalism had been as strong in Canada as is sometimes suggested, it would be hard then to understand why the concept of a parliament on the other side of the Atlantic Ocean directing policy held much appeal.

The other view, dubbed the laurentian camp by Robin Winks, argues that tory conservatism influenced and modified the liberalism of the nineteenth century and explains the strong importance placed on communalism and serving the common good.[57] Janet Ajzenstat and Peter Smith have already commented on the limitations and inadequacies of the liberal-laurentian paradigm. Ajzenstat and Smith note the obvious problem that under the traditional paradigm scholars must "include under the aegis of tory conservatism two tendencies that are not easy to reconcile: a selfless sense of the common good and a ruthless dedication to commerce and economic development."[58] A more coherent view of Canadian history will acknowledge the range of ideologies that coloured and shaped the transition to responsible government. Including the role of civic republicanism perhaps complicates the neatness of the liberal-laurentian view, but in return it offers a more cogent explanation of the primacy of the common-good argument in nineteenth-century colonial debates and even suggests an ideological base for the socialism that would shape Canada in the twentieth.

It is hard to reconcile the arguments of the laurentian camp with the history of the Family Compact, the Château Clique, and the various tory cabals that held such sway under the 1791 constitutional arrangement. One need only look to the howls of protest that came not only from radicals such as Mackenzie but from moderate reformers such as Baldwin. Even moderate tories like Howe could not deny the fact that the tory cabals and the colonial elites who comprised them were nepotistic, often blatantly self-serving, and concerned with restricting power to a small base. The spirit that united the diverse group of reformers can be identified as civic republican. Just as the Commonwealthmen of the eighteenth century would find justification for their civic republicanism in the British constitution, so too would the colonial reformers of the nineteenth.

By the end of the 1840s, the British government and public took part in serious debate over management of the colonies. The *Glasgow Herald* compared the British government to an abusive mother: "the British public, like the evil-tempered [mother's] neighbours, are... disturbed, at all hours, by the piercing lamentations of our transmarine fellow subjects."[59] The *Manchester Times* commented in late 1849 that "it would be difficult, at this moment, to point out a single Colony in which the spirit of disaffection is not daily expanding into open hostility."[60] The prospect of colonial representation in the Imperial Parliament was discussed as a possible remedy. Joseph Howe would champion this idea on behalf of the Canadians, while John Dunmore Lang would denounce it for Australia.[61] As the decade wound to a close, Durham's grand compromise was established in British North America and thoughts there turned to confederation. The Australian colonies would take up where their Canadian brethren left off, demanding responsible government and a type of democracy with no little civic republican influence.

By 1850 the colonies of British North America, with the sole exception of Newfoundland, would enjoy responsible government. The transition under Russell and Grey was complete, and the conclusion was reached that the common good could only realistically be determined by local parliaments comprised of virtuous members held regularly to account by the court of public opinion. The principle would take less than five years to extend to the vast majority of Australian colonists. The following chapters will examine the role of civic republicanism in the transition to responsible government in these southern colonies, so distant from Canada geographically, yet connected through culture, through politics, and through history.

7

The Future America of the Southern Hemisphere: Dr Lang and the Failure of Separatism

> The Christian citizen of America – a country which has risen so recently to the rank and dignity of a great and independent nation, from the comparatively humble condition of a mere series of British colonies – can scarcely fail to sympathize with a people of kindred origin, who are still labouring under all the disadvantages of that humbler condition.
> Lang, *The Future America of the Southern Hemisphere*

An aficionado of social history would have to search laboriously to find an example of more profound and lasting change in a shorter period than the experience of New South Wales in its first half century of European settlement. Dispossessing the Indigenous inhabitants, New South Wales began its existence in 1788 as a military dictatorship. The early military governors were, of course, men under the authority of the Crown. Be that as it may, the "tyranny of distance," as Geoffrey Blainey so eloquently phrased it, and the convict status of the vast majority of the white population ensured that the new colony was a virtual fiefdom.[1] It is remarkable to consider that the first generation of white Australians were born into a prison system and by middle age were living in a free society engrossed in vigorous public debate about the nature of their new democratic constitution. The granting of the first partially elective house of parliament on Australian soil in 1842 was a sign of things to come. It was the first clear indication that a social transformation had taken place and was continuing to take place. In little over half a century the shackles of convictism were both literally and metaphorically thrown off, and the civic republican impulse would ensure that democracy was the norm by the middle of the nineteenth century.

The cause of separatist republicanism was never more than a marginal interest in colonial Australia. In the early 1850s, however, it was championed by a Sydney leader with such passion, energy, and tenacity that for a brief moment radicals in Australia, Britain, and the United States dared to believe that an Australian republic truly was a "coming event."[2] It seemed possible for a fleeting moment in the middle of the nineteenth century that the "artful dodger of Sydney," the firebrand leader of the Scots Church, Dr John Dunmore Lang, might bring about the political separation of Britain and her Australian colonies by sheer willpower if nothing else.[3] Lang was certainly one of the most significant figures in Eastern Australian colonial politics. He arrived in Sydney in 1823 with the objective of establishing a Presbyterian church on the Australian mainland, but his vision was far greater than this. Determined, opinionated, and never burdened with humility, he used first his pulpit, then newspapers, books, and public office to spread his Antipodean vision of a free and virtuous society.

Lang's radicalism was of a gradual nature. He remained attached to Britain and the British monarchy, but his continual frustrations with the colonial office and his trips to the United States led him to firmly advocate local rule. In Australia, Lang was a leading voice calling for the separation of Port Phillip and Moreton Bay from New South Wales (now the Australian States of Victoria and Queensland). On a grander scale, he would call for the complete legal separation of the Australian colonies from the mother country. For Lang, the shared history, language, and culture of British people around the world would always unite them as an imagined race. There was no need for these bonds of mutual affection to be mirrored by bonds of legislation. Quite the contrary, Lang felt that only a free and independent Australia could produce virtuous British citizens worthy of the legacy bestowed by their immortal ancestors. No one in the nineteenth century, or arguably in the century to follow, did more to bring about an Australian republic. The failure of separatist republicanism is in stark contrast to the enormous popularity Lang enjoyed both as a preacher and a politician. The vehement loathing by his enemies and the unveiled adoration of his supporters tells of a man whose finger was, for good or ill, on the pulse of the Eastern Australian colonies at their most defining moment. This chapter will suggest that Lang should be seen not simply as the chief advocate for a failed separatist republican scheme but also as the vocal ambassador of a civic republican philosophy that was widely accepted and ultimately legislated in 1855.

Lang arrived in Sydney in May 1823. He engaged actively in public life where his sharp tongue quickly earned him the disdain of Governor Brisbane (and virtually every governor thereafter). His purpose was to found a Presbyterian church on the Australian mainland, but his ambition was far greater than this. Intimately concerned with the politics, morality, and future of the nascent colony of New South Wales, the fiery Scot was an active participant in many areas of public life and vociferously opinionated in every area. Through his pulpit, papers, and public office, he lectured on issues ranging from education and emigration to anti-transportation and anti-Catholicism. Lang was a colonial behemoth comparable to the likes of Parkes and Wentworth (the former a great ally, the latter a fierce opponent). Yet for his myriad political interests and achievements (not least his active role in securing the separation of Victoria and Queensland from New South Wales), it is republicanism with which his name is forever associated.

The great shaper of Lang's moral compass was, of course, the Bible and, true to the radical tradition of Nonconformist preaching politicians, he would pursue his reformist agendas with religious zeal. Although this chapter traces Lang's civic republicanism (as opposed to separatist republicanism), it could fairly be called Christian civic republicanism, since his worldview was inextricably linked to his faith. Typical of the nineteenth century "moral radical party," Lang championed a host of reforms and was convinced that each was blessed by the Divine will.[4] The intersection of good works, reform, and civic virtue was clearly displayed in his campaign to bring a "copious stream of Protestant emigration" to Australia.[5] London's *Examiner* understood his mission: "In point of special design, his project is to forward Emigration in connection with Christian Nonconformist missions; and to show that by the proper application of free white labour in the Moreton Bay district, Great Britain might create for herself a sugar and cotton-field, and inflict a final blow on the atrocities of American slavery. Benevolent and worthy designs, both; supposing them practicable."[6]

For Lang, the moral condition of society was directly proportionate to the prevalence of "real Christians" and true Christianity. In the manual he authored for his Protestant migration he commented: "I have much greater confidence in the influence of a few Christian men for the preservation of the public peace, and the maintenance of order in a mixed community, than in any number of bayonets and batons." Lang asked his emigrants to remember "what the Lord Jesus said to His disciples, (for He still says precisely the same to real Christians of whatever denomination,) 'Ye are the salt of the earth.'" He goes on to explain precisely how that verse should be interpreted: "ye are those whose peculiar function is to preserve the mass of society from corruption."[7] When examining Lang's campaigns for democratic reform, separatist republicanism, franchise extension, Protestant migration, or any other thing, it is vital to understand it as an outpouring of religious conviction. He was won over to democracy later in life not because he sought individual rights but because he saw it as a means of restricting the greed of a corrupt ruling oligarchy and advancing the cause of a moral Christian society.

The demand for a more democratic and representative government heightened in the late 1840s. As with the Canadians before them, many New South Wales reformers viewed the idea of sanctioning a military governor to rule over a largely free population as despotic at best and draconian at worst. Lang even went so far as to draft a Declaration of Independence for New South Wales. He wrote: "The galling and degrading yoke under which we have so long groaned as a British colony governed by absolute Secretaries of State and tyrannical governors, is broken at last. Peace! Freedom! and the Republic of New South Wales! In the name and on behalf of the League of Liberators of New South Wales. Sydney, AD, 1845, First Year of the Republic!" While this revolutionary rhetoric was not published during Lang's lifetime, it is indicative of the dissatisfaction felt with the current government, particularly among many democrats.

The year 1850 saw a sharp acceleration in the intensity of civic republican agitation in Australia. A series of Sydney lectures by Lang known as the Coming Event marked the most sophisticated, politically aggressive and popularly received republican campaign hitherto seen in the colonies. During the lectures, Lang argued that the creation of colonial republics, and eventually a united continental republic, was not an extreme revolutionary act but a natural maturation and graduation into nationhood. He announced to a rapturous Sydney audience on 11 April: "In short, full-grown communities, like several in the present British colonies in both hemispheres, have just as good a right to their entire freedom and independence, as Her Majesty has to her crown, (cheers) and I am sure you will not accuse me of disloyalty, even if I add, a great deal better. (laughter)." Through Lang's humorous and disarming oratory, he was addressing a fundamental reservation many held concerning republicanism. He carefully disassociated republicanism from the violence that, following the American and French revolutions, was often synonymous with the word. Lang insisted that the potential Australian republic, which he baptized the United Provinces of Australia, would be achieved through peaceful democratic means.

Lang clearly was in favour of political separation from Britain. This position, however, was a particularly hard sell, since most colonists were proud of their British heritage and indeed considered themselves to be British. Lang was only too aware of this and consistently argued that the creation of an Australian republic also benefited England. As he told the packed Theatre of the School of Arts in Sydney, the "coming event" should not "cost our mother dear one single throe, one moment's agony." "I wish not a man from England to be shot on the occasion," he continued, "nor a single sixpence of English money to be lost."[8] Although we have no reason to doubt his sincerity, it was nonetheless politically prudent of Lang to take every opportunity to insist on his affection for Britain, and he was always the loudest to cheer whenever the Queen was toasted.

Despite Lang's best efforts, separatist republicanism remained on the fringes of New South Wales politics. This was demonstrated by the lethargic response to the Australian League. Committed to land reform and against transportation, the League was a statedly republican organization that hoped to unite radicals, democrats, and other opponents of the "dung-hill aristocracy of Botany Bay."[9] Lang immediately thrust himself into the work of promoting the League. He declared in the second Coming Event lecture: "Fellow colonists of New South Wales, is it necessary, after these explanations, that I should now call upon you to join the Australian League, to give freedom and independence to your adopted country? There is clearly nothing else worth agitating for in our present circumstances, and be assured that if you do agitate for this great boon with earnestness and determination, you will certainly obtain it."[10]

Political democrats such as Henry Parkes, James Wilshire, and Archibald Michie, all future members of the New South Wales Legislative Council, helped found the Australian League with other radicals. Popular support, however, proved more elusive. Following the great success of Lang's lectures, Parkes supposed that the Sydney chapter could attract between eight and ten thousand supporters. There was probably more than a little disappointment when the inaugural Sydney meeting at the Australian College, which could accommodate 250 people, failed to fill the building beyond half capacity.[11] The Australian League never evolved into the large transcolonial nationalist movement that Lang envisioned.

In June 1850, just two months after the Coming Event lectures and the formation of the Australian League, Lang offered himself as a candidate for a City of Sydney seat on the Legislative Council, despite having recently failed to secure a seat representing the Port Phillip district.[12] Lang's Sydney campaign, backed by a large and powerful committee of democratic reformers, including the politically astute and increasingly influential Henry Parkes, was highly efficient and professional.[13] A campaign to discredit Lang, mounted by the conservative press, especially the *Sydney Morning Herald*, was countered by the *People's Advocate and New South Wales Vindicator*, edited by the noted radical Edward John Hawksley.

Employing rhetoric that was indicative of the growing tensions between the proponents of the status quo and the agents of civic republican reform, Hawksley painted Lang as the "most indomitable advocate of Australian liberty" and denounced his enemies who "have in every possible way endeavoured to crush the rising liberties of Australia; and whose every aim has been to keep her people in the vilest bounds of political subjection."[14] In addition, Parkes and noted Chartist David Blair produced their own mini-paper for the duration of the campaign, titled *The Representative: A Daily Journal of the Election*, to counter the venomous abuse circulated by Lang's opponents. Don Baker notes that "the half-penny paper contain[ed] not only serious articles but also squibs, jokes, satirical verse and so on."[15] The paper poked fun at Wentworth who, having previously made thinly veiled threats of colonial separation had since assumed a constitution of staunch conservatism. *The Representative* cheekily asked its readers, "Q. Why is Mr. Wentworth like a spoiled child? A. Because he is frightened at The Doctor."

An indefatigable campaigner, Lang spent the month of July delivering speeches to large and enthusiastic audiences in every tavern, hall, and hotel that would have him. Such was the zeal of Lang's supporters that extra police and military were assigned for election day because officials feared a potential riot.[16] It was difficult to find someone willing to run against Lang and expose themselves to the slings and arrows of his vulpine wit. A petition signed by 320 Sydney citizens and published in the Irish Catholic *Freeman's Journal* on 11 July requested that John Rose Holden run for the vacated seat. The petition said they were satisfied that Holden would exercise his influence to serve the colony during this "present important crisis." Holden responded favourably to the request in the same paper on 18 July.[17]

It is highly significant that Lang appealed only to civic republicanism, rather than separatist republicanism during the election campaign. Separatism, it seems, was not a vote winner but civic republicanism was. Lang subscribed not only to the classic civic republican theory of political participation but also to the British civic republican tradition that insisted the voice of the third estate must be heard by the first and second (*id est*, the monarchy and the aristocracy). Lang informed his supporters, "I should advocate a great extension of the franchise, so as to include whole classes of the community who are at present debarred from all political rights." Both as a preacher and a politician, Lang was intimately concerned with shaping the moral character of the colony. As evidenced by his many electoral victories, he found great public sympathy in his mission to denounce government corruption and champion the common good. Civic republicanism centres around the promotion of virtue, and when Lang announced he would "strenuously oppose" the resumption of convict transportation "in whatever form, and under whatever pretensions," he was sure he was doing just that.

The political rhetoric of Henry Parkes leading up to the election can also be seen as an appeal to the civic republican ethos. He boasted in the pages of the *Herald* that Lang's campaign committee numbered nearly one hundred diverse citizens, few of which were personal acquaintances of Lang, but all were united in a desire to promote the "common welfare of their country." Parkes described Lang as the champion of the Sydney *comuyns*, the "suffering poor," and predicted the election would be a "national triumph."[18] No hint of separatist republicanism came from either Parkes or Lang during the campaign period, nor was the Australian League mentioned.

Nomination day was 23 July at Macquarie Place. In the end there were no riots, though the *Freeman's Journal* commented that "the attendance on the whole was as large as we have ever seen assembled on a like occasion," with an estimated five thousand persons present. It noted also that, considering the mud was a foot deep, the numbers strongly confirmed "that the event excited a good deal of interest."[19] On the whole, the crowd supported Lang, cheering emphatically when he spoke and jeering loudly at the moral criticisms Holden levelled against him. The ensuing debate can certainly be seen through the prism of civic republicanism. R.M. Pite (who seconded Lang's nomination) clearly articulated the contest as a struggle for political freedom requiring "a representative who was deeply imbued with the love of freedom." Rather than promoting their own candidate, the Holden team dedicated the bulk of their speeches to attacking Lang, particularly over his perceived anti-Irish, anti-Catholic opinions. This turned out to be a pyrrhic tactic, however, since it resulted in the entire debate being about Lang, an outcome that would have doubtless pleased the doctor.

Lang appealed to the current class antagonism when he described the gross parliamentary overrepresentation of the rural bourgeoisie compared with the urban masses as a "grand evil." He further affiliated himself with the *comuyns* by making the "somewhat ominous" observation that Holden had been nominated by two lawyers, while he was proud to be endorsed by "two plain citizens." Lang stood on three primary platforms. He argued against transportation and for equal electorates. He also argued for the civic republican ideal of political participation of virtuous citizens. He claimed, in keeping with the first point of the People's Charter, that "everyman not under sentence as a felon, and not receiving public charity, should have the right to vote." This civic republican argument was embedded in British tradition as Lang added, "this [is] the constitutional right of England," and 'it was the right they experienced under Alfred."[20] Lang's reference to a king is no small indication that his election platform did not entertain separatist but only civic republican theory.

Lang's civic republican message was meekly rebutted by Holden's Burkean ethos, that the only election promise he need make was to act according to his conscience. He was nebulous and unconvincing on several key issues. Although he had denounced transportation, he maintained that it might be reintroduced under certain conditions.[21] Lang's hard-line anti-transportation stance juxtaposed this quite favourably with the urban voters. Similarly, Holden spoke vaguely about the electoral boundaries, leading many to think he would support the wealthy squattocracy. Lang vowed to uphold the utilitarian ideal to deliver the "greatest possible good to the greatest possible number."[22] He argued eloquently, again with Chartist undertones, that Sydney, containing one-third of the New South Wales population, was under-represented and vowed to fight Wentworth to secure the people's rights.

Despite Lang's considerable support from the disenfranchised laypeople, the electors of Sydney granted him only a marginal victory, 987 votes to Holden's 931. That evening Lang stood at the window of the committee room at the Star Hotel acknowledging the wild applause from the large crowd that had gathered in the rain to offer their congratulations. When Lang prepared to enter the Council chambers for the first time on 30 July 1850, he was greeted by a rowdy and excitable crowd of eight thousand that hurled abuse at Wentworth and lavished praise on Lang with equal enthusiasm.[23]

How is it then, that Lang was so popular with the people and yet separatist republicanism, which became synonymous with his name, never flowered into the large-scale political movement that would explain such adoration? Lang's promotion of civic republicanism holds the key. Despite the prima facie case his publications and lectures on the topic may present, Lang was not seen by his contemporaries as a one-dimensional separatist. The *Sydney Illustrated News*, for example, was tenaciously anti-separatist, yet it was able to mourn the death of Lang in 1878, stating thta "no man ever died in Australia more worthy of gratitude than the lamented John Dunmore Lang."[24] Lang was certainly a passionate separatist republican, but above even that, he was a committed democrat. The democracy he believed in was not simple freedom from interference; it was the creation of a free society governed by virtue and honour bound to serve the common good. It was Lang's promotion of civic republicanism that earned him fame during his lifetime and an honoured place in the history of democracy in Australia.

In 1851 Lang embarked on the seventh of the numerous voyages to Britain he would make in his lifetime. During March and April he composed a political tome that would encapsulate his vision for Australia. Aptly titled *Freedom and Independence for the Golden Lands of Australia*, the work was undeniably a call for a separatist republicanism. Inspired by his time in America, he dreamt of the United Provinces of Australia, the new Southern power that would dominate and civilize the Pacific Islands. This work was not only an argument for a type of government but must also be considered a blueprint for a specific type of society. Lang was a radical democrat by the standards of the day; however, it was not so much a classically liberal democracy but rather a civic republican democracy he petitioned for. In plain yet confronting language he explains in the introduction that "in short, it is the object of the writer to show, that Great Britain hitherto has been all wrong in her principles and practice in the matter of colonization."[25] Lang goes on to exhibit a classic whig interpretation of history. All British policy, he argues, had been essentially wrong until the passing of the Reform Act and the repeal of the Corn and Navigation Laws. In the grand passage of history it was as if Britain had realized her folly only yesterday. A complete overhaul of colonial administration, deduced the doctor, should be next on the imperial agenda.

Lang has been dubbed a prophet without honour by Ken Elford, and it is true that his work is rarely acknowledged as the tour de force in Australian political literature that it is.[26] *Freedom and Independence* is arguably the greatest political treatise ever to be written about Australia, and yet Don Baker mentions it only in passing in his gargantuan biography of Lang. This lack of acclaim is perhaps owing to the view that it is a failed pitch for separatist republicanism. Although it certainly is that, it is much more as well. It is a highly sophisticated vision of a democratic Australia run along civic republican principles. It is true that Lang held the deepest of convictions that Australia needed to imitate the United States and evolve into the great America of the South Seas, a goal that, for no lack of zealousness on his part, was never realized. Nevertheless, the vast majority of the objectives in *Freedom and Independence* were achieved within a decade of its publication. Although Lang's full vision may have stretched beyond the grasp of most of his contemporaries; his finger was clearly on the pulse of this young British society.

In *Freedom and Independence* Lang dedicated very little space to discussing monarchy in general and none whatsoever to criticizing the British monarchy in particular. Thomas Paine's *Rights of Man*, which Lang was doubtless aware of, defended the separatist republicanism of the French with biting sarcasm. Paine famously ridiculed hereditary rulers, insisting that the concept was as absurd as a "hereditary mathematician, or a hereditary wife man; and as ridiculous as a hereditary poet laureate."[27] Lang took a more measured approach and was equally wary of history's "ill-balanced republics."

It may seem strange in a text with a central theme of separatist republicanism, but *Freedom and Independence* was in no way an assault on monarchy. Lang had a specific civic republican vision of a virtuous communal society. Separatist republicanism, quite frankly, was the best avenue to achieve a civic republican utopia.

Lang saw in Australia, just as Machiavelli had seen in Florence, a desperate need to instil and grow patriotism for the defence and success of society. National pride is even referred to as a "gift from God" by the Scots preacher. The emphasis on patriotism is crucial in the civic republican tradition, since it is the emotional force that causes citizens to value the common good over individual gain. "Must the young Australian," Lang asked, "be debarred from the exercise of the generous and manly feeling... when he exclaims with deep emotion, this is my own, my native land!" Lang would go on to outline the democratic political institutions he felt were needed in the Australian colonies but the underlying spirit must be a sense of patriotic duty. That is what would inspire Australians to "virtuous actions." Lang described patriotism as the heart of the system, "give us *this*, and you give us everything to enable us to become a great and glorious people. Withhold *this*, and you give us nothing."

As Machiavelli had done centuries earlier, Lang looked to the ancients for inspiration and wisdom. He saw in the Greek city-states a ready analogy for modern British politics. He praised the republican-minded Greeks and lambasted the "miserable affair" that was British colonization. Lang noted that in Greek colonization (or, in any case in his imagination of it), "Men of all ranks in society, of all professions and occupations, went forth on the great undertaking, and staked their character and fortunes on the issue... As an embryo community, they had all from the first the same interesting associations, and the same endearing recollections of the land they had left... they all left the same locality in the *old* country, and they all settled together in the *new*." The crucial factor for Lang was the sense of communalism, which marks civic republicanism but is all but absent in both tory conservative and liberal philosophy. The Australian convicts and immigrants were assembled from all corners of the three kingdoms and often had little shared identity. Without the civic republican goal of a shared patriotic identity reinforced by civic institutions, the colonies could lose that priceless social capital called virtue. If the colonists continue to settle randomly among utter strangers, then "the moral restraints of their native vicinage are gradually weakened, and perhaps completely lost."

Next Lang considered the history of Roman colonization and in particular the colonization of Britain. Unlike the Greeks, who colonized to transplant redundant populations, the Romans colonized to expand their imperial borders. As with Britain and Australia, the Romans would offer land, travel, and other incentives for colonists to settle on the frontier of the empire. Relying on Cicero's letters, Lang concludes that the Roman cities in Britain soon grew, obtained limited self-government, and quickly came to exhibit "in no inconsiderable degree the civilization and refinement of Rome." Lang asks, "if the Roman colonists of Britain were entitled to their freedom and independence, under the reign of Emperor Honorius, when they seized upon that freedom and independence themselves, why should we, the British colonists of Australia, be refused our freedom and independence under the reign of Queen Victoria?"

Ultimately, Lang was concerned with that most patriarchal of British philosophical epigrams: make the world England. Lang held the same idealized vision of British history and the British constitution that had inspired the Commonwealthmen of the eighteenth century and the regicides of the seventeenth century. This was a civic republican vision, and it was crucial that it be replicated successfully in the Australian colonies. The Aristotelian mixed constitution needed to be maintained by encouraging migrants of all classes, rather than creating a population almost exclusively from the working class. Lang insisted that "the tree of English society must be carefully taken up, with a good ball of earth round the roots, and transplanted whole and entire to Canada or Australia"[28]

Lang's work received mixed reviews in Britain. In a letter dated 2 May 1853, Lang recalled a "pleasant evening" spent with radical statesmen Richard Cobden and John Wright. In his own typically immodest style he went on to state that "they both consider that I have been doing a great work in this country, both for the mother country and for the colonies." In *Freedom and Independence*, he saw himself as "sowing seed" that would ultimately flourish in a British-style, civic republican democracy.[29] The *Westminster Review*, although quick to felicitate Lang, whom they called Australia's Joseph Hume, the "tribune of the people," felt the good doctor was too ambitious in seeking change before the colony was ready. His ideas were acknowledged as sound, but the timing was wrong, since nothing can be achieved by shaking the branches in hope that the apple may drop before it is ripe. The map of the hypothetical United Provinces of Australia drew particular attention. "As if this was already settled," the *Review* chastened, "a map is prefixed, altered to suit the new state of things, and with its coloured divisions, presenting so much the respectable appearance of a *fait accompli*, as somewhat to prepossess the reader in favour of the work." Somewhat unfairly, the conclusion was drawn that "having now declared for a republic, he probably means to finish off by being its first President!"[30]

The *Duchess of Sutherland* returned Lang to Sydney on 16 November 1853. He was more convinced than ever that the spirit of the British constitution was most certainly a civic republican one. He declared in a letter to the *Empire* that the Australian colonies had not been established according to the principles of the British constitution but rather on a "rotten foundation" that was "utterly unworthy." He continued, "the advocates for popular rights ought to agitate for *constitutional* reform; for I consider freedom and independence for the colonies, the most constitutional thing in the world."[31] For Lang, mixed government, local representation, and a society in which virtuous citizens actively participate for the *commune bonum* was the good soil in which the seeds of colonial democracy must be planted. Much like the reformers of Canada, Lang and his supporters would argue that it was not their hatred but in fact their love of Britain that drove them to these civic republican demands.

Although completed a year earlier, *Freedom and Independence*, published in England and targeted at a British market, reached Australia only in late May 1853. The conservative grandparent of Australian news media, the *Sydney Morning Herald*, made no secret of its objection. Not wishing to afford Lang any courtesies that might add legitimacy to his work, a savage review from 31 May began by noting that the grossness and vulgarity of *Freedom and Independence* was suitable enough, since they were characteristics shared with the author. The *Herald* went on to insist that it would rather make no mention of the work, except that it feared the people of England might be misled by Lang and his "noisy friends." Lang's greatest crime was to imply that the colonists of New South Wales were panting for separation when, in the *Herald*'s summation, it was only the "tag-rag and bob-tail" who listened to him pontificating at Malcom's Circus and Macquarie Place. The editors did concede, however, that the future destiny of Australia was to be free. But this was not likely until the colonists numbered in the millions.[32] In a crushing blow for Lang, the only other daily paper in Sydney, run by ally and Australian League founder Henry Parkes, sided with the *Herald* on this issue.

What bitter reading it must have been for Lang when the *Empire* posited that the central leitmotif of *Freedom and Independence* would be discussed with more seriousness in two hundred years.[33]

Although Lang was eager to grow the paltry figures that comprised the Australia League and bring life to his theoretical republic, the bulk of New South Wales society was engaged in excited debate over the form and content of the forthcoming constitution. On 20 May a Select Committee charged with making recommendations on a new constitution was appointed by the Legislative Council. Wentworth chaired, and from what we can ascertain from the incomplete minutes, dominated proceedings.[34] Wentworth's ideal constitution appears to have been coloured by an 1852 pamphlet released by Judge John Nodes Dickinson.[35] The *Report* of the Select Committee was published in the *Herald* on 29 July. The *Report* claimed that having traded correspondence with Sir John Pakington and the Duke of Newcastle, the new constitution should be "similar in its outline to that of Canada."[36] The fact that the Canadian constitutions with their nominated upper houses had attracted fierce protests seemed not to deter Wentworth and his backers.

The *Report* was ruthlessly undemocratic in its recommendation for electing the Lower House, and the *Herald* noted that the committee members clearly had "no wish to sow the seeds of a future democracy."[37] Although the Select Committee endorsed an increase of the franchise to all with freehold property worth £100 or paying £10 per annum for lodging, a change that it boasted would equate to virtual "universal suffrage" for white males, the grossly uneven electoral boundaries were fixed and required a two-thirds vote in the Legislative Assembly to be altered. The net result of the proposals was to entrench the rural bourgeoisie in a position of oligarchic dominance over the Assembly. By keeping the Electoral Act of 1851, the committee was asking the sprawling metropolis of Sydney to be content with six seats, while rotten boroughs under the sqattocracy's orbit could return a member though numbering their constituents in the hundreds. The lesson of 1832 seemed not to matter to the Select Committee, who would see Sydney as unrepresented as Manchester or Birmingham before the passing of the Great Reform Act.

The most extraordinary of the Select Committee's recommendations was not that the Upper House should be nominated but that the Crown should confer hereditary titles on leading colonists, with a view to creating an Antipodean House of Lords. The *Report* suggested that a colonial nobility would "Lay the foundation of an aristocracy which, from their fortune, birth, leisure and the superior education these advantages would superinduce, would soon supply elements for the formation of an Upper House, modeled, as far as circumstances will admit, upon the analogies of the British Constitution." [38] Even for Lang, the push for separatist republicanism had to take a backseat to opposing a bill that would potentially see his bête noire promoted from the moniker he had bestowed, Old Lottery, and ennobled as Baron Wentworth.[39] Wentworth of course would have expected nothing less than fierce opposition from the doctor. He must have felt some disappointment, however, when the *Herald* disowned the idea, concluding that "unless we are very much mistaken, a colonial baronetcy would be an object of ridicule rather than deference."[40]

The *Herald* was to be proved absolutely correct in its assessment as a growing class of urban democrats banded together to oppose Wentworth's vision of an Australian nobility. The Sydney correspondent for the *Melbourne Morning Herald* apologized to his readers that he could not help but jest when he considered Wentworth as Lord Vaucluse, John Macarthur as the Duke of Camden, and Terence Aubrey Murray as the Marquis of Malwaree and Lord of the Ponds.[41] Lang, anticipating this recommendation, had already set the tone for mockery in *Freedom and Independence*. With derisive laughter he asked, "are we to have colonial Peers of Parliament ... the Marquis of Parramatta, for instance, Lord Wollongong, and Viscount Curraducbidgee?"[42] Although Dickinson's pamphlet had eloquently presented colonial hereditary title as a worthy goal, Lang ridiculed it without mercy. In the *Empire* he charged with venomous sarcasm, "fall down and worship these Australian Bunyips, ye Plebeians of New South Wales."[43]

Wentworth's dream was conclusively ridiculed out of serious consideration at a large rally the day before the bill was to be debated in the Legislative Council. Led by Parkes and W.R. Piddington, opponents of the bill had formed a protest group called the New South Wales Constitution Committee. On 15 August 1853 some four thousand Sydney locals filled the Royal Victoria Theatre on Pitt Street. The large turnout was assisted by the shrewd decision by the committee to hold the meeting on a Monday. In Sydney, Mondays were often referred to as Saint Monday on account of the Australian working class habit of unofficially extending the weekend.⁴⁴ The business owners of Sydney may well have cursed their recalcitrant employees, who were absent from work but present at 1:00 P.M. to see the Scottish merchant John Gilchrist open the meeting.

There was an electric atmosphere in the room akin to a revival meeting. The preacher on stage would play off the energy of the congregation as they engaged in call and response worship. Piddington shouted to the crowd, "COLONISTS! Will you submit to be robbed of your rights?" From the crowded pit to the upper and lower boxes came a universal shout, "NO!" Piddington outlined several aspects of the proposed bill, including the uneven electoral boundaries, and the crowd voiced their disapproval. The loudest groans were saved for mention of hereditary title. To this the crowd howled in protest.

The keynote address was delivered by John Bayley Darvell. Educated at Eton and Cambridge, the Yorkshire barrister and politician added great respectability to the Constitution Committee. Though a textbook loose fish, Darvell was still a nominal tory and hence a prized convert. He spoke at length, denying that Wentworth's plan would recreate the institution of the British House of Lords and denying that a nominated Upper House could hold the people's confidence. Revealing how far under Lang's gambit he was, albeit temporarily, he made the astonishing statement that it was of little consequence whether New South Wales was under a limited president or a limited king or queen so long as the people's rights were maintained. He poured fierce scorn on the Wentworth apologia, which suggested that any imperfections in the Select Committee's bill could always be altered in the future. Darvell was offended at this small-minded notion. Did they not realize, he cried, that the colonists had "the most glorious opportunity [ever] offered to any free and enlightened community in the world?" This was not some bill of minor consequence that could later be tinkered with. This special moment in history was chosen "to frame a Constitution for the great Australian empire – not for the present only, but to last, and probably determine the destiny of that empire for all time." The crowd erupted in thunderous applause.

When Darvell had concluded, Parkes took the floor with some fine oratory of his own. Following these lengthy addresses, the audience could have been excused for displaying impatience as the final speaker took the floor. A diminutive twenty-four-year-old philomath named Daniel Deniehy had neither the clout nor the experience of his predecessors, and he began by meekly confessing that his inclusion in the panel was a mystery even to him. The audience promptly jeered him for speaking too softly. He replied with gracious humour informing the crowd that he might compensate for the small volume of his voice by calling things by their right names. Deniehy began to speak louder and with greater confidence, and it would be his speech, rather than those of his distinguished colleagues, that would be seen as the *coup de grâce* to the hereditary title clause and be revered as one of the greatest ever in Australian political history.

Quick-witted and sharp-tongued, Deniehy questioned whether the "democratic escapades" of his youth still entitled Wentworth to respect given the extreme measures he was resorting to in his political twilight to stem the democratic impulse. To great cheers from the crowd, Deniehy lambasted the "serpentine movements" of Wentworth's bloc, those "political oligarchs, who treated the people at large as if they were cattle to be bought and sold in the market place." Deniehy had the rambunctious crowd bent over in fits of laughter with his colourful insults. Wentworth and his acolytes were described as "harlequin aristocrats," "Botany Bay magnificos," and "Australian mandarins." Most famously of all, Deniehy would borrow Lang's analogous use of the mythical Aboriginal creature and decry the creation of a "Bunyip aristocracy." Deniehy went on to propose an alternative vision of a civic republican meritocracy. In discernibly Christian civic republican language, he charged that "there is an aristocracy worthy of our ambition. Wherever man's skill is eminent, wherever glorious manhood asserts its elevation, there is an aristocracy that confers honour on the land that possesses it. That is God's aristocracy (Great cheering). That is an aristocracy that will grow and expand under free institutions, and bless the land where it flourishes."[45]

In his fascinating and ambitious biography of democracy, John Keane insists that Deniehy "deserves to stand among the unsung, forgotten heroes of the era of Australian democracy."[46] Public memory has not been kind to Deniehy, and he certainly can be considered an unsung hero.[47] Like Arthur O'Connor in Ireland, he was one of the most important radicals, but few people in the country he served would even recognize his name.[48] Keane concludes, however, that the Bunyip Aristocracy failed in cementing power in the new constitution "by a whisker." More generally, he attributes democratic advances in Australia (and Canada) to fate, noting that "for reasons of politics and money, or accident or whim, things were done abroad that could not be done at home."[49] This sentiment does not do justice to the hard work of colonial reformers. Far from accident or whim, there was design and purpose in the reform movement and a determination to usher in the Durhamite grand compromise. Wentworth did not come within a whisker of becoming Lord Vaucluse. The idea would not even make it to London.

Although Wentworth would defend the draft constitution the day after the protest meeting in the Legislative Council, even he seemed to accept that the public meeting had ipso facto buried some of the clauses. In the end the Select Committee's most controversial recommendation would never be debated in the British parliament, because the hereditary title clause was removed from the bill sent to London. This was just as well, since the influential *Times* had already been highly effective in turning English opinions against the proposed colonial nobility. The squattocracy was scorned as unworthy opportunists, and the paper noted that "the proprietary class are intoxicated by the change, and men who a few years ago were meditating a composition with their creditors are now not content with demanding the life-long tenure of the office of legislator, but require... hereditary peerage."[50] Nonetheless, it was not English but Australian agitation that defeated the proposal.

The ultimate result of the 1853 debates would be the New South Wales Constitution Act 1855 (UK). The act was a great leap forward for democracy in Australia, yet it also sounded the death knell for separatist republicanism. Two issues had the potential to push the Australians down the same revolutionary road that the Canadians, however half-heartedly, had set on in 1837: first, the issue of anti-transportation and second, the more general issue of a lack of democracy in a society that was panting for it. The fierce local opposition to transportation combined with the discovery of gold effectively ended any prospect of a reintroduction of that system in the 1850s. The following two chapters will look at the anti-transportation movement and the gold rushes, respectively. The granting of responsible government in 1855 removed the last agitation that could conceivably goad the colonists into forming Lang's great federal republic. Yet the rejection of separatist republicanism did not follow the rejection of civic republicanism.

On the contrary, civic republicanism was accepted to such an extent that separatist republicanism was not needed or even wanted.

The Australian colonists were clearly proponents of democracy and democratic reform. This much is *res ipsa loquitur* and can be gleaned through the support not only of radicals but also of moderate conservatives for democratic reform. The conservative *Sydney Morning Herald*, for example, rejoiced that the fixed electorate idea was to be scrapped from the new constitution, calling this development a "step in the right direction." It commented, "the more nearly we can approximate in practice to the principle of having electoral districts of equal population, the more thoroughly do we establish representative institutions."[51] A spectacle at the Royal Victoria Theatre provided a beautiful visual metaphor of the various political positions showing a general commitment to democratic principles. As Gilchrist made his introductory remarks, there sat together on stage the conservative Darvell, the moderate reformer Parkes, and the republican radical Deniehy. The only colour of Australia's political mural that was absent was the hard-line toryism that Wentworth had adopted. This was the same strain of toryism that fought the Canadian reformers and consequently saw men like Joseph Howe switch sides. But if Australia was committed to democracy by the middle of the nineteenth century, what kind of democracy was it to be?

Although the Australian colonists most certainly took note of the great liberal philosophers of the eighteenth and nineteenth century, civic republicanism was a constant ideological presence and could fairly be considered the more influential of the two. Negative liberty was only ever a great theme in Australian political discourse when the colonists felt they were being faced with tyranny, as in the punishment of Joseph Sudds and the Eureka Stockade. On the whole, the Australians wanted a democracy founded on positive liberty. They wanted to maintain the British connection and to rejoice in the sense of virtue and communalism that came with it. Yet simultaneously, they wanted control over their own affairs and freedom to resist the imperial voice when its commands were found to be without virtue. The colonists in Australia and Canada wanted to have their cake and eat it too, and Lord Durham and the civic republican grand compromise allowed them to do just that.

Dual-patriotism did not mean that the colonists loved Australia and Britain in the same way. One was the land of their imagination, the source of their heritage and culture. The other was the land of the adoption and for increasing numbers, the land of their birth. It was in Australia that they hoped to build a virtuous society based on the best principles of Britain. They were truly loath to see their new home develop into anything short of a paragon of British values guided by the sacred rights and liberties of free people enshrined in the British constitution. Perhaps the Australians were particularly motivated to create and exhibit a colony of virtue to cover the embarrassment of their penal origins. The Canadians too, however, without this motivation, were equally keen to prove they were in no way second-class Britons. The next chapter will explore the tenacity with which the Australians would fight to see their colony of virtue become a reality.

8

A Colony of Virtue:
The Anti-Transportation League

Lord Grey evidently thinks that crime is in danger of becoming extinct, and delivers premiums for its encouragement. A little larceny is a dangerous thing. Dive deep into your neighbour's pocket, if you wish to visit El Dorado. Small crimes are henceforth to be punished, large ones to be rewarded.

Launceston Examiner, 25 February 1852

For the entire span of the nineteenth century, there was no single greater influence on the way Britain and the world saw the Australian colonies or how the colonists saw themselves than the convict stain. Such was the enormity of this psychological trauma that were it not for the immense power of sport and war, the same could likely be said of the twentieth century. From the earliest days of settlement, those free British settlers known as the sterling and pure merinos recoiled with horror at the black mark that besmirched this new British society.[1] It is little wonder then that the emerging large and free population demanded that the source of this shame be removed from the colony. In doing so, the colonists were making stern demands that can be seen through the prism of civic republicanism. On the one hand, the colonists were making clear that they would not meekly accept any ordinance from Britain for no other reason than that it had managed to pass through the houses of the Imperial Parliament. On the other hand, a vision of a particular kind of society was beginning to emerge. In arguing against transportation, the colonists were, at least in part, arguing for a society of virtue. This chapter will explore the campaign against transportation and its implications for Australian nationalism and civic republicanism.

The campaign against transportation is a staple of early Australian historiography, and the pan-colonial nature of the Australasian League is generally interpreted, to varying degrees, as a precursor or early example of Australian nationalism.[2] It is telling that in his history of Australia, Henry Parkes, often dubbed the "Father of Federation," dedicates the opening chapter to the anti-transportation movement.[3] While the story of anti-transportation is well told both by contemporary and by modern historians, this chapter will pay particular attention to the sort of language used to encapsulate the movement. In 1992, Dan Huon named his speech on anti-transportation for the Tasmanian Historical Research Association, "By Moral Means Only," a reference to the Launceston League's constitution.[4] A few years later Sister Veronica Brady titled her John West lecture "Conviction and Conscience."[5] The rhetoric, both of the protesters themselves and of their subsequent historians, implies a firm belief in the perceived morality of their cause. The very language of this well-told story suggests more was at stake than an unpopular policy or even the rights of the colonists to influence the policy-makers. The colonists were commencing battle over the spirit of the society. They had a particular vision of what a virtuous British society should look like. This chapter will conclude that the movement was very much influenced by civic republican thought in its moral agitation.

Was the anti-transportation movement an example of Lockean liberalism triumphing over an autocratic British imperialism? If one is to adopt such a view, there are numerous historical inconsistencies to be overcome. The first and most glaring is the deep devotion to Britain and Britishness regularly displayed by the opponents of transportation, even in their protests against British policy.[6] The second problem is the distinctly anti-Lockean stance the protesters took with regard to landowners. Rather than allowing independent landowners to freely carry out their business, the movement sought to severely curtail the labour supply for the greater good of the community. Finally, the rhetoric and spirit of the protests were communitarian, not individualistic. The cause was centred on the *bonum commune communitatis* not individual rights. This chapter will look at the literature surrounding the convict debate, the formation of the Australasian League and select protests to examine the role of civic republican thinking.

The merits of convict transportation to Australia were widely debated in the early years of the nineteenth century. During the 1830s, transportation and the costs and benefits involved were regularly discussed in Britain. In Australia, however, the issue had galvanized to the point where only the squattocracy and a handful of mercantilists who directly benefited from the supply of cheap labour spoke favourably of the system in Australia. The public humiliation of accommodating Britain's criminal class became increasingly unbearable as Sydney, Melbourne, and Hobart evolved into mature British metropolises. John Dunmore Lang would gain wide admiration in the 1830s for his personal zealousness and entrepreneurial creativity in countering the evil of transportation with migration programs aimed at bringing virtuous, protestant citizens to the colonies.[7]

Over the next two decades, Lang became increasingly radical in his thinking and increasingly contrarian in his actions, earning the title "the chaplain of pandemonium."[8] In November 1834, however, as the latest boatload of hand-picked, virtuous protestant workers, teachers, and clergy arrived on the *James*, the conservative *Sydney Herald* happily concluded that "there are few men to whom the Colony is more indebted, in reference to correct views on emigration."[9] The moral state of New South Wales was a topic of grave concern for many of the respectable elements, especially the clergy. The blame for the high incidence of drunkenness and sexual promiscuity was, perhaps unfairly, assigned almost exclusively to the convicts. Applauding Lang, the *Herald* stated, "this Colony requires a constant infusion of moral worth... we require a continuous flow and gushing stream of virtuous industrious emigration, to neutralize the corruption of Convictism."[10]

In 1837 four important works dealing with convict transportation were published. Lang released *Transportation and Colonization; or, the causes of the comparative failure of the transportation system in the Australian colonies: with suggestions.*[11] He also released a second edition of *An Historical and Statistical Account of New South Wales.*[12] The Catholic Vicar-General of New Holland and Van Diemen's Land, William Bernard Ullathrone, released *The Catholic Mission in Australasia.*[13] James Macarthur, the son of the great pastoralist John Macarthur, released a tome titled *New South Wales; its present state and future prospects: being a statement with documentary evidence.* Taken as a whole, these publications represent the wide-ranging views on transportation. While Macarthur would argue for its continuation, Lang and Ullathrone would argue against, for very different reasons.

James Macarthur's work was a basic apologia for the tory clique known as the squattocracy and a championing of transportation as a means of cheap labour. Macarthur argued that the "radical fault" with British transportation policy was not the influx of convicts but rather the dearth of "settlers of respectability." Macarthur acknowledged the "lamentable depravity of manners" and "fearful prevalence of crime" in New South Wales and also laid the blame squarely at the feet of the convicts and former convicts.[14] Yet he insisted this was no reason to cease transportation. Without transportation keeping the price of labour artificially low, the free settlers and especially the landowners would suffer by having to pay increased wages to former convicts, who would then be profiting from their crimes. The problem was the lack of respectable settlers, which allowed convicts to rise to positions that would otherwise be unattainable. The lack of religious instruction and the easy availability of alcoholic spirits were also problematic. The *Sydney Monitor* was quick to dismiss Macarthur's work and its "oligarchical scheme."[15] The emancipist Dr William Bland was incensed enough to publish an eighty-page "review" of the work in response to what he considered erroneous facts and opinions.[16]

Ullathrone's work represented a humanitarian view that had some following in Britain. Following the abolition of slavery, there was a school of thought that was sensitive to the plight of anyone in chains and keen to differentiate British policy from that of the Americans.[17] In promoting migration in 1849, Lang urged British subjects to choose Australia over "Slaveland."[18] Catherine Hall has noted that for respectable English gentlemen in the mid-nineteenth century, "to be a supporter of the weak and dependent... constituted precisely the 'independence' of middle-class masculinity."[19] Ullathrone concluded that the transportation of convicts was an unjust punishment, the cruelty of which was disproportionate to the crimes committed and an affront to Christian justice. While Macarthur spoke of the economic rationale for continuing transportation, Ullathrone spoke of the moral prerogative for its cessation. The *Catholic Mission in Australasia* had a considerable impact both in Europe and in the colonies. The work sold some eighty thousand copies in six editions and was translated into German, French, Italian, and Dutch.[20] A letter to the *Launceston Examiner* from December 1850 bore the clear mark of Ullathrone's thinking. Writing under the alias "Christian," the author commented that "whilst the colony is waging war with that greatest of all evils, transportation, the prisoners are the greatest sufferers."[21]

Ullathrone's time in Australia, though often frustrating and shorter than he would have liked, had clearly affected him deeply. He spoke of the sacred bonds and personal relationships he had formed with the "daughter of crime" and "the dark-faced man." In particular, he felt a special affinity with the suffering male convicts who "like a brother to afflicted brother" would pour out their "whole soul into my breast." The chief and fatal flaw with transportation was that it did nothing to reform criminals but rather placed them together to learn each other's habits and become worse still. Ullathrone makes clear his dystopian vision for Australia if this grand evil is not stopped: "We have been doing an ungracious and ungodly thing. We have taken a vast portion of God's earth, and have made it a cess-pool; we have taken the oceans, which, with their wonders, gird the globe, and have made them the channels of a sink; we have poured down scum upon scum, and dregs upon dregs, of the offscourings of mankind, and, as these harden and become consistent together, we are building up with them a nation of crime, to be, unless something is speedily done, a curse and a plague, and a by-word to all the people of the earth."[22]

Lang took a different approach in condemning transportation. While Ullathrone wept for the convicts who had little chance of reformation in Botany Bay, Lang wept for the free settler and the native born, who were thrust into a society where drunkenness and sexual immorality were the rule and not the exception. Lang did not initially call for transportation to be completely abolished, although he soon would, but rather for it to be scaled back and reformed. Like Macarthur, Lang insisted the colonies were starved of respectable persons. In a major point of contention, however, Lang called for an end to convict assignment to private landholders, since the practice allowed an enormous discrepancy between the treatment of various convicts. One might be severely punished while the other was virtually rewarded for having committed a similar crime. Above all, it was the deleterious impact of transportation on the morality of the colonies that goaded Lang the most. Without immediate reform, the current system would destine New South Wales to remain indefinitely "a mere gaol and dunghill for the British empire."[23]

Lang's weekly paper, the *Colonist*, praised his own "sober and dispassionate inquiry" while attacking the "gross personal allusions and injudicious statements which disgrace the volume of a recent writer on New South Wales."²⁴ Lang received generally positive assessments in the *Sydney Gazette,* the *Perth Gazette,* and the *Hobart Town Courier* (which was itself based on a favourable review from London's *Atlas*).²⁵ The *Sydney Monitor* published objections from Edward Hall thta pertained only to the accuracy of his stories rather than the tenor of his argument.²⁶ Lang's works were lauded in London's *Times,* whose editors were grateful for being informed of the absurdity of transportation as a punishment. The *Times* was horrified to learn that convicts and former convicts were earning fortunes, buying property, and even influencing public morals through the news media when they should have been subjected to "punishment, and gloom, and repentance." The lamentation continued: "We find in place of these an absolute rouge's saturnalia, a scouting of the common decencies of the law; convict attorneys conducting suits, convict editors inculcating morals, convict politicians spouting about the rights of man, convict Lovelaces with harems of convict women – all the debauchery and drunkenness, all the swindling and thievery... the opportunities for vice (the chance of earning money to pamper it) are a thousand times greater than in the parent country!"²⁷

In the same year that these comments were published, Sir William Molesworth headed a British parliamentary committee that concluded with Lang and Ullathrone that the policy was unequal and benefited neither the mother country nor the colonies.²⁸ The squattocracy and their London lobbyists were unsuccessful against such strong colonial opposition and on 22 May the Order-in-Council Ending Transportation of Convicts 1840 (UK) removed New South Wales from the list of places where British convicts could be sent. This was a significant recognition of the progress New South Wales had made from a convict society to a society with convicts. Having been declared a penal settlement over half a century ago by an Order-in-Council from 6 December 1786, New South Wales stood in the 1840s on the precipice of freedom and democracy.²⁹ Transportation continued, however, to Van Diemen's Land, much to the chagrin of both Vandemonians and the mainland colonists, especially those in Port Phillip district, who feared that Tasmanian convicts would simply cross Bass Strait and continue to pollute their communities. The status of New South Wales was also precarious, as a strong attempt to reintroduce transportation would take place in 1848.

Although Botany Bay was the popular synonym in the English-speaking world for penal settlement, it was the island colony of Van Diemen's Land that would give birth to the great movement that would unite for the first time the Australian colonies in political protest. The history of Van Diemen's Land is a tragic one. The Indigenous population was decimated through disease and violence following white contact.[30] Van Diemen's Land had a reputation for being a violent society and Aboriginals, women, and the convicts themselves were particularly vulnerable.[31] In his popular fiction work from 1874, *His Natural Life,* Marcus Clarke described the brutal ill-treatment inflicted on Tasmanian convicts.[32] Despite often being the victims, the respectable citizens of Van Diemen's Land considered convicts to be the cause of colonial violence and other vices. They were outraged that transportation to their distant island was to continue. As with New South Wales, the free population cared not for weighing economic benefits or academic deliberations in a cold London office. They cared about the place where they were born and lived, they cared about the state of their society, and they wanted the moral leprosy of convictism to finally be gone.

An early Australian folk song published in England in 1830 warned would-be criminals of the hellish fate that awaited them should they end up transported to Van Diemen's Land. The tune claimed:

Oh when that we were landed upon that fatal bay,
The planters they came flocking round full twenty score or more.
They ranked us up like horses and sold us out of hand,
They yoked us up to the plough my boys to plough Van Diemen's Land…

Come all you gallant poachers give ear unto my song,
It is a bit of good advice although it is not long.
Lay by your dog and snare to you I do speak plain,
If you knew the hardship we endure you ne'er would poach again.[33]

The ballad made reference to the cruelty of the land owners, the rough life of the male convicts, and the sexual promiscuity of the female convicts. With such an extreme gender imbalance in the colony, even the female convicts who married were of "good usage" to the male population. The song continued, "As for our wretched females, see them we seldom can. There are twenty to one woman upon Van Diemen's Land." The connection between convict transportation, moral laxity, and sexual immorality was clearly implied in the song and others like it. The negativity associated with Van Diemen's Land was such that a writer for Hobart's *Colonial Times* lamented that the free colonies "urge strongly upon free women of ordinary respectability not to come here, being that they would be assailed to their destruction in every possible way."[34] Real or imagined, there was no question in the minds of the free population from where this societal degradation came.

Perhaps it was the threat of reintroducing transportation to mainland Australia in 1848 that sparked the Tasmanians into action. In any case their patience with a strongly disliked system was wearing thin, and the talk of expansion only confirmed the wide-spread suspicion that British colonial policy was heading in the wrong direction and the time for firm action was nigh. The Tasmanians drew heavily from the experience of British radicals and were doubtless influenced in the style and form of their protest by the Chartists. The influence of British radical protesters on their Australian brethren has been largely overlooked by historians. Paul Pickering has noted that Henry Parkes praised the British movement as a useful "example" worthy of emulation and has theorized that even the suffix "League" was almost certainly an inheritance from the British Anti-Corn Law League.[35] Parkes himself hinted at the link when he predicted in 1851 that transportation was "as certainly doomed to speedy extinction as were the Corn Laws."[36] The prospectus of the Anti-Transportation League was published in the *Launceston Examiner* on 6 January 1849. Supporters were called on to use "every means in their power" to oppose transportation and the employment of convicts who did arrive. This was a spiritual and moral battle, and the prospectus ended with a declaration that should their mere human attempts fail to end these "horrors and vices" their cause would be taken up by "Him who judgeth right."[37]

On Wednesday 24 January 1849, three hundred people gathered at Launceston's Cornwall Assembly Room to form the Anti-Transportation League. The excitable company included powerful banker Thomas Walker, public servant and farmer Theodore Bartley, Brighton-born pastoralist William P. Weston and his close friend, the gifted orator and Congregationalist minister, John West.

James Cox, who owned a property of nearly seven thousand acres at Morven, known as Clarendon, declared to those gathered that in the light of the Crown's betrayal by attempting to revive transportation, the time had come to "not only speak but act." The group were in firm agreement that "convictism in any shape is an evil destructive of their best interests."

The fight against transportation was very much fought on moral grounds, and it is no coincidence that such a large number of Christian ministers were among the leading critics of transportation. Apart from Reverend West, fellow Congregationalist Charles Price, Wesleyan William Butters, Anglican Dr William Henry Browne, and Chaplain Henry Plow Kane were in attendance at the formation of the league. Membership of the league was based not on monetary contribution but simply a gentlemen's written agreement "not to engage any convict, whether probationer or ticket-of-leave, who shall have arrived in this colony since the first day of January."[38] This would have seemed pure madness to the mind of James Macarthur, since the landowners were being asked to forfeit their access to cheap and in some cases free labour. Nevertheless, several large landowners were active foundation members. Along with Walker, Bartley, and Cox, Richard (later Sir Richard) Dry, the native-born inheritor of Elphin Farm near Launceston, was one of the loudest voices at Cornwall Room. These men were acting against their economic interest in favour of the moral interest of the colony. Democratic liberalism, of course, offers no incentive or explanation for this kind of selfless communalism. Rather, this triumph of the greater good over self-gain is textbook civic republicanism.

In his *History of Tasmania*, John West emphasized the moral bankruptcy that marked Australia's origins. Unlike the American pilgrims seeking freedom of religion, the white settlers in Australia burned down their first church "to escape the tedium of attendance." While the first leaders of America were the clergy, in Australia it was a group of soldiers who made money from the sale of liquor and were guilty of both alcoholism and fornication. It was inevitable that Australia would have to begin its white existence with a despotic system of government, argued West. Despite this unfortunate beginning, "the genius of British freedom has ever overshadowed the British colony, and awed the despotic ruler." The establishment of British laws, British courts of justice, British principles of liberty and, crucially, free British immigrants transformed the colonies once so wrapped in vice into thriving British communities. It was little short of a miracle for West that the honest British citizens had shown that a colony of virtue could be created even from such scandalous beginnings. West praised the democratization of the colonies and insisted they were "indebted to the whigs." And yet, men like Wentworth or any others who attempt to curb democracy or allow transportation were the most dangerous of all.[39]

It is noteworthy that in Van Diemen's Land, as in New South Wales, Nova Scotia, the Canadas, and elsewhere, democracy was presumed to be normative before the granting of responsible government. It was only the oligarchic cliques of the British Empire, the rural bourgeoisie, the Family Compact, and the other tory cabals who held out against democracy and, like Sir Francis Bond Head, considered it their aristocratic duty to combat this plebeian philosophy. This brand of toryism, the radicals and whiggish liberals insisted, simply did not understand the spirit of the British constitution. The *Examiner* indignantly informed its readers that "it is an axiom in British rule, that none can take from the people what they do not grant."[40] Years before responsible government would be introduced and at a time when Van Diemen's Land was still an active penal settlement, Bartley threw his arms up in exasperation and questioned how the people could be ignored when they had made a unified supplication to both houses of parliament and the foot of the throne. Durham's seed had found fertile grounds in the Australian colonies, and the people's right to dictate local policy would not be compromised. Bartley bellowed this question to the crowded room: "will you employ the prisoners sent to this country?" The reply was passionate and heartfelt: "No, no, we won't!"

Richard Dry commented on the general attitude of those present, and of the colony at large, towards the behaviour of the British government. He described the mood as one of "indignation, astonishment and regret."[41] Australia's feelings towards Britain in the middle of the nineteenth century were nothing if not complicated. As Lang, Deniehy, and Charles Harpur would discover, the appetite for separatism was frustratingly elusive. Yet even that was more appealing than to persevere under the direction of Earl Grey and the Downing Street gang, men who understood little of Van Diemen's Land's woes and, so it appeared, cared even less.

Pickering is quick to highlight that anti-transportation rallies often bore witness to a seemingly odd juxtaposition. He notes that an event in Hobart Town on 25 August 1851 began with a hearty rendition of "God Save the Queen" followed by the effigy burning of her minister (Grey) and governor (Denison) and the slandering of her government.[42] Dry paints the picture of a people who felt their loyalty was going unappreciated. They were indignant that they were not receiving the rights or respect owed to them as a free British society. They were astonished that the people's clear and unified voice could be disregarded. Finally, it was with regret that they considered the disgraceful attitude of the Colonial Office, which acted in their good Queen's name. It felt as though the chains on every convict transported to Van Diemen's Land had, through mismanagement, been placed by Earl Grey over the wrists of every freeman on the island. The *Examiner* called for that patriotic virtue so central to the civic republican tradition. If patriotism did not cause the virtuous citizens to rise up with "terrible force on the enemies of the colony," then it would be doomed to become "a great gaol, with one merchant and three shopkeepers to supply the families of the gaolers."[43]

Despite these strong sentiments from Van Diemen's Land, on the other side of the world plans were being set in place to see transportation continued to the southern island and reintroduced on the mainland. On 12 April 1850 Earl Grey gave a speech to the House of Lords in which he defended transportation to Australia and outlined his plans for its expansion. Acknowledging the problems in the colonies, Grey insisted that the "balance of evil" would have been far greater had the convicts been kept in Britain.[44] So strongly did he feel about the issue that he proposed separating New South Wales into two provinces and to resume transportation to the squattocracy's hinterland while avoiding the urban metropolis.

Grey informed the Lords that "New South Wales and Van Diemen's Land are completely the creation of transportation," adding that Port Phillip, soon to be separated and baptized Victoria was "hardly less so." Inwardly, Grey had probably accepted that the free population of the bourgeoning cities of Sydney and Melbourne would never allow transportation to the Eastern mainland. Instead he focused on Van Diemen's Land, perhaps hoping that the powerful mainland lobby would be indifferent to the fate of their southern neighbour. He explained: "I consider the colonists of Van Diemen's Land to have no just right to call upon this country to discontinue the practice of sending convicts there… This country has spent millions of money in fitting it for the reception of convicts; and the free population which has established itself there for the sake of the pecuniary advantages of that expenditure, has no right whatever to expect that the policy of this country should be altered when they think proper to demand it." In the closing of his speech Grey revealed that despite the Canadian experience, he was still not fully at ease with the concept of responsible government. In frustration he lambasted the cocksure Tasmanians for thinking that the presence of representative institutions in their colony meant that the parliament of Britain was superseded. In Grey's estimation, the authority of the Crown "ought to be firmly maintained and asserted" by continuing transportation to Van Diemen's Land.[45]

If Grey's strategy was to play what we would now call wedge politics with the colonies, it failed in spectacular style. Australian nationalism often seemed an oxymoron during the colonial period. The issue of convict transportation, however, seemed to spark in the colonists an intense feeling of patriotism. Although this patriotism was interwoven with the British embrace, the colonists regularly displayed love for their adopted country and a willingness to fight for it. On 16 September 1850 a monster meeting was held in Sydney, the likes of which had rarely been witnessed. Some six thousand people gathered at Barrack Square, now Wynyard Park, to voice their discontent.[46] The *Sydney Morning Herald* praised the protesters, who conducted themselves with "propriety and dignity, which did high honour to the people of Sydney." It was common knowledge in Sydney that the peelite and future British prime minister William Gladstone had written to Governor Fitzroy on 30 April 1846 suggesting the resumption of transportation to New South Wales. Grey's subsequent approval of this plan sent the city into hysterics. That this could even be considered just as the convict stain was beginning to be replaced by a society of free British subjects was the gravest of imperial insults.

The intriguing display of loyalty described by Pickering in Hobart Town was seen in Sydney also. A large wooden platform was erected for the speakers at the centre of Barrack Square with the British Ensign and Union Flag raised at each corner. As the thousands of protesters situated themselves on the grass, the band began to play God Save the Queen. Before Charles Cowper, who had resigned his seat on the Legislative Council earlier that year, began his speech, "three hearty cheers" were offered for the Queen.[47] After the battle against transportation was finally won, the patriotic duality continued as the victorious Leaguers joyfully sung these words: "Hurra for the noble Leaguers! Hurra for our British Queen! / Hurra for the trend of freemen, Where bondsmen erst have been!"[48] It is perfectly clear that neither the protesters in Sydney nor their Tasmanian counterparts can be called disloyal. This was not a fight for separatist republicanism but for a civic republican interpretation of the British constitution.

At the heart of the anti-transportation protests was the desire to create a colony of virtue, a living replica of the highest ideals of Great Britain. It was not mere rhetoric when Cowper described the issue as "the most important question which has ever fallen under [our] attention."[49] But why was this question so crucial? Transportation was debated with such zealousness not because of its impact in mere pounds, shillings, and pence but because it cut to the very soul of these new British societies. Cowper, it must be remembered, was himself a huge landowner with some sixty-eight thousand acres in Argyle, Lachlan, Camden Park, and Sydney real estate.[50] His biographer, Alan Powell, very fittingly called his work about Cowper *Patrician Democrat*, since he was both an aristocratic gentleman and a champion of reform.[51] Cowper's passionate denunciation of transportation can be best understood in civic republican terms since his public life is generally acknowledged to have been motivated by ideological conviction for the greater good rather than by self-gain. As David Clune and Ken Turner note, "not even Cowper's most rabid opponents suggested that his years in power brought him any financial gain... or that his personal life was other than irreproachably moral."[52] Although his reputation for political adroitness earned him the sobriquet "slippery Charlie" in the case of anti-transportation, we find a wealthy pastoralist agitating not for his personal advancement but for the common good and for democracy.[53] It was not for money but for morals that he took the stage at Barracks Square and urged his fellow employers to refuse the services of convicts.

In his speech, Cowper began with an economic defence of the anti-transportation movement. His true passion and the heart of the protest were revealed, however, when he exclaimed that "the colonists would reject the system, although their material prosperity might be dependent upon it." It is not possible to reconcile these sentiments with Lockean liberalism. This commitment to always value the common good over individual gain finds its home in the civic republican tradition. Cowper was adamant that there was no "worldly advantage" a man could gain that would justify pouring "moral evils" over the heads of his fellow colonists.[54] The song of patriotism, sacrifice, and active service, which Aristotle sang for Athens, Cicero for Rome, Machiavelli for Florence, and the Commonwealthmen for England, Cowper now sang for Sydney, indeed for Australia.

It is worth reflecting on this powerful sentiment. The anti-transportation protesters made it perfectly clear that they were fighting a moral battle, for a cause greater than money. Even if the end of transportation was to negatively affect the colonial economies, it was still a step they overwhelmingly wanted to take because they were committed to the idea of a virtuous society. This is exactly what Cicero was speaking of when he theorized that "Nature has implanted in the human race so great a need of virtue and so great a desire to defend the common safety that the strength thereof has conquered all the adherents of pleasure and ease."[55] The Australian colonists responded so passionately to the anti-transportation movement because, more than financial gain, they wanted to live in a virtuous British society that they could be proud of. They were not content with individual gain but wanted their whole community to be seen as a paragon of virtue holding to the highest principles of the British constitution. Their reputation was clearly important to them.

The anti-transportation movement saw for the first time on Australian soil significant evidence of a trans-colonial nationalism.[56] Half a century before federation, the colonists banded together in a display of nationalist solidarity, realizing that their strength lay in unity. The pioneering work of the Van Diemen's Land protesters was mirrored in New South Wales, New Zealand, South Australia, and, following its creation in 1851, Victoria. With Queensland still part of New South Wales, it was Western Australia alone that bucked the trend and requested that convicts be sent (although the sheep ranchers of Moreton Bay were also pro-transportation). The New South Wales protesters at Barracks Square publicly swore to defend from transportation not only themselves but "their brethren in that colony [Van Diemen's Land]." The following year, leaders of the anti-transportation movement from the various colonies would assemble in Melbourne to make their wishes known to the world.

John West and League members from Van Diemen's Land arrived in Hobson's Bay, Victoria, aboard the *Shamrock* on 1 January 1851. Cowper soon arrived with fellow pastoralist and merchant Robert Campbell, and the best part of a month was spent discussing the nationalization of the movement with their Melbourne hosts, including Mayor William Nicholson. On 1 February 1851 the Australasian League was officially proclaimed. The constitution of the league vowed to fight transportation to any Australasian colony "by moral means only."[57] Again, it is emphasized that this was not an economic or even a political but a moral struggle. The league excited the colonial imagination and was seen as the forebear to greater things. The *South Australian Register* said of the league (yet to be officially formed), "we see in it the germ of that federal union which is so desirable, and without which a number of states... cannot be powerful, or rather will inevitably be weakened by mutual jealousy, distraction, and alienation."[58]

At its inauguration the league unfurled "a very beautiful banner" that would represent the movement.[59] With the Union Jack in the top right-hand corner, the royal blue material was adorned with golden stars representing the colonies. It is appropriate that this early display of Australian nationalism should produce a flag of strikingly similarity to the national flag designed in 1901. It was not without cause that Charles Blackton described the league's formation as the "dawn of Australian national feeling."[60] Although the sentiment was nationalist, the imposing Union Jack served as a reminder that the movement was not separatist. As with residents of the Canadian provinces, residents of the Australian colonies felt an intense form of dual patriotism. They loved and valued the place where they lived but that very love spilled over from national pride in being members of a British society and part of the British Empire. This is where the true genius of Durham's assessment of the Canadian rebellions reveals itself. Durham was adroit enough to glean that it was loyalty to the British constitution that caused these colonists to be disloyal to the British government. They would fight any British governor or minister in defence of their right to be treated as British subjects.

This complex well of emotions can be explained most easily by looking at the civic republican tradition. The colonists held a passion for their British heritage and homeland that the so-called tyranny of distance could not dampen.[61] It was their veneration of

Britain and their steadfast belief in the divine righteousness of (the whig interpretation of) the British constitution that made them naturally desire to transplant the values and morality of the land of their past to the land of their future. From its inception, the league was desperate to make their case heard in England. One of the earliest resolutions decried the fact that the "great evils" suffered in Australia were "unknown to the people of England." It was considered paramount that their position be explained to their "fellow-subjects."[62] The colonists saw themselves as "independent Australian Britons," and they wanted nothing more than the rights and liberties enjoyed by their kinsmen in the mother country.[63] If only the people of England were aware of their plight, it was felt that they would support them completely. To this end, the league released an "address to the English people" in which they reaffirmed that "the native Australasians are entitled to all the rights and privileges of British subjects, and to the sympathy and protection of the British nation."[64]

The League appointed agents to press their case in England. An initial board of nine members was set up in London. There was equal representation for New South Wales, Victoria, and Van Diemen's Land.[65] The London agents were charged with raising awareness in every major English city. Significantly, each agent, no matter which colony sponsored him, was to act as a representative of all Australia. The London agents were charged with presenting the Australian colonies the way they wanted to be seen, as mature British societies that provided vital resources and foodstuffs for the empire. Far from the depraved reputation of Botany Bay, the agents were to present to the English public British colonies of virtue.

In April and May 1852 the Australasian League held a conference in Launceston and Hobart with delegates from New South Wales, Victoria, South Australia, Van Diemen's Land, and New Zealand. Cowper, who was the president of the conference, gave an impassioned opening speech in which he attacked a despatch from Denison to Grey. Denison had hoped the despatch would remain confidential, since he was "obliged to state circumstances and opinions in reference to the character and habits of the people of these colonies, which it would be by no means desirable to make public." The governor's fear was realized, and the League was outraged by his comments. Denison used New South Wales as a case study and concluded that the cessation of transportation had a negative impact on the moral state of the colony. His reasoning was that the decrease in labour caused an increase in pay for the working class, which in turn led to greater disposable income to be spent on alcohol, gambling, and other vices. He predicted that should transportation to Van Diemen's Land end, "the tone of moral feeling would become worse and worse, drunkenness and debauchery... would spread like a moral pestilence over the land."[66]

Cowper insisted that the vastly improved moral condition of New South Wales since the end of transportation was undeniable proof that convictism was a form of civic cancer. He noted that since the end of transportation criminal convictions had fallen from 725 in 1841 to 665 in 1850, despite a population increase from 149,669 to 265,503 in the same period. Executions had fallen from 15 in 1841 to 4 in 1850. Although perhaps not strictly relevant, it was added that during the same period wool exports had quadrupled and total exports had increased by more than a million pounds from 1,023,397 to 2,399,580. By Cowper's summation, "with regard to the charge of the deterioration in morals, this council is utterly at a loss to imagine any plausible grounds for such a calumny; and cannot regard without indignation, the proof this correspondence affords, of the reckless misrepresentation by which a colonial governor can place in jeopardy the dearest interests of these colonies, and the honour of the British name in the southern hemisphere." Cowper closed by thanking the British press, who he felt had finally begun taking their side. He spoke of Australia as the abused younger brother of the British family, fully entitled to the rights of the family but often overlooked. He finished by saying, "accustomed, heretofor, to neglect, unused to sympathy, we are at last inspired with the hope that our own earnest efforts, aided by advocacy... will accomplish our deliverance from Colonial Office oppression." It was hoped that British journalists supporting their "reasonable claims and constitutional rights" would be the "harbinger... of brighter and happier days."[67]

Again, it needs to be emphasized that the struggle was not economic but moral. This was a battle not for improved conditions but for the spirit of the society. Denison noted in his despatch to Grey that "the main objection... will be based upon the amount of moral evil" caused by transportation. He added that "some economic objections will be urged too... but these will be so closely connected with the moral question as hardly to admit of separation or distinction."[68] Denison understood that movement was geared towards creating a virtuous society that the colonists could be proud of, a moral commonwealth that would bring glory to themselves and to the empire. The governor disagreed, of course, that ending transportation was the best policy. Nonetheless, it is clear that he understood the movement to be a moral campaign. The communitarian overtones to this debate are striking. Establishing a moral collective is the highest goal of civic republicanism, and the rhetoric of both the governor and the protesters strongly suggests that the struggle against transportation was understood in these terms.

The *coup de grace* for Eastern transportation would not technically come until 6 January 1854, when an order-in-council removed Van Diemen's Land as a convict destination. Nevertheless, the transportation question was effectively settled during a speech from the throne of "unusual length" when the British parliament met on 11 November 1852. The speech recognized that the pressure from Van Diemen's Land and her neighbours had created a situation requiring transportation to be stopped completely to Eastern Australia.[69] The discovery of vast goldfields along the East Coast was well known in Britain by 1852, and this doubtless had some bearing on or perhaps hastened the decision to end convict transportation. It simply made no sense for the British government to pay the fares of criminals to travel to a destination that was beginning to rival California as the gold capital of the world. London's *Times* ridiculed the logic of sending criminals to "El Dorado."[70]

Did the gold rushes end transportation? The short answer is no.[71] Even if gold had not been discovered, it is inconceivable that the colonists, having taken such a dramatic stand, would have allowed transportation to continue. The gold rushes need to be seen as a historical coincidence that aided the existing protest movement and hurried the end of a highly unpopular policy. Lang's separatist mission may seem with the subsequent passage of 150 years of constitutional connection to have been the ranting of a mad prophet. During those crucial years of 1850–53, however, the spectre of separatist republicanism seemed very real to some, particularly in Britain.[72] In September 1850, Leeds' *Northern Star* ran an article titled "The United States of the Australian Republic." The author commented that "to many ears this title will sound strange, if not ridiculous, as that of the 'Independent United States of North America' did to our ancestors."[73] Grey had already conceded in his 1846 despatch to Nova Scotia's Governor Harvey that "it is neither possible nor desirable to carry on the government of any of the British provinces in North America in opposition to the opinion of the inhabitants."[74] Hidden on the other side of the world, it was even more unrealistic to hope to rule the Australian colonies against their wishes. "Australia is too far distant, its colonists too widely spread, for us to dream of holding them in subjection by mere brute force," concluded the *Northern Star*.[75] The British government had little to gain in maintaining transportation but an entire continent to lose should the Boston Tea Party be recreated at Sydney Cove. To credit the discovery of valuable minerals with ending transportation is to deny the hard work and influence of a powerful social movement that made steadfast demands. The reformers clearly articulated what kind of society they wished to be.

News of the Queen's speech reached the colonies in February 1853. A change of government in Britain had seen the Duke of Newcastle assume control of the Colonial Office under the administration of the Earl of Aberdeen. Earl Grey made some attacks on Newcastle's policy of cessation, but by May the issue was settled. The news reached Australia in August, and Wednesday the tenth became an unofficial holiday in Van Diemen's Land.[76] At Launceston, the spiritual home of the anti-transportation movement, emotions spilled over as the colonists rejoiced. The clearly elated Launceston correspondent for Hobart's *Courier* beamed that "the inhabitants at early dawn were preparing for the day's rejoicing, and flags of every hue flouted bravely in the brilliant rays of the glorious sun!"

An "elegant structure" made of large wattle branches was constructed at St John's Square and stood proudly among the colourful banners that were waved. The "gaily dressed ladies" and their "attentive chaperones" all gathered together to hear the mayor begin proceedings. He introduced the first speaker, Richard Dry, as the speaker of the Legislative Council and "a native youth to boot."[77] Both factors were warmly approved of by the glowing crowd. Following a procession of statesmen and League leaders, the people bellowed out a newly composed Jubilee Anthem to the tune of God Save the Queen:

Sing! for the hour is come! Sing! for our happy home, Our land, is free!
Broken Tasmania's chains; Wash'd out the hated stain; Ended the strife and pain!
Blest Jubilee!

Sons of Tasmania, sing! Daughters, sweet garlands bring; All joyful be!
Raise, raise your banner high; star of the Southern sky!
Banner of victory!
Cross of the free!

God bless our Fatherland; God bless our patriot band!
Staunch have they been.
Truth has confounded spite; Justice has conquered might;
Heav'n has maintain'd the right; God Save the Queen![78]

The choice of music and lyrics have great meaning. Since the crowd conceptualized themselves as British people, the British anthem seemed an obvious inclusion in the festivities. The adaptation of the lyrics, however, reveals the colonial mindset. The popular imagination understood "our land" and "our happy home" to be under the "Southern sky." The blessings of British heritage and the British constitution proved to be transportable, and so in a new and distant land they were able to praise the "Fatherland," the symbol of the virtuous society they wished to become. The colonists' ideas, language, and culture were British, but their "happy home" and their free land was Tasmania. The celebrations would take the same form as the protests. Dual patriotism would allow the Fatherland and the patriot band, the noble Leaguers and the British Queen to be celebrated together. Durham's grand compromise would ensure they could do so, and Australians and Canadians continue even today to respect their British Queen in nations both patriotic and independent.

It is generally accepted that the anti-transportation movement was driven by democratic passion. By the middle of the nineteenth century, democracy was functionally normative in the Australian colonies. Wentworth had championed representative government in his youth to great acclaim, only to leave Australia as a pariah for his loudly voiced objections to "pure democracy."[79] This attitude resulted in his acclaimed poem *Australasia* being satirically vandalized by Charles Harpur in Henry Parkes' *Empire* on 6 August 1853:

May this thy last born daughter then arise
A barbarous Britain under other skies,
And Australasia spread, with flag unfurled,
All thy worst features in a wider world.[80]

As has been shown, throughout the anti-transportation demonstrations, the colonists clearly understood democracy to be an accepted norm and felt it was a basic British right that the wishes of the people be accepted. The terminology for describing Australian colonial democracy, however, has been nebulous and changeable.

Defining the role of liberalism in the development of Australian democracy has always been difficult. Far from liberalism, the French writer Albert Metin, described Australian democracy in his work of 1901 as *le socialisme sans doctrines* (socialism without doctrines).[81] Writing in the 1930s, Keith Hancock reinterpreted Metin through a liberal framework. The origins of *le socialisme sans doctrines*, he insisted, were individualistic. Hancock goes on to say, "To the Australian, the State means collective power at the service of individualistic 'rights.' Therefore he sees no opposition between his individualism and his reliance upon Government."[82] Hancock is describing a hybrid of liberalism mixed with something else. In the campaign against transportation, this book would argue that the "something else" is civic republican ideas.

Discussing the early federation period, Gregory Melluish distinguishes between New South Wales liberalism and Victorian liberalism.[83] The former was a free trade philosophy championed by George Reid; the latter was the Deakinite liberalism that embraced state intervention. So appalled was contemporary free trade politician and political theorist Bruce Smith with the hijacking of liberalism that he used the term "true liberals" in his notable 1887 work, *Liberty and Liberalism*.[84] The true liberals championed individual freedom, whereas "the whole Liberal Party and the whole Liberal press of the colony of Victoria… are professing one policy and practicing another." Smith describes Victorian, Deakinite liberalism as "opposite and contradictory," because he identifies a communitarian, positive liberty at its core.[85] It seems likely, however, that Victorian liberalism was in fact liberalism to which civic republican ideology had been grafted. As this chapter has suggested, civic republicanism was already finding political expression along with liberalism as early as the mid-nineteenth century. Rather than acknowledging a civic republican tradition, many historians have attempted to unpack these ideas by creating further variants and subsections in the theoretical realm of liberalism.

Terry Irving, for example, distinguishes between constitutional radicalism, civic radicalism, and plebeian radicalism. When dealing with civic radicalism he acknowledges republicanism as the philosophical home of the "active citizenship," with which he defines it. Choosing William Augustine Duncan as its patron saint, Irving speaks of a philosophy that requires the people to have knowledge, public spirit, and settled political principles in order to make representative government viable.[86] There is nothing wrong with making these distinctions, but it needs to be remembered that these classically republican ideals were hardly exclusive features of radicalism, civic or otherwise. Paul Pickering refers to "popular constitutionalism," defining it as the "set of ideas that set the Australian colonies on a path not to independence in the form of republican separatism, but to a 'comfortable' constitutional monarchism."[87] When examining the broader history of ideas that goaded the anti-transportation movement, Irving's civic radicals and Pickering's popular constitutionalists can be seen as natural allies under the banner of civic republican democrats. Without identifying the unifying philosophy, there is a risk of separating colonial thinkers who were almost always on the same side of the political debate against toryism. Using civic republicanism as a broader school of thought allows people who had a shared vision of Australia (though perhaps disagreeing on the method of attainment) to be viewed together. Whether their bent was more towards moderate democratization under the auspices of the British constitution or a radical challenge to the aristocracy, civic republicanism allows the many whose ultimate goal was a society of virtuous active and informed patriotic citizens to stand in the camp.

Australian historiography, like Canadian historiography, has a tradition of seeing liberalism as the catalyst behind every democratic improvement. Broadly speaking, the colonial periods are seen as a great duel between tory-conservatism and progressive-liberalism that ultimately led to the modern democratic state. To use Irving again: he refers to the Mutual Protection Association as a breeding place for "liberal politics" and the fight for self-government as a "long-standing liberal campaign."[88] His PHD thesis, which formed the basis of his book, was titled "The Development of Liberal Politics."[89] In fact, almost every progressive, reformist, and democratic impulse seems to be housed in the wide philosophical halls of liberalism. One of the chief reasons historians employ the term so liberally (if the pun may be excused) is that the term was used so frequently by the colonists themselves. By the second half of the nineteenth century, whig and tory had been largely replaced by their modern equivalents, liberal and conservative respectively. The reason, though, why contemporaries would have avoided the term republican is plainly obvious. The United Empire Loyalists in Canada, Australia's squattocracy, and tory governors in both hemispheres used republicanism as a by-word for disloyalty. Republicanism was clearly defined in the nineteenth century by those two world-changing events in the eighteenth century, the revolutions in America and France. Even if they had wanted to, in this heady environment, few ambitious reformers were willing to sabotage their cause by trying to distinguish between the civic republicanism of Aristotle and Cicero and the separatist republicanism of Paine.

With the benefit of hindsight and the passage of history and ideas that open before us like a scroll, we can now look back and see a particular dominating ideology woven into the anti-transportation protests. The form of protest and the argumentation used was clearly democratic, but it does not sit comfortably under the banner of liberalism. In particular, the behaviour of large property owners, whose rights were championed by John Locke, goes against the natural grain of the liberal school and the principles of negative liberty. Particularly given Earl Grey's determination to continue and expand transportation, the landowners and other employers were quite plainly acting against their self-interest for the common good of the community. Cowper expressly stated that the colonists would insist on the cessation of transportation even if it was against their economic interest. Denison confirmed that economic arguments fell into insignificance, since this was a moral issue. The rhetoric and spirit of the movement had an undeniable communitarian flavour. The desire to foster a society of virtue and to improve the moral condition of the community through policy can be seen as positive liberty in practice. Acknowledging the role of civic republican thought in the anti-transportation campaigns allows us to better understand a burgeoning colonial democracy that made frequent calls, not just for the rights of a free man but for the rights of a free British society and not just for individual freedom but for the greater good of the whole community.

9

Eureka Revisited: How Republican Was the Great Stockade?

I looked around me; I saw brave and honest men, who had come thousands of miles to labor for independence. I knew that hundreds were in great poverty, who would possess wealth and happiness if allowed to cultivate the wilderness which surrounded us. The grievances under which we had long suffered, and the brutal attack of that day, flashed across my mind; and, with the burning feelings of an injured man, I mounted the stump and proclaimed "Liberty."

Peter Lalor

In 1838, Scottish pioneers Archibald Yuille and his brother William set up a camp at Black Swamp, known today as Lake Wendouree, in Victoria. The large sheep run established by the Yuille brothers would come to be known by its Indigenous name, Ballarat, which in the language of the Kulin nation means a good resting place.[1] It is with no little irony, then, that Ballarat would be the scene of Australia's most famous episode of civil unrest leading to armed civil rebellion. Australian public memory has struggled to find a clear place for the Eureka Stockade. On 27 March 1998 the premier of Victoria, Jeff Kennett, opened the Eureka Stockade Centre in Ballarat following intense debate about how events should be interpreted and historical players portrayed.[2] Historians of great reputation and influence in Australia have come to perfectly opposite views on the topic.[3] For Russell Ward, the Stockade was part of the Australian legend, epitomizing the diggers' "unconventional yet powerful collectivist morality."[4] Manning Clark has condemned the excessive veneration of Eureka as "the great Australian illusion" and claimed this "bubble of… conceit" has distorted our conception of the period.[5] Neville

Meaney complains it has been given "a ludicrously inflated importance."[6] This chapter will not weigh into that debate more than is absolutely necessary but will rather seek to demonstrate that, like the anti-transportation protests, the Eureka Stockade can be seen as a violent climax of a sustained protest for a democracy shaped, not just by liberalism, but civic republicanism also.

Just as it was for the anti-transportation protests that immediately preceeded it, the Eureka Stockade held separatist republicanism only as a peripheral, last resort. The project was clearly to obtain an address for colonial grievances, not the independent republic endorsed by John Dunmore Lang's Australian League. Although separatist republicanism remained at the extreme ebb of the reformist agenda, civic republicanism can be shown to be a noteworthy influence leading up to the Eureka storm. The Battle of Ballarat was not only a mere argument about gold licences but also a much broader struggle for the perceived rights of free Victorians and the kind of society they wished to create and preserve. As the *Argus* insisted, this was "constitutional agitation," and again, the meaning of the British constitution was being contested.[7] The flow of history and ideas would place Eureka as the final kick against the goads of the penal mentality that some colonial governors and British politicians still held. The battle was lost militarily, but it was won in the courts, in the minds and hearts of Australians, and in the responsible government that was granted the following year. Victoria was separated from New South Wales in 1851, only three years before the Stockade. The newest of the Australian colonies can be seen as a social experiment of sorts. How would a group of British people wish themselves to be ruled in a free society on the other side of the world? Examining the impact of the Gold Rush, the speeches and sentiments of the diggers, and the radical press before Eureka and the public and judicial reaction afterwards, this chapter will acknowledge the role of liberalism but suggest that civic republicanism was the ideology that most shaped the democracy Victoria would become in 1855.

Before discussing Eureka, it is important to make plainly clear that the meaning and impact of the events were contested at the time and have been ever since by academics, politicians, and the general public.[8] In early 1855, once the dust had settled and the battle had moved from a Ballarat fortress to a Melbourne court, the *Sydney Morning Herald* spoke of the outbreak that could have fanned into the "Victorian revolution."⁹ The *Argus* was indignant about such an account, claiming that the *Herald*'s reporters' "success in mastering [the Victorian] political condition is by no means proportionate to their meritorious assiduity in discussing it." The stockade was "an unusually bloody riot, but no more."¹⁰ Elsewhere it was described as "riots," an "affray," an "insurrection," a "fatal collision," and the "Ballarat disturbances."¹¹ The *Geelong Advertiser*'s reporting of a "scene of carnage and death!" was matched for emotion only by the *Ballarat Times*' description of "a foul massacre" complete with a call for vengeance.¹² News of the stockade reached Britain in March, and the press there were equally conflicted on how to conceptualize the events. The rhetoric of the radical press suggested an epoch-making event had occurred. The *Leader* reported a "positive rebellion," while the Chartist *People's Paper* spoke of the "Australian Revolution."¹³ The headline for London's *Morning Chronicle* read "Loss of Life," but the same article republished in Ireland's *Freeman's Journal* upgraded the title to "Great Loss of Life."¹⁴ The *Times*, on the other hand, referred more calmly to the "difficulty" on the gold fields, and other journals used a range of descriptors implying varying levels of severity.¹⁵

Just as the contemporary press struggled to define and explain the importance (or insignificance) of Eureka, so too have journalists, politicians, and the general public since. In the vexed war year of 1940, H.V. Evatt, soon to enter federal parliament as a Labor member, famously declared that "Australian democracy was born at Eureka."[16] In 1949, the Labor Chifley government created the electorate of Lalor in honour of the Eureka leader.[17] On 3 December 1973, the 119th anniversary of Eureka, Labor prime minister Gough Whitlam claimed Eureka as a "symbol of pride" and an expression of the "democratic traditions and the strong nationalist aspirations for which Labor had always stood."[18] As Labor's Victorian premier Steve Bracks prepared to celebrate the 150th anniversary of Eureka in 2004, conservative commentator Gerard Henderson lamented then Liberal prime minister John Howard's apparent lack of interest.[19] Henderson objected to such a powerful cultural legend being surrendered to the political left and expressed hope that by the bicentenary in 2054 the federal Liberal leadership would realize its enduring significance.[20] Whatever contribution the events at Eureka may have made to the embryonic Australian democratic tradition, it is beyond question that the legend of Eureka has featured prominently in that tradition. What this chapter will do is question whether the democratic impulse exhibited through the mining protests reveals a liberal or civic republican thinking.

Although the Australian gold rushes began in New South Wales, by 1852 it was clear that the Victorian gold fields were far richer.[21] During the 1850s, this nascent colony would produce more than one-third of the world's gold. The population of Victoria between 1851 and 1861 would increase sevenfold from seventy-seven thousand to well over half a million.[22] It is worth considering what so sudden a population change would mean for a small and new colony, for the merchants, pastoralists, government, and police. With a tidal wave of migrants and the prospect of enormous fortunes, a recipe for anarchy seemed prepared. Despite this dystopian potential, the remarkable thing about the Victorian gold rush initially was the very lack of lawlessness and civil disobedience. The mob rule and lynch justice that made the '49ers in California so infamous was not to be repeated in Australia to any comparable degree.[23]

Lieutenant-Colonel Godfrey Mundy commented on this odd contrast in his 1852 *Rambles*. Of course he was writing before the turbulent year of 1854, but his assessment is supported by that of Governor Hotham, who arrived in Victoria on 22 June 1854. Touring the Ballarat goldfields, Hotham concluded that they were "an orderly well conducted people," the mass of which were "true hearted and loyal."[24] Mundy offers historians an interesting firsthand insight into the different atmospheres in California and Victoria. In California, he noted, "A heterogeneous crowd, rushing from different countries, with every tie broken, without laws or leaders, without experience, converged madly upon the gold-bearing Thule – producing gold alone to sustain life – a bare wilderness, with a severe climate and a fierce race of aborigines." The Victorian situation differed greatly: "Here – the gold, as it were, comes to a community already firmly established, the machinery of government, of the law, of social protection complete, with a fair share of agriculture in the golden land itself, and a knot of sister colonies close around her, able to assist her augmented population with the necessaries of life."[25]

Mundy's explanations are far from unreasonable. The relative proximity of the gold finds to Melbourne (and Sydney) would certainly have made the diggings feel less like the Wild West. An important point also is that the Australian gold rushes were less of an international affair than those in California. The presence of Americans, Europeans, and Chinese is of course well noted by historians, but the numeric supremacy of British diggers was overwhelming. Paul Pickering has challenged the "inward-looking" approach of the historical orthodoxy and argued that a strong "symbiotic relationship" existed between British and Australian radicals.[26] The shots fired from the Eureka fortification should not be divorced from the radical press in Victoria and the ongoing campaign for democratic reform. Unlike the truly "heterogeneous crowd" in California, Australia experienced a British gold rush and a British rebellion.

The perception that the Eureka Stockade was an international affair was one Governor Hotham was keen to promote. In his despatch to George Grey on 20 December 1854, he blames the rebellion largely on "foreign democratic opinions" and notes of the agitators and promoters of sedition that "foreigners are to be found amongst the most active."[27] The *Sydney Morning Herald*'s Melbourne correspondent reported that "the announcement that the late outbreak was caused by foreigners, has caused a very great sensation; and by many the fact is doubted."[28] A.G.L. Shaw's terse analysis was simply that "there was no foreign flood."[29] Serle notes that of the forty-one killed or injured only three were foreigners and that the Hanoverian Frederick Vern and Italian Rafaello Carboni were the only foreigners among the leadership.[30] The thirteen who eventually stood trial certainly gave some weight to Hotham's claim, including representatives from the United States, Italy, Holland, Denmark, Jamaica, Ireland, Scotland, Australia, and England. The Irish were the best represented, with five in the dock and, more generally, it was the Irish who seemed most eager for active rebellion; it was an Irishman, Peter Lalor, who would ultimately lead the Stockaders. It is important to bear in mind, however, that in the typology of mid-nineteenth century Victoria, the Irish would not have been deemed foreigners. As Patrick O'Farrell has argued, "the Irish in Australia identified proudly with the power and prestige of the Empire."[31]

This perception of an international rebellion divorces Eureka from the much larger diggers' protest movement from which it sprang. The *Age* saw a battle of ideas with only two outcomes: "self-government or Downing-street domination." Far from being influenced by foreigners, this was the same struggle British colonists were facing all over the empire: "It would seem to be the fate of our fatherland, whilst in all hemispheres sowing the seed of vigorous and promising states, to succeed nowhere in attaching them to it by bonds of endearing affection. Imperial authority, stretching itself beyond the bounds of right and reason, excites to a natural antagonism every feeling of self respect and every instinct of liberty." Few diggers ultimately resorted to physical agitation; the greater movement for reform and democracy by moral means only had nearly universal support on the diggings and strong sympathy in Melbourne also. The champions of reform and diggers' rights in the press and in the lobby groups were British men following the example of other British protests. As the *Age* put it, "we are Englishmen still, and have brought with us the traditions of freedom."[32]

The classic protest cry of "No Taxation without Representation" is eminently British. It was the famous catchphrase that propelled the thirteen American colonies to revolution in 1776. In the remaining North American colonies, the sentiment remained as strong as ever, and the previous chapters have discussed how this sentiment led to fierce protests. On the Victorian gold fields the sentiment was being championed by English Chartists George Black and Henry Holyoake. Their mouthpiece, the *Gold Diggers Advocate and Commercial Advertiser* stated in January 1854 that "if there is one thing which is admitted more clearly than another in England, it is the right of those who are taxed to have a voice in electing the men by whom the revenue thus collected is spent."[33] The *Advocate* prided itself on being "the only newspaper devoted entirely to the social and commercial interests of the digging community."[34] The title page sported a magnificent banner depicting an eagle with spread wings over a seal. In the seal two bearded diggers stand, shovel and pitchfork in hand, next to an emblem of kangaroo and emu, surrounded by the words "friends I shelter, foes I crush." The defiant motto of the paper was "I will not look silently on and see our liberties invaded, nor remain a passive spectator of public robbery." Black and Holyoake had a utopian vision of the new colony. Free from the "precedents of bygone ages," which still curtailed democracy in Europe, Victoria was destined to become a place where anything less than democracy, universal suffrage, and the Chartist principles would be "almost unthought of."[35] In order to protect this vision, the *Advocate* declared war against the "ellete flunkeyism of England" and the "snobbism" of the privileged classes.[36]

Although, as Mundy insists, there was no violent or erratic predisposition to be found among the diggers, the political situation they encountered was anathema to many, and the calls of the *Advocate* were not unheeded.[37] The colony of Victoria was separated from New South Wales by the Australian Constitutions Act 1850 (UK) and given a single-chamber parliament.[38] The Victorian Legislative Council was modelled on the New South Wales Constitution Act 1842 (UK) and allowed one-third of the House to be nominated and the remainder elected with the franchise set at £100 freehold or £10 per annum rental for male citizens over the age of twenty-one.[39] The population of diggers with a licence on the Victorian gold fields was around 35,000 in 1842 and 40,000 in 1843 (let alone the many without a licence). The government census in the fateful year of 1854 revealed the figure as 66,697.[40] With the population of Victoria just over 270, 000, the diggers officially comprised about one-quarter of the colony, and if the unlicensed miners, shopkeepers, publicans, women, and children of the gold fields were added, then the figure would be much more. Together, they were perhaps the most significant section of the community bringing extreme wealth to Victoria and Britain, and they were completely unrepresented in parliament. This contributed in no small way to the prevailing feeling on the gold fields that the licence fee was an unfair tribute demanded by an unrepresentative government, in opposition to the constitution of Britain. As the *Advocate* succinctly put it, "Are the diggers content? The Government answers, Yes... we reply No!"[41]

Following the discoveries in 1851, diggers applied their craft without governmental interference, and great fortunes were made. By the end of the year, Victoria's inaugural lieutenant-governor, Charles La Trobe, decided to establish some government regulation, and an Act to restrain by summary Proceeding unauthorised Mining on Waste Lands of the Crown was assented to on 6 January 1852. The act required any persons "mining or digging" to have a government licence or face a fine of up to £5 for a first offence, up to £15 for a second, and up to £30 for a third or any subsequent offences. Should they not be able to pay, guilty persons would face jail time of up to one month, two months, or six months respectively. The law allowed any "Commissioner Inspector Constable or any other person specially appointed by the Lieutenant-Governor... to apprehend any person who shall be found offending."

It was not only the fines and penalties but also the impetus given to Commissioners of Crown Lands and police troopers that created such bitter tension between the diggers and the government authorities. Clause VIII stated that " all fines and penalties recovered under this Act not specially appropriated shall be applied and go one moiety to Her Majesty Her Heirs and Successors for the public uses of the said Colony and in support of the Government thereof and the other moiety to the use of the informer or party prosecuting."[42] With one-half of the fines being paid to the trooper or official, a bounty hunter mentality seeped into the police force, and diggers were often presumed to be guilty outlaws. Clause VII provided a great temptation for corruption and overzealousness on the trooper's part and contributed to the sense of mistrust and resentment among diggers.

The ferociousness with which the law was enforced and the lack of clemency and in some cases common sense created an atmosphere of mutual antagonism. In late 1852, the *South Australian Register* paid a special correspondent to live among the diggers and report on their lifestyle. Apart from startling the housewives of Adelaide by informing them that a four-pound loaf of bread could fetch 3s in Bendigo and that a £5 note failed to purchase two ducks, he felt it vital to inform his readers what becomes of the "large party of unfortunates" caught by the police without a licence. William Probert desperately explained that he was a cook, not a digger, who had arrived only a week ago from Manchester and his master had not told him he needed a licence. The judge fined him £2, sternly adding that "your master deserves to be himself fined." James Cole had lost his licence and pleaded that the register be checked to verify that he had abided with the law. He was fined £2 10s. Owen Egan had arrived only the previous night and claimed he had no intention of working till he had acquired a licence. He was fined £2 10s. Frederic Irving was only a boy in the care of his uncle, a licensed digger. For not obtaining a licence for his nephew, he was fined £1. John Crickley's licence was in his tent when he went to see a doctor, and Roger Sheehan explained his mine had collapsed and his licence was buried under tons of earth (he had barely escaped with his life). Both men insisted that a reference to the books would absolve them. Both were fined 10s.[43]

Little consideration was given to poverty or desperation. A digger whose good luck had won him some early fortune could easily pay the 30s per month. Many others had not a farthing to their name or worse yet had taken on a high-interest loan to pay for food and equipment. For these people, the licence fee was prohibitively expensive. At The Ovens on 8 January 1853, a large hunting party of police on foot and horseback stormed the diggings in search of unlicensed miners. Irrespective of wealth or poverty, sixty-seven diggers were given fines totalling £204.[44] In August, some three thousand diggers at The Ovens met to protest the perceived injustice of the tax and the way it was enforced. The protesters carried many colourful flags, including one that bore the slogan "taxation without representation is robbery." A digger named John Whitelaw received great cheers when he insisted the assembly demanded only "the privilege which belongs to British subjects, of assembling together for the purpose of fairly representing to the Government the grievances under which we labor."[45] This would become an important theme at subsequent larger and more emotional meetings. The question was not restricted to individual rights but explored the notion of how a British community should live.

Although the grievances were centred on local administration and tax policies, they were tied to, or at the very least used as a pretext to promote, far loftier democratic ambitions. In April 1853, it was decided that each licence would entitle a man to dig an area of twelve feet by twelve feet only. Geoffrey Blainey has emphatically insisted that "without this decision, the rebellion in Eureka in 1854 would not have occurred."[46] It is impossible to verify such an assertion one way or the other; however, it is clear that the diggers and their urban supporters were concerned with far more than a specific mining policy. At a great public meeting in Melbourne's Protestant Hall, the diggers' representatives spoke of their recent interview with Governor La Trobe on 1 August. After listing their specific complaints against the licence fee, it was the "question of representation" that they pressed most earnestly on the governor.

George Thompson addressed the crowd, insisting that none but a digger could fully contemplate "the tyranny and the system of terror under which people lived at the diggings."[47] Thompson conceptualized the diggers as a distinct and valuable but unrepresented and oppressed class that yearned for democracy. Black and the *Advocate* would also employ this language. Letter writer "The Eagle" lamented that the ruling elite could not get "the idea... into their heads that the diggers are really an important class."[48] After Thompson resumed his seat, English doctor John Downes Owens prompted great cheering from the excitable crowd by declaring that the only satisfactory policy La Trobe had introduced was his own resignation. Owens spoke favourably of the revolutions of 1848 in Europe but insisted that the diggers must restrict themselves to "moral not physical force."[49]

The members of the Irish community on the diggings were quick to organize and list their grievances formally.[50] Although labouring under the same hardships as other diggers, the Irish felt they had been singularly insulted by the unjust treatment of Father Smyth, whose servant was abused and fined for not having a licence despite being disabled and clearly not a miner.[51] This blatant miscarriage of justice led to a heated meeting at the Roman Catholic Chapel and three resolutions were angrily passed:

1. That this meeting are of opinion that their respected pastor has been insulted by the disgraceful maltreatment endured by his servant at the hands of a Government official.
2. That the meeting, alive to their position, feel that an insult has been offered as well to themselves as to the aggregate Catholic body of the colony, by the uncourteous conduct by Mr. Commissioner Johnston towards our reverend pastor.
3. That this meeting are of opinion that the magistrates of Ballaarat have been premature in the decision at which they have arrived on the matter, and that we therefore call for a revision of the sentence.

The diggers were becoming politicized and radicalized in 1854, and before the year's end the meetings and resolutions being passed would become more dramatic. In the words of the *Argus*, "instead of wanton rioters, the people arise as justified avengers, stepping in to administer the law – the law of nature, when the law of conventionalism has been abused and failed to affect justice."[52]

On 17 October, a new six-pence daily began publication in Melbourne. The political stance taken by the *Age* was representative of the political climate in which it was birthed. The inaugural issue of the *Age* included a front-page column that plainly stated the editorial philosophy: "The politics of The Age will be liberal, aiming at a wide extension of the rights of free citizenship and a full development of representative institutions. Believing that public order is essential to the preservation of national liberties, it will in all cases uphold the inviolability of law, and urge the reform of abuses and the redress of grievances by means purely constitutional. It will advocate the removal of all restrictions upon freedom of commerce, freedom of religion, and – to the utmost extent that it is compatible with public morality – upon freedom of personal action." This is clearly identifiable as a liberal democratic doctrine. The emphasis is on the negative liberty and the rights of the individual. What is especially noteworthy, however, is that the *Age* clearly calls on positive liberty in the civic republican tradition also. It continues: "Whilst boldly asserting the rights of citizenship in a free state, it will faithfully point out its duties, and aim at the creation of a high-toned public spirit amongst all classes of society. Convinced that our further and permanent progress is to be looked for, more from the settlement and the cultivation of the Colony, than from the wonderful mineral wealth that would seem to have answered its purpose in attracting hither the elements of a great people, its conductors will give their unremitting advocacy to every scheme that promises, by attaching that people to the soil, to give them a powerful and lasting interest in the well being of their adopted country."[53]

The politics of the *Age* can be described as a marriage of liberalism and civic republicanism. On the one hand there is a strong belief in negative liberty, manhood suffrage, representative government and freedom from interference in the areas of commerce, religion, or personal actions. But there is something else. The *Age* championed liberalism with duties. It was necessary to promote a sense of civic duty, public spirit, and patriotism and a personal investment in the common good. The journalists at the time would not have employed the term civic republicanism to describe this collectivist ideal, but that is not the point. It can now be identified as a continuation of the ancient political tradition of communitarian positive liberty. This politics of the *Age* in 1854 should come as no surprise under the editorship of Chartists Thomas Bright and David Blair. Blair, in particular, had a fine pedigree for such a position, originally coming to Australia as a disciple of Lang. Some of the Australian Chartists on or around the Victorian gold fields had come to reassess their political position. Under the influence of Italian politician and journalist, Giuseppe Mazzini, they sought "Chartism and something more."[54]

Mazzini was an international celebrity at the time of the Australian gold rushes. Famous for his activism in the cause of Italian unification and popular democracy, his decade-long exile in London from 1837 and his London-based Friends of Italy group made him particularly accessible and prominent in the English-speaking world. To the conservative *Times*, Mazzini's republican doctrine was "reckless, impractical, irritating, and imbecile."[55] The radical *Leader*, however, spoke of the "ludicrous light" in which some commentators sought to cast Mazzini.[56] The hagiography of Mazzini by English radicals is best exhibited by William Edwin Adams' *Memoirs of a Social Atom*, which lauds its hero as "the greatest teacher since Christ." Adams notes that many English Chartists felt they had an incomplete agenda: "Chartism was not satisfying. We were Chartists and something more... The Charter, as a declaration of rights, was excellent. It covered the whole ground of political demand. But popular power proclaimed – what then?" Adams points to Mazzini as the pedagogue who finally articulated what the elusive "something more" was. Ideal republicanism required not only individual rights but civic duty also, a marriage of negative and positive liberty. Mazzini's 1850 "Proclamation to the People" declared that fraternity was vital, since without it "Liberty and Equality would be only means without end." "It was reserved for Mazzini," concluded Adams, "to preach the higher doctrine, Duty, which meant sacrifice, service, endeavour, the devotion of all the faculties possessed and all the powers acquired to the welfare and improvement of humanity."[57]

It should come as no surprise that the veneration of the Mazzinian doctrine by British radicals would be repeated in Australia. Ideas, opinions, and even personnel were freely exchanged between the radical presses in both hemispheres. Henry Richard Nicholls, for example, was active in Chartist circles in London before emigrating to Australia with his fellow activist brother, Charles. Growing up, Nicholls' father had taken him to hear speeches by Chartist leader, Feargus O'Connor, and the pioneer of British socialism, Robert Owen.[58] Henry was a talented poet and used his skill for the Chartist cause. After arriving in Australia, Henry was offered a job by George Black as an assistant editor for the *Advocate*. It is more than likely that Nicholls' influence led to the publication of letters from Mazzini and Hungarian nationalist Lajos Kossuth.[59] Along with Nicholls, Scottish journalist and regular contributor to the *Argus* Ebenezer Syme helped launch and edit the *Advocate*.[60] In London, Syme had been acquainted with men such as Joseph Cowen, who numbered both Mazzini and Kossuth among his friends, and George Jacob Holyoake, whose paper, *The Reasoner*, was a vocal advocate of

Mazzini and his compatriot Giuseppe Garabaldi.[61] Thinking the *Argus* not radical enough, Syme would join Blair at the *Age* and eventually buy the paper with his brother David (a Ballarat prospector who would ultimately edit the paper for half a century).[62]

It is difficult to say with authority what impact Mazzinian thought had on the Victorian goldfields. One direct link is the fiery Italian leader Raffaello Carboni, who was involved in the Italian rebellions against Austria in 1848 and 1849 and, according to some accounts, was at one point a secretary to Mazzini.[63] Certainly, Mazzini had a great influence on the British Chartists, and they in turn affected the movement in Australia. In one of its frequent attacks on the "La-Trobian dynasty" the *Advocate* lamented that some diggers were not engaged in the battle for democratic rights. In an article titled "The Franchise" it claimed: "In the eager race for riches, few have yet had time to think upon those topics which occupied perhaps much of their attention when in Europe."[64] As with Dr Owens approving the "revolutionary principles" of Europe in 1848, it is hard to imagine that Mazzini and the Italian revolutionaries were not among those Europeans being endorsed. Mazzini's fame among British Chartists must have had some impact in Australia. Although their direct impact on Eureka was limited, it is still worth noting that in addition to the many Chartist journalists and sympathizers who willingly emigrated to Australia around the middle of the nineteenth century, some 102 were transported to Van Diemen's Land as prisoners for involvement in various public protests between 1839 and 1848.[65] There was certainly an appetite for Chartist ideas in Australia, and ultimately the principles of the Great Charter, save annual parliaments, would be accepted in Victoria by 1857, well before they became normative in Britain. Keith Hancock made the point that "within ten years of the discovery of gold, practically the whole political programme of the Chartists is realised in the Australian colonies."[66] When the diggers formalized their protest in a political lobby, the impact of the Chartist press in Australia and England was plainly evident.

On 11 November the Ballarat Reform League was constituted and launched.[67] Some ten thousand diggers gathered at Bakery Hill to witness the formation of the league and hear the manifesto that would be sent to La Trobe's successor, Lieutenant-Governor Charles Hotham. It had been with great difficulty that La Trobe had juggled the demands of the diggers, the Legislative Council, and the Colonial Office. Privately at least, he seemed to be sympathetic to the diggers' cause and had budgeted for a deficit rather than increase gold field revenue. When Hotham took power in June 1854, he saw the colony's debt as his first duty to attend to. He ordered the police to dramatically increase their efforts at enforcing the licence fee just at the time when easily mined gold was scarce and the diggers were reaping far less reward than in the previous three years. Hotham's impolitic decision to use the diggers to return the budget to surplus ensured that the ongoing feud would end in confrontation. No longer content with tricks and ruses to outwit the hated Joes, the Leaguers at Bakery Hill made their protest open and defiant.[68]

The Irish journalist and author William Kelly stumbled across the great meeting quite accidentally when he made a detour to Bakery Hill to pick up a copy of the *Argus*. Kelly recalled the great excitement among the throngs of diggers assembled in a large tent before a wooden stage. The meeting came to order with the ringing of a bell. Goldfields doctor Alfred Carr gave a lengthy opening speech about the principle of representation that, in Kelly's summation, failed to approach mediocrity. Eventually a restless digger loudly yelled, "what about the b[lood]y licence-tax," and Dr Carr promptly concluded, "to the apparent delight of the crowd." Several other speakers were greeted by the rowdy crowd with chants of "shut up." It was the imposing figure of Thomas Kennedy that demanded the respect of the crowd. His rough but honest demeanour, open shirt, mud-stained hair, and unshaved face informed the crowd that he not only spoke for them but was one of them also. All were attentive as he opened his speech with two strong yet simple words that marked the spirit of the League, "brother diggers!"

Kennedy gave an impassioned speech in which he insisted over and over again that the diggers must be united against the "tyranny of officials." As with the Anti-Transportation League before them, separatist republicanism did not feature strongly, if at all, in the reformers' agenda. Kennedy declared loudly to his ecstatic audience that he would lay down his life for his noble Queen. Yet with his very next breath he declared that he would "shed the last drop of his blood before he would pay another licence." Kennedy's words brought forth a well-spring of emotion from all who listened. Sitting on the edge of the stage, Kelly was deeply moved as he witnessed the speech and its reception: "The burst of enthusiasm that followed this declaration is altogether indescribable. It seemed to lift the great tent into mid-air, and, inoculated with the glow of feeling around me, I could almost imagine that I had a cloud for a footstool."[69] The diggers rushed forward and grabbed Kennedy. They placed him triumphantly on their shoulders and carried him outside. The meeting had not ended, Kennedy had probably not finished his speech, but a wave of ecstasy overwhelmed the diggers, who now had a formal political lobby and worthy leaders to defend their rights. The chairman, veteran Welsh Chartist John Basson Humffray, happily dissolved the meeting.

The Ballarat Reform League composed a manifesto to explain to Hotham their grievances and demands. The document borrowed strongly from eighteenth-century American revolutionaries (even using Americanized spelling). It began by stating:

> That it is the inalienable right of every citizen to have a voice in making the laws he is called upon to obey. That taxation without representation is tyranny.
>
> That, being as the people have been hitherto, unrepresented in the Legislative Council of the Colony of Victoria, they have been tyrannized over, and it becomes their duty as well as interest to resist, and, if necessary to remove the irresponsible power which so tyrannized over them."[70]

The document is unashamedly democratic, and the authors clearly identified democracy as a principle of the British constitution. It was not, however, pure liberalism that guided the Victorian democratic impulse. The rhetoric of the manifesto and the movement at large married rights and diggers' interests to that most sacred of civic republican concepts – duty. The common good was presented as a higher law than any specific law passed by any parliament anywhere in the empire. Again the guiding philosophy was virtue over corruption and the common good over individual gain: "This colony has hitherto been governed by paid officials, upon the false assumption that the law is greater than justice, because, forsooth, it was made by them and their friends, and admirably suits their selfish ends and narrowminded views."[71] Unsurprisingly, the Leaguers also demanded "the total abolition of the diggers' and storekeepers' licence tax."

It may be tempting to reduce the rebellion itself to a minor skirmish concerned with a localized tax dispute, yet it is nigh on impossible to do the same with the resolutions of the Reform League. These were not minor regional complaints but broad demands stemming from a fundamental commitment to a particular political philosophy. The goldfields of Victoria bore witness to a battle of ideas in a virgin colony. Miles Taylor has convincingly argued that Britain did not escape the rebellions of 1848 if the colonial empire is included.[72] Duly acknowledging that "constitutional reform rather than the revolutionary nationalism of Europe" was the primary goal for Australian radicals, they still must be seen in the same cohort of democratic protesters.[73] As the phalanx of democratic warriors battled across Europe in the mid-nineteenth century, the Victorian radicals were attempting to answer a very basic social question, "how best should British subjects live?" Chartism and something more, was the answer offered by radicals, not only to address the diggers' grievances but to usher in a new dawn and a better Britain.[74] The community of diggers were as loyal as any other, but they demanded their rights under a democratic interpretation of the British constitution. They would not kowtow to corrupt officials who placed individual gain before the common good.

Like the Anti-Transportation League, the Ballarat Reform League held no strong separatist republican sentiments, seeing it only as a political threat and a last resort. In an article for the *Age* commemorating the 150th anniversary of Eureka, John Molony argued that the manifesto "had forceful [separatist] republican elements." Identifying the "British monarchy" as the "the ultimate source of the diggers' discontent," Molony subscribes enthusiastically to Evatt's thesis, titling his article "Dawn of Democracy."[75] What is perhaps overlooked in this interpretation is the fact that on the very same flagpole where the Southern Cross flew, there was also a Union Jack.[76] Kennedy's comment that he would die for the Queen but also die before paying the licence tax is probably a more accurate summary of the diggers' sentiment. For them, there was no contradiction in this. The principles they were fighting for, the rights of British subjects and the spirit of the constitution, were not in opposition to their monarch. Their fight was with the petty officials who corrupted the principles that the Queen should be defending. The Leaguers made it clear that separatism was something they would not embrace but might be driven to: "That it is not the wish of the league to effect an immediate separation of this colony from the parent country, if equal laws and equal rights are dealt out to the whole free community; but that, if Queen Victoria continues to act upon the ill advice of dishonest ministers… the Reform League will endeavour to supersede such Royal prerogative by asserting that of the people, which is the most royal of all prerogatives, as the people are the only legitimate source of all political power."[77]

The spirit and tenor of the Leaguers was clearly far larger than the "bloody" licence tax. In one of the articles that would be used against him in a libel case, *Ballarat Times* editor Henry Seekamp wrote that "the league is nothing more or less than the germ of Australian independence." He added that the "die is cast" and "no power on earth can now restrain the united might and headlong strides for freedom of the people of this country."[78] The Leaguers and their Chartist leadership were advocates of democratic reform, which, although not requiring separatism, did require a far greater degree of independence. They argued for political reform along Chartist lines:

1 A full and fair representation.
2 Manhood suffrage.
3 No property qualification of members for the Legislative Council.
4 Payment of members.
5 Short duration of Parliament.[79]

The battle lines in an ideological war had been clearly drawn, and history would prove that the advantage was always with the diggers. The government had the armed police and soldiers, but the diggers had an infinitely stronger weapon, the democratic zeitgeist that had enveloped the British Empire and much of Europe.

With the formation of the Ballarat Reform League, the diggers committed themselves to a path that they could not easily change. Like the rebels in Canada and the Chartists in Britain they had made the bold claim "peaceably if we can, violently if we must," and they could not back down, even in the face of the latter eventuality.[80] Following the formation of the league, notices were placed around the Ballarat diggings with the bold heading, "Down with the Licence-Fee! Down with despotism! Who so base as to be a slave?" A great meeting was advertised for 29 November to petition for "the immediate abolition of the licence-fee." Giving hint to the civil disobedience that was to follow the notice included a telling postscript: "bring your licences, they may be wanted."[81]

The meeting on 29 November surpassed even the heightened passions that characterized the meeting two and a half weeks before. Thousands assembled on Bakery Hill to hear from their delegates to Melbourne and to applaud the new resolutions to be passed on behalf of their beloved league. Mr Reynolds was met with wild cheers when he emphatically denounced the assessment of the acting chief justice (the assessment also of some historians) that the diggers were taking part in a petty riot. Far from it, declared the speaker. Reynolds likened the diggers' spirit to that which protested King George III. They were engaged in nothing less than the "persevering and indomitable struggles for freedom of the brave people of England and Ireland for the last eighty years."

It was the Hanoverian sailor turned digger Frederick Vern who put forward the radical resolution that would invite certain conflict. With a thick German accent he announced to the crowd: "That this meeting, being convinced that the obnoxious licence-fee is an imposition and an unjustifiable tax on free labour, pledges itself to take immediate steps to abolish the same, by at once burning all their licences. That in the event of any party being arrested for having no licences, that the united people will, under all circumstances, defend and protect them."[82] Thousands of guns fired into the evening air. The rapturous crowd created two large bonfires kindled by piles of mining licences. Many paid the five shillings to become members of the League, conscious perhaps of the threat that non-members would not be guaranteed safety after 15 December. As the smoke from burning licences filled the night sky, it seemed clear that Humffray and the advocates of "moral force" or "constitutional means" had lost their grip on the leadership. The *Geelong Advertiser* noted the day before the rebellion that "Humffray and all the other respectable 'moral force' members of the Reform League have withdrawn their names, and the movement is now headed by some persons hitherto unknown, whose object seems to be less the redress of grievances than the gratification of their evil passions and thirst for plunder."[83]

Again the diggers gathered at Bakery Hill, and some two hundred metres away from Bentley's Eureka Hotel, a stockade was being constructed. They were determined to defend themselves and were divided into five divisions of eighty, all armed with rifles. A sixth division was formed also; however, a dozen of the men were armed only with pistols.[84] An Irish digger, Peter Lalor, was pronounced leader, and while confessing no military experience, he promised his brethren, "once I pledge my hand to the diggers, I will neither defile it with treachery, nor render it contemptible by cowardice."[85] A remarkable ceremony then took place as the diggers witnessed the unveiling of what the *Argus* christened the "Australian flag."[86] The majestic blue flag bore a white cross and five stars for the five colonies. Full of emotion, Carboni believed that "there is no flag in old Europe half so beautiful as the Southern Cross of the Ballarat miners."[87] The *Argus* marvelled at the "wild romance" of the occasion and accurately predicted that the unfolding events "must form an important picture in the future history of Australia."[88]

Lalor took his place next to the flagpole, and the digger army circled attentively around him. He explained to his troops that they were to be sworn in. He gave this moral warning: "the man who, after this solemn oath does not stand by our standard, is a coward in heart." Hearing this, some of the onlookers did retreat quietly. Some five hundred diggers moved in closer to confirm their participation, and the captains of each division gave Lalor a military salute. The whole congregation followed Lalor's example as he knelt down in reverence to the flag. In a "firm measured tone" he led his men in their sacred oath: "WE SWEAR BY THE SOUTHERN CROSS TO STAND TRULEY BY EACH OTHER, AND FIGHT TO DEFEND OUR RIGHTS AND LIBERTIES." The diggers stretched out their hands to the flag and shouted in unison, "AMEN." Carboni's satisfied eyes looked around at the different faces, all united in their determination to fight a common enemy to secure the common good. He recalled that it was "one of those grand sights, such as are recorded only in the history of the Crusaders in Palestine."[89]

The euphoria of that moment, with the diggers united by common cause and determined to stand together, was soon to be contrasted with the stark reality that from a militaristic point of view the mouse had challenged the lion to a duel. The story of "our own little rebellion" has been extensively told and retold and needs no mention here.[90] Whilst many Stockaders distinguished themselves with personal bravery in the face of overwhelming odds, the breaking dawn of 3 December 1854 saw their beloved Southern Cross torn from its pole by trooper John King and carried away as a trophy. Twenty-two diggers and seven military were killed. Many more were wounded, and some 120 arrests were made. The aftermath of Eureka was nearly as bloody as the rebellion itself. It was certainly more brutish. "Maddened by success," the troopers seemed determined to take indiscriminate revenge on all who called them Joe.[91]

The definitive battle between the diggers and the government was not to take place at the Eureka Stockade on 3 December 1854 but in the hearts and minds of the people of Victoria. It was the court of justice and ultimately the court of public opinion that granted the diggers a victory on the moral field that they could never gain on the field of battle. Thirteen of the ringleaders were accused of high treason and sent to Melbourne to face the Victorian Supreme Court. Despite the great public sympathy for the diggers and even a recommendation of clemency from the royal commission into the administration of the goldfields, Hotham insisted that the trial go ahead. In January Seekamp was found guilty of sedition for his inflammatory tone in the *Ballarat Times,* and the governor hoped this indicated the fate of the Eureka ringleaders. He was desperate to see his course of action against the Ballarat Reform League and his general handling of the goldfields justified by a guilty verdict that would see his enemies hanged as traitors.

The trials began on 22 February 1855 and quickly descended into an embarrassment for Hotham. Several talented lawyers offered their services for the defence *pro bono public*. Among them was prominent anti-transportation campaigner and founding member of Dr Lang's republican Australian League, Archibald Michie. After seven acquittals, the outcomes seemed inevitable, and the prosecution took on an air of pointlessness. Michie told the jury that the case had become so "weary, stale, flat, dull, and unprofitable" that he barely saw the point in addressing them at all. He continued only because he saw the case as momentous, not only to the prisoners but to "the colony at large." The last six defendants were to be tried together. The case against Thomas Dignum was dismissed owing to lack of evidence, so five men took the stand on 27 March. The jury took seven minutes to return a not guilty verdict for all the accused. The jury was dismissed, and the diggers were free. The supportive crowd outside was not as large or as noisy as they had been a month earlier following the first acquittal. Perhaps by this stage the result seemed a foregone conclusion. Together with their followers the diggers cheerfully marched from the court to celebrate at a house on Little Lonsdale Street.[92]

Noel McLachlan quite rightly describes the state trials as "the most popular miscarriage of justice in Australian history."[93] The Crown could produce evidence that the thirteen were at the stockade, had sworn an oath to a rebel flag, and had fought against the Queen's soldiers. What the Crown could not produce was twelve men willing to find the diggers guilty. The diggers were not seen as disloyal to the Queen but as loyal to the true principles of the British constitution. Dr Owens poetically phrased this sentiment in his *Diggers' Song*: "Will show what you want in your new constitution / Will show you are loyal, but have resolution."[94] A new paper appropriately titled the *Democrat* sprang up in Melbourne by the end of the year. The front page of its inaugural issue triumphantly declared that "the men and women of Victoria are democrats."[95] This simple declaration truly captured the mood of a people in a year that began with the acquittal of the Eureka rebels and concluded with the granting of responsible government and a new democratic constitution. In the pages of history the line between the traitor and the patriot is sometimes paper thin. Despite Hotham's best efforts, the diggers had landed safely in the latter camp and public memory has kept them there ever since.[96] The *Age* described them as heroes who had the courage to say to the tyrant, "hitherto shalt thou go, and no farther."[97]

The Eureka Stockade was not a manifestation of separatist republicanism. The notion was certainly in circulation, but it was the first choice of very few.[98] The stockade and its aftermath can more easily be understood along democratic and civic republican lines. It was not the diggers only but the farmers and city population also who dreamt of a specific kind of society governed by the laws of virtue and committed to the common good. This was the dream for Victoria but far from the reality. The *Age* emphatically stated that the Victorians must be treated as "Colonial Britons," not "British Colonists." In other words, they must not be demeaned by autocratic government but be treated as equal members of the universal British family. The *Age* insisted, "we would therefore tell our brethren, that we only demand these rights and privileges we were reared to enjoy; but we sicken at being treated as a harlot class."[99] It was not simply the unfair licence tax but the entire situation where honest citizens had no political representation and no forum for the airing of grievances that set the colony on the path to conflict.

The near-monopoly of land enjoyed by the squatters caused bitter resentment, and the slogan "a vote, a rifle and a farm" became popular.[100] In its comprehensive etiology of the riots, the report of the gold commission highlighted the desire for land as one of three primary causes of discontent (the others being the licence fee and want of political rights).[101] One letter writer to the *Argus* described the limited availability of land as the "alpha and omega" of grievances. Fed up with perceived elitism at the expense of the common good, the letter writer demanded, "why is not the land opened to the man of industry, though unfortunately no capitalist?"[102] As with the Family Compact in Canada, the diggers saw a corrupt oligarchy enjoying a stranglehold on power and wealth and working against the common good. David Day has suggested that when Peter Lalor spoke of independence he "did not mean independence from Britain but financial independence."[103] It was with ideals far loftier than a mere tax dispute that the Ballarat Reform League was founded. The league leaders used the same language of democratic reform that was being preached all over the empire. As Humffray told his fellow leaguers, "with truth and justice on your side, the knell of colonial tyranny will be rung."[104]

The events that transpired in Ballarat in the dying weeks of 1854 made an impression far beyond Victoria. The *New York Times* ran the Eureka story as a headline at the expense of news on the Crimean War.[105] Karl Marx had been monitoring the events with great interest from London. He was convinced that the fight concerned the very structure of society in which the diggers wished to live. He wrote in *Die Neue-Oder Zeitung:* "We must distinguish between the riot in Ballarat (near Melbourne) and the general revolutionary movement in the State of Victoria. The former will by this time have been suppressed; the latter can only be suppressed by far-reaching concessions. The former is merely a symptom and an incidental outbreak of the latter."[106] Mark Twain described the stockade as "the finest thing in Australasian history." He insisted, like Marx, that the violence itself was a mere symptom of the great and noble struggle: "It was a revolution – small in size; but great politically; it was a strike for liberty, a struggle for a principle, a stand against injustice and oppression. It was the Barons and John, over again; it was Hampden and Ship-Money; it was Concord and Lexington; small beginnings, all of them, but all of them great in political results, all of them epoch-making. It is another instance of a victory won by a lost battle."[107] Perhaps it was not the same kind that Marx and Twain envisaged, but a revolution was taking place in Victoria, just as it was in New South Wales and Canada. The diggers achieved their immediate goal and saw the licence fee abolished and replaced with an export tax in 1855. Of far more significance, however, was the democratic voice that was heard all the way in London and the responsible government that was granted in the Victorian Constitution Act 1855 (UK).[108]

Tracing the history of the secret ballot in Victoria, John Hirst notes that the struggle for greater democracy had been gaining momentum before the discovery of gold. Nonetheless, the Eureka rebellion inflamed passions and accelerated the democratic program of the League and other leaders in the mining community. Hirst argues reasonably that "if the new constitution had not been on its way back to Victoria after approval in London, the reaction against the governor would have been even more intense."[109] The mood was for change. The royal commission concluded that "happily there seems not at present any difference of opinion in any quarter upon the question of conferring the franchise upon the industrious population of the gold-fields."[110] In May 1855, the *Argus* trumpeted that the bill to extend the franchise to the diggers in the mining districts, "having circumnavigated the globe, is now the law of Victoria." At long last that "important class of the community, altogether excluded from the rights of self government, might receive some instalment of the power they claimed."[111] With the diggers enfranchised, virtually all white males in Victoria were included in the political community. Hirst comments that universal male suffrage was no longer a radical pursuit; "it had virtually come into existence."[112] Interestingly, in an article dedicated to the gold fields commission and general democratic reform, Ireland's *Freeman's Journal* paused to mention that at great expense, teaching had begun at the University of Melbourne around the same time.[113] This was a period of radical transition. Victorians on and off the gold fields were making clear what kind of society they wished to be. Educated and democratic, they were determined that the early years of their proud colony should be the very opposite of the early years of their convict-stained northern neighbour.

One of Manning Clark's primary complaints against the Eureka myth is that it necessarily overlooks or undervalues the democratic movement and its champions before 1854. Like Hirst, Clark insists that the "germ of belief in equality" is to be found before the discovery of gold.[114] Geoffrey Serle would concur, noting that "all or almost all the reforms that followed Eureka must in any case soon have occurred."[115] As the previous chapters have shown, the move to responsible government was already happening all over the British Empire, and the wheels were already in motion to provide a more democratic constitution for Victorians. Nevertheless, the Eureka rebellion must still be seen as a continuation of the push for democracy and, particularly, the civic republican ideal of a society based on the principles of civic duty and virtue. The *Argus* linked the diggers' resistance to Canada's rebellions of 1837–38. It noted that "Canada could not get a British statesman to listen to her grievances till she broke out into rebellion." Because of "stubborn resistance" against reform in Canada and Australia, rebellion became "essential to the progress of liberty and good government."[116] To what degree Eureka hastened the move to democracy in Victoria is debatable. What is suggested here is that the kind of democracy advocated at Eureka was more civic republican than liberal in philosophy.

The language of the rebels was telling. The same pattern of argument surfaced in Eureka that had been so prominent with the anti-transportation movement, Joseph Howe's campaign, and the rebellions of 1837–38. In all cases, separatist republicanism was always the least preferred option. Neither in Australia nor Canada did the colonists petition with any great fervour or success to end British involvement in their affairs.[117] This was not about freedom from interference but freedom from domination.[118] The spirit of Britishness, the culture, art, law, tradition, and history of their ancestral homeland was a treasured inheritance that the colonists were loath to surrender. The British constitution was sacrosanct. What they desired was both to control their own local affairs and to be joined to the mother country. Lord Durham gave them their wish.

Following the state trials, Peter Lalor resurfaced in the public eye. Demonstrating the complete popular vindication of the diggers' actions, both he and Humffray would be elected to the Legislative Council. Lalor was quick to assert that the diggers were not fighting for their individual right to work and earn money. It was not a liberal but a civic republican argument he used when offering an apologia for the diggers. He and his brethren were acting collectively for the common good against a corrupt and self-serving government. He implored his fellow colonists, "can you say that the Government did not trample on the constitution... I am satisfied that you can not." Lalor insisted that "neither anarchy, bloodshed, nor plunder were the object of those engaged in that late outbreak." Rather, they were compelled to mount some response to the "unconstitutional and bloodthirsty" attacks under which the diggers found themselves. Lalor clearly took democracy and communalism as a given when he pressed the government about why it did not heed the popular voice and respond to public demands: "Why did not the Government take steps to alter the land system, to amend the mode of collecting the gold revenue, and to place the administration of justice into the hands of honest men before this bloody tragedy took place? Is it to prove to us that a British Government can never bring forth a measure of reform without having first prepared a font of human blood in which to baptise that offspring of their generous love? Or is it to convince the world that, where a large standing army exists, the Demon of Despotism will have frequently offered at his shrine the mangle bodies of murdered men?"[119]

The Eureka legend immediately took on a life of its own. The impact and importance of that brave and doomed stockade is debated back and forth. What is clear is that the myth has become as real as the events and that it holds an integral spot in the history of Australian nationalism. What has been argued here is that the Eureka Stockade was both a symptom of the ongoing push for democratic reform in Australia and around the empire and that the democratic philosophy of the digger's leaders and sympathisers in the press had more of a civic republican flavour than liberal. The final chapter of this book will expound further on the place of Eureka in the fierce battle of ideas that affected all British colonies in the first half of the nineteenth century.

10

Responsible Government: A Liberal or a Civic Republican Legacy?

The triumph of those principles, which distinguish freedom from
despotism, and constitutional government from political thraldom
is now complete.

Banner, 28 January 1848

The history of ideas is not an exact science and humans by nature do not fit neatly into ideological boxes. It is without controversy to say that the first half of the nineteenth century was characterized by a push for greater democracy in the British Empire. This book has examined the cases of Australia and Canada, but the argument for reform was being articulated everywhere, from Ireland to India, South Africa to New Zealand, and in Britain itself. By the middle of the century, democracy was normative in Australia and Canada, and by the end of the century both were federated commonwealth nations. These two nations, divided by oceans and hemispheres, followed a remarkably similar path. They looked to each other and to the mother country for inspiration, and the metropole itself was influenced by the theories and examples of the colonies. A famous passage in Cicero's *De Re Publica* states, "populus autem non omnis hominum coetus quoquo modo congregatus, sed coetus multitudinis iuris consensu et utilitatis communion sociatus" (a people is not any group of humans gathered together in any old way, but a multitude of people who take an oath and agree to serve the common good of the society).[1] This definition of a people applies perfectly to diaspora of British subjects who left for North America and Australasia. Important questions were being asked about the nature of citizenship, the ideal society and the meaning of the British constitution. How would these two societies, separated from Britain by waves but joined in spirit, wish to live?

In Nova Scotia today, there is a modest stone memorial that commemorates the granting of responsible government. The tablet reads: "First responsible government in the British Empire overseas. The first Executive Council, chosen exclusively from the party having a majority in the representative branch of a colonial legislature, was formed in Nova Scotia on the 2nd February 1848."[2] This humble tribute does not compare to the myriad of parks, statues, buildings, and other memorials that dot the United States in celebration of their Revolutionary War. Nonetheless, this development in Nova Scotia would prove as epoch-making as any revolution. In Charles Smith's play demonizing the passing of the Rebellion Losses Bill, one scene sees La Fontaine asking the governor general for his opinion. Smith has Elgin reply, "Gentlemen, you may do just as you wish on the matter for I maintain that its one of the prerogatives of my office to know nothing, see nothing, do nothing, feel nothing; therefore I shall maintain a 'dignified neutrality.'"[3] As odious as this dignified neutrality was to the tories, it emphatically marked the establishment of a new concept of freedom that had been gaining momentum for over half a century. The colonists were not, and largely did not wish to be, free from the British connection but simply free from domination. The new democratic interpretation of freedom enabled them to control their own local affairs while still being duty bound to create and protect the British nature of their society.

This book has not argued that liberalism played little or no role in the development of democracy in Australia and Canada. It does, however, veer from orthodoxy by identifying civic republicanism as a major ideological force during the transition to responsible government and asserts that of the two it was probably the more prominent. The traditional dichotomy saw the nineteenth century as a constant duel between toryism and liberalism, the conservatives and the reformers, with the latter crowned as the eventual winner. The problem with this interpretation is that the language of the reformers repeatedly invokes civic virtue, collectivism, and the need for a democratic check on government officials to ensure that they acted for the common good. The British radicals, who influenced their colonial brethren so greatly, were speaking of the moral superiority of classical republicanism before the Rebellions of 1837–38 took place in the Canadas. The *Brighton Patriot* looked to ancient Rome, noting that "the Romans began their career by the establishment of Monarch, but they soon found that that species of government was ill suited to the freedom of their mind or the vigour of the character... they vowed eternal hatred to kings, and established a republic in which the most virtuous and most eminent citizens were eligible by the people to the office of consul."[4] In many respects, the democratic putsch was seen as a moral prerogative. As William Baldwin confided to his son, "I really believe the fight is with the power of darkness."[5] This rhetoric is more at home in the republican lexicon.

It is with the benefit of hindsight and a displacement from the emotions and passions of the day that the philosophy of civic republicanism can be identified as integral to the understanding of citizenship and the British constitution during the transition to responsible government in Australia and Canada. A number of considerations explain why this term has not been widely used before. For the contemporary figures (and to a great extent today's academics and the general public) the term "republicanism" was inextricably tied to separatist republicanism. The revolutions in America and France saw the term smeared with blood and left as a political insult, a synonym for anarchy, disloyalty, and treason. Republicanism, then and now, is understood primarily as separatist republicanism, a theory that is mutually exclusive of monarchy.

There is no small irony in branding republicanism in all forms an anti-monarchical theory, since liberalism by its very nature is more antagonistic to hereditary rule than civic republicanism. Contemporary figures are excused from this oversight on the very reasonable grounds that it was almost exclusively tories who brandished republicanism as an insult, and they were equally against liberalism as they were against republicanism. When Sir Francis Bond Head christened his reformist opponents the "republican party" in Upper Canada's election of 1836, it was hardly because he supported a liberal party. For modern readers the paradox is less easily explained. The rise of liberalism accompanied the demise of absolute monarchs and championed the rights of the individual. Liberalism does not require the absence of monarchy in the way separatist republicanism does, but it is certainly far from conducive to it. To put it another way, liberal philosophy would not necessarily remove a monarchy in a society that had one, but it would never create a monarchy in a society that did not. Derek Heater characterized liberalism well when he described its rise as a shift away from a "monarch-subject relationship to a state-citizenship relationship."[6]

Civic republicanism holds no prejudice against monarchy as an institution. The ideal mixed constitution of Aristotle saw it as an important element in an ideal society. The rise of liberalism and the declining political power of hereditary monarchs did not, however, make civic republicanism a redundant theory. Rather, civic republicanism adapted itself to the democratic mood of the late eighteenth and early nineteenth centuries. In the United States, John Adams adapted the mixed constitution so that a president or chief executive would replace the king, leaving the upper and lower houses to represent aristocracy and democracy respectively.[7] In the British world, the power of the monarch had been fundamentally challenged in the English Revolution of 1649 and the Glorious Revolution of 1688. By the reign of Queen Victoria, the transformation was complete. In his celebrated treatise on the English constitution, Walter Bagehot commented in 1867, "the sovereign has, under a constitutional monarchy such as ours, three rights – the right to be consulted, the right to encourage, the right to warn. And a king of great sense and sagacity would want no others."[8] Speaking of this transformation a century later, Australian prime minister Sir Robert Menzies noted that "the Monarch is no longer the tyrant, but the symbol."[9] But what was the monarch a symbol of? For many Australian and Canadian colonists the answer was clear: virtue.

The liberalism that grew out of the philosophy of Immanuel Kant and John Locke is intrinsically tied to the notion of individual rights. In this paradigm of thought, freedom from interference is paramount, and even the greater good of society is not imperative enough to violate the individuals' right to peacefully and lawfully conduct their affairs. In his famous critique, Michael Sandel refers to this as "deontological liberalism."[10] Civic republicanism turns this theory on its head and argues that freedom from domination is paramount and that the common good of society needs to be advanced even at the expense of individual rights. Political scientists identify all shades of liberalism, particularly libertarian and egalitarian, just as civic republicanism can be divided into moderate and socialist camps. Looking at the birth of colonial democracy in Australia and Canada, however, we must first ask, did these British societies seek a democracy based on individual rights or on community welfare? Were the rebellions of 1837, the stockade at Eureka in 1854, and all the passionate lobbying in between seeking freedom from interference or freedom from domination? This book concludes that the latter was the primary concern. The good preceded the right.

Although civic republican and liberal theory both endorsed greater democracy in mid-nineteenth-century Australia and Canada, the balance of emphasis was quite different. For Australia the focus was more on duty to the community, while the latter placed greater importance on the rights of the individual. The campaign for responsible government took over half a century if it is to be traced from the debates in the aftermath of the American War of Independence. During that time democratic reformers of all stripes emerged. Liberalism and separatist republicanism were certainly endorsed by various players with various motives. Taken as a whole, the single most consistent argument was not advocating individual rights but the right of the community to live under the British constitution. The prospectus of Howe's *Novascotian* summarized well the popular feeling when it demanded the constitution, the whole constitution, and nothing but the constitution.[11] The meaning of the British constitution, of course, was a contested idea, fiercely fought for in the debates of Mackenzie and Head, Howe and Johnstone, Wentworth and Deniehy, and so many others. Nonetheless, it was a communitarian debate and the central questions concerned not just how a British community should be governed but how British citizens should behave.

This book has also introduced the term "Christian civic republicanism" to describe reformers who saw the Bible and the Christian faith as the logical foundation of a virtuous society. The seamless merging of religious and democratic rhetoric by some reformers is striking. One banner that was typical of this ideology was proudly waved at a reform rally in Lower Canada. It read, "Liberty, The bread of the people and the will of God."[12] Men like Mackenzie and Lang were convinced that their democratic agitation was not simply a good thing but God's will for their respective colonies and the world. Christian civic republicanism is a topic that could warrant its extensive research. This book, while acknowledging the openly religious nature of some reformers, has focussed instead on the broader ideology, including civic republican reformers for whom religion was not central.

In his final book, *On Duties*, Cicero offers this wisdom to his son: "we are not born for ourselves alone, to use Plato's splendid words, but our country claims for itself one part of our birth, and our friends another."[13] This sense of civic duty and the obligation to promote the greater good of society over individual gain is central to civic republican thinking. The same sentiment was expressed by Howe when he addressed the Mechanics' Institute on 5 November 1835. He insisted that it was "the duty of each individual to cast into the public treasury of Nova Scotia's reputation something to make her 'loved at home, revered abroad.'"[14] John Dunmore Lang was similarly convinced that the people had a civic duty to place the community before the individual. Lang dedicated a great deal of time, effort, and money (often other people's) towards bringing virtuous British citizens to Australia. In his *Australian Emigrant's Manual* he warned that "your adopted country also expects you to do your duty to her," because "Australia will soon date her existence as a great nation."[15] The reformers in Australia and Canada believed a great destiny awaited their homelands, but it was incumbent on the people to act virtuously for the common good to realize it.

What we often find in the speeches and sentiments of prominent reformers is contractarian thinking. It is not a liberal demand for democratic rights but rather a complex system of rights and responsibilities in the ultimate social contract, the British constitution. The concept of Britishness proved to be transportable to the far reaches of the red-painted globe. Linda Colley has argued that "impressive numbers of Britons did make the step from passive awareness of a nation to an energetic participation on its behalf." She insists, however, that British race patriotism did not simply spread because it was "recommended from above, but also because [average people] expected to profit from it in some way."[16] Reform leaders in Canada and Australia certainly expected to profit when they contested the meaning of the British constitution with their tory opponents. They used the rhetoric of Britishness to pursue a democratic agenda, fully expecting a society of virtue to be their reward. They demanded that the colonial office and the British parliament allow them their rights and liberties, but crucially, they made demands also of their own communities. They were required to behave in a manner worthy of Britishers. They were duty bound to both the mother country and their home colony to maintain the international reputation of British people by keeping alive the spirit of virtue for which they celebrated their ancestors so joyfully.

Dual patriotism is a phenomenon that manifests itself almost exclusively in immigrant nations. In the cases of Australia and Canada the feeling was particularly intense since the concept of Britishness proved it could be transported across the seas and the oak of British liberty could find fertile soil in foreign lands. When the Young Men's Debating Society met in Mason's Hall on 3 February 1848, they toasted Nova Scotia with these words: "our Country, our Birthplace, our Home. May the energy and independence of her sons be commensurate to her resources". Then they toasted Britain, "our Fatherland – the Cradle of Nations, land of Statesmen, Poets and Philanthropists. The dispenser of knowledge and the diffuser of civilization. 'We hail thee.'"[17] They truly loved both places, just in different ways. It was not simply the case that they had warm feelings of attachment to their old country while living in a new country. These people considered themselves without qualification to be British citizens living in British communities abroad. They were British Canadians and British Australians. The bogey of separatist republicanism has served to artificially divide the Australian and Canadian colonists into two camps, loyalists and (separatist) republicans. To adhere to this forced binary is to uncritically accept the propaganda from the mid-nineteenth-century tory election machine.

Alexander Mackay argued in the wake of the Rebellion Losses Bill that separatism was in fact a "false issue." He wrote in 1849: "The only real issue between the parties was whether or not the colony was to have the Parliamentary government which was promised it. But the false issue raised was whether the colony was to remain connected with the Mother Country or not. "No separation" was emblazoned on the electioneering banners of the Tories, and "no separation" was the cry at their electioneering meetings. But all this time, no one talked of separation but themselves. By means of this cry, however, and by other acts, the liberals were overborne and the British government and people were cheated into the belief that a great service had been rendered them by those, who were working only for themselves."[18] Mackay is highlighting the fact that separatist republicanism was only ever on the outer periphery of colonial debates and that the alarm bells rung by the conservative press were little more than an exercise in what modern linguistics would call wedge politics.

Mackay would have found a handy ally in Henry Parkes, who voiced his frustration at the "bugbear" of republicanism in 1853.

Given the minimal support for political separation from Britain, Parkes decried the conservative tactic of using republicanism to "frighten the sober politicians of New South Wales out of their righteous demands." Parkes goes on to praise the "doctrine of representation" in England and lament the fact that when colonial reformers attempt to introduce it locally it is "dreaded and impugned under the terrible name of republicanism."[19] Joseph Howe evoked Cato, the great Roman symbol of civic republicanism, when refuting L.M. Wilkins' claim in February 1846 that democratic principles would sever the relationship between Britain and her colonies. Howe replied: "The learned gentleman tells us self-government will terminate our allegiance; I tell him it will preserve it. Cato required his wife to suckle the children of his servants that they might become more attached to the family; and I say, let us suck liberty that we may love England."[20] The Australian and Canadian colonists were dual patriots. They loved the law and spirit of the homeland, and they wanted to see it firmly planted in their new land, a land they also loved.

Dual patriotism had taken such firm root in Australia and Canada because the colonists were able to express both a love of their native land and a pride in their heritage. Their identity was an indissoluble blend of love of country and love of legacy. Britishness can be understood as a secular religion that provided the colonists with a culture, language, and history of which they were immensely proud and which they thought to be unique among the nations of the world. In 1840 the *Perth Gazette and Western Australian Journal* argued against free trade and for a British preferential trade system, highlighting that the former relied on the whims of fortune while there was no limit on "the growing demand for articles of British production from the men of British race and British habits in the Colonies."[21] This is far more than a friendly nostalgia towards their former country. They believed the British race to be a real and living thing, a spirit of virtue that travelled with them even to the ends of the world. Mackay was correct to deduce that political separation was not the burning issue of the day. The real bone of contention between the tory and reformist packs concerned the place of democracy in British society.

It was in this struggle that the *Durham Report* proved truly to be a grand compromise. Durham's call for responsible government reveals a masterful understanding of the nature of dual patriotism, specifically in Canada, but also all over the British Empire. Durham perceived that directly from the colonists' firmly rooted identity as Britishers sprang the desire to be treated the same as their brethren at home and a violent refusal to submit to arbitrary government. The *Durham Report* recognized also that the Imperial Parliament gained nothing from micro-managing these distant colonies and that it was only on a world stage that the mother country desired control. By separating local governance from international policy Durham created a proposal that recreated in legislation the heartfelt desires of the colonists. On the one hand, they gained what they desired most, the freedom to conduct their own affairs and control their own money and the power to determine their destiny, which they saw as nothing less than the rights of freemen under the British constitution. On the other hand, they remained joined in spirit and in legislation to their ancestral home. They remained duty bound to their Queen to defend and advance the British race all over the world.

The mid-nineteenth century was an exciting time in the history of the British world. Between 1848 and 1856 colonies all over British North America and Australasia demanded and received responsible government. The transformative effect on the British Empire of this fundamental policy shift can hardly be overstated. It is no exaggeration to say that the granting of responsible government birthed a new British Empire with Durhamite principles as its guiding light. Democracy had become normative in the British world but, as the *Weekly Despatch* cautioned in 1850, "democracy is ruined by democrats." Was it a desire for liberal democracy that spurred the reformers to advocate responsible government so forcefully? To an extent liberalism played a role, certainly, but time and again we find positive liberty and contractarian, community-minded thinking woven into the concept of British freedom. The *Despatch* sternly warned that freedom from interference was not enough, for "you may easily give a bull the run of a china shop – but what would become of the crockery?" In addition to personal rights must come a duty to pursue the common good, for "virtue, intelligence, goodness, are the conditions precedent to liberty."[22]

When the historian considers the writings, speeches, and actions of the colonial reformers in Australia and Canada, the underlying context seems to be a battle of ideas over what it meant to be British and how a British community abroad should live. The power of this stalwart conceptualization of Britishness is sometimes difficult for the modern scholar to disentangle from the cacophony of rhetoric, but even a century after the granting of responsible government the sentiment remained firmly rooted in public consciousness. In 1949 the Australian politician and United Nations president Dr H.V. Evatt defended the retention of the term "British" in "British Commonwealth of Nations." The *Times* lauded Evatt, noting: "The word is an historically right description which can be retained without implying the slightest claim of people from the British Isles to authority over their fellow subjects in other self-governing realms. It is an epithet, once national, which has so far changed its connotation that it now commemorates the historical origin of a system of ideas and a way of life by which members of an international community are linked."[23] Britishness was central to the colonists not because it located their origins but because it tied them into a system of ideas and values that after the 1850s included representative and responsible local government. Britishness was a powerful fount of identity from which flowed concepts of both how they should be governed fairly and how they should conduct their affairs with virtue. This book has argued that civic republicanism was a primary philosophical prism through which local colonial patriotism and filial loyalty were reconciled.

In their heterodox work, *Canada's Origins,* Janet Ajzenstat and Peter J. Smith argue that the whiggish, linear interpretation of Canada's democratic evolution is deeply flawed. The standard view acknowledged Lockean liberalism as the dominant ideological force of the nineteenth-century British world and viewed democratic advancements such as the granting of responsible government as important milestones on the journey from toryism to liberalism. Ajzenstat and Smith argue that a powerful third ideology was at play and that "the challenge to nineteenth-century liberalism arose from a republican ideology on the political left, rather than toryism on the right." They conclude that "the formative influence in Canada's past was not solely liberalism, or the combination of liberalism and tory conservatism, but a lively opposition between liberalism and civic republican philosophy with a progressive agenda."[24] Ajzenstat has since taken a more Lockean position, arguing that "scholars rewrote Canadian history and the story of Confederation, ascribing to the Fathers a preference for collective provision and the regulatory state."[25] This work has not challenged Ajzenstat's new position directly, since it focuses on an earlier period. By examining the rhetoric of reformers during the campaign for responsible government in British North American and the Australasian colonies, however, ample evidence of civic republican thought shaping and influencing the emerging democracy in these British communities has been found, and it is likely that this continued to have an impact during the confederation and federation debates in Canada and Australia respectively.

The people and communities who shaped the world centuries ago were complex, compelling, and often contradictory. It is important to avoid crude caricatures and stringent ideological labelling. A helpful starting point is to appreciate the rich bricolage of thought and emotion that must have been present at a time of great social and political change. In highlighting the influence of republican thought on the American Revolution, J.G.A. Pocock commented on the infinite combinations of political ideas that were always present in both the individual and the collective minds at a time of crisis and instability. He concludes that "the commitment to virtue, to the Machiavellian moment, had a way of producing this result; it made men aware that they were centaurs."[26] This book has made no attempt to claim figures or communities as civic republicans as opposed to liberals. Rather, it has attempted to reconceptualize the history of ideas that led to democracy in general and responsible government in particular becoming established and accepted in the British world.

The extent to which civic republican and liberal thought affected the nascent democracies of the British world in the mid-nineteenth century is something that can be debated ad nauseam. The research for this book leads to the conclusion that, of the two, civic republicanism was probably the more dominant idea. In any case, the purpose here has simply been to re-examine the place of republicanism in colonial Australian and Canadian thought and to present it as an overlooked or lost history. Vickie Sullivan has recently argued that so many eighteenth-century English thinkers were demonstrably influenced by both traditions that the term "liberal republicanism" should be employed.[27] Pocock's metaphoric centaur is helpful in conceptualizing the history of ideas leading to the democratization of Australia and Canada. Part liberal, part civic republican, the beast of democracy left the stable of toryism to roam uncharted places. Whatever the makeup, it must acknowledge that there was a tension between the individualistic, rights-based, negative liberty of liberalism and the communitarian, duty-based, positive liberty of civic republicanism in the history of democratic ideas in Australia and Canada.

The fight for responsible government in the British world is sometimes dismissed as, at best, the gradual progression to a historical inevitability and, at worst, simply boring. This is largely due to the fact that it was never really a physical fight. There was no grand oppressor to take up arms against. The Rebellions of 1837–38 and the Eureka Stockade stand out as anomalies. They were physical manifestations of what must be considered a battle of ideas that was fought not with cannon and bayonet but with oratory, petition, and the press. Why did Mackenzie and the reformers of Upper Canada fight to democratize their constitution: to fight the corruption of the Family Compact. Why did Howe lead the Nova Scotians towards responsible government: to allow them to live with the freedoms they believed were inherent in British citizenship. Why did John West and his Tasmanians mount such a ferocious campaign against convict transportation? To create a society of virtue. Why did Peter Lalor risk his life in the Eureka Rebellion? To reject arbitrary government and insist that the voice of the people must be heard in parliament. In every instance examined in this book, the pattern is repeated. In those crucial few years before the granting of responsible government, the reformers continually petitioned not for individual rights but for the collective good of the community. Even when traditional rights-based ideas like manhood suffrage and elected Upper Houses were championed, the emphasis was not on the right but on the common good. These democratic advances were made in order to establish a British society abroad founded on virtue and with safeguards against corruption.

Plotting the murder of the tyrant Caesar for the common good of Rome, the bard imagined Cassius offering these words to his reluctant co-conspirator: "men at some time are masters of their fates: the fault, dear Brutus, is not in the stars, but in ourselves."[28] This advice was echoed in the faraway lands that would become Australia and Canada. The British colonists in those places were convinced that they were indeed masters of their own fate. The dagger of change was in their hands, and they collectively thrust it deep into the heart of what they deemed a corrupt colonial policy. The Roman experience formed a powerful analogy in the English-speaking world, and Cato, the champion of virtue and the Roman republic, was looked to for guidance as British colonists faced their own Machiavellian moment. While the pages of colonial journals were littered with wisdom from anonymous writers using this prestigious moniker, it was the enormously influential letters of John Trenchard that did the most to ensure that the legend of Cato was kept alive centuries after his death.[29] In his letter *Considerations on the Weaknesses and Inconsistencies of Human Nature*, Cato agreed with Machiavelli that the law must suppose "all men naturally wicked."[30] Holding the Ciceronian ideal of *aequalitas*, Cato insisted that "if therefore we would look for Virtue in a Nation, we must look for it in the Nature of Government."[31] Durham's grand compromise and the granting of responsible government allowed the British colonists of Australia and Canada to enjoy a system of government that they felt helped virtue and hindered corruption.

Over a century and half after the granting of responsible government, Australia and Canada are still not constitutional republics. The gradual breakup of the British Empire and the establishment of both countries as independent nations did not result in a complete unravelling of the Durhamite bonds that once held the universal family of Britishers together so closely. Despite a wave of Australian and Canadian neo-nationalism stemming from the 1960s, separatist republicanism remained on the political fringe, and it seems no more likely to eventuate today than it did in the 1840s and 1850s.[32] And yet Australia and Canada do have a lengthy republican tradition that powerfully shaped their colonial experience and affected the nature of the democracies they would become. Civic republican thought played a largely uncredited role in the tempering of Lockean liberalism with a form of British communitarianism. Concepts of Britishness and the rights and responsibilities encompassed in British citizenship were central to the agitation and granting of responsible government. The question was not, however, what rights men are entitled to but how a British community abroad should live. The fearless pursuit of this question led the colonists down the road to democracy, and reformist ideas from the ends of the empire would rebound to shape the metropole itself. The history of ideas in the mid-nineteenth-century British world must consider civic republicanism a powerful, formative influence. In the pursuit of positive liberty, the adoration of civic virtue, and the primacy of *bonum commune communitatis* over *bonum commune hominis*, the lost republican history of Canada and Australia is revealed.

APPENDIX ONE

Timeline of the Rebellions of 1837–1838

19 June 1791   The Constitution Act is given the royal assent. The act authorized the separation of Quebec into Protestant, English-dominated Upper Canada and Roman Catholic, French-dominated Lower Canada. It gave both provinces a bicameral legislature and representative but not responsible government.

21 February 1834   Louis-Joseph Papineau releases the Ninety-Two Resolutions protesting the undemocratic nature of government in Lower Canada.

October 1834   Upper Canadian Reformers win control of the Legislative Assembly. There is great tension between the democratic reformers and the oligarchical clique, the Family Compact who dominate the Executive Council.

December 1835   Francis Bond Head is appointed Lieutenant Governor of Upper Canada. Head is an ultra-conservative with little political experience.

15 April 1836   Upper Canadian Reformers in the Assembly vote to block supply in protest of Head and the Family Compact.

June 1836	New elections are held. Bond campaigns vigorously for the conservatives, claiming that the reformers are disloyal republicans. The conservatives take control of the Legislative Assembly. Reforms complain of corruption and Head's influence.
4 July 1836	William Lyon Mackenzie, having lost his seat at the election, launches the *Constitution* and advocates radical agitation.
March–May 1837	Lord Russell's Ten Resolutions pass through the British Houses of Parliament. The Resolutions reject responsible government.
23 October 1837	Five thousand French Canadians from six counties gather to petition for greater democracy.
13 November 1837	Upper Canadian Reformers draft a new constitution for the province. Plans for a rebellion are discussed.
16 November 1837	Arrest warrants are issued for Lower Canadian Reform leaders, including Papineau and Wolfred Nelson.
23 November 1837	Rebel forces defend Saint-Denis against British attack.
25 November 1837	British forces defeat the rebels at Saint-Charles.
4 December 1837	Upper Canadian rebels assemble at Montgomery's Tavern after the rebellion date is brought forward. Many rebels did not hear about the late change. A small confrontation between rebels and a loyalist militia takes place.

7 December 1837	Government forces defeat the Upper Canadian rebels at Montgomery's Tavern. Mackenzie and other leaders flee to the sympathetic United States.
14 December 1837	British forces defeat Lower Canadian rebels and burn the village of Saint-Eustache.
November 1838	Following the resignation of Lord Durham, rebellion breaks out again in Lower Canada but is quickly crushed.
July 1840	The Act of Union unites Lower and Upper Canada in one united Province of Canada.

APPENDIX TWO

Timeline of the Eureka Stockade[1]

1 July 1851	Following agitation from reformers including Lang, New South Wales and Port Phillip separate creating the Colony of Victoria.
August 1851	Gold is discovered at Ballarat, and the gold licence system is introduced.
Nov–Dec 1853	Many diggers are angry with the licence fee because it is expensive and is payable whether or not any gold is found. The heavy-handed nature and perceived corruption of the police further agitates the miners. Many protest as the fee is increased.
22 June 1854	Governor Charles Hotham replaces La Trobe. Hotham increased the frequency of licence hunts to every week in a bid to counter government debt.
13 September 1854	Licence hunts are increased again to bi-weekly.
7 October 1854	James Scobie is murdered outside the Eureka Hotel. Inn keeper James Bently is believed by many diggers to be responsible.

10 October 1854	The disabled servant of Fr Smyth (parish priest) is beaten and arrested for not holding a licence. Irish diggers see this as a personal insult.
12 October 1854	Bentley is released owing to lack of evidence. Many diggers suspect corruption.
15 October 1854	A monster meeting is held on Bakery Hill to protest the treatment of Fr Smyth's servant.
17 October 1854	A meeting of up to ten thousand diggers is held near the Eureka Hotel to protest Bentley's acquittal. The meeting results in the burning of the hotel.
23 October 1854	The diggers send a deputation to Commissioner Rede seeking to have the police involved in the arrest of Fr Smyth's servant removed.
11 November 1854	The Ballarat Reform League is formed.
20 November 1854	James Bentley, Thomas Farrell, and William Hence are convicted of the manslaughter of James Scobie.
29 November 1854	A monster meeting is held on Bakery Hill attended by more than ten thousand diggers.
30 November 1854	Diggers refuse to show their licences and throw rocks at the troopers The Riot Act is read. Approximately six diggers are arrested and taken. Another meeting is held on Bakery Hill, and Peter Lalor becomes leader of the diggers. Hundreds of volunteers swear an oath to defend their rights and liberties under the Flag of the Southern Cross. A number of diggers erect a barricade.

2 December 1854	Father Smyth tries to persuade Catholics to lay down their arms.
3 December 1854	Soldiers and police attack the stockade and quickly defeat the diggers. Twenty-two diggers and seven military are killed. Many others are wounded and arrested.
4 December 1854	Martial Law is proclaimed in Ballarat. Henry Seekamp, the editor of the Ballarat Times, is arrested.
6 December 1854	Thirteen prisoners are charged with treason.
23 January 1855	Henry Seekamp is tried and found guilty of seditious libel.
Feb-March 1855	The thirteen Stockaders excluding Thomas Dignum are tried and found not guilty of treason. The charge against Dignum is withdrawn.
27 March 1855	The Gold Fields Commission Report is presented. It recommends a duty on gold and the abolition of the license. It also advocates greater rights for diggers.
10 November 1855	Peter Lalor and John Basson Hummfray are elected to the Legislative Council.

Notes

CHAPTER ONE

1 G.K. Raudzens, "Upper Canada and New South Wales."
2 Some of the noteworthy works comparing Australia and Canada include Bruce W. Hodgins et al., *Federalism in Canada and Australia*; Oliver, *The Constitution of Independence;* and Brown, *Three Rebellions.*
3 To borrow Peter Oliver's expression. See Oliver, *The Constitution of Independence*, 1.
4 Anna Clark concludes in her recent illuminating work on history in schools that "for too many students, Australian history is 'repetitive' or 'boring' or both. But is that their fault or ours?" Clark, *History's Children*, 141.
5 Manning Clark's influential *History of Australia* is typical of the Australian orthodoxy. The distinction is made between tory and whig, exclusive and emancipist, sterling and currency, but the progressive reformers sit together under the philosophical umbrella of liberalism. For example, see Clark in reference to the arrival of the "liberal" Governor Bourke. Clark, *History of Australia*, 138–9.
6 Headon et al., *Crown or Country*, 1.
7 The Australia Acts 1986 (Cth and UK) removed any remaining power of the United Kingdom to legislate for or interfere with Australia. As a result, republicanism in the 1990s was largely conceptualized as the process of removing the last constitutional link to Britain and taking the final step towards "true" independence.
8 Smith, *The Republican Option in Canada*, 3.
9 Headon, *Crown or Country*, 4.
10 Berlin, *Four Essays on Liberty.*

11 This definition is not accepted by all. Quentin Skinner, in particular, would contest that republicanism should be seen as a unique type of negative liberty differentiated from liberalism by its emphasis on virtue. This will be addressed more fully later in the chapter.
12 Pettit, *Republicanism*.
13 Michael Sandel, *Liberalism*.
14 It is important to remember that the colonists in Australia and Canada did indeed view Britain not as a geographical location but as a distinct race to which they belonged. This was a powerful cultural identifier and goes some way to explaining the intense dual patriotism readily exhibited by reformers in both places.
15 Curtis, "After 'Canada,'" 182.
16 Inspired by McKay's essay, the McGill Institute for the Study of Canada hosted the Liberal Order in Canadian History symposium in March 2006. The lectures were subsequently published as a book. McKay, "The Liberal Order Framework," and DuCharme and Constant, *Liberalism and Hegemony*.
17 For example, in *Liberalism and the Australian Federation* (a work commissioned by the Liberal Party of Australia), Greg Melleuish argues convincingly that turn-of-the-century Victorian liberalism was entirely different from New South Wales liberalism. Nethercote, *Liberalism and the Australian Federation*.
18 McKay, "The Liberal Order Framework."
19 When the *Report* reached Sydney in mid-1839 the *Sydney Monitor and Commercial Advertiser* proclaimed that Durham had taught the colonies the "difference between bad and good government." *Sydney Monitor and Commercial Advertiser*, 21 June 1839.
20 The astonishingly diverse historiography of Eureka is explored in chapter 8.
21 See, for example, Bridge and Fedorowich, *The British World*; Colley, *Britons*; Ward, *Britishness since 1870;* Arnold, *Cultural Identities and the Aesthetics of Britishness*; Darian-Smith, Grimshaw, and Macintyre, *Britishness Abroad*.
22 Marshall, *Citizenship and Social Class*.
23 For specific criticisms that Marshall's theory applies imperfectly to British settler societies such as Australia and Canada, see Barbalet, "Developments in Citizenship Theory"; and Pearson. "Theorising Citizenship." For more general criticisms see Bulmer and Rees, *Citizenship Today*.
24 The anti-transportation protests discussed in chapter 7 provide a case in point.

25 Anderson, *Imagined Communities*, 6.
26 Colley, *Britons*, xvi, 5, 6, 11, 55, 369.
27 Or in the case of convicts heading to Australia, their sense of Britishness was virtually their only possession.
28 Bridge and Fedorowich, *The British World*, 7–10.
29 Again, the juxtaposition of patriotic songs and effigy burning is discussed in chapter 7.
30 Lipset, *Political Man*.
31 *Canadian Freeman*, 24 July 1828.
32 Lindsay and Lindsay, *William Lyon Mackenzie*, 37.
33 See, for example, Lyon, *Politicians in the Pulpit;* Shaw and Kreider, *Culture and the Nonconformist Tradition*; Rix, *William Blake*; Latham, *Search for a New Eden*.
34 Pickering and Tyrrell, "'In the Thickest of the Fight,'" 473–9.
35 Tyrrell, *Joseph Sturge and the Moral Radical Party*.
36 All these figures and their Biblical language will be explored throughout this book.
37 Beck, *Joseph Howe: Conservative Reformer*, 16.
38 Headon and Perkins, *Our First Republicans*, 129. West, *History of Tasmania*, 261.
39 Wilson, *The Clergy Reserves*, 3.
40 *St. Thomas Liberal*, August 1837, reprinted in Lindsay, *The Life and Times of Wm. Lyon Mackenzie*, 391.
41 Kierkegaard, *Either/or*.
42 Insofar as these societies and individuals are bound to hold multiple contrasting views that, nevertheless, combine to create a synthesis. See Hegel, *The Science of Logic*.
43 John Mee and Paul Pickering have used the concept of bricolage with regard to nineteenth-century radicals. See Mee, *Dangerous Enthusiasm*; Pickering, *Feargus O'Connor;* and Lévi-Strauss, *The Savage Mind*.

CHAPTER TWO

1 Glare, *Oxford Latin Dictionary*, 329.
2 Aristotle, *The Politics*, 59.
3 Liddell and Scott, *A Greek-English Lexicon*, 1058.
4 The *Ekklesia* was a large decision-making assembly that all adult males citizens were encouraged to attend. There were around thirty thousand adult male citizens in the mid-400s. A quorum of six thousand was required for the *Ekklesia* to conduct business, emphasizing the Athenians' commitment to participatory democracy in the classical period.

5 Thucydides, *History of the Peloponnesian*, 111.
6 Aristotle, *The Politics of Aristotle*, 94-6.
7 The term *polis* (πόλις) has a generic meaning referring to a state or community, but it particularly refers to a free state or republic. See Liddell and Scott, *Lexicon*, 1433-4.
8 Aristotle, *Nicomachean Ethics*, 7.
9 Cicero, *De Re Publica De Legibus*, 15.
10 Cicero, *On the Commonwealth and On the Laws*.
11 The dates of Polybius' birth and death are a subject of debate among classical historians. It is, however, of little consequence here, since this study is interested in his legacy rather than his life. The dates used are taken from William Smith's 1870 dictionary of ancient Greek and Roman personalities. See Smith, *Dictionary of Greek and Roman Antiquities*.
12 Polybius, *The Histories of Polybius*, 468.
13 Sellers, *American Republicanism*, 46-9.
14 Peek Jr, *The Political Writings of John Adams*, 105-7.
15 Sellers, *American Republicanism*, 70.
16 Wirszubski, *Libertas as a Political Idea*, 9.
17 Honohan, *Civic Republicanism*, 48.
18 Machiavelli, *The Discourses*, 111-12.
19 Machiavelli, *Selected Political Writings*, 96.
20 Gallagan, *A Federal Republic*, 24.
21 Koritansky, "Thomas Paine," 72.
22 Collinson, *Elizabethan Essays*, 31-57.
23 It should be noted, however, that Paine did think that republic and absolute monarchy were "naturally opposed," since the former sought the good of the people and the latter the good of the monarch. In this, Paine's republicanism is of a different shade from that of the civic republican thinkers who were more willing to accept a monarchy provided that it was also tempered by the power of the second and third estates and provided the common good was still the highest goal. Had Paine lived to see the granting of responsible government to British colonies and the birth of the second empire with its limited monarchy, it is doubtful his opposition to any form of monarchy would have remained as intense. See Paine, *Rights of Man*, 75.
24 Machiavelli, *Discourses*, 109.
25 Peek, *The Political Writings of John Adams*, xvi-xvii.
26 Hobbes, *Leviathan*, 137, 162, 481.
27 Locke, *Two Treatises of Government*.
28 Harrington, *The Commonwealth of Oceana*, 8-10.

29 The patriotic militia is a particularly Machiavellian tact for producing citizens who will fight for the common good rather than individual gain.
30 Honohan, *Civic Republicanism*, 68.
31 Hobbes, *Leviathan*, 167.
32 Harrington, *Commonwealth*, 20.
33 This was how Hobbes described the views put forward in Milton's *Pro Populo Anglicano Defensio* (1651).
34 Armitage, Himy, and Skinner, *Milton and Republicanism*, 6, 16, 25.
35 Morison, *Milton and Liberty*, 56.
36 Taken from his 1634 masque "Comus."
37 To use Pocock's terminology. This idea will be elaborated on later in the chapter.
38 Armitage, Himy, and Skinner, *Milton and Republicanism*, 26.
39 Filmer, *Patriarcha*.
40 Sidney, *Discourses Concerning Government*, 104–6.
41 Scott, *Algernon Sidney*.
42 Ibid., 210.
43 The "Locke and none else" paradigm could be considered the dominant orthodoxy in American historiography before the republican revisionism of the 1970s. The revisionists and their impact will be considered later in this chapter. See also Shalhope, "Towards a Republican Synthesis," 49.
44 Gough, "Review," 695.
45 Mitchell, "A Liberal Republican 'Cato,'" 588.
46 Anonymous, *Cato's Letters*, 37.
47 Mitchell, "A Liberal Republican "Cato,'" 588.
48 Typifying the caustic nature of Anglo-French relations at the time, Macaulay qualified his comment by attributing Montesquieu's renown to good "fortune." He notes that "The English at that time considered a Frenchman who talked about constitutional checks and fundamental laws, as a prodigy not less astonishing than a learned pig or the musical infant." Macaulay, *The Modern British Essayists*, 33.
49 Montesquieu, *The Spirit of the Laws*, 155.
50 Honohan, *Civic Republicanism*, 81
51 Montesquieu, *The Spirit of the Laws*, xxi, 68, 150–2
52 Richter, *The Political Theory of Montesquieu*, 3.
53 In 1886 the *Sydney Morning Herald* lamented that Harrington's *Oceana*, once so prominent and controversial, had become virtually unknown. It expressed further displeasure that the works of Hobbes, Sidney, and even Milton were also slipping into obscurity. *Sydney Morning Herald*, 11 October 1886.

54 Paul Pickering has been one of the only historians to highlight the impact of Mazzini on colonial radicals. Mazzini's impact on the Victorian goldfields is discussed in chapter 8. See Pickering, "'Glimpses of Eternal Truth'"; Pickering, "Garibaldi's Shirt."
55 Canadian negative identity theory was famously articulated by S.D. Clark in the 1930s. Clark suggested that "Canadian national life can almost be said to take its rise in the negative will to resist absorption in the American republic." Now an established school, proponents of negative identity theory include Seymour Lipset, Leslie Pal, Barry Cooper, Neil Bissoondath, and Jack Granatstein. See Clark, " Anti-Americanism in Canadian National Feeling"; James, *Constitutional Politics*, 44.
56 *Empire*, 19 November 1853.
57 McKenna, "Tracking the Republic," 4.
58 Arendt, *The Human Condition*.
59 Lovett, "Republicanism," *Stanford Encyclopedia of Philosophy*.
60 Viroli, *Republicanism*, 7–8.
61 Burckhardt, *Die Kultur*; Voigt, *Die Weiderbelebung des classischen Alterthums*.
62 Burckhardt, *Die Kultur* (translation mine), 4.
63 Baron, *The Crisis of the Early Italian Renaissance*.
64 Ferguson, "The Interpretation of Italian Humanism," 19.
65 Baron, *The Crisis*, 28.
66 Fubini, "Renaissance Historian."
67 Ferguson, "The Interpretation of Italian Humanism, 24.
68 Bernard Bailyn, *Ideological Origins*, vi, viii, 95, 130.
69 Pocock, *The Machiavellian Moment*, 506–7.
70 Moulakis, "Civic Humanism," *Stanford Encyclopedia of Philosophy*.
71 Pocock, *The Machiavellian Moment*, 454, 545.
72 Skinner, *The Foundations of Modern Political Thought*, vol. 1, *The Renaissance*, 152–61.
73 Skinner, "The Idea of Negative Liberty," 197.
74 With the obvious exception of the separatist republican tradition in Australia, which gained significant academic interest in the early 1990s.
75 Ajzenstat and Smith, *Canada's Origins*, 1.
76 Ajzenstat, *The Canadian Founding*.

CHAPTER THREE

1 Greer, "1837–38."
2 Baehre, "Trying the Rebels," 41.
3 After amnesty was granted to the rebels in exile, Mackenzie returned to become Toronto's first mayor before returning to parliament. His

grandson, William Lyon Mackenzie King went on to become Canada's longest-serving prime minster, and his image appears on the nation's fifty-dollar notes. Owing partly to intervention by his esteemed descendant and partly to the positive mythology built around him, William LeSueur's critical biography of Mackenzie was repeatedly rejected for publication. Although penned in 1907–08, it was rejected by the Makers of Canada series and not published till 1979. LeSueur, *William Lyon Mackenzie*. See also Gates, *After the Rebellion*, 321–3.

4 *Advocate*, 18 January 1834.
5 Bullion, "George III on Empire," 306.
6 Craig, *Upper Canada*, 3.
7 Allen, *Tories*.
8 Jasanoff, *Liberty's Exiles*, 8.
9 Knowles, *Inventing the Loyalists*, 14.
10 Coupland, *The Quebec Act*, 40.
11 Following the 1713 Peace of Utrecht, French Acadia was ceded to the British and renamed Nova Scotia. Despite swearing an oath of loyalty and living peaceably under British rule for decades, the Acadians were viewed as "enemies to the laws and religion of their country." The Seven Years War triggered a brutal case of ethnic cleansing. In 1755 the British governor of Nova Scotia, Charles Lawrence, confiscated the Acadians' land and forcibly transported them to hostile English colonies, separating families in the process. See *South Carolina Gazette*, 1 January 1756; Lowe, "Massachusetts and the Acadians."
12 The seigneurial regime was a system of land distribution dating back to Gallo-Roman times. Eventually integrated into the monarchic system, it was used in America as early as the sixteenth century as part of New France's colonization program. Persons of rank would receive titles and land grants known as a fiefs. These seigneurs would then be expected to recruit settlers, known as censitaires, and develop the new colony. After New France was ceded to the English the seigneurial regime began to die out. While it had served Quebec well in its formative years, the industrialization of the mid-nineteenth century revealed its semi-feudal inefficiencies. It was formally abolished on 18 December 1854 when the government paid $5 million to the remaining seigneurs to release the censitaires from their obligations. See Trudel, *The Seigneurial Regime*.
13 Wilson, *The Clergy Reserves of Upper Canada*, 3.
14 Gerald Craig offers an excellent overview of the Pitt-Fox debates concerning the constitution Act. See Craig, *Upper Canada*, 13–19.
15 *General Evening Post*, 7 April 1791.
16 *E. Johnson's British Gazette and Sunday Monitor*, 15 May 1791.

17 *Diary or Woodfall's Register*, 13 May 1791.
18 *General Evening Post*, 7 April 1791.
19 *Royal Standard*, 9 September 1836, 2.
20 McNairn, *The Capacity to Judge*, 23.
21 Fierlbeck, *Political Thought in Canada*, 45, 51.
22 In a celebrated and contested 1966 essay, Gad Horowitz used the phrase "red tory" to describe an "ideological Conservative with some 'odd' socialist notions… or an ideological socialist with some 'odd' tory notions." He specifically identified Canadian philosopher George Grant as a red tory since he had combined "elements of socialism and toryism so thoroughly into a single integrated Weltanschauung." Horowitz, "Conservatism, Liberalism, and Socialism." See Dart, *The Red Tory Tradition;* Taylor, *Radical Tories*.
23 Dunham, *Political Unrest in Upper Canada*, 136.
24 *Kingston Gazette*, 29 January 1811.
25 Mackenzie's comments on the British constitution were glowing until 1834. See *Colonial Advocate*, 16 July 1829, 13 December 1832, and 16 May 1833.
26 Wise and Brown, *Canada Views the United States*, 21.
27 This quote from John Lindsay was referring specifically to the treatment of African slaves (intriguingly, it was penned long before the abolition of slavery in Britain): "whatever the barbarous Americans may do with their African dependents; nature ne'er designed one to play the tyrant over another." More generally, however, the phrase does sum up the feeling of British people towards the American colonists. The British constitution was viewed as an ancient, proven system of governance that compared entirely favourably to the "barbarous" attempts of republican government in the American colonies. See *Memoirs of Sir Thomas Hughson and Mr Joseph Williams*, 14.
28 Smith, "*Le Canadien* and the British Constitution," 18.
29 *Le Canadien*, 23 September 1809 and 11 November 1809.
30 *Le Canadien*, 22 November 1806.
31 *Canadian Freeman*, 31 July 1828.
32 *Advocate*, 22 May 1834. Mackenzie had also used this tactic to great advantage in the election of 1828.
33 *Advocate*, 22 May 1834.
34 Glenelg to Head, 5 December 1835, 1.
35 Glenelg to Head, 5 December 1835, 3.
36 Head seems in many ways an odd choice as governor by the Colonial Office. In his own *Narrative*, he recalls the "utter astonishment" of his posting, noting he was "altogether at a loss to conceive why

this appointment should have been offered to me." One theory is that the colonial secretary, Lord Glenelg, had confused Sir Francis with his cousin Edmund Walker Head. He had no experience in colonial government and none even in politics. He was a former military engineer, manager of a semi-successful silver mine in South America, author of travel books, and assistant poor-law commissioner in Kent. He was given a knighthood by William IV in 1831 for demonstrating the military usefulness of the lasso. Although it is certainly possible Head was offered the post by accident, it should be remembered that Upper Canada was not a particularly alluring post for qualified British civilians and that the whig government had decided against sending another high-ranking military officer. William Kilbourn notes that "several refusals had already been received" and imagines that at a frustrated meeting, "someone suggested 'young Head' the brilliant thirty-year-old Oxford don." Head also refused the post initially. Under the circumstances, Sir Francis Bond Head was perhaps the best man who could be found. See Head, *Narrative*, 23–4; Kilbourn, *The Firebrand*, 161–2.

37 Kilbourn, *The Firebrand*, 164.
38 Head, *Narrative*, 110.
39 Craig, *Upper Canada*, 233.
40 In contrast he referred to the tories as the Constitutionalists. Head, *Narrative*, 110.
41 Mills, *The Idea of Loyalty*, 7.
42 The Orange Order was a vehemently Protestant group that fought to maintain British loyalty and Protestant dominance. For their presence in Upper Canada, see Senior, "A Bid for Rural Ascendancy."
43 The *Constitution* dubbed them "infuriated demons under the name of Orangemen." See *Constitution*, 16 August 1837.
44 Anonymous, *History of the County of Middlesex*, 103.
45 Makenzie reprinted this article, which appeared initially in the *St Thomas Liberal*. See "Terrible Orange and Government Riot at Middlesex," *Constitution*, 19 July 1836, 2.
46 *Manchester Advertiser*, 27 August 1836, reprinted in *Constitution*, 16 November 1836.
47 Glenelg to Head, 26 February 1837, 138.
48 John Sewell has noted that "although Head, as the Crown's representative, was expected to stay out of local politics, he played a forward role in this election, blaming the Reformers for all the problems." Sewell, *Mackenzie*, 131.
49 *Constitution*, 19 July 1836.

50 *Spectator*, 18 March 1837.
51 *Constitution*, 12 October 1836.
52 *Constitution*, 13 November 1837. This phrase would become something of a battle cry for the English Chartists the following year. It is unclear but certainly possible that, given Mackenzie's infamy, the radical press in England seized on his words. Mackenzie himself had borrowed the phrase. Paul Pickering notes that a similar phrase was used by Henry Clay in the American Congress in 1813. Clay himself mistakenly attributed the phrase to Josiah Quincy. See Pickering, "Peaceably If We Can," 324.
53 Mackenzie's concept of republicanism was intimately connected to the Bible and could fairly be termed Christian civic republicanism. During his election speeches he would read long passages from the Bible that, according to his opponents, were painfully boring for the audience. See *Canadian Freeman*, 24 July 1828.
54 *Colonial Advocate*, 16 May 1833.
55 *Advocate*, 4 November 1834.
56 Rousseau himself is borrowing the logic from the civic republican mind of Machiavelli. *Constitution*, 15 February 1837; Rousseau, *A Treatise on the Social Compact*; Machiavelli, *The Discourses*.
57 Kilbourn, *The Firebrand*, 178–9.
58 Mackenzie commented on his ancestry in a defence case: "Colin Mackenzie, my paternal grandfather, was a farmer under the Earl of Airly in Glenshee, in the highlands of Perthshire; he, at the command of his chieftain, willingly joined the Stuart standard, in the famous 1745, as a volunteer. My mother's father, also named Colin Mackenzie, and from the same glen, has the honour to bear a commission from the prince and served as an officer in the Highland army." See Lindsey and Lindsey, *William Lyon Mackenzie*, 36.
59 Glenelg to Head, 24 August 1836, 73.
60 Head, *Narrative*, 65.
61 *The London Dispatch and People's Political and Social Reformer*, 17 September 1837.
62 Greer, *The Patriots and the People*, 138.
63 Kennedy, *Statutes*, 270–1.
64 This is how Fox described the original bill. See *General Evening Post*, 7 April 1791.
65 Kennedy, *Statutes, Treaties and Documents*, 271–2.
66 *Diary or Woodfall's Register*, 13 May 1791.
67 Kennedy, *Statutes*, 272.
68 *The London Dispatch and People's Political and Social Reformer*, 23 July 1837.

69 *Correspondent and Advocate*, 14 June 1837.
70 Kennedy, 271–2.
71 Peter Mandler opines, "He was not… the architect of his own return to the premiership in April 1835 [and] was not much more the architect of the new government. On one point, the exclusion of Durham and Brougham – who had offended him on personal as well as political grounds – he was insistent. But otherwise much of the running in the appointment of ministers and the determination of policy was to be made by Russell, and in foreign affairs by Palmerston." See "Mandler, Lamb, William, second Viscount Melbourne (1779–1848)," *Oxford Dictionary of National Biography*.
72 Kinchen, *Lord Russell's Canadian Policy*, 1, 33–5.
73 De Lolme, *The Rise and Progress of the English Constitution*, 591.
74 Burke, *Reflections on the Revolution in France*.
75 Kinchen, *Lord Russell's Canadian Policy*, 35–6.
76 The fourth resolution, rejecting an elective Legislative Council, was almost completely unopposed, passing 144 to 14. In Britain the radical *Brighton Patriot* referred to the "atrocious resolutions of Lord John Russell." In Canada, Mackenzie's article on the Resolutions was titled "Slavery For Canada." See Scherer, *Lord John Russell*; Jonathan Scott, *Algernon Sidney and the Restoration Crisis*, 360; *Brighton Patriot and South of England Free Press*, 13 June 1837; *Constitution*, 19 April 1867.
77 *Constitution*, 27 April 1837.
78 *Constitution*, 7 June 1837.
79 *La Minerve*, 13 April 1837.
80 *Spectator*, 11 March 1837.
81 Manning, "Who Ran the British Empire 1830–1850?" 97.
82 Scherer, *Lord John Russell*, 108.
83 *The London Dispatch and People's Political and Social Reformer*, 23 July 1837.
84 *Correspondent and Advocate*, 14 June 1837, taken from the *Montreal Vindicator*.
85 *Correspondent and Advocate*, 14 June 1837, taken from the *Montreal Vindicator*.
86 Arendt, *The Human Condition*.
87 *Correspondent and Advocate*, 14 June 1837.
88 Davis, *The Canadian Farmer's Travels*.
89 The *Constitution* boasted that "six hundred copies are already purchased and paid for." *Constitution*, 12 July 1837; *Constitution*, 19 July 1837; Paine, *Common Sense*.
90 *Constitution*, 22 August 1837.

91 Collin and Stagg, *The Rebellion of 1837*, xxviii.
92 *Constitution*, 22 August 1837.
93 *Constitution*, 16 August 1837.
94 *Constitution*, 4 October 1837.
95 *Bristol Mercury*, 18 November 1837.
96 *Constitution*, 15 November 1837.
97 Ouellet, *Lower Canada*, 294.
98 Thompson, "Nelson, Wolfred," *Dictionary of Canadian Biography*.
99 Ouellet, *Lower Canada*, 294.
100 *Vindicator*, 31 October 1837.
101 Christie, *A History of the Late Province of Lower Canada*, 509.
102 *Tait's Edinburgh Magazine for 1838*, 269.
103 Wilson, "Colborne, John," *Dictionary of Canadian Biography Online*.
104 Jean-Paul Bernard, *The Rebellions of 1837 and 1838*, 5.
105 Ouellet, *Lower Canada*, 292.
106 *Constitution*, 27 September 1837, 2.
107 Greer, *The Patriots and the People*, 296–8.
108 Thompson, "Nelson, Wolfred."
109 Greer, *The Patriots and the People*, 305.
110 *Morning Chronicle*, 27 December 1837.
111 *Northern Star and Leeds General Advertiser*, 13 January 1837.
112 George Bell, *Rough Notes*, 50.
113 Mackenzie, *Mackenzie's Own Narrative of the Late Rebellion*, 8.
114 Kilbourn, *The Firebrand*, 196–7.
115 *Constitution*, 6 December 1837.
116 On 20 February 1836, Head placed three men outside the tory ranks on the Executive Council: Rolph, Robert Baldwin, and John Henry Dunn. It took less than a month before Head's dictatorial style led the men to resign in protest on 12 March. See Craig, "Rolph, John," *Dictionary of Canadian Biography*.
117 Bell, *Rough Notes*, 56.
118 Gates, *After the Rebellion*, 17.
119 McLaughlin, "The Patriot War," 17.
120 Boissery, "The Punishment of Transportation," 383.
121 *Daily Buffalo Journal*, 8 December 1837.
122 Mills, *The Idea of Loyalty*, 10.
123 McLaughlin, "The Patriot War," 15.
124 Horowitz claims that "because the new societies, other than Canada, are unfamiliar with legitimate ideological diversity, they are unable to accept it." The presumption that liberalism was a dominant, monolithic national

ideology was powerfully challenged by John Pocock and Bernard Bailyn, who argued republicanism at the expense of Lockean liberalism. Horowitz, *Canadian Labour in Politics*, 17; Pocock, *The Machiavellian Moment*; Bailyn, *Ideological Origins of the American Revolution*.
125 Mills, *The Idea of Loyalty*, 10.
126 *Upper Canada Gazette*, 13 March 1800.
127 Trenchard, *Cato's Letters*.
128 The Australian chapters will detail the many Catos who appeared in New South Wales, Victorian, and Tasmanian newspapers arguing for reform.
129 *Upper Canada Gazette*, 1 April 1822.
130 *Colonial Advocate*, 16 July 1829.
131 Australian references to 1776 in their demand for responsible government, the end of transportation, and other protests will be discussed in the later chapters.
132 Peter Burroughs, *British Attitudes towards Canada*, 56.
133 *Colonial Advocate*, 6 February 1834.
134 Berry, *Cicero: Political Speeches*, 28.
135 Mackenzie, *The Legislative Black List of Upper Canada*.
136 Lindsey, *The Life and Times of Wm. Lyon Mackenzie*, 6.
137 DeCelles, *Louis Joseph Papineau*, 150.
138 Papineau to Bancroft, 18 December 1837.
139 *Colonial Advocate*, 18 January 1834, 1.
140 Cicero, *Selected Works*, 7–8.
141 The Conservatives, of course, even adopted the name Constitutionalists.
142 Ouellet, *Lower Canada*, 284.
143 *Freeman's Journal and Daily Commercial Advertiser*, 6 January 1838.
144 Burroughs, *British Attitudes towards Canada*, 55.

CHAPTER FOUR

1 *Spectator*, 9 February 1839.
2 *Sydney Monitor and Commercial Advertiser*, 21 Junes 1839.
3 Craig, *Lord Durham's Report*, 1.
4 Lucas, *Lord Durham's Report*, 316–17.
5 The standard interpretation of Durham's assimilation program varies from condemning his racism to highlighting his naivety. Kenneth McNaught, for example, sees "Anglo-Saxon racism," whereas Carl Wittke sees ignorance, noting that "Durham never fully appreciated the force of the French-Canadian nationality." See McNaught, *The History of Canada*, 94; Wittke, *A History of Canada*, 115.

6 Wade, *The French Canadians, 1760–1945*, vol. 1, 210.
7 Craig, *Lord Durham's Report*, x.
8 Ajzenstat, *The Political Thought of Lord Durham*.
9 Bayly, *Imperial Meridian*, 246.
10 Martin, "Lambton, John George," *Oxford Dictionary of National Biography*.
11 New, *Lord Durham*, 3.
12 Martin, "Lambton, John George."
13 Reid, *Life and Letters of the First Earl of Durham*, 68.
14 Trevelyan, *Lord Grey of the Reform Bill*, 187.
15 *Newcastle Chronicle*, 23 October 1819.
16 New, *Lord Durham*, 109.
17 New, *Lord Durham*, 128.
18 In an open letter to Grey, Durham said of his illness, "I cannot anticipate any relief, or even the chance of it, unless from a temporary change of climate and abstinence from the cares and anxieties of office." *The Times*, 14 March 1833.
19 Gollin, "Review," 93–4.
20 George Woodbridge has written a comprehensive history of the club. See Woodbridge, *The Reform Club*.
21 *Weekly Chronicle*, 5 March 1837.
22 Bentham, *Canada: Emancipate Your Colonies*, xii–xvi.
23 Greville, *The Greville Memoires*, 7.
24 Smith, *The Durham Papers*, Appendix B, 21–2.
25 McGilchrist, *The Life and Career of Henry, Lord Brougham*, 197.
26 Newbould, "Lord Durham, the Whigs and Canada, 1838," 360.
27 New, *Lord Durham*, 352.
28 Richard Cobbett, "Lord Durham," *The Champion and Weekly Herald*, 22 July 1837, 328.
29 *Times*, quoted in Cobbett, "Lord Durham," 327.
30 *Le Canadien*, 23 March 1838.
31 The delay may have been due to weather concerns or to allow Durham, meticulous in preparation, to learn as much as possible about the Canadian situation. Nevertheless, he received fierce tory criticism for assembling a large entourage, including eight aides-de-camp, expensive furniture, horses, the family plate, and even musical instruments to accompany him. James Fraser drily noted, "Lord Durham sailed in the Hastings, having turned out the ship's clergyman to provide accommodation for his private band." Sydney Smith mockingly suggested that Durham's plan was to win the Canadian people over with overtures. See Fraser, "Little Men and Little Measures," 364; Reid, *Life and Letters of the First Earl of Durham*, vol. 2, 165; Martin, "Lambton, John George."

32 Spencer, "Buller, Charles," *Oxford Dictionary of National Biography*.
33 Gibbon, *A Letter From Sydney*.
34 Curtis, "The Most Splendid Pageant," 75.
35 *Mackenzie's Gazette*, 11 August 1838.
36 *Times*, 17 January 1838.
37 *Freeman's Journal and Daily Commercial Advertiser*, 2 February 1838.
38 Fox, *The Holland House Diaries*, 93.
39 Curtis, "The Most Splendid Pageant," 62.
40 Reid, *The Life and Letters*; New, *Lord Durham*; Martin, *The Durham Report*.
41 Martin, "Lambton, John George."
42 Colborne had already released some 326 prisoners from the Rebellion in Lower Canada; most who remained were believed to be highly involved. New, *Lord Durham*, 387.
43 New, *Lord Durham*, 29.
44 *Northern Star and Leeds General Advertiser*, 13 January 1837.
45 *Ordinances made and passed by the Governor General and the Special Council*, vol. 2, 8.
46 New, *Lord Durham*, 392.
47 Smith, *The Durham Papers*, appendix B, 352.
48 Mackenzie insists that Nelson and his comrades were tricked into pleading guilty to high treason and that Durham had destroyed "all confidence in his honestly, justice or promises." *Mackenzie's Gazette*, 14 July 1838.
49 One-time friends, Henry Brougham, later Lord Brougham, and Lord Durham developed a strong dislike for one another in the summer of 1830, and according to Queen Victoria's journal, the two had "hated each other ever since." Brougham, jealous of Durham's influence with the Radicals, regularly attacked his "envied rival" in the press. In 1868, John McGilchrist suggested that "it needed the influence of the King and of Earl Grey to prevent the feud being fought out, at Brougham's challenge, on the floor of the House of Lords." After the formation of the second Melbourne government in 1835, Brougham was ostracized from Whig circles and bitterly swore revenge. He declared to Melbourne, "my life will henceforth be devoted to vengeance which I shall exact most fully against the creatures who have disgraced themselves and abandoned me." When news of the Bermuda ordinance reached England in late July 1838, Brougham saw his chance to attack both Durham and Melbourne. In Greville's words he was "animated with nothing but the delight of firing a double shot into Durham there and the Ministry here, and as to the consequences he cared not a straw." See New, *Lord Durham*, 428; Newbould, *Lord Durham*, 361; McGilchrist, *Life and Career*, 183.
50 Murray, *Quarterly Review*, 252–3.

51 Fraser, "Little Men and Little Measures," 361–5.
52 Newbould, *Lord Durham*, 366.
53 Martin, "Lambton, John George."
54 New, *Lord Durham*, 444.
55 *Montreal Herald*, 4 October 1838.
56 Martin, "Attacking the Durham Myth," 54.
57 Charles Buller, "Sketch of Lord Durham's Mission to Canada in 1838," 345.
58 *Le Canadien*, 1 June 1838.
59 *Montreal Transcript*, 2 June 1838.
60 This case will be made through an examination of the *Report* itself.
61 Bacon, *The Works*, vol. 3, 278.
62 Colley, *Britons: Forging The Nation*, 5, 368.
63 John Heraud, "Canadian Squabbles" *The Monthly Magazine*, 1 January to June (1839), 585.
64 Since Coupland coined the phrase, the term "second British empire" has been broadened and used by historians to describe the policy changes in the late-eighteenth century in response to the American Revolution. The most significant work was that of Vincent Harlow, who succeeded Coupland as Beit Professor of Commonwealth History at Oxford. Coupland, *The Durham Report*, xlvi; Harlow, *The Founding of the Second British Empire*.
65 *Church of England Quarterly Review*, vol. 5 (London: William Edward Painter 1839), 478.
66 Durham and Buller were the only people really making that claim in any case.
67 McGilchrist, *Life and Career*, 199.
68 Russell to Melbourne, 9 December 1838, quoted in Martin, *The Durham Report*, 28.
69 Lucas, *Lord Durham's Report*, vol. 1, 3.
70 For an overview of the authorship debate see Garnett, "The Authorship of Lord Durham's Canada Report," 268–75.
71 Lambton, *Report*, 7.
72 Possibly leaked by Wakefield, huge sections of the *Report* appeared first in the *Times* and then other papers also. See *Times*, 8, 9, 11 February 1839.
73 Lambton, *Report*, 11–20, 125–8.
74 And de Tocqueville in turn was influenced by Montesquieu. Lambton, *Report*, 40.
75 de Tocqueville, *Democracy in America*, 428–30.
76 de Tocqueville, *De la démocratie en Amérique*.
77 Wade, *The French Canadians*, 195–7.

78 de Tocqueville, *Democracy in America*, 431–2.
79 Lambton, *Report*, 28, 126–7.
80 de Tocqueville, *Democracy in America*, 429; and Lambton, *Report*, 128.
81 Lambton, *Report*, 17.
82 Ajzenstat, *Political Thought*, 100.
83 Lucas, *Lord Durham's Report*, vol. 1, 125.
84 It should be noted that Durham was not governor-in-chief of Newfoundland. The same commission appointed Henry Prescott, captain of the Royal Navy, as governor.
85 Lucas, *Lord Durham's Report*, vol. 2, 2–3.
86 Lambton, *Report*, 4, 89–90.
87 Craig, *Upper Canada*, 263–4.
88 Lambton, *Report*, 5, 35–6, 65–7, 112, 121–2.
89 Greene, "Empire and Identity," 228.
90 New, *Lord Durham*, 497.
91 Head, *A Narrative*, 471.
92 *Eclectic Review* 5 (January–June 1839), 558.
93 He was so described by his biographer, Patrick Brode. See Brode, *Sir John Beverley Robinson*.
94 Robinson, *Canada and the Canada Bill*, 149.
95 Brode, *John Beverley Robinson*, 214.
96 Hunt, *Canada and South Australia*, vi.
97 *Belfast News-letter*, 15 February 1839.
98 *Bristol Mercury*, 16 February 1839.
99 Thomson Buckner, "Charles Poulett," *Oxford Dictionary of National Biography*.
100 New, *Lord Durham*, 554–63.
101 Snow, "Review," 671–2.

CHAPTER FIVE

1 Shortt and Doughty, *Canada and Its Provinces*, 107.
2 *Novascotian*, 4 May 1847.
3 W.S. Macnutt was referring specifically to the Atlantic provinces and the rapid progress of commerce, communication, and technology, but he notes that development in other parts of North America was greater still. He comments that "progress came rapidly to the Atlantic Provinces as they passed into the vibrant and hungry forties of the nineteenth century, but according to North American standards, it could be reckoned as slow." Macnutt, *The Atlantic Provinces*, 214.
4 *Upper Canada Herald*, 28 May 1839.

5 *Christian Guardian*, 5 June 1839.
6 Beck, *Joseph Howe*, vol. 1, 6.
7 This is how one of Howe's fellow Sandemanian loyalists described Halifax in comparison to Boston. See Charles St. C. Stayner, "The Sandemanian Loyalists," 108.
8 Beck, *Joseph Howe*, 20.
9 Martin, *Empire and Commonwealth*, 165.
10 Harvey, "The Intellectual Awakening," 9–10.
11 MacMechan, "The Nova-Scotia-ness of Nova Scotia," 556.
12 Burroughs, "Ramsay, George," *Oxford Dictionary of National Biography*.
13 MacMechan, "Nova Scotia: General History," 62.
14 Harvey, "The Intellectual Awakening," 112.
15 Buckner and Reid, *The Atlantic Region to Confederation*, 266.
16 McCulloch, *The Nature and Uses of a Liberal Education Illustrated*, 24.
17 MacMechan, "The Nova-Scotia-ness of Nova Scotia," 269.
18 Harvey, "The Intellectual Awakening," 112–17.
19 *Novascotian*, 9 July 1829.
20 Beck, "Joseph Howe," *Dictionary of Canadian Biography*.
21 Beck, *Joseph Howe: Conservative Reformer*, 103.
22 *Novascotian*, 23 April, 1834.
23 Patterson, *History of the County of Pictou*, 377.
24 In 1826 a bill was passed requiring a duty of one shilling and fourpence on a gallon of brandy. Owing to an error, only one shilling was charged between 1826 and 1830. Towards the end of session the Assembly passed a bill correcting this error, which the Council rejected. The Council demanded a series of amendments to other duties in return for passing the brandy bill. Both the Assembly and Howe were horrified at this abuse of power. Howe spoke bitterly of the meddling councillors, who could "jeopardize the peace, and destroy the Revenue of the Country; who can abruptly break up the consideration of public business, and inflict evils of a nature so multifarious and extensive as to require the passage of years to repair." See *Novascotian*, 20 May 1830.
25 *Novascotian*, 1 January 1835.
26 Beck, "Joseph Howe: Mild Tory," 467–9.
27 For an extensive account of the trial see Chisholm, *Speeches and Public Letters*, vol. 1, 22–83.
28 Howe noted in a letter to his half sister that the room was "crammed to overflowing, and as hot as a furnace." See Beck, "A Fool for a Client," 33.
29 Annand, *Speeches and Public Letters*, vol. 1, 14.

30 The libel law at the time was not concerned with the truth of the claims but rather with whether the motive of the claims was to defame one's reputation.
31 Annand, *Speeches and Public letters*, vol. 1, 22.
32 Macnutt, *The Atlantic Provinces*, 200.
33 Annand, *Speeches and Public letters*, vol. 1, 66–8.
34 Chisholm, *Speeches and Public Letters*, 82.
35 Beck, "A Fool for a Client," 39.
36 *Novascotian*, 17 November 1836.
37 *Novascotian*, 22 December 1836.
38 Annand, *Speeches and Public Letters*, vol. 1, 96.
39 *Novascotian*, 31 January 1939.
40 Campbell, *A History of the County of Yarmouth*, 154.
41 A.A. MacKenzie, "Herbert Huntington," *Dictionary of Canadian Biography*.
42 Edgar Mcinnis, *Canada*, 232–3.
43 *Colonial Gazette*, 29 January 1840.
44 Annand, *Speeches and Public Letters*, vol. 2, 234.
45 Martin, *Empire and Commonwealth*, 175–82.
46 Annand, *Speeches and Public Letters*, vol. 2, 236–8.
47 Macnutt, *The Atlantic Provinces*, 221.
48 Annand, *Speeches and Public Letters*, vol. 2, 236–42.
49 *Colonial Gazette*, 13 October 1841.
50 *Times*, 14 November 1843.
51 See votes for the first month of sitting. *Journal and Proceedings of the House of Assembly of the Province of Nova Scotia, Session 1844* (Halifax 1844), 12–71.
52 Longley, *Sir Francis Hincks*, 153.
53 Egerton and Grant, *Canadian Constitutional Development*, 297.
54 Grey, *Colonial Policy*, vol. 1, 227.
55 Martin, *Empire and Commonwealth*, 229.
56 "Howe to Buller, 16 September 1846," *Joseph Howe Papers*, vol. 6, 76. See also Beck, *Joseph Howe*, 299.
57 Beck, *Joseph Howe: Conservative Reformer*, 299.
58 *Novascotian*, 16 November 1846.
59 Chisolm, *The Speeches*, 636.
60 *Novascotian*, 17 May 1847.
61 Martin, *Empire and Commonwealth*, 234.
62 Chisolm, *The Speeches*, 657–64.
63 *Novascotian*, 7 February 1848.
64 In the article "An Incident in the Life of Cromwell" a story is told of a "poor, unlearned woman" who pleads for the life of her Cavalier husband.

"Away! Away!" was the initial and repeated stern response. The woman continued to plead in a manner reminiscent of the parable of the persistent widow (Luke 18:1–8). Cromwell then agrees to her demand. Taking the part of Jesus Christ, Cromwell decrees, "her husband shall be free; for 'verily I say unto you, I have not found such great love – no, not in all Israel.'" See *Novascotian*, 7 February 1848.

65 See *Morning Chronicle*, 28 February 1848; *Liverpool Mercury*, 29 February 1848; *London Gazette*, 7 April 1848; *Glasgow Herald*, 10 April 1848; *Caledonian Mercury*, 10 April 1848.
66 Chisolm, *The Speeches*, 69.
67 Saul, *Joseph Howe and the Battle for Freedom of Speech*, 7.
68 Wise and Brown, *Canada Views the United States*, 30.
69 When Sir Colin Campbell was recalled after he had refused to change his Council following objections in the Assembly, Howe mistakenly believed and celebrated responsible government being granted. See Harvey, *The Heart of Howe*, 102.
70 Beck, *Joseph Howe*, 113–14.
71 Bliss, *Canadian History in Documents*, 71.
72 *Novascotian*, 22 October 1840.

CHAPTER SIX

1 Machiavelli, *The Discourses*, 111–12.
2 Grey, *The Colonial Policy of Lord John Russell's Administration*, vol. 1, 200.
3 Lambton, *Report on the Affairs of British North America*, 127.
4 3 & 4 Vict. c. 35. *An Act to re-unite the Provinces of Upper and Lower Canada, and for the Government of Canada* (Quebec: John Charlton Fisher and William Kemble 1841), 7–15.
5 Wilton, *Popular Politics and Political Culture in Upper Canada*, 194.
6 Lambton, *Report*, 7.
7 Baldwin and Baldwin, *The Baldwins*, 23.
8 Born in India, Roebuck spent most of his childhood in Canada before moving to England at age twenty-two. Throughout his parliamentary career he was a passionate supporter of Canadian democracy.
9 Baldwin and Baldwin, *The Baldwins*, 146.
10 Bergeron, *Lire Étienne Parent*, 278.
11 Monet, "Sir Louis-Hippolyte La Fontaine," *Dictionary of Canadian Biography*.
12 *Examiner*, 3 July 1838.
13 Baldwin and Baldwin, *The Baldwins*, 164–5.

14 Leacock, *Baldwin, La Fontaine, Hincks*, 117.
15 Careless, *The Union of the Canadas*, 75.
16 *Quebec Gazette*, 9 October 1842.
17 Bliss, *Canadian History in Documents*, 70.
18 Writing to Russell in 1840, Metcalfe expressed his earnest desire that the happiness of the former slaves who had suffered so much be "greatly increased."
19 Kaye, *Selections*, 335–405.
20 Wilson, *The Life of Robert Baldwin*, 257.
21 Ryerson, *Sir Charles Metcalfe Defended*.
22 Buckner posits that the distinction between Stanley and Grey is unfairly overdrawn to the latter's advantage. See Buckner, *The Transition to Responsible Government*, 294.
23 Stephenson and Marcham, *Sources of English Constitutional History*, 786–7.
24 Parliamentary Debates, 233–4.
25 Pope, *The Poetical Works of Alexander Pope Esq.*, 128.
26 Edgar, *Lord Elgin and Responsible Government*, 4.
27 Bliss, *Canadian History*, 71–2.
28 Smith, *Rebels Rewarded?* 5–6, 12.
29 *Montreal Pilot*, reprinted in *Globe*, 10 March 1849.
30 McNairn, *The Capacity to Judge*, 273.
31 A good contemporary account of the riot can be found in McMullen's *History of Canada*.
32 McMullen, *History of Canada*, 491.
33 *Pilot*, 27 April 1849.
34 *Pilot*, 28 April 1849.
35 *Daily News*, 20 April 1849
36 *Examiner*, 19 May 1849.
37 *Manchester Times*, 19 May 1849.
38 It noted also the cruel irony that had seen the Reform Party constantly branded as disloyal. The article concludes with the observation that "it is to that very long abused party that the mother country has now solely to look for the maintenance of her authority on Canada."
39 *Liverpool Mercury*, 18 May 1849. See also Dyck, *A Commentary on Cicero*, 459.
40 *Liverpool Mercury*, 18 May 1849.
41 *Pilot*, 27 April 1849.
42 Wilson, *The Life of Robert Baldwin*, 270.
43 Mackay, *The Crisis in Canada*, 10–11, 48.
44 *Manchester Times*, 1 May 1849. Lang's impact on Australian politics is thoroughly discussed in the second section, particularly chapter 6.

45 It was also printed in the *Montreal Transcript* and was subsequently produced as a pamphlet. See *Montreal Gazette*, 11 October 1849; *Montreal Transcript and Commercial Advertiser*, 13 October 1849; *Annexation Manifesto of 1849*.
46 Ibid., 3.
47 Stewart, *My Dear Friend*, 286.
48 Edgar, *Lord Elgin*, 8–14.
49 *Examiner*, 7 January 1838.
50 *Daily News*, 6 April 1849.
51 *Novascotian*, 6 December 1847.
52 *Globe*, 5 May 1849.
53 Wilson, *The Life of Robert Baldwin*, 247.
54 Two notable exceptions to this rule are Chester Martin and Donald Creighton. See Martin, *Empire & Commonwealth*; Creighton, *The Empire of the St. Lawrence*.
55 Buckner, *The Transition*, 293.
56 Robin Winks claimed in 1966 that Canadian historians fall into either the liberal or the laurentian camp. In the liberal camp Winks places historians such as Chester Martin and Aileen Dunham. Winks, *The Historiography of the British Empire-Commonwealth*.
57 Ibid.
58 See Ajzenstat and Smith, *Canada's Origins*, 3–7.
59 *Glasgow Herald*, 26 November 1849.
60 *Manchester Times*, 21 November 1849.
61 *Daily News*, 14 January 1848.

CHAPTER SEVEN

1 Geoffrey Blainey, *The Tyranny of Distance*.
2 This was the name Lang gave to his republican lecture series that will be discussed later in the chapter.
3 The "artful dodger of Sydney" is but one of numerous colourful and often derogatory monikers applied to Lang. This particular one appeared in the *Illustrated Sydney News*, 3 June 1854.
4 Alex Tyrrell has used this term with regard to Joseph Surge and the anti-slavery campaign. Tyrrell, *Joseph Sturge*.
5 Lang, *Cooksland*, 44.
6 It is significant that *Examiner* deemed Lang's project benevolent and worthy, since it was the single piece of praise in a scathing review of his emigrant booklets. The review opened with the observation that "the books

have the decisive merit, we should say, of very much resembling their author. They are full of information, in the worst possible condition." *Examiner*, 18 September 1847.
7 Lang, *The Australian Emigrant's Manual*, 37–8.
8 Headon and Perkins, *Our First Republicans*, 11, 20–8.
9 As Henry Parkes described the Sydney powerbrokers in a letter to Lang. See Martin, "Parkes, Sir Henry," *Australian Dictionary of Biography*.
10 Headon and Perkins, *Our First Republicans*, 26.
11 Baker, *Days of Wrath*, 95.
12 Baker notes that Lang might have been more successful in Port Phillip had he stayed there to campaign rather than returning to Sydney. In any case it was Lang's only electoral defeat for the Legislature.
13 Baker, *Days of Wrath*, 299–304.
14 *People's Advocate and New South Wales Vindicator*, 8 June 1850, 6–7. On Hawksley's career, see Diamond, "Edward Hawksley."
15 Baker, *Days of Wrath*, 304.
16 *The Representative: A Daily Journal of the Election*, 25 July 1850.
17 *Freeman's Journal*, 11 July 1850, 8, and 18 July 1850, 8.
18 *Sydney Morning Herald*, 20 July 1850.
19 *Freeman's Journal*, 25 July 1850.
20 *Sydney Morning Herald*, 24 July 1850.
21 Baker, *Days of Wrath*, 305.
22 *Sydney Morning Herald*, 24 July 1850.
23 *Freeman's Journal*, 25 July 1850; Baker, *Days of Wrath*, 306–8.
24 *Illustrated Sydney News*, 7 September 1878.
25 Lang, *Freedom and Independence*, vi–vii.
26 Elford, *A Prophet without Honour*, 161–75.
27 Paine, *Rights of Man*, 75.
28 Lang, *Freedom and Independence*, 42, 115–20, 131, 157, 162.
29 *Maitland Mercury & Hunter River General Advertiser*, 30 July 1853.
30 *Westminster Review*, vol. 59, January and April 1853, 308–9.
31 *Colonial Times*, 29 November 1853.
32 *Sydney Morning Herald*, 31 May 1853.
33 *Empire*, 24 May 1853.
34 *Votes and Proceedings of the Legislative Council of New South Wales*, vol. 2 (Sydney 1853), 123–8.
35 Dickinson, *A Letter to the Honourable the Speaker of the Legislative Council*.
36 *Sydney Morning Herald*, 29 July 1853.
37 *Sydney Morning Herald*, 30 July 1853.
38 *Sydney Morning Herald*, 29 July 1853.

39 Lang began sarcastically, referring to William Wentworth as Old Lottery in response to a bill Wentworth had introduced in 1844 to salvage assets from the failed Bank of Australia by lottery. See *Colonial Times*, 20 September 1850; Ferguson, *Biography of Australia*, 314.
40 *Sydney Morning Herald*, 30 July 1853.
41 *Melbourne Morning Herald*, 2 August 1853.
42 Lang, *Freedom and Independence*, 36.
43 *Empire*, 14 January 1852.
44 This was a centuries-old tradition brought over from Britain.
45 Headon, *Our First Republicans*, 127–9.
46 John Keane, *The Life and Death of Democracy*, 515.
47 David Headon and Elizabeth Perkins identified him as one of three pioneering republicans worthy of inclusion in their collection of primary speeches and writings. See Headon and Perkins, *Our First Republicans*.
48 Clifford D. Conner gave his biography of Arthur O'Connor the telling subtitle "The Most Important Irish Revolutionary You May Never Have Heard Of." Similarly, Deniehy may well be the most important Australian radical few have heard of. Lang has similarly been largely forgotten; however, he is immortalized through his statue in Sydney and through John Dunmore Lang Place in Canberra, and Queenslanders still refer to Suncorp Stadium as Lang Park. See Connor, *Arthur O'Connor*.
49 Keane, *Life and Death of Democracy*, 510–16.
50 *Times*, 31 October 1853.
51 *Sydney Morning Herald*, 26 August 18.

CHAPTER EIGHT

1 These names were used by free British settlers to distinguish themselves from the local currency lads and lasses, the native-born white Australians who were predominantly the children of convicts. The earliest sporting rivalry in Australia was likely between the first two cricket clubs, one made up of Stirling and the other of Currency. Their first game on 17 October 1832 was marred when the Stirling made a dubious appeal for leg before wicket. Convinced he was not out, the Currency batsman left the pitch only when the bowler challenged him to a dual. See *Sydney Gazette and New South Wales Advertiser*, 18 October 1832.
2 Linda Cardinal and David Headon, for example, describe the anti-transportation movement as "early Australian federalism." John Hirst calls it "quasi-nationalist"; Peter Cochrane calls it an "intercolonial" movement; Frank Crowley notes the "nationalist theme" of the Australasian

League; Ken Inglis calls it a "national movement"; and Stefan Berger and Angel Smith describe the movement as part of the "emergence of a national consciousness." See Cardinal and Headon, *Shaping Nations*, 75; Hirst, *Freedom on the Fatal Shore*, 202; Cochrane, *Colonial Ambition*, 253; Crowley, *A New History of Australia*, 109; Inglis, *The Australian Colonists*, 46; and Berger and Smith, *Nationalism, Labour and Ethnicity*, 197.

3 Parkes, *Fifty Years in the Making of Australian History*. Helen Irving has questioned Parkes' popular moniker, the father of federation, in her work. Irving, *The Centenary Companion*, 60–2.
4 Although the phrase "moral means" had a narrow definition in opposition to violent means, the evocation of morality remains significant. This theme will be expanded on later in the chapter. Huon, "By Moral Means Only."
5 Brady, "To set the people free."
6 This chapter will examine one such event in Hobart Town on 25 August 1851.
7 Lang spent three years in England between 1847 and 1849 encouraging the emigration of virtuous British working class people to Australia. In an open letter to Earl Grey in 1849 he boasted that despite "not receiv[ing] the slightest assistance from the Colonial-office," he organized the emigration of three ships and nearly six hundred people of "superior character." See *Morning Chronicle*, 19 November 1849.
8 This description of Lang appears in Pickering, "The Highway to Comfort and Independence," 1.
9 *Sydney Herald*, 20 November 1834. During the 1830s Lang openly campaigned to bring honest, protestant workers to Australia, since he felt this would help relieve the poverty in England while providing Australia with labour and a counterbalance to the loose morals of the convicts.
10 *Sydney Herald*, 20 November 1834.
11 Lang, *Transportation and Colonization*.
12 Lang, *A Historical and Statistical Account of New South Wales*.
13 Ullathrone, *The Catholic Mission in Australasia*.
14 Macarthur, *New South Wales*, 32–3.
15 *Sydney Monitor*, 29 December 1837.
16 Bland, *Examination of Mr. James Macarthur's Work*.
17 Lang took particular advantage of this sentiment when promoting British emigration to Australia. Unlike America, he boasted, Australia had "no foul blot of slavery to defile [the] national escutcheon." See his open letter to Earl Grey in London's *Morning Chronicle*, 19 November 1849. For a general history of the British anti-slavery movement after abolition see Temperley, *British Antislavery*.

18 *Manchester Times*, 27 February 1849.
19 As examples of the weak and dependent, Hall mentions women, children, slaves, and animals. Australian convicts could very reasonably be included in this group. See Hall, "Imperial Man," 133.
20 T.L. Suttor, "Ullathorne, William Bernard," *Australian Dictionary of Biography*.
21 *Launceston Examiner*, 18 December 1850.
22 Ullathrone, *The Catholic Mission*, 3–5.
23 Lang, *Transportation and Colonization*, 226.
24 A clear stab at James Macarthur. *Colonist*, 31 August 1831.
25 *Sydney Gazette and New South Wales Advertiser*, 30 November 1837; *Perth Gazette and Western Australia Journal*, 17 November 1838; *Hobart Town Courier*, 25 August 1837.
26 *Sydney Monitor*, 27 December 1837.
27 *Times*, 26 September 1837.
28 Ullathrone influenced proceedings directly, since he was in England in February 1837 and gave evidence to Molesworth's committee. See Suttor, "Ullathorne, William Bernard," 544–6.
29 The New South Wales Constitution Act 1842 (UK) would establish the first partially elected legislature in Australia, while full responsible government would be granted with the passing of the New South Wales Constitution Act 1855 (UK), just sixty-eight years after the colony was founded as a penal settlement.
30 The violent and tragic history of Tasmania's Indigenous inhabitants was investigated by Lyndall Ryan and Henry Reynolds in their 1981 works *The Aboriginal Tasmanians* and *The Other Side of the Frontier*, respectively. These works and other subsequent releases were castigated by some for allegedly exaggerating the negative impact of European contact in what came to be known as Australia's History Wars. The most notable refutation of Ryan and Reynolds is Keith Windshuttle's *Fabrication of Aboriginal History*. See Ryan, *The Aboriginal Tasmanians*; Reynolds, *The Other Side of the Frontier*; and Windshuttle, "The Fabrication of Aboriginal History."
31 For violence against Aboriginals see Ryan, *The Aboriginal Tasmanians*; Reynolds, *The Other Side*. For violence against women in Tasmania see Boyce, *Van Diemen's Land*, 128–33.
32 Clarke, *His Natural Life*.
33 *Van Diemen's Land/Sweet Home* (Newcastle: Fordyce 1830). An original copy of this broadside is kept at the National Library of Australia.
34 *Colonial Times*, 2 November 1841.
35 *Empire*, 15 February 1851. See Pickering, "Loyalty and Rebellion," 91–2.

36 *Empire*, 13 February 1851.
37 *Launceston Examiner*, 6 January 1849.
38 *Launceston Examiner*, 27 January 1849.
39 West, *History of Tasmania*, 339–42.
40 *Launceston Examiner*, 1 December 1849.
41 *Launceston Examiner*, 27 January 1849.
42 Pickering, "Loyalty and Rebellion," 87–9.
43 *Launceston Examiner*, 1 December 1849.
44 Grey's address to the House of Lords, *Great Britain Parliamentary Debates*, third series, vol. 110, 217–18. Also in Crowley, *Colonial Australia*, vol. 2, 173–5.
45 Crowley, *Colonial Australia*, vol. 2, 173–5.
46 In a letter to Earl Grey, Governor FitzRoy commented that he had heard reports from people with "no interest in misleading" that there were three to five thousand people present. The *Sydney Morning Herald* put the number at six thousand. In his own letter to Grey, Cowper confidently put the figure at eight thousand. See FitzRoy to Grey, 9 October 1850, *Further Correspondence on the Subject of Convict Discipline and Transportation*, House of Common Papers, vol. 45 (London: William Clowes and Sons 1851), 188–9. Suitably enough, a large statue of Dr John Dunmore Lang, who was so vocal in his opposition to transportation, dominates modern-day Wynyard Park.
47 *Sydney Morning Herald*, 18 September 1850.
48 *Courier*, 11 August 1853.
49 *Sydney Morning Herald*, 18 September 1850.
50 John M. Ward, "Cowper, Sir Charles," *Australian Dictionary of Biography*.
51 Alan Powell, *Patrician Democrat*.
52 Clune and Turner, *The Premiers of New South Wales*, vol. 1, 43.
53 Parkes notes that the dubious term was no slight on Cowper, whom he describes as "a gentleman of good address and high personal character." Rather it was a comment on his political cunning and general ability. See Parkes, *Fifty Years*, 116–17.
54 *Sydney Morning Herald*, 18 September 1850.
55 Cicero, *De Re Publica De Legibus*, 15.
56 As noted earlier, for histories that interpret the anti-transportation movements as the precursor to Australian nationalism. See Cardinal and Headon, *Shaping Nations*, 75; Hirst, *Freedom on the Fatal Shore*, 202; Cochrane, *Colonial Ambitions*, 253.
57 *Sydney Morning Herald*, 18 September 1850.
58 *South Australian Register*, 2 January 1851.

59 *Courier*, 11 February 1851.
60 Blackton, "The Dawn of Australian National Feeling," 121–38.
61 Blainey, *The Tyranny of Distance*.
62 *Courier*, 11 February 1851.
63 "Independent Australian Britons" is a well-known phrase by Keith Hancock and a chapter title from his influential 1930 work, *Australia*. He argues that each of those three words is embedded with meaning, as is their order. See Hancock, *Australia*, 39–51.
64 *Launceston Examiner*, 5 February 1851.
65 Blackton, "The Australasian League," 391.
66 Denison to Grey, 2 May 1850, "Transportation to Van Dieman's Land: 1846–50," Mitchell Library, Sydney, New South Wales, 1–4.
67 *Sessional papers of the Australasian League Conference: Held in Hobart Town and Launceston, Van Dieman's Land in the months of April and May 1852*, Tasmania: Published by order of conference, 1852, 6.
68 Denison to Grey, 2 May 1850, 1.
69 *South Australian Register*, 1 February 1853.
70 *Times*, reprinted in *Launceston Examiner*, 25 February 1852.
71 Paul Pickering has argued convincingly that the discovery of gold was a major pretext used by radicals to demand progressive reform and the end of transportation. He rightly contends that "gold transformed the image of Australia in the eyes of the international community, especially in Britain." What is argued here, however, is that the social movement and the general dissatisfaction with transportation in the Eastern colonies was so intense that, despite the discovery of gold, it was a policy doomed to be ended, either willingly by the British government or, less likely, by the colonies separating from the empire. See Pickering, "The Finger of God," 37–51.
72 Following Lang's Coming Event lectures, the British press released a frenzy of articles about the imminent separation of the Australian colonies. See, for example, *Northern Star and National Trades' Journal*, 14 September 1850; *Freeman's Journal and Daily Commercial Advertiser*, 3 September 1850; *Manchester Times*, 21 November 1849; *Morning Chronicle*, 19 November 1849; and *Belfast News-Letter*, 6 September 1850.
73 *Northern Star and National Trades' Journal*, 14 September 1850.
74 Stephenson and Marcham, *Sources of English Constitutional History*, 787.
75 *Northern Star and National Trades' Journal*, 14 September 1850.
76 Governor Denison, whom the league had ridiculed and slandered for his support of transportation, was not prepared to grant an official holiday despite the obvious emotional outpourings of his citizens.

77 *Courier*, 12 August 1853.
78 *Colonial Times*, 13 August 1853.
79 During the heat of the anti-transportation debate, Wentworth argued loudly against an increase of the franchise, which in his mind constituted "pure democracy." See *Sydney Morning Herald*, 16 September 1850.
80 Headon and Perkins, *Our First Republicans*, 87.
81 Albert Metin, *Socialism without Doctrines*.
82 Hancock, *Australia*, 55.
83 Melleuish, "Australian Liberalism," 28–9.
84 The entire ninth chapter is dedicated to understanding *The Principles of True Liberalism*. See Smith, *Liberty and Liberalism*, 133–70.
85 Ibid., 13–14.
86 Irving, *The Southern Tree of Liberty*, 127–49.
87 Pickering, "Loyalty and Rebellion," 98.
88 Irving, *Southern Tree of Liberty*, 135–7.
89 Irving, "Development of Liberal Politics.

CHAPTER NINE

1 The spelling of Ballarat in contemporary newspapers varies. For the purpose of this book, all spelling has been standardized to conform with the accepted modern version.
2 Anne Beggs Sunter's PhD dissertation deals extensively with the debates surrounding the Eureka Centre and the Eureka legend more broadly. Sunter, *Birth of a Nation?* See also Sunter, "Contested Memories of Eureka," 29–45.
3 For example, Geoffrey Serle, Geoffrey Blainey, A.G.L. Shaw, and Manning Clark are all either dismissive of the significance of Eureka or at least feel that its importance has been overstated. Compare them with John Molony, Henry Gyles Turner, Clive Turnbull, Russell Ward, or R.D. Walshe: see Serle, *The Golden Age*, 180–5; Blainey, *A Shorter History of Australia;* Shaw, *The Story of Australia*, 123–36; Clark, "Re-writing Australian History"; Molony, *Eureka;* Turner, *Our Own Little Rebellion;* Turnbull, *Eureka;* and Walshe, "The Significance of Eureka."
4 Ward, *The Australian Legend*, 117
5 Clark, "Re-writing Australian History," 136. Another notable example of nearly opposite conclusions about the significance of Eureka would be Geoffrey Serle's dismissive account of Eureka in contrast to John Molony's work. See Serle, *The Golden Age*, 180–5; Molony, *Eureka*.
6 Meaney, *Search for Security*, vii.

7 *Argus*, 27 October 1854.
8 Again, Anne Beggs Sunter's account of the fierce debates and problems surrounding the opening of the Eureka Centre is telling. Sunter, "Contested Memories of Eureka."
9 *Sydney Morning Herald*, 30 March 1855.
10 *Argus*, 24 March 1855.
11 See, respectively, *South Australian Register*, 4 December 1854; *The Cornwall Chronicle*, 9 December 1854; *Bell's Life in Sydney and Sporting Reviewer*, 16 December 1854; *Moreton Bay Courier*, 19 December 1854; and *The Maitland Mercury & Hunter River General Advertiser*, 13 December 1854. The *Age* also ran with the heading, "Disturbances at Ballarat," 5 December 1854.
12 The editor of the *Ballarat Times*, Henry Seekamp, was arrested as he was preparing the special edition of the paper. *Ballarat Times*, 3 December 1854; *Geelong Advertiser* in *Age*, 5 December 1854.
13 *Leader*, 10 March 1855; *People's Paper*, 3 March 1855. Paul Pickering has given a full account of the response to Eureka in the British radical press. See Pickering, "Ripe for a Republic," 69–90.
14 Both articles were a composite of reports from Melbourne. See *Melbourne Morning Herald*, 5 December 1854; *Argus*, 4 December 1854; *Morning Chronicle*, 7 March 1855; *Freeman's Journal and Daily Commercial Advertiser*, 7 March 1855.
15 *Times*, 8 March 1855. Pickering, "Ripe for a Republic," 71.
16 This is the title of one of Evatt's essays. See *Golden Jubilee Souvenir of the Australian Labor Party* (Sydney: Workers Trustees 1940).
17 The seat is currently held by Labor Prime Minister Gillard.
18 Whitlam, *Eureka*, 3. For a discussion of the speech in the broader context of prime ministerial rhetoric and a comparison to Evatt's statement see Curran, *The Power of Speech*, 119.
19 Curiously, Henderson ignores the fact that it was Victorian Liberal premier Jeff Kennett who opened the Eureka Centre. *Age*, 30 November 2004.
20 *Age*, 30 November 2004.
21 Paul Pickering has written on the disparity between the gold yields in New South Wales and Victoria and the resulting political implications. See Pickering, "The Finger of God."
22 Macintyre, *Concise History*, 87.
23 David Goodman's celebrated work, *Gold Seeking*, contrasts the Californian and Victorian gold rushes and discusses the unique national identities that were shaped by their respective experiences. See Goodman, *Gold Seeking*.
24 Hotham to Secretary of State for the Colonies, 10 September 1854.

25 Mundy, *Our Antipodes*, 312.
26 Pickering, "Ripe for a Republic," 69–70.
27 Hotham to Grey, 20 December 1854, *Historical Studies: Eureka Supplement* (Melbourne: Melbourne University Press 1954).
28 *Sydney Morning Herald*, 14 December 1854.
29 Shaw, *The Story of Australia*, 124.
30 Serle, *Golden Age*, 181.
31 O'Farrell, *The Irish in Australia*, 163.
32 *Age*, 3 October 1854
33 Hereafter, the newspaper will be referred to as the *Advocate* in the main text. *Gold Diggers Advocate and Commercial Advertiser*, 27 January 1854.
34 *Gold Diggers Advocate and Commercial Advertiser*, 20 January 1854.
35 *Gold Diggers Advocate and Commercial Advertiser*, 27 January 1854.
36 In a display of anti-authoritarian, classist humour that would later come to be seen by radical nationalists as quintessentially Australia, Black said of the privileged classes that their "only privilege seems to be the privilege of making greater asses of themselves than other people." *Gold Diggers Advocate and Commercial Advertiser*, 27 January 1854.
37 Later this chapter will discus some of the monster meetings and their broad democratic agenda.
38 13 & 14 Vict. C.59. Clark, *Select Documents in Australian History*, vol. 1, 377–85.
39 Ibid.
40 Clark, *Select Documents in Australian History*, vol. 2, 78–9.
41 *Gold Diggers Advocate and Commercial Advertiser*, 17 February 1854.
42 Legislative Council of Victoria, *Act to restrain by summary Proceeding unauthorised Mining on Waste Lands of the Crown*. Melbourne: John Ferrers, Government Printer 1852.
43 *South Australian Register*, 31 January 1853.
44 *Argus*, 14 January 1853.
45 *Argus*, 26 August 1853.
46 Blainey, *A History of Victoria*, 44.
47 *Argus*, 5 August 1853.
48 *Gold Diggers Advocate and Commercial Advertiser*, 27 January 1854.
49 *Argus*, 5 August 1853.
50 Again, see Patrick O'Farrell's work for a unique look at the Irish experience on the gold fields. O'Farrell, *The Irish in Australia*.
51 The Roman Catholic Church had appointed Father Smith to the chapel at Bakery Hill, and he took with him a servant named John Gregory. One day in October 1854, Gregory, being fluent in a foreign language, went to

the gold fields on a visit of charity. While he was conversing with a non-English-speaking Catholic, a zealous trooper named Lord demanded the pair produce their licences in language so foul the *Argus* would not print it. Not having a licence and not being allowed to explain his presence, Gregory was ordered to follow Lord on his round before being locked up in a camp. Being disabled (the *Argus* described him as a cripple), Gregory pleaded to be allowed to go directly to the camp. For appearing unwilling to follow his orders, Lord violently beat Gregory, stopping only when Father Smith intervened and posted £5 bail. The following morning, the police magistrate charged Gregory the £5 as a fine for mining without a licence. When it was brought to his attention that Gregory was not a miner, the charge was changed to assaulting a trooper, and the £5 penalty was upheld. See *Argus*, 27 October 1854.
52 *Argus*, 27 October 1854.
53 *Age*, 17 October 1854.
54 For the relationship between Mazzini and the Chartists and Australia's political development see Pickering, "Garibaldi's Shirt."
55 *Times*, 2 August 1856.
56 *Leader*, 8 November 1856. In an article titled "Pens and Daggers," the Leader again bemoaned the perceived character assassination of Mazzini by the conservative press. *Leader*, 13 December 1856.
57 Adams, *Memoirs of a Social Atom*, 261–5.
58 Pickering, "Glimpses of Eternal Truth," 54–5.
59 *Gold Diggers Advocate and Commercial Advertiser*, 13 May 1854.
60 Sayers, "Syme, Ebenezer," *Australian Dictionary of Biography*.
61 Both Cowen and Holyoake were subjects for the biographer's pen in the 1920s (and at various other times). New biographies of both have recently been published. See Allen, *Joseph Cowen*; McCabe, *George Jacob Holyoake*. See also Rae, "Cowen, Joseph," *Oxford Dictionary of National Biography*; Royle, "Holyoake, George Jacob," *Oxford Dictionary of National Biography*.
62 Sayers, "Syme, Ebenezer." See also Sayers, "Syme, David," *Australian Dictionary of Biography*.
63 The details of Carboni's early life are frustratingly sketchy. Geoffrey Serle notes only that he had "revolutionary experience" and that it "may be that he took part" in the rebellions against Austria. Jennifer Lorch notes that he was encouraged to join the Young Italy movement by Mattia Montecchi, a firm supporter of Mazzini. Following the Eureka rebellion, several Australian papers reported that he was at one time Mazzini's secretary. See Serle's introduction to Carboni, *The Eureka Stockade*, ix–x; Lorch, "Carboni, Raffaello," *Australian Dictionary of Biography*; *Sydney Morning Herald*, 18 December 1854; *Argus*, 11 December 1854.

64 *Gold Diggers Advocate and Commercial Advertiser*, 27 January 1854.
65 Moore, *Death or Liberty*.
66 Hancock, *Australia*, 54.
67 Like the Anti-Transportation League, the suffix of the Ballarat Reform League is significant for its connection to England's Anti-Corn Law League.
68 "Joe" was the well-understood cry on the diggings to warn of a hunting party. Men with licences would flee and attract the attention of the troopers, while men without would hide. Or men with licences would stay by the windlass while their unlicensed mates would descend deep underground. Licences were also forged or shared among several men. The diggers felt quite justified in doing so because to their mind the licence system itself and especially the collection method were a breach of British liberty. See Raffaello Carboni's contemporary account of the Eureka Stockade. Carboni, *The Eureka Stockade*, 74.
69 Kelly's account of the meeting at Bakery Hill on 11 November 1854 was published in his 1859 memoir. See Kelly, *Life in Victoria*, 251–3
70 *Argus*, 16 November 1854. Ballarat Reform League, *Resolutions of the Diggers at Bakery Hill, Ballarat*, in Clark, *Select Documents in Australian History*, vol. 2, 58.
71 Clark, *Select Documents in Australian History*, vol. 2, 58–9.
72 Taylor, "The 1848 Revolutions."
73 Taylor adds that "to judge colonial discontent by the yardstick of European nationalism is to apply the benefit of hindsight. As much scholarship on the 1848 revolutions in Europe has shown, the idea of nationalism was not a conspicuous feature of the early stages of the revolutions." Taylor, "The 1848 Revolutions," 174.
74 Many historians have described the agenda of Chartists, socialists, and other radicals in Australia as building a "better Britain." See, for example, Hirst, *Sense and Nonsense*, 74; Partington, *The Australian Nation*, 190; Galligan and Roberts, *Australian Citizenship*, 122; Buckner, *Canada and the End of Empire*, 2.
75 *Age*, 27 November 2004.
76 *Argus*, 4 December, 1854; *Colonial Times*, 8 December 1854; *Empire*, 9 December 1854. The flying of the Union Flag by Stockaders was also commented on in the British press. See *Leader*, 10 March 1855; *Leeds Times*, 10 March 1855; *Freeman's Journal and Daily Commercial Advertiser*, 7 March 1855. Paul Pickering notes that this crucial fact has been "virtually erased" from Australian histories of Eureka. See Pickering, "Ripe for a Republic," 80.
77 Clark, *Select Documents*, 58–9.

78 *Ballarat Times*, 17 November 1854.
79 Clark, *Select Documents*, 59.
80 The previous chapter comments extensively on the origins of this solemn vow.
81 *Argus*, 27 November 1854.
82 *Empire*, 6 December 1854.
83 *Geelong Advertiser*, 2 December 1854.
84 *Argus*, 5 December 1854.
85 Carboni, *Eureka Stockade*, 65.
86 *Argus*, 5 December 1854.
87 Carboni, *Eureka Stockade*, 67.
88 *Argus*, 5 December 1854.
89 Carboni, *Eureka Stockade*, 68.
90 Turner, *Our Own Little Rebellion*.
91 One particularly hapless victim of the troopers was a young digger from Creswick's Creek named Henry Powell. Powell was not involved with the Ballarat Reform League or the Eureka Rebellion but was visiting some friends and family on the diggings. On Sunday morning he was woken by the firing and got out of his tent to observe the commotion. Powell soon found himself surrounded by mounted troopers including the clerk of the bench, Arthur Purcell Akehurst. Although Powell offered no resistance, Akehurst struck him on the head with his sword. As he was lying defenceless on the ground the troopers shot at him and rode their horses over him. Powell clung to life for the next week. He lived just long enough to convey his story to the coroner before dying on 10 December. Powell's fate drew widespread sympathy for the diggers and reinforced the popular opinion that the police were antagonizing and largely to blame for the violence. See *Argus*, 14 December 1854; *Argus* 15 December 1854; Carboni, *Eureka Stockade*, 107–8.
92 *Argus*, 28 March 1855.
93 McLachlan, *Waiting for the Revolution*, 101.
94 *Gold Diggers Advocate and Commercial Advertiser*, 27 January 1854.
95 *Democrat*, 1 December 1855.
96 Although, as was mentioned earlier, the Liberal Party and its leaders, aside from Kennett, have generally been less enthusiastic about the Eureka legend than their Labor counterparts.
97 *Age*, 4 November 1854.
98 The *Age* raised the spectre of separatist republicanism towards the end of 1854. Clearly caught up in the revolutionary atmosphere of the time, it published a lead article in November titled "Colonial Empire." "What is

the destiny of the Australian Colonies?" it asked; "are these colonies to remain a part of the United Kingdom? Or is the day drawing near where we shall be irrevocably disunited?" The previous month had seen the *Age* menacingly comment that "one might have supposed that the thirteen colonies of North America had taught the imperial government a lesson never to be forgotten." This kind of rhetoric, however, was an aberration. It was far more revolutionary than that of the *Argus* or the *Gold Diggers Advocate* or even than anything said by the Ballarat Reform League. See *Age*, 15 November 1854 and 23 October 1854.

99 *Age*, 15 November 1854.
100 McQuilton, *Kelly Country*, 47.
101 Report from the Commission Appointed to Inquire into the Condition of the Goldfields of Victoria. To His Excellency, Sir Charles Hotham, K.C.B., Lieutenant-Governor of the colony of Victoria, Melbourne, 1855. See also *Argus*, 30 March 1855.
102 *Argus*, 9 February 1855.
103 Day, *Claiming a Continent*, 146.
104 *Age*, 2 November 1854.
105 *New York Times*, 24 March 1855.
106 Karl Marx, "News from Australia," *Die Neue-Oder Zeitung*, 7 March 1855. The article is reprinted Sharkey, Australia Marches On, 2–3.
107 Mark Twain, *Following the Equator*, 107
108 18 & 19 Vic. No. 184
109 Hirst, *Looking for Australia*, 111.
110 *Argus*, 30 March 1855.
111 *Argus*, 29 May 1855.
112 Hirst, *Looking for Australia*, 111.
113 It noted in particular that the government of Victoria had given a generous land grant and annual endowment and had constructed a magnificent building at great expense for the matriculation of just sixteen students. *Freeman's Journal and Daily Commercial Advertiser*, 27 July 1855.
114 Clark, "Re-writing Australian History," 136.
115 Serle, *The Golden Age*, 184.
116 *Argus*, 28 November 1854.
117 Although Lang was in Ballarat in November 1854, he declined an invitation to speak at the monster meetings. Lang was far too respectable to get caught up with the physical-force agitators, and his trip to Ballarat was personal since his son George was being charged with embezzlement following his tenure as manager of Ballarat branch of the Bank of New South Wales. See Baker, *Days of Wrath*, 385.

118 To again call on Petite's definitions of republicanism and liberalism. See Pettit, *Republicanism*.
119 *Argus*, 10 April 1855.

CHAPTER TEN

1 Cicero, *De Re Publica: Selections* (translation mine), 53. There is some debate over the correct translation of *iuris consensus* and *utilitatis communion*. For our purposes here, the general idea of partnership and the common good is all that needs to be conveyed. For a detailed commentary of the translation see Gorman, *The Socratic Method*, 42.
2 Harvey, *The Winning of Responsible Government*.
3 Smith, *Rebels Rewarded?*, 28.
4 *Brighton Patriot and South of England Free Press*, 5 July 1836.
5 William Baldwin to Robert Baldwin, 12 August 1841, in Yolande, *My Dear Friend*.
6 Dwyer, *Understanding Social Citizenship*, 20.
7 Peek Jr, *The Political Writings of John Adams*, xvi–xvii.
8 Bagehot, *The English Constitution*, 103.
9 Menzies, *Afternoon Light*, 250.
10 Sandel, *Liberalism*, 1.
11 *Novascotian*, 2 January 1828.
12 *Correspondent and Advocate*, 14 June 1837.
13 Cicero was quoting Plato's ninth letter. See Cicero, *On Duties*, 9–10.
14 Harvey, *The Heart of Howe*, 56.
15 Lang, *The Australian Emigrant's Manual*, 38.
16 Colley, *Britons*, 371.
17 *Novascotian*, 7 February 1848.
18 Mackay, *The Crisis in Canada*, 16.
19 *Empire*, 19 November 1853.
20 Howe's speech in the Legislative Assembly of Nova Scotia on 5 February 1846 can be found in Harvey, *The Heart of Howe*, 107–8.
21 *Perth Gazette and Western Australian Journal*, 25 January 1840.
22 *Weekly Despatch*, reprinted in *South Australian Register*, 26 July 1850.
23 *Times*, reprinted in *Morning Bulletin*, 15 January 1949.
24 Ajzenstat and Smith, *Canada's Origins*, 1.
25 Ajzenstat, *The Canadian Founding*, ii.
26 Pocock, *The Machiavellian Moment*, 531–2.
27 Sullivan, *Machiavelli, Hobbes*.
28 Shakespeare, *Julius Caesar* (act 1, scene 2), 18.

29 For example, in the late 1840s a "Cato" frequented the pages of the *Times,* Cato the Censor contributed to the *Sydney Morning Herald,* and the *Tasmanian Daily News* of the mid-1850s took swipes at its rival *Courier* under the moniker of Cato.
30 Trenchard was referring to Machiavelli's passage in *Discourses*: "it must needs be taken for granted that all men are wicked." See Machiavelli, *The Discourses,* 111–12; and Trenchard, *Cato's Letters,* 238.
31 Trenchard, *Cato's Letters,* 238.
32 The crucial exception is the lively republican debates in Australia in the 1990s culminating in the referendum of 1999.

APPENDIX TWO

1 This timeline is an abridged version of a timeline created by the Eureka Centre. Accessed online February 2013 at http://www.eurekaballarat.com/media/209212/eureka_timeline.pdf.

Bibliography

CONTEMPORARY SOURCES

Annand, William. *The Speeches and Public Letters of the Honourable Joseph Howe.* Vols. 1 and 2. Boston: John P. Jewett 1858.

Annexation Manifesto of 1849: reprinted from the original pamphlet with the names of the signers. Montreal: D. English 1881.

Anonymous. *History of the County of Middlesex, Canada.* Toronto: W.A. and C.L. Goodspeed 1889.

Anonymous [Edward Wakefield Gibbon]. *A Letter From Sydney, the principal town of Australasia: together with the outline of a system of colonization.* London: Joseph Cross 1829.

Anonymous [John Lindsay]. *Memoirs of Sir Thomas Hughson and Mr Joseph Williams, with the remarkable history, travels, and distresses, of Telemachus Lovet. The whole calculated for the improvement of the mind and manners; and for a becoming and useful entertainment for the youth of both sexes.* London: L. Davis, T. Waller, T. Osborn, J. Shipton, W. Strahan, R. Griffiths, and W. Fenner. Vol. 2. 1757.

Anonymous [John Trenchard and Thomas Gordon]. *Cato's Letters; Or, Essays on Liberty, Civil and Religious, and other important Subjects.* Vol. 1. New York: Russell and Russell 1969.

Bell, George. *Rough notes by an old soldier during fifty years' service.* Vol. 2. London: Day and Son 1867.

Bentham, Jeremy. *Canada: Emancipate Your Colonies, an unpublished argument.* London: Effingham Wilson 1838.

Bland, William. *Examination of Mr. James Macarthur's work, "New South Wales, its present state and future prospects."* Sydney: Abraham Cohen 1839.

Carboni, Raffaello. *The Eureka Stockade.* Melbourne: Melbourne University Press 1963.

Clarke, Marcus. *His Natural Life.* Melbourne: G. Robertson 1874.

Christie, Robert. *A History of the Late Province of Lower Canada: Parliamentary and Political, From the commencement to the close of its existence as a separate Province; Embracing a period of fifty years.* Vol. 4. Quebec: John Lovell 1853.

Creevey, Thomas. *The Creevey Papers: A Selection from the Correspondence and Diaries of the Late Thomas Creevey.* Vol. 1. Edited by Herbert Maxwell. London: John Murray 1904.

Cunningham, Peter. *Two Years in New South Wales.* Vol. 2. London: Henry Colburn 1827.

Davis, Robert. *The Canadian farmer's travels in the United States of America: in which remarks are made on the arbitrary colonial policy practised in Canada, and the free and equal rights, and happy effects of the liberal institutions and astonishing enterprise of the United States.* Buffalo 1837.

De Lolme, Jean-Louis. *The Rise and Progress of the English Constitution: The treatise of J.L. De Lolme, LL.D, with a historical and legal introduction, and notes, by A.J. Stephens M.A., F.R.S., Barrister-at-Law.* London: John W. Parker 1838.

Dickinson, John Nodes. *A Letter to the Honourable the Speaker of the Legislative Council, on the Formation of a Second Chamber in the Legislature of New South Wales.* Sydney 1852.

Fairfax, William. *Handbook to Australasia: Being a brief historical and descriptive account of Victoria, Tasmania, South Australia, New South Wales, Western Australia and New Zealand.* Melbourne: William Fairfax 1859.

Fraser, James. "Little Men and Little Measures." *Fraser's Magazine for Town and Country*, vol. 18 July-December 1838.

Greville, Charles. *The Greville Memoires: A Journal of the Reign of Queen Victoria from 1837 to 1852.* Vol. 1. Boston: Elibron Classics 2005.

Grey, Henry George. *The Colonial Policy of Lord John Russell's Administration.* Vol. 1. London: Richard Bentley 1853.

Griffith, Charles. *The Present State and Prospects of the Port Phillip District of New South Wales.* Dublin: William Curry 1845.

Head, Francis Bond. *A Narrative.* London: William Clowes and Sons 1839.

Henderson, John. *Observations on the Colonies of New South Wales and Van Diemen's Land.* Calcutta: Baptist Mission Press 1832.

Hunt, Thornton Leigh. *Canada and South Australia: a commentary on that part of the Earl of Durham's report which relates to the disposal of waste lands and emigration.* London: A. Gole and Co. 1839.

Kaye, John William. *Selections from the Papers of Lord Metcalfe.* London: Smith, Elder and Co. 1855.

Kelly, William. *Life in Victoria or Victoria in 1853, and Victoria in 1858.* London 1859.

Lang, John Dunmore. *The Australian Emigrant's Manual: Or, A guide to the gold colonies of New South Wales and Port Phillip.* London: Partridge and Oakey 1852.

– *Cooksland in North-Eastern Australia: The future cotton-field of Great Britain: Its characteristics and capability for European colonization. With a disquisition of the origin, manners and customs of the Aborigines.* London: Longman 1847.

– *Freedom and Independence for the Golden Lands of Australia; The right of the colonies and the interest of Britain and of the world.* London: Longman, Brown, Green and Longmans 1852.

– *A Historical and Statistical Account of New South Wales both as a Penal Settlement and as a British Colony.* Vol. 1. London: Cochrane and McCrone 1834.

– *Transportation and Colonization; or, the causes of the comparative failure of the transportation system in the Australian colonies: with suggestions.* London: A.J. Valpy 1837.

Lindsey, Charles. *The Life and Times of Wm. Lyon Mackenzie: With an account of the Canadian rebellion of 1837, and the subsequent frontier disturbances, chiefly from unpublished documents.* Vol. 1. Toronto: P.R. Randall 1862.

Macarthur, James. *New South Wales; its present state and future prospects: being a statement with documentary evidence, submitted in support of petitions to His Majesty and Parliament.* London: D. Walther 1837.

Mackay, Alexander. *The Crisis in Canada; or vindication of Lord Elgin and his cabinet as to the course pursued by them in reference to the Rebellion Losses Bill.* London: James Ridgway 1849.

Mackintosh, James. *Memoirs of the Life of the Right Honourable Sir James Mackintosh.* Vol. 2. London: Edward Moxon 1835.

Marjoribanks, Alexander. *Travels in New South Wales.* London: Smith, Elder and Co. 1847.

McCulloch, Thomas. *The Nature and Uses of a Liberal Education Illustrated: Being a lecture delivered at the opening of the building erected for the accommodation of the classes of the Pictou Academical Institution.* Halifax: A.H. Holland 1819.

McGilchrist, John. *The Life and Career of Henry, Lord Brougham: with extracts from his speeches, and notices from his contemporaries.* London: Cassell, Petter and Galpin 1868.

McMullen, John Mercier. *The History of Canada from its First Discovery to Present Time.* Brockville: J. M'Mullen 1855.

McNairn, Jeffery L. *The Capacity to Judge: Public Opinion and Deliberative Democracy in Upper Canada, 1791–1854*. Toronto: University of Toronto Press 2000.

Mundy, Godfrey Charles. *Our Antipodes: or residence and rambles in the Australian colonies with a glimpse of the gold fields*. London: Richard Bentley 1855.

Ordinances made and passed by the Governor General and the Special Council. Vol. 2. Quebec: John Charlton Fisher and William Kemble 1838.

Paine, Thomas. *Rights of Man: Being an Answer to Mr Burke's Attack on the French Revolution*. London: J.S. Jordan 1791.

Parkes, Henry. *Fifty years in the making of Australian history*. London: Longmans 1892.

Pope, Alexander. *The Poetical Works of Alexander Pope Esq: including his translation of Homer to which is prefixed the life of the author by Dr Johnson*. Philadelphia: J.J Woodward 1830.

Robinson, John Beverley. *Canada and the Canada Bill; being an examination of the proposed measures for the future government of Canada*. London: J. Hatchard and Son 1841.

Ryerson, Egerton. *Sir Charles Metcalfe Defended against the Attacks of his Late Counsellors*. Toronto: British Colonist 1844.

Smith, Charles. *Rebels Rewarded? Or the Rebellion Losses Bill signed and the destruction of both houses of parliament by fire!* Montreal, 1849.

Therry, Roger. *Reminiscences of Thirty Years' Residence in New South Wales and Victoria*. London: Sampson Low 1863.

Tocqueville, Alexis de. *De la démocratie en Amérique*. Brussels: Louis Hauman 1835.

– *Democracy in America*. Trans. Henry Reeve. New York: George Adlard 1839.

Townsend, Joseph Phipps. *Rambles and Observations in New South Wales*. London: Chapman and Hall 1849.

Ullathrone, William Bernard. *The Catholic Mission in Australasia*. Liverpool: Rockliff and Duckworth 1837.

Wentworth, William. *A Statistical, Historical, and Political Description of the Colony of New South Wales and Its Dependent Settlements in Van Diemen's Land*. 2d ed. London: G & W.B Whittaker 1820.

West, John. *History of Tasmania*. Vol. 2. Launceston: Henry Dowling 1852.

SECONDARY SOURCES

Adams, W.E. *Memoirs of a Social Atom*. New York: Augustus M. Kelley 1968.

Ajzenstat, Janet. *The Canadian Founding: John Locke and Parliament*. Montreal: McGill-Queen's University Press 2007.

– *The Political Thought of Lord Durham.* Montreal: McGill-Queen's University Press 1988.
Ajzenstat, Janet, and Peter J. Smith. *Canada's Origins: Liberal, Tory, or Republican?* Montreal: McGill-Queen's University Press 1995.
Allen, Joan. *Joseph Cowen and Popular Radicalism on Tyneside.* London: Merlin Press 2004.
Allen, Thomas B. *Tories: Fighting for the King in America's First Civil War.* New York: Harper 2011.
Anderson, Benedict. *Imagined Communities.* London: Verso 2006.
Arendt, Hannah. *The Human Condition.* Chicago: University of Chicago Press 1958.
Aristotle. *Nicomachean Ethics.* Trans. H. Rackham. London 1982.
– *The Politics.* Trans. T.A. Sinclair. London: Penguin 1982.
– *The Politics of Aristotle.* Trans. Peter L. Phillips. Chapel Hill: University of North Carolina Press 1977.
Armitage, David, Armand Himy, and Quentin Skinner. *Milton and Republicanism.* Cambridge: Cambridge University Press 1995.
Arnold, Dana. *Cultural Identities and the Aesthetics of Britishness.* Manchester: Manchester University Press 2004.
Atkinson, Alan. "The Political Life of James Macarthur." PhD diss., The Australian National University 1976.
Bacon, Francis. *The Works of Francis Bacon.* Vol. 3. London: J. Crowder and E. Hemfled 1803.
Baehre, Rainer. "Trying the Rebels: Emergency Legislation and the Colonial Executive's Overall Strategy in the Upper Canadian Rebellion." In F. Murray Greenwood and Barry Wright, eds., *Canadian State Trials.* Vol. 2, *Rebellion and Invasion in the Canadas, 1837–1839.* Toronto: Osgoode Society for Canadian Legal History 2002.
Bagehot, Walter. *The English Constitution.* London: Chapman and Hall 1867.
Bailyn, Bernard. *The Ideological Origins of the American Revolution.* Cambridge: Harvard University Press 1967.
Baker, D.W.A. *Days of Wrath.* Melbourne: Melbourne University Press 1985.
Baldwin, R.M., and J. Baldwin. *The Baldwins and the Great Experiment.* Toronto: Longmans 1969.
Barbalet, Jack. "Developments in Citizenship Theory and Issues in Australian Citizenship." *Australian Journal of Social Issues* 31 (1996), 55–72.
Baron, Hans. *The Crisis of the Early Italian Renaissance.* Princeton: Princeton University Press 1966.
Bayly, Christopher A. *Imperial Meridian: The British Empire and the World, 1780–1830.* London: Longman 1989.

Beck, J. Murray. "'A Fool for a Client': The Trial of Joseph Howe." *Acadiensis: Journal of the History of the Atlantic Region* 3, no. 2 (1974).
- *Joseph Howe: Conservative Reformer, 1804–1848*. Vol. 1. Montreal: McGill-Queen's University Press 1982.
- "Joseph Howe: Mild Tory to Reforming Assemblyman." In J.M. Bumsted, ed., *Canadian History before Confederation: Essays and Interpretations*. 2d ed. Georgetown: Irwin-Dorsey 1979.
- *Joseph Howe: Voice of Nova Scotia*. Toronto: McClelland and Stewart 1964.
Berger, Stefan, and Angel Smith. *Nationalism, Labour and Ethnicity: 1870–1939*. Melbourne: Melbourne University Press 1999.
Bergeron, Gérard. *Lire Étienne Parent: Notre Premier Intellectual, 1802–1874*. Quebec: Presses de l'Université du Québec 1994.
Berlin, Isaiah. *Four Essays on Liberty*. London: Oxford University Press 1969.
Bernard, Jean-Paul. *The Rebellions of 1837 and 1838 in Lower Canada*. Ottawa: The Canadian Historical Association Booklets 1996.
Berry, D.H. *Cicero: Political Speeches*. Oxford: Oxford University Press 2006.
Blackton, Charles S. "The Australasian League," *Pacific Historical Review* 8, no. 4 (1939).
- "The Dawn of Australian National Feeling." *Pacific Historical Review* 24, no. 2 (1955).
Blainey, Geoffrey. *A History of Victoria*. Melbourne: Cambridge University Press 2006.
- *A Shorter History of Australia*. Melbourne: William Heinemann 1994.
- *The Tyranny of Distance: How Distance Shaped Australia's History*. Sydney: Macmillan 2001.
Blair, R.S., and J.T. McLeod. *The Canadian Political Tradition: Basic Readings*. Toronto: Nelson 1993.
Bliss, J.M. *Canadian History in Documents, 1763–1966*. Toronto: Ryerson 1966.
Boissery, Beverley. "The Punishment of Transportation as Suffered by the Patriotes Sent to New South Wales." In F. Murray Greenwood and Barry Wright, eds., *Canadian State Trials*. Vol. 2, *Rebellion and Invasion in the Canadas, 1837–1839*. Toronto: Osgoode Society for Canadian Legal History 2002.
Bowen, Brett, and Michael T. Davis, eds. *Terror: From Tyrannicide to Terrorism in Europe, 1605–2005*. St Lucia: University of Queensland Press 2008.
Boyce, James. *Van Diemen's Land*. Melbourne: Black 2010.
Brady, Veronica. "'To set the people free': Conviction and Conscience, John West at the End of the Twentieth Century." *Papers and Proceedings of the Launceston Historical Society*, 1996.

Bridge, Carl, and Kent Fedorowich. *The British World: Diaspora, Culture, and Identity.* London: Frank Cass 2003.

Brode, Patrick. *Sir John Beverley Robinson: Bone and Sinew of the Compact.* Toronto: Osgoode Society 1984.

Brown, Richard. *Three Rebellions: Canada 1837–1838, South Wales 1839, and Victoria, Australia 1854.* Southampton: Clio 2010.

Buckner, Phillip. *Canada and the End of Empire.* Vancouver: University of British Columbia Press 2006.

– *The Transition to Responsible Government: British Policy in British North America, 1815–1850.* Westport: Greenwood Press 1985.

Buckner, Phillip, and John G. Reid. *The Atlantic Region to Confederation: A History.* Toronto: University of Toronto Press 2005.

Buller, Charles. "Sketch of Lord Durham's Mission to Canada in 1838." In W.M. Smith, *The Durham Papers: Appendix B.* Ottawa: Public Archives 1924.

Bullion, John L. "George III on Empire, 1783." *William and Mary Quarterly.* 3d series, 51, no. 2 (1994).

Bulmer, Martin, and Anthony M. Rees. *Citizenship Today: The Contemporary Relevance of T.H. Marshall.* London: University College London 1996.

Bumsted, J.M. *Canadian History before Confederation: Essays and Interpretations.* Georgetown: Irwin-Dorsey 1979.

Burckhardt, Jacob. *Die Kultur der Renaissance in Italien.* Leipzig: Alfred Kröner Verlag 1929.

Burke, Edmund. *Reflections on the Revolution in France.* Oxford: Oxford University Press 1999.

Burroughs, Peter. *British Attitudes towards Canada, 1822–1849.* Scarborough: Prentice-Hall 1971.

Campbell, J.R. *A History of the County of Yarmouth, Nova Scotia.* J. & A. McMillan 1876.

Cardinal, Linda, and David Headon. *Shaping Nations: Constitutionalism and Society in Australia and Canada.* Ottawa: University of Ottawa Press 2002.

Careless, J.M.S. *The Union of the Canadas: The Growth of Canadian Institutions.* Toronto: McClelland 1967.

Chisholm, Joseph Andrew. *The Speeches and Public Letters of Joseph Howe (Based upon Mr. Annand's edition of 1858).* Vol. 1. Halifax: Chronicle Publishing 1909.

Cicero. *De Re Publica De Legibus*, Trans. C.W. Keyes. London 1977.

– *De Re Publica: Selections.* Cambridge: Cambridge University Press 1998.

– *On the Commonwealth and On the Laws*, ed. James E.G. Zetzel. Cambridge: Cambridge University Press 2005.

- *On Duties*, eds. M.T. Griffin and E.M. Atkins. Cambridge: Cambridge University Press 2003.
- *Selected Works*. Trans. Michael Granttrans. Harmondsworth: Penguin 1971.

Claeys, Gregory. *Utopias of the British Enlightenment*. Cambridge: Cambridge University Press 1994.

Clark, Anna. *History's Children: History Wars in the Classroom*. Sydney: University of New South Wales Press 2008.

Clark, C.M.H. *Select Documents in Australian History*. Vol. 1, *1788–1850*. Sydney: Angus and Robertson 1970.

Clark, Manning. *History of Australia*. Melbourne: Melbourne University Press 1993.
- "Re-writing Australian History." In Imre Salusinszky, ed., *Oxford Book of Australian Essays*. Oxford: Oxford University Press 1999, 129–38.

Clark, S.D. "The Importance of Anti-Americanism in Canadian National Feeling." In *Canada and Her Great Neighbour*, ed. H.F. Angus. Toronto: Ryerson Press 1938.

Clune, David, and Ken Turner. *The Governors of New South Wales: 1788–2010*. Sydney: Federation Press 2009.
- *The Premiers of New South Wales, 1856–2005*. Vol. 1. Sydney: Federation Press 2009.

Cochrane, Peter. *Colonial Ambitions: Foundations of Australian Democracy*. Melbourne: Melbourne University Press 2006.

Colley, Linda. *Britons: Forging The Nation, 1707–1837*. London: Yale University Press 2005.

Collinson, Patrick. *Elizabethan Essays*. London: Hambledon Press 1994.

Connor, Clifford B. *Arthur O'Connor: The Most Important Irish Revolutionary You May Never Have Heard Of*. New York: iUniverse 2009.

Cook, Ramsay, et al., eds. *Constitutionalism and Nationalism in Lower Canada*. Toronto: University of Toronto Press 1969.

Coupland, Reginald. *The Durham Report: An Abridged Version with Introduction and Notes*. Oxford: Oxford University Press 1945.
- *The Quebec Act: A Study in Statesmanship*. Oxford: Oxford University Press 1925.

Craig, Gerald M. *Lord Durham's Report*. Toronto: McClelland and Stewart 1971.
- *Upper Canada: The Formative Years, 1784–1841*. Toronto: McClelland and Stewart 1963.

Creighton, Donald. *The Empire of the St. Lawrence: A Study in Commerce and Politics*. Toronto: University of Toronto Press 2002.

Crowley, Frank. *Colonial Australia*. Vol. 2, 1841–1874. Melbourne: Thomas Nelson 1980.
- *A New History of Australia*. William Heinemann: Melbourne 1986.
Curtis, Bruce. "After 'Canada': Liberalisms, Social Theory, and Historical Analysis." In *Liberalism and Hegemony: Debating the Canadian Liberal Revolution*, eds. Michel DuCharme and Jean-François Constant. Toronto: University of Toronto Press 2009.
- "The 'Most Splendid Pageant Ever Seen': Grandeur, the Domestic, and Condescension in Lord Durham's Political Theatre." *Canadian Historical Review* 89, no.1 (2008).
Darian-Smith, Kate, Patricia Grimshaw, and Stuart Macintyre. *Britishness Abroad*. Melbourne: Melbourne University Press 2007.
Dart, Ron. *The Red Tory Tradition: Ancient Roots, New Routes*. Dewdney: Synaxis 1999.
Davidson, John. "England's Commercial Policy towards Her Colonies since the Treaty of Paris." *Political Science Quarterly* 14, no.1 (1899).
Day, David. *Claiming a Continent: A New History of Australia*. Sydney: Angus and Robertson 1997.
DeCelles, Alfred D. *Louis Joseph Papineau*. Whitefish: Kessinger 2004.
Diamond, Marion. "Edward Hawksley: A Catholic Radical in Journalism." In D. Cryle, ed., *Disreputable Profession: A History of Australian Journalists*. Rockhampton: Central Queensland University Press 1997, 41–54.
DuCharme, Michael, and Jean-François Constant, eds. *Liberalism and Hegemony: Debating the Canadian Liberal Revolution*. Toronto: University of Toronto Press 2009.
Dunham, Aileen. *Political Unrest in Upper Canada, 1815–1836*. Toronto: McClelland and Stewart 1963.
Dwyer, Peter. *Understanding Social Citizenship: Themes and Perspectives for Policy and Practice*. Bristol: Policy Press 2003.
Dyck, Andrew R. *A Commentary on Cicero, De Legibus*. Ann Arbor: University of Michigan Press 2007.
Edgar, J.F. *Lord Elgin and Responsible Government: An Address presented to Lord Elgin by the St. Andrew's Society of Toronto, May, 1849, and His Reply*. Toronto: J.F. Edgar 1924.
Egerton, H.E., and W.L. Grant. *Canadian Constitutional Development: Shown by Selected Speeches and Despatches, with Introduction and Explanatory Notes*. New Jersey: Lawbook Exchange 2006.
Elford, Ken. "A Prophet without Honour: The Political Ideals of John Dunmore Lang." *Royal Australian Historical Society Journal* 54, no. 2 (1968).

Ferguson, John Alexander. *Biography of Australia*. Vol. 3. Canberra: National Library of Australia 1986.

Ferguson, Wallace K. "The Interpretation of Italian Humanism: The Contribution of Hans Baron." *Journal of the History of Ideas* 19, no.1 (1958): 19.

Fierlbeck, Katherine. *Political Thought in Canada: An Intellectual History*. Broadview Press: Peterborough 2006.

Filmer, Robert. *Patriarcha and Other Writings*. Cambridge: Cambridge University Press 1991.

Fisher, John. *The Australians: From 1788 to Modern Times*. London: Robert Hale 1968.

Fox, Henry Richard Vassall. *The Holland House Diaries, 1831–1840: The Diary of Henry Richard Vassall Fox, third Lord Holland.*, edited by Abraham D. Kriege. London: Routledge and Kegan Paul 1977.

Fubini, Riccardo. "Renaissance Historian: The Career of Hans Baron." *Journal of Modern History* 64, no. 3 (1992).

Galligan, Brian. *A Federal Republic: Australia's Constitutional System of Government*. Cambridge: Cambridge University Press 1995.

Galligan, Brian, and Winsome Roberts. *Australian Citizenship*. Melbourne: Melbourne University Press 2004.

Garnett, R. "The Authorship of Lord Durham's Canada Report." *The English Historical Review* 17, no. 66 (1902).

Gascoigne, John. *The Enlightenment and the Origins of European Australia*. Cambridge: Cambridge University Press 2002.

Gates, Lillian, F. *After the Rebellion: The Later Years of William Lyon Mackenzie*. Toronto: Dundurn Press 1988.

Glare, P.G.W. *Oxford Latin Dictionary*. Oxford: Oxford University Press 1982.

Gollin, Alfred. "Review." *Albion: A Quarterly Journal Concerned with British Studies* 11, no.1 (1979): 93–4.

Goodman, David. *Gold Seeking: Victoria and California in the 1850s*. Sydney: Allen and Unwin 1994.

Gorman, Robert. *The Socratic Method in the Dialogues of Cicero*. Wiesbaden: Franz Steiner Verlag 2005.

Gough, J.W. "Review" *English Historical Review* 75, no. 297 (1960).

Gourlay, Robert. *Statistical Account of Upper Canada*. Toronto: McClelland and Stewart 1974.

Grant, William Lawson. *The Tribune of Nova Scotia*. Toronto: Glasgow, Brook and Company 1915.

Greene, Jack P. "Empire and Identity from the Glorious Revolution to the American Revolution." In *The Oxford History of the British Empire*, vol. 2,

The Eighteenth Century, ed. P.J. Marshall. Oxford: Oxford University Press 1998.
Greer, Allan. "1837–38: Rebellion Reconsidered." *Canadian Historical Review* 76, no. 1 (1995).
– *The Patriots and the People: The Rebellion of 1837 in Lower Canada*. Toronto: University of Toronto Press 2003.
Griffiths, Phillip Gavin. "The Making of White Australia: Ruling Class Agendas, 1876–1888." PhD diss., The Australian National University, 2006.
Hall, Catherine. "Imperial Man: Edward Eyre in Australasia and the West Indies, 1833–66." In Bill Schwarz, *The Expansion of England: Race, Ethnicity and Cultural History*. London: Routledge 1996, 133.
Hancock, W.K. *Australia*. Brisbane: Jacaranda 1961.
Harlow, Vincent T. *The Founding of the Second British Empire, 1763–1793*. Vol. 1, *Discovery and Revolution*. London: Longmans, Green 1952.
Harrington, James. *The Commonwealth of Oceana and A System of Politics*, ed. J.G.A. Pocock. Cambridge: Cambridge University Press 1992.
Harvey, D.C. *The Heart of Howe: Selections from the Letters and Speeches of Joseph Howe* Toronto: Oxford University Press 1939.
– "The Intellectual Awakening of Nova Scotia." In *Historical Essays on the Atlantic Provinces*, ed. G.A. Rawlyk. Toronto: McClelland and Stewart 1971.
– *The Winning of Responsible Government in Nova Scotia*. Halifax: Centenary Celebration 1948.
Headon, David, and Elizabeth Perkins. *Our First Republicans*. Sydney: Federation Press 1998.
Headon, David, et al. *Crown or Country: The Traditions of Australian Republicanism*. Sydney: Allen and Unwin 1994.
Hegel, G.W.H. *The Science of Logic*. London: Routledge 2002.
Hirst, John. *Freedom on the Fatal Shore: Australia's First Colony*. Melbourne: Black 2008.
– *Looking for Australia*. Melbourne: Black 2010.
– *Sense and Nonsense in Australian History*. Melbourne: Black 2009.
Hobbes, Thomas. *Leviathan: Or the Matter, Forme and Power of a Commonwealth Ecclesiasticall and Civil*. New York: Touchstone 1997.
Hodgins, Bruce W., et al. *Federalism in Canada and Australia: The Early Years*. Waterloo: Wilfred Laurier University Press 1978.
Honohan, Iseult. *Civic Republicanism*. London: Routledge 2002.
Horowitz, Gad. *Canadian Labour in Politics*. Toronto: University of Toronto Press 1968.

- "Conservatism, Liberalism, and Socialism in Canada: An Introduction." *Canadian Journal of Economics and Political Science / Revue canadienne d'Economique et de Science politique* 32, no. 2 (1966): 143–71
Huon, Dan. "By Moral Means Only: The Origins of the Launceston Anti-transportation Leagues, 1847–1849." In *Papers and Proceedings of the Tasmanian Historical Research Association*, 1992.
Inglis, K.S. *The Australian Colonists: An Exploration of Social History, 1788–1870*. Melbourne: Melbourne University Press 1974.
Irving, Helen. *The Centenary Companion to Australian Federation*. Cambridge: Cambridge University Press 1999.
Irving, Terry. "The Development of Liberal Politics in New South Wales, 1843–1855." PhD diss., University of Sydney, 1967.
- *The Southern Tree of Liberty: The Democratic Movement in New South Wales before 1856*. Sydney: Federation Press 2006.
James, Patrick. *Constitutional Politics in Canada after the Charter: Liberalism, Communitarianism and Systemism*. Vancouver: University of British Columbia Press 2010.
Jasanoff, Maya. *Liberty's Exiles: American Loyalists in the Revolutionary World*. New York: Knopf 2011.
Johnson, J.K. *Historical Essays on Upper Canada*. Toronto: McClelland and Stewart 1975.
Keane, John. *The Life and Death of Democracy*. London: Simon and Schuster 2009.
Kennedy, W.P.M. *Statutes, Treaties and Documents of the Canadian Constitution, 1713–1929*. Oxford: Oxford University Press 1930.
Kierkegaard, Søren. *Either/or: A Fragment of Life*. Trans. Alistair Hannay. London: Penguin, 1992.
Kilbourn, William. *The Firebrand: William Lyon Mackenzie and the Rebellion in Upper Canada*. Toronto: Dundurn Press 2008.
Kinchen, Oscar A. *Lord Russell's Canadian Policy: A Study in British Heritage and Colonial Freedom*. Lubbock: Texas Tech Press 1945.
Knowles, Norman. *Inventing the Loyalists: The Ontario Loyalist Tradition and the Creation of Usable Pasts*. Toronto: Toronto University Press 1997.
Koritansky, John. "Thomas Paine: The American Radical." In Bryan-Paul Frost and Jeffrey Sikkenga, eds., *History of American Political Thought*. Maryland: Lexington 2003.
Latham, J.E.M. *Search for a New Eden: James Pierrepont Greaves (1777–1842), the Sacred Socialist and His Followers*. Cranbury: Associated University Presses 1999.

Leacock, Stephen. *Baldwin, La Fontaine, Hincks: Responsible Government.* Toronto: Morang 1912.

LeSueur, William. *William Lyon Mackenzie: A Reinterpretation.* Toronto: Macmillan 1979.

Lévi-Strauss, Claude. *The Savage Mind.* Chicago: University of Chicago Press 1968.

Liddell, H.G., and R. Scott. *A Greek-English Lexicon.* Oxford: Oxford University Press 1968.

Lindsay, Charles, and G.G.S Lindsay. *William Lyon Mackenzie.* Whitefish: Kessinger 2004.

Lipset, Seymour Martin. *Political Man.* New York: Doubleday 1960.

Livingston, W. Ross. *Responsible Government in Nova Scotia: A Study of the Constitutional Beginnings of the British Commonwealth.* Iowa: Iowa University Press 1930.

Locke, John. *Two Treatises of Government.* New York: Hafner 1947.

Longley, J.W. *Joseph Howe.* Toronto: Morang 1906.

Longley, Ronald Stewart. *Sir Francis Hincks: A Study of Canadian Politics, Railways, and Finance in the Nineteenth Century.* Toronto: University of Toronto Press 1943.

Lowe, Richard G. "Massachusetts and the Acadians." *William and Mary Quarterly* 25, no. 2 (1968).

Lucas, C.P. *Lord Durham's Report on the Affairs of British North America.* Vols. 1 and 2. Oxford: Oxford University Press 1912.

Lyon, Eileen Groth. *Politicians in the Pulpit: Christian Radicalism in Britain from the Fall of the Bastille to the Disintegration of Chartism.* Aldershot: Ashgate Publishing 1999.

Macaulay, Thomas Babington. *The Modern British Essayists: Macaulay, T.B. Essays.* Philadelphia: A. Hart, Carey and Hart 1852.

Machiavelli, Niccolò. *The Discourses.* Trans. L.J. Walker. London 2003.

– *Selected Political Writings.* Trans. David Wootton. Indianapolis: Hackett 1994.

Macintyre, Stuart. *A Concise History of Australia.* Melbourne: Cambridge University Press 2003.

MacMechan, Archibald. "Nova Scotia: General History, 1775–1867." In Adam Shortt and Arthur G. Doughty, eds., *Canada and its Provinces: A History of the Canadian People and Their Institutions by One Hundred Associates.* Toronto: Glasgow, Brook and Company 1914.

– The Nova-Scotia-ness of Nova Scotia." *Canadian Magazine* 25 (1905).

Macnutt, W.S. *The Atlantic Provinces: The Emergence of Colonial Society.* Toronto: McClelland and Stewart 1968.

Magocsi, Paul Robert. *Encyclopaedia of Canada's People.* Toronto: University of Toronto Press 1999.

Manning, Helen Taft. "Who Ran the British Empire 1830–1850?" *Journal of British Studies* 5, no. 1 (1965).

Marshall, T.H. *Citizenship and Social Class.* London: Pluto Press 1992.

Martin, Chester. *Empire and Commonwealth: Studies in Governance and Self-Government in Canada.* Oxford: Oxford University Press 1929.

Martin, Ged. "Attacking the Durham Myth: Seventeen Years On." *Journal of Canadian Studies* 25, no.1 (1990).

– *The Durham Report and British Policy: A Critical Essay.* Cambridge: Cambridge University Press 1972.

McCabe, Joseph. *George Jacob Holyoake.* New York: General Books 2010.

Mcinnis, Edgar. *Canada: A Political and Social History.* Toronto: Rinehart 1947.

McKay, Ian. "The Liberal Order Framework: A Prospectus for a Reconnaissance of Canadian History." *Canadian Historical Review* 81, no. 4 (2000).

McKenna, Mark. *The Captive Republic: A History of Republicanism in Australia, 1788–1996.* Cambridge: Cambridge University Press 1996.

– "Tracking the Republic." In David Headon et al., *Crown or Country: The Traditions of Australian Republicanism.* Sydney: Allen and Unwin 1994.

McLachlan, Noel. *Waiting for the Revolution.* Victoria: Penguin 1989.

McLaughlin, Shaun J. "The Patriot War: Attempts by Canadian Rebels and American Citizen Allies to Establish a Republic." *Australasian Canadian Studies* 29, nos. 1–2 (2011).

McNaught, Kenneth. *The History of Canada.* London: Heinemann 1970.

McQuilton, John. *Kelly Country: A Photographic Journey.* St Lucia: University of Queensland Press 2001.

Meaney, Neville. *The Search for Security in the Pacific, 1901–1914.* Vol. 1, *A History of Australian Defence and Foreign Policy, 1901–23.* Sydney: Sydney University Press 2009.

Mee, John. *Dangerous Enthusiasm: William Blake and the Culture of Radicalism in the 1790s.* Oxford: Oxford University Press 1992.

Melleuish, Gregory. "Australian Liberalism." In J.R. Nethercote, ed., *Liberalism and the Australian Federation.* Sydney: Federation Press 2001.

Menzies, Robert. *Afternoon Light.* Melbourne: Cassell 1967.

Metin, Albert. *Socialism without Doctrines.* Trans. Russell Ward. Sydney: Alternative Publishing Co-operative 1977.

Mills, David. *The Idea of Loyalty in Upper Canada: 1784–1850.* Montreal: McGill-Queen's University Press 1988.

Mitchell, Annie. "A Liberal Republican 'Cato.'" *American Journal of Political Science* 48, no. 3 (2004).
Molony, John. *Eureka*. Melbourne: Melbourne University Press 2001.
Montesquieu, Charles de Secondat. *The Spirit of the Laws*. New York: Cosimo 2011.
Moore, Tony. *Death or Liberty: Rebels and Radicals Transported to Australia: 1788–1868*. Sydney: Murdoch 2010.
Morison, William. *Milton and Liberty*. Edinburgh: William Green 1909.
Nethercote, J.R. *Liberalism and the Australian Federation*. Sydney: Federation Press 2001.
New, Chester W. *Lord Durham: A Biography of John George Lambton, First Earl of Durham*. London: Dawsons of Paul Mall 1968.
Newbould, I.D.C. "Lord Durham, the Whigs and Canada, 1838: The Background to Durham's Return." *Albion: A Quarterly Journal Concerned with British Studies* 8, no. 4 (1976).
O'Farrell, Patrick. *The Irish in Australia*. Sydney: New South Wales University Press 1993.
Oliver, Peter C. *The Constitution of Independence: The Development of Constitutional Theory in Australia, Canada, and New Zealand*. Oxford: Oxford University Press 2005.
Ouellet, Fernand. *Lower Canada, 1791–1840: Social Change and Nationalism*. Toronto: McClelland and Stewart 1980.
Paine, Thomas. *Common Sense; Addressed to the Inhabitants of America*. Philadelphia: W. and T. Bradford 1776.
Partington, Geoffrey. *The Australian Nation: Its British and Irish Roots*. Piscataway: Transaction Publications 1997.
Patterson, George. *A History of the County of Pictou, Nova Scotia*. Montreal: Dawson Brothers 1877.
Pearson, David. "Theorising Citizenship in British Settler Societies." *Ethnic and Racial Studies* 25, no. 6 (2002), 898–1012.
Peek, George A. Jr. *The Political Writings of John Adams*. Indianapolis: Hackett 2003.
Pettit, Philip. *Republicanism: A Theory of Freedom and Government*. Oxford: Oxford University Press 2000.
Pickering, Paul. *Feargus O'Connor: A Political Life*. London: Merlin Press 1998.
– "The Finger of God: Gold's Impact on New South Wales." In Iain McCalman et al., eds., *Gold: Forgotten Histories and Lost Objects of Australia*. Cambridge: Cambridge University Press 2001.

- "Garibaldi's Shirt: The Influence of Garibaldi and Mazzini on Popular Politics after 1850." Unpublished paper, Network of Italian Scholars Abroad Conference, Australian National University, April 2011.
- "'Glimpses of Eternal Truth': Chartism, Poetry and the Young H.R. Nicholls." *Labour History* 70 (1996).
- "The Highway to Comfort and Independence: A Case Study of Radicalism in the British World." *History Australia* 5, no. 1 (2008).
- "Loyalty and Rebellion in Colonial Politics: The Campaign against Convict Transportation in Australia." In *Rediscovering the British World*, ed. Phillip Buckner and R. Douglas Francis. Calgary: University of Calgary Press 2005.
- "Peaceably If We Can, Forcibly If We Must: Political Violence and Insurrection in Early Victorian Britain." In *Terror: From Tyrannicide to Terrorism in Europe, 1605–2005*, eds. Brett Bowen and Michael T. Davis. St Lucia: University of Queensland Press 2008.
- "'Ripe for a Republic': British Radical Responses to the Eureka Stockade." *Australian Historical Studies* 34, no. 121 (2003).

Pickering, Paul, and Alex Tyrrell. "'In the Thickest of the Fight': The Reverend James Scholefield (1790–1855) and the Bible Christians of Manchester and Salford." *Albion: A Quarterly Journal Concerned with British Studies* 26, no. 3 (1994): 473–9.

Pike, Douglas. *Australia: The Quiet Continent*. Cambridge: Cambridge University Press 1970.

Pocock, J.G.A. *The Machiavellian Moment: Florentine Political Thought and the Atlantic Republican Tradition*. Princeton: Princeton University Press 1975.

Polybius. *The Histories of Polybius*. 2 vols. Trans. Evelyn S. Shuckburgh. Bloomington: Indiana University Press 1962.

Powell, Alan. *Patrician Democrat: The Political Life of Charles Cowper, 1843–1870*. Melbourne: Melbourne University Press 1977.

Rasporich, Anthony W. *William Lyon Mackenzie*. Toronto: Holt, Rinehart and Winston 1972.

Raudzens, G.K. "Upper Canada and New South Wales to 1855: The Feasibility of Comparative Colonial History." *Journal of the Royal Australian Historical Society* 67, no. 3 (1981).

Rawlyk, George A. *Joseph Howe: Opportunist? Man of Vision? Frustrated Politician?* Toronto: Copp Clark 1967.

Read, Collin, and Ronald J. Stagg. *The Rebellion of 1837 in Upper Canada*. Ottawa: Carleton University Press 1988.

Reid, S.J. *Life and Letters of the First Earl of Durham, 1792–1840*. Vols. 1 and 2. London 1906.

Reynolds, Henry. *The Other Side of the Frontier: Aboriginal Resistance to the European Invasion of Australia.* Sydney: University of New South Wales Press 2006.

Richter, Melvyn. *The Political Theory of Montesquieu.* Cambridge: Cambridge University Press 1977.

Riddell, William Renwick. "Upper Canada – Early Period." *Journal of Negro History* 5, no. 3 (1920).

Rix, Robert. *William Blake and the Cultures of Radical Christianity.* Aldershot: Ashgate Publishing 2007.

Rousseau, Jean-Jacques. *A Treatise on the Social Compact, or, The Principles of Political Law.* London: D.I. Eaton 1795.

Rorty, Richard, J.B. Schneewind, and Quentin Skinner. *Philosophy in History: Essays on the Historiography of Philosophy.* Cambridge: Cambridge University Press 1984.

Roy, James, A. *Joseph Howe: A Study in Achievement and Frustration.* Toronto: Macmillan 1935.

Ryan, Lyndall. *The Aboriginal Tasmanians.* Sydney: Allen and Unwin 1996.

Ryerson, Stanley B. *Unequal Union: Confederation and the Roots of Conflict in the Canadas, 1815–1873.* New York: International Publishers 1968.

Salusinszky, Imre. *Oxford Book of Australian Essays.* Oxford: Oxford University Press 1999.

Salutin, Rick, and Theatre Passe Muraile. *1837: William Lyon Mackenzie and the Canadian Revolution.* Toronto: Playwrights Canada Press 1997.

Sandel, Michael. *Liberalism and the Limits of Justice.* Cambridge: Cambridge University Press 1998.

Saul, John Ralston. *Joseph Howe and the Battle for Freedom of Speech.* Kentville: Gaspereau 2006.

– *Louis-Hippolyte LaFontaine and Robert Baldwin.* Toronto: Penguin 2010.

Scherer, Paul. *Lord John Russell: A Biography.* Cranbury: Associated University Presses 1999.

Scott, Jonathan. *Algernon Sidney and the Restoration Crisis, 1677–1683.* Cambridge: Cambridge University Press 1971.

Schwarz, Bill. *The Expansion of England: Race, Ethnicity and Cultural History.* London: Routledge 1996.

Sellers, M.N.S. *American Republicanism: Roman Ideology in the United States Constitution.* New York: New York University Press 1995.

Senior, Hereward. "A Bid for Rural Ascendancy: The Upper Canadian Orangemen, 1836–1840." *Canadian Papers in Rural History* 5 (1986): 224–34.

Serle, Geoffrey. *The Golden Age.* Melbourne: Melbourne University Press 1963.

Sewell, John. *Mackenzie: A Political Biography of William Lyon Mackenzie*. Toronto: James Lorimer 2002.

Shakespeare, William. *The Tragedy of Julius Caesar*. Chicago: Lorenz 2003.

Shalhope, Robert E. "Towards a Republican Synthesis: The Emergence of an Understanding of Republicanism in American Historiography." *William and Mary Quarterly* 29, no.1 (1972).

Sharkey, Laurence Louis. *Australia Marches On*. Sydney: New South Wales Legal Rights Committee 1942.

Shaw, A.G.L. *The Story of Australia*. London: Faber and Faber 1972.

Shaw, Jane, and Alan Kreider. *Culture and the Nonconformist Tradition*. Cardiff: University of Wales Press 1999.

Shortt, Adam, and Arthur Doughty. *Canada and Its Provinces: A History of the Canadian People and Their Institutions by One Hundred Associates*. Toronto: Edinburgh University Press 1913.

Sidney, Algernon. *Discourses Concerning Government: To Which Are Added Memoires of His Life and an Apology for Himself.* 3d ed. London: A. Millar 1751.

Skinner, Quentin. *The Foundations of Modern Political Thought*. Vol. 1, *The Renaissance*. Cambridge: Cambridge University Press 1980.

– "The Idea of Negative Liberty." In *Philosophy in History: Essays on the Historiography of Philosophy*, eds. Richard Rorty, J.B Schneewind, and Quentin Skinner. Cambridge: Cambridge University Press 1984.

Smith, Bruce. *Liberty and Liberalism*. New York: Cosimo 2006.

Smith, David E. *The Republican Option in Canada, Past and Present*. Toronto: University of Toronto Press 1999.

Smith, William. *Dictionary of Greek and Roman Antiquities*. Boston: C. Little and J. Brown 1870.

Snow, A.H. "Review." *The American Journal of International Law* 7, no. 3 (1913): 671–2.

Stayner, Charles St. C. "The Sandemanian Loyalists." *Collections of the Nova Scotia Historical Society* 29 (1951).

Stephenson, Carl, and Frederick George Marcham. *Sources of English Constitutional History*. New York: Harper and Row 1937.

Stewart, Yolande. *My Dear Friend: Letters of Louis Hyppolyte La Fontaine and Robert Baldwin*. Whitby: Plum Hollow 1979.

Sullivan, Vickie B. *Machiavelli, Hobbes, and the Formation of a Liberal Republicanism in England*. Cambridge: Cambridge University Press 2004.

Sunter, Anne Beggs. *Birth of a Nation? Constructing and De-constructing the Eureka Legend*. PhD diss., University of Melbourne, 2002.

- "Contested Memories of Eureka: Museum Interpretations of the Eureka Stockade." *Labour History* 85 (2003).
Taylor, Charles. *Radical Tories: The Conservative Tradition in Canada.* Toronto: Anansi 1982.
Taylor, Miles. "The 1848 Revolutions and the British Empire." *Past and Present* 166 (2000): 146–80.
Temperley, Howard. *British Antislavery: 1833–1870.* London: Longmans 1972.
Thucydides. *The History of the Peloponnesian War.* Trans. Richard Livingstone. Oxford: Oxford University Press 1960.
Trenchard, John. *Cato's Letters; or, Essays on Liberty, Civil and Religious, and other important subjects.* 4th ed. London: W. Wilkins, T. Woodward, J. Walthoe and J. Peele 1737.
Trevelyan, G.M. *Lord Grey of the Reform Bill.* London 1920.
Trudel, Marcel. *The Seigneurial Regime.* Ottawa: The Canadian Historical Association Booklets 1971.
Turnbull, Clive. *Eureka: The Story of Peter Lalor.* Melbourne: Hawthorn Press 1946.
Turner, Henry Gyles. *Our Own Little Rebellion: The Story of the Eureka Stockade.* Melbourne: Whitcombe and Tombs 1913.
Twain, Mark. *Following the Equator.* Stilwell: Digireads 2008.
Twomey, Anne. *The Constitution of New South Wales.* Sydney: Federation Press 2004.
Tyrrell, Alex. *Joseph Sturge and the Moral Radical Party in Early Victorian Britain.* London: Christopher Helm 1988.
Viroli, Mario. *Republicanism.* Trans. Antony Shugaar. New York: Hill and Wong 2002.
Voigt, Georg. *Die Weiderbelebung des classischen Alterthums oder das erste Jahr-hundert des Humanismus.* Berlin: Reimer 1859.
Wade, Mason. *The French Canadians, 1760–1945.* Vol. 1. Toronto: Macmillan 1968.
Walshe, R.D. "The Significance of Eureka in Australian History." In *Historical Studies: Eureka Supplement.* Melbourne: Melbourne University Press 1954, 103–27.
Ward, Paul. *Britishness since 1870.* New York: Routledge 2004.
Ward, Russell. *The Australian Legend.* Melbourne: Oxford University Press 1974.
Warhurst, John, and Malcolm Mackerras. *Constitutional Politics: The Republic Referendum and the Future.* St Lucia: University of Queensland Press 2002.

Whitlam, Gough. *Eureka: Saga of Australian History: Speeches by the Prime Minister the Hon. E.G. Whitlam and the Hon. A.J. Grassby at Ballarat, 3 December 1973*. Canberra: Department of Immigration 1973.

Wilson, Alan. *The Clergy Reserves of Upper Canada*. Ottawa: The Canadian Historical Association Booklets 1969.

Wilson, George. *The Life of Robert Baldwin*. Toronto: Ryerson Press 1933.

Wilton, Carol. *Popular Politics and Political Culture in Upper Canada: 1800–1850*. Montreal: McGill-Queen's University Press 2000.

Windshuttle, Keith. "The Fabrication of Aboriginal History: Van Diemen's Land, 1803–1847." Sydney: Macleay Press 2002.

Winks, Robin. *The Historiography of the British Empire-Commonwealth*. Durham: Duke University Press 1966.

Wirszubski, C.H. *Libertas as a Political Idea at Rome during the Late Republic and Early Principate*. Cambridge: Cambridge University Press 1950.

Wise, S.F., and Robert Craig Brown. *Canada Views the United States: Nineteenth Century Political Attitudes*. Washington: University of Washington Press 1967.

Wittke, Carl. *A History of Canada*. New York: Alfred A. Knopf 1928.

Woodbridge, George. *The Reform Club, 1836–1938*. New York: Clearwater Publishing 1978.

Yolande, Stewart. *My Dear Friend: Letters of Louis Hippolyte LaFonatine and Robert Baldwin*. Whitby: Plum Hollow 1978.

Index

Aboriginal Australians, 174
Act of Union, 127–9
Adams, John, 24, 219
Adams, Samuel, 65, 104
Adams, William Edwin, 202
Age (newspaper), 200–1
Annexation Manifesto, 142–3
Anti-Transportation League, 175–85; rally in Hobart 1851, 177–8; rally in Sydney 1850, 179–81
Aristotle, 19–21, 24–5, 94, 181, 219; *Politics*, 20
Arthur, George, 70–1
Assemblée des six-comtés, 63–4
Australian League, 152–3

Bagot, Charles, 133
Bailyn, Bernard, 35–6
Baldwin, Robert, 129–30
Baldwin, William, 47
Ballarat Reform League, 203–7
Baron, Hans, 34–5
Berlin, Isaiah, 7, 33
Black, George. *See* Gold Diggers Advocate
Britishness, 9, 11, 13–14, 52, 74, 88, 97, 115, 126, 169, 214, 221–5, 228

Buller, Charles, 81–7, 99, 112, 114, 120, 130
Bunyip Aristocracy, 162–4
burning the parliament building in Lower Canada. *See* Montreal Riots

Canada Act (1791), 42–5
Canadas. *See* Province of Canada
Carboni, Rafaello, 195, 203, 209
Catholicism, 42–3, 50–1, 88, 143, 150, 154–5, 170–1, 200
Cato (alias), 72, 223, 227–8
Cato's Letters, 29, 60, 72
Chartism, 156, 175, 193, 196, 201–7
Château Clique, 10, 45, 47, 54, 59, 75, 87
Christian civic republicanism. *See* republicanism
Cicero, 19–23, 68, 74–5, 141, 159, 181, 216, 220–1
civic republicanism. *See* republicanism
Clark, Marcus, 174
Colborne, John, 48, 50, 64, 70, 84
Coming Event lectures. *See* Lang, John Dunmore
Common Sense. See Paine, Thomas

Commonwealth of Oceana. See Harrington, James
Commonwealthmen, 29–31, 36, 60, 72–3, 146, 159, 181
Confederation, 9, 38, 141, 226
Constitution (newspaper), 51, 68
Constitution Act (1791), 42–5
Crisis of the Early Italian Renaissance, 34–5

Deniehy, Daniel, 15, 163, 166, 177, 220
Discourses Concerning Government, 27–8
Durham, Lord (John George Lambton), 79–87
Durham *Report. See Report on the Affairs of British North America*

effigy burning, 13–14, 86, 140, 142, 178
Elgin, Lord (James Bruce), 136–8, 140
Eureka Stockade: aftermath and legacy, 112–15; Ballarat Reform League, 203–7; contested meaning, 192–4; Eureka oath, 209; grievances of the diggers, 207; trials, 210–11

Family Compact, 10, 45, 47–8, 53, 59, 63, 74–5, 95, 98, 101, 103, 227
federation of Australia, 169, 181, 188, 226
Filmer, Robert, 27
Fox-Pitt debates, 42–5
Freedom and Independence for the Golden Lands of Australia. See Lang, John Dunmore
French Canadians: Buller on French Canadians, 84–5;
creation of Lower Canada, 42–3; discrimination under the Canada Act, 47; discrimination in the Durham Report, 78; fight against the Château Clique, 54; grievances with the Act of Union, 128; pillars of French Canadian culture, 41–2. *See also* rebellion in Lower Canada

Glorious Revolution of 1688, 28–32, 73, 102, 121, 219
Gold Diggers Advocate (newspaper), 196–7
Grey, Charles (second Earl Grey), 80
Grey, Henry George (third Earl Grey), 119, 127, 135; despatch to Governor Harvey, 119–20, 134, 177–9

Harpur, Charles, 187
Harrington, James, 24–7
Harvey, John, 119
Head, Francis Bond, 48–50, 76
Hincks, Francis, 103–31, 140, 144
His Natural Life, 174
History of Tasmania. See West, John
Hobbes, Thomas, 24–6
Holyoake, Henry, 196–7
Howe, Joseph, 104–9, 123–5; libel trial, 109–10; letters to Lord Russell, 114–17

Johnston, James William, 117–18, 121–2

Kierkegaard, Søren, 16–17

La Fontaine, Louis-Hippolyte, 130–1, 217

La Trobe, Charles, 197–200
Lalor, Peter, 193, 195, 209, 212–15
Lang, John Dunmore, 149–62, 170–3, 221; Coming Event lectures, 151–2; influence of Christianity, 150–1; election campaign, 153–6; *Freedom and Independence*, 157–61
Leviathan, 24–6
liberal-laurentian paradigm, 145–7
liberalism: Canadian liberal revolution, 9; difference between liberalism and civic republicanism, 7–9; deontological liberalism, 219; meaning of liberal in nineteenth-century Britain, 118–19. *See also* Locke, John
Liberalism and the Limits of Justice, 7, 219
Locke, John, 25, 28–9, 38, 60, 62–3, 73; Lockean liberalism, 5, 16, 31–2, 36, 60, 131, 145–6, 169, 180, 190, 219, 225, 228; *Two Treatises of Government*, 25, 28–9
Lower Canada: anti-coercion meetings, 58–9; Assemblée des six-comtés, 63–4; campaign for greater democracy, 54–5; Château Clique, 10, 45, 47, 54, 59, 75, 87; creation and debates in Britain, 42–3; Durham on Lower Canada, 93–4; fighting in Beauharnois, 70; fighting in Saint-Denis and Saint-Charles, 65–6; fighting in Saint-Eustache, 70; electoral success of the Parti Patriote, 53–4; establishment of an oligarchy, 45; protest meetings and the cult of Papineau, 58–9; solidarity with Upper Canada, 62; suspending the constitution, 81–2; tensions between loyalists and reformers, 65; Tocqueville on Lower Canada, 91; transportation of rebels, 71; union with Upper Canada, 127–8
Loyalists, 41

Macarthur, James, 170–1
McKay, Ian, 8–9
Machiavelli, 22–7, 37, 126, 158, 226–8
Machiavellian Moment, 35–7, 226
Mackenzie, William Lyon: *Constitution*, 51, 68; early career 46, 48; exile in America, 83–5; influence of Christianity, 14–15; in public memory, 40; radicalizing, 51–3; rebellion leadership, 60–76; relationship with Baldwin, 129; return to Canada, 140
Mazzini, Giuseppe, 201–3
Memoirs of a Social Atom, 202
Metcalfe, Charles Theophilus, 133–4
Milton, John, 26–7
mixed constitution, 10, 20–1, 24, 27–8, 44, 76, 102, 124, 131, 136–7, 159, 160, 219
Montesquieu, Baron (Charles-Louis de Secondat), 30–1
Montreal Riots (1849), 140–1

Nelson, Wolfred, 63–5, 74, 76, 84
Ninety-Two Resolutions, 54–6
New South Wales: British settlement, 148–9; constitution debates, 161–5; declaration of independence, 151; fight against

transportation, 178–9, 181–3; moral character, 170–3, 184; separation of Victoria, 197; transportation of rebels from Lower Canada, 77

Nova Scotia: 1847 election, 121; appointment of Governor Harvey in 1846, 119; attempt to merge the Reform and Official parties, 117–18; conservative and reformist newspapers, 108; first responsible ministry in the British empire, 121–2; impact of the *Novascotian*, 107–9; impact of the Rebellions of 1837–38, 111; intellectual awakening, 105–7; letters of Joseph Howe, 114–17; trial of Joseph Howe, 109–10

Novascotian, 107–9

Orangemen, 50–1

Paine, Thomas, 23, 56, 59, 63, 71–3, 157, 190

Papineau, Louis-Joseph: arrest warrant, 65; influence on La Fontaine, 130–2; leadership of the reform movement, 53–8; pardon, 71; in public memory, 40; rebellion and legacy, 73–6, 84, 114; solidarity with Upper Canada, 60–1

Parkes, Henry, 9, 32, 150; anti-transportation, 169, 175, 187; campaign for greater democracy, 166; changing opinion on republicanism, 160–3, 222–3; support for Lang, 153–4

Parti Canadien, 48

Parti Patriote, 53–9, 63–6, 70

Patriacha, 27

Pettit, Philip, 7

Pictou Academy, 105–6

Pitt the Younger, William, 42–5

Pocock, J.G.A., 35–7, 226

Port Phillip. *See* Victoria

Politics (Aristotle), 20

positive and negative liberty, 7

Province of Canada: attempt to join the United States, 142; creation, 127–9, first parliament, 132. *See also* Montreal Riots, Rebellion Losses Bill

Quebec Act, 41

rebellion in Lower Canada: anti-coercion meetings, 58–9; fighting in Beauharnois, 70; fighting in Saint-Denis and Saint-Charles, 65–6; fighting in Saint-Eustache, 70

rebellion in Upper Canada: 1836 Upper Canada Election, 49–53, Ninety-Two Resolutions, 54–6; planning the rebellion, 66–7; reform meetings, 60–2; seizure of Navy Island, 70; Toronto skirmish, 69

Rebellion Losses Bill, 138–41, 222

Report on the Affairs of British North America (Lord Durham), 77–9, 89–98

republicanism: Christian civic republicanism, 14–16; civic republicanism, 7–9; difference between liberalism and civic republicanism, 7–9, mixed constitution, 10, 20–1, 24, 27–8, 44, 76, 102, 124, 131, 136–7, 159,

160, 219; republicanism in ancient Greece, 18–20; republicanism in ancient Rome, 20–2; republicanism in England, 24–9; republicanism in Florence, 22–3; republicanism in the United States, 35–6; separatist republicanism, 6, 33
Rolph, John, 61, 67, 69, 129
Ryerson, Egerton, 103, 134

Sandel, Michael, 7, 219
separatist republicanism. *See* republicanism
Sidney, Algernon, 27–8
Skinner, Quentin, 36–7
Sons of Liberty, 64–5
Sydenham, Lord (Charles Poulett Thomson), 132

Tasmania, 70, 169, 173; anti-transportation movement, 175–8; Launceston meeting, 186–7; reputation, 174–5. *See also* West, John
Ten Resolutions (Lord Russell), 56–7
Toronto Declaration (1837), 62–3
Turton, Thomas, 83
Two Treatises of Government (Locke, John), 25, 28–9

Ullathrone, William Bernard, 170–2
Uniacke, John Boyle, 117, 121–2
Upper Canada: 1836 election, 49–53; attitude to America, 46; creation and debates in Britain, 42–3; establishment of an oligarchy, 45; establishment of Orange lodges, 50; growing reform movement, 48; Ninety-Two Resolutions, 54–6; reform meetings, 60–2; union with Lower Canada, 127-8. *See also* Family Compact; rebellion in Upper Canada

Van Diemen's Land. *See* Tasmania
Vern, Frederick, 208
Victoria, 13, 135–6; anti-transportation movement, 182–3; gold rush, 194; opinion of Earl Grey, 178; separation from New South Wales, 192–3, 197. *See also* Eureka Stockade
Viscount Howick. *See* Grey, Henry George (third Earl Grey)

Wakefield, Edward Gibbon, 83
Wentworth, William, 150, 153, 156, 161–6, 177, 187, 220
West, John, 175–7, 181–2